CALDERÓN

CALDERÓN

THE SECULAR PLAYS

ROBERT TER HORST

THE UNIVERSITY PRESS OF KENTUCKY

Editorial and Sales Offices: Lexington, KY 40506-0024

Library of Congress Cataloging in Publication Data

Ter Horst, Robert, 1929–
   Calderón, the secular plays.

   Includes bibliographical references and index.
   1. Calderón de la Barca, Pedro, 1600-1681—Criticism and interpretation.   I. Title.
PQ6312.T43   862'.3   82-4747
ISBN 0-8131-1440-3   AACR2

CONTENTS

ACKNOWLEDGMENTS

My thanks go first to the University of Arizona. It has provided the generous subvention that has helped to make publication possible. This generosity, both moral and material, is personified in Professor Paul Rosenblatt, Dean of the College of Liberal Arts and Acting Provost of the University. His support and encouragement have materially advanced my work at every stage. Especially valuable was a year in France as Fulbright visiting professor of Spanish at the Université de Lille III, obtained mainly through Dean Rosenblatt's recommendation. The major portion of this book was written in Lille, where freedom from extraneous care made intense labor possible.

My thanks also go to Professor Patricia Kenworthy of Vassar College, to Professor Jean-Jacques Demorest of the University of Arizona, and to Professor Harry Sieber of the John Hopkins University. All three have read the manuscript in its earlier stages and have made many valuable observations and suggestions. Any defects in the book as now published are of course mine, not theirs.

And if the book has merit, much of it is owed to Professor Bruce W. Wardropper, who awakened me years ago to the irresistable attractions of Spanish literature and whose own scholarship is that model of the non-pareil which one vainly strives to equal.

INTRODUCTION

The purpose of this book is to bring, for the first time, a large number of Calderón's non-allegorical plays under critical discussion so as to gain something of a sense of the whole of his drama. But theatre hardly is a discrete kind of literature. It draws considerable nourishment from companions in poetry and in prose fiction. I have accordingly tried to see Calderón's drama in the context of its great Golden-Age congeners.

The large number of these plays of itself poses an acute critical problem which neither the descriptive nor the representative method has been able to solve. I have not attempted to classify overall, and I have selected plays in such abundance—about eighty of them are examined in some manner in the book— that the procedure fails of being representative. Instead, I have proposed, after the fashion of the medieval *roman,* three major *matières,* or subject areas, as prime sources for Calderón's craft. They are myth, honor, and history.

The mythological *comedias* come first in this study because they provide the clearest insights into Calderón's art at maturity. It emerges from them as remarkably unfettered, at once imaginative and passionate. Among the mythological plays are some of Calderón's finest achievements as well as a masterpiece, *La estatua de Prometeo.* It has peculiar importance for the whole body of Calderón's theatre because it rehearses an etiological myth, is a genesis of those principal woes against which the plays generally struggle. Consequently, I have examined *La estatua de Prometeo* as a model of Calderonian dramaturgy. In addition, *La estatua* engenders the disturbance or disease that provides a second large subject area. The quadrangle made up of Minerva, Prometheus, Epimetheus, and Pandora is a prototype of the honor situation. Thus the transition from myth to honor is a natural progression, for Calderón saw honor as myth in contemporary dress, myth made modern.

The honor situation in drama allowed Calderón to learn a lesson in its potential from his great predecessor Cervantes, who in effect presides over all the early honor plays. The *Quijote* and the *Novelas ejemplares* revealed to Calderón the psychological possibilities of honor, which brought male and female into a new intimacy. By means of honor, Calderón completely redefines maleness and femaleness in terms of each other, using the classical and stereotyped situation as the way to a new understanding of woman and man.

But the basic interplay in the honor plays is that between conventional maleness and conventional femaleness, man public in the outer world, woman private in the inner. The ultimate honor play is *El alcalde de Zalamea,* which so commingles the basic elements as to make them indistinguishable. It is also remarkable for introducing into the private sphere of honor a great public figure, Philip II.

With him begins my investigation of a group of plays that are historical in the special sense that they feature an eminent public figure, often a sovereign, in the dual perspective that the honor plays so beautifully conjugate, the inner and the outer, the public individual at variance with the private person. The shift from the honor plays to the historical plays is a shift from conflict among individuals to conflict in one supreme individual. Real heroism for Calderón requires a mastery of private emotion as well as of public circumstance, and it is the richness of its psychological conflict that makes of a play like *El segundo Escipión* a masterpiece on a level with *La vida es sueño.* Indeed, they are of the same species.

The unity of the book is a unity of progression, of argumentation, of idea. Its method of discussion is roundabout rather than direct. It is a willed Senecan amble in which the reader is meant to find meaning and purpose.

PART I

"AMOR ES GUERRA"

La estatua de Prometeo as the
Model of Calderonian Dramaturgy

Seventeen mythological plays by Don Pedro Calderón de la Barca survive.[1] Of the traditional classifications of Calderonian drama, this is the most nearly acceptable. Aside from *El mayor encanto, amor* and *Los tres mayores prodigios,* all belong to their author's later years and are verse dramas in three acts in which music and spectacle have especially significant functions. *El golfo de las sirenas* and *La púpura de la rosa* vary the pattern slightly by having only one act, while *El laurel de Apolo* has two. Every play conforms to Calderón's high technical standards, but several clamor to be ranked among his finest works. Some of the most rewarding are *Los tres mayores prodigios; La fiera, el rayo, y la piedra;* the diptych formed by *Apolo y Climene* and *El hijo del sol, Faetón; Fineza contra fineza;* and the supreme achievement in this area, *La estatua de Prometeo.*

Love as both a creative and a destructive force is the great theme of these plays, and they are mythological because in each of them the gods of classical antiquity meddle with men while, reciprocally, humans involve themselves with the immortals. Generally the emotion that brings gods and men together is sexual passion, so that Calderón is able to use the mythological as his psychological casebook. The seventeen *comedias* thus constitute a dramatic phenomenology of love, so extraordinarily rich, subtle, and diverse that, because of them, Calderón deserves to be placed along with La Rochefoucauld, Pascal, Stendhal, and Proust as an exceptionally penetrating observer of the major passion. This Calderón, one might almost call him *Calderón enamorado,* is virtually unknown. Yet he is the author of the wonderfully erotic *Ni amor se libra de amor,* a retelling of the story of Cupid and Psyche. Beginning with the erotic, then, of which he is a master, Calderón demonstrates a range of amorous virtuosity that in its way parallels Titian's, a spectrum that advances from the altogether profane to the near sacred.

At the same time that he probes in the mythological plays the passions of the body, Calderón also explores the passions of the mind with more than equal distinction. Each urge, the physical and the intellectual, displays the highest intensity; but mind does ever so slightly prevail over body, even though they are extremely well matched. The prime thematic impulse of love thus divides on the dramatic level into opposite and nearly equal forces, corporeal on the one hand, spiritual on the other. The encounter between these attracted adversaries—in the individual human or divinity, among siblings, lovers, and friends, and above all in the divine descent to the human together with the human ascent to the divine—provides the fundamental mythological *agon.* The Calderonian conflict between gods and men is in essence a conflict between nature and culture. The gods possess a far greater degree of civilization and knowledge than men do. Lacking these, men desire ardently to appropriate them. Yet mortality incites among humans a kind of total intensity and brevity of beauty that the gods, in their urbane ennui, covet. This beguiled antagonism between the human and the divine is the special feature of the mythological plays, their greatest charm, despite their rich diversity.

Tragedy in Calderón is a vexed question which manifests itself here because several of these plays end in death for their human protagonists. And here as elsewhere in the theatre of Calderón, a fundamental seriousness infuses his art. But I would deny any mythological play true tragic classification for a number of reasons. One is that the traditional matter of myth dictates a fixed conclusion. Calderón does modify myth as conveyed to him by manuals in strikingly original ways. For example, *El hijo del sol, Faetón,* Phaeton *alias* Eridano drives the chariot of the sun quite expertly until he witnesses the abduction and attemped rape of the woman he loves, Thetis. His consternation is what causes the fatal plunge to earth. Nonetheless, the fatal conclusion was unalterable. In addition, drawing upon Ovid, Calderón frequently lessens potential tragic impact through metamorphosis. Narciso is changed into a flower, Eco into vibrations. Instead of intensifying the tragic mood, he lessens it.

Even more significantly, the complicity that binds the gods to men in the mythological play prevents that human alienation from the divine which creates the tragic possibility by making mortal life forfeit to some imperishable hostility. Calderón's Olympians are all too human, but they cannot be made to pay the human price. At the most, tragedy in the mythological plays is a partial and mitigated phenomenon, as in *Los tres mayores prodigios,* where, to be sure, Hercules dies in jealous agony but Jason and Theseus survive. To be denied such status in no way detracts from the greatness of Calderón's mythological. His emphasis is higher than disaster. Although accuracy compels him to portray how badly men mishandle their relations with deities, as well as the fact that the pagan gods are not guiltless, the benefits of supernatural civilization on the whole tend to overbalance its terrors and risks. Calderón's gods are awful at the same time that they are indispensably benign. For men to seek them out and confront them is a heroic endeavor worth venturing upon, not only because such undertakings reveal a vaster scale in mankind but also because contact with the divine can bring real advantages, such as fire and law. It is this commitment, at all costs, to civilization that raises the mythological plays above the tragic. They all, implicitly and explicitly, point to a higher law, which we know but they do not.

The greatest critical problem in connection with these plays, particularly in the absence of any substantial analysis or number of analyses of them,[2] is their interpretation. For that effort, *La estatua de Prometeo* will be the guide. But first some descriptive observations:

The mythological play was a highly localized and specialized dramatic subgenre. It flourished at court, which afforded it the occasions and resources necessary for its realization. The Spanish mythological play was almost entirely a function of the court of Philip IV. Philip's predecessors did not have his taste for the theatre, and it did not occur to them to use lavish theatrical productions as a propaganda agency demonstrating to Spaniards and foreigners the wealth and determination of the monarchy. Philip may have learned this tactical justification of costly court functions from Olivares, his suicidally great first minister during the first portion of his reign. At all events, Calderón's mythological plays were almost a personal adjunct to the dynasty, marking with festive rites its supreme individual moments. His rhythm of creation followed the chart of Spanish Hapsburg fortunes. After the first two works came a hiatus of at least fifteen years, doubtless occasioned by the revolt of the Catalans and the secession of Portugal. Next came a period of ten or more years of abundance, twelve plays between 1650 and 1662. Succeeding it was a gap of seven years, at the center of which occurred Philip's death in 1665. At the last we find a mild mythological revival, three plays, during the early years of the reign of Charles II. The genre disappeared with the extinction of Charles and the dynasty.

Mythological plays were thus essentially "occasional" pieces. Calderón wrote *El mayor encanto, amor* as a vehicle for spectacular effects created on the lake and in the park of Philip's palace of the Buen Retiro. *Los tres mayores prodigios* was composed for a similar celebration the following year. *La fiera, el rayo y la piedra* helped to celebrate the birthday of Philip's niece and queen, Mariana of Austria, in 1652. *La púrpura de la rosa* was performed in connection with the wedding of princess María Teresa to Louis XIV in 1669. *Eco y Narciso* was another birthday offering to Mariana in 1661.

Calderón's predecessors in the field were Lope de Vega and the nascent Italian opera. From his later years, Lope left eight mythological efforts: *Adonis y Venus,* 1604; *Las mujeres sin hombres,* 1613–1618; *El Perseo,* also known as *La fábula de Perseo,* 1611–1615; *El Laberinto de Creta,* 1610–1615; *El vellocino de oro,* 1622; *El marido más firme, Orfeo,* 1617–1621; *La bella Aurora,* 1612-1625; *El amor enamorado,* 1625-1635.[3] Lope's subjects thus are Venus and Adonis, the Amazon women, Perseus, Theseus in Crete, the golden fleece, Orpheus and Eurydice, Aurora, and Cupid and Psyche. Calderón used all of these subjects except the Amazons and Orpheus. Orpheus does, however, figure in Calderón's one-act play of Christian allegory, *El divino Orfeo,* as indeed do several other personages from myth.

The other source for Calderón's mythological production was Italy and Italian opera. Since the Church occupied the talents of the great composers, it was mainly the performers who devised and improvised opera. The style of singing was recitativo, thus intoned and dramatic, exactly what we find in the *zarzuelas* and what Calderón prescribes in *La estatua de Prometeo.* The titles of the early operas are instructive: Jacopo Peri's *Dafne* (1597) and *Euridice* (1600), Giulio Caccini's *Il rapimento de Céfalo* (1600), and Claudio Monteverde's *La favola d'Orfeo* (1607), *Arianna* (1608), *Il combattimento di Tancredi e di Clorinda* (1624), *Il ritorno di Ulisse in Patria* (1641), and finally *L'incoronazione di Poppea* (1642). Myth overwhelmingly predominates here, but history has begun to creep in. Calderón's technical artistic collaboration on court spectacles with the Italian Cosme Lotti, as well as Spain's many intimate links with Italy, makes it certain that he was well informed about new developments abroad.

So it was that Calderón over the years created what must be the largest group of mythological plays written by any single non-ancient author. Although they were commissioned works that were intended to unite with music and machine spectacle, they have autonomy, and some rank very high on the scale of Calderón's literary achievement. Nor has the species entirely disappeared. Molière's *La Princesse d'Elide* is reminiscent of Calderón's plays set in the eastern Mediterranean, and his *Amphitryon* is exactly a mythological comedy, the originality of which cannot be fully savored without reference to the works and circumstances of Spanish court art, since the French and Spanish courts were extremely close. And, somewhat feebly perhaps, Molière and Calderón to an ironic degree live on in Giraudoux's *Amphitryon 38.* Eugene O'Neill's *Mourning Becomes Electra* is a radical and unique restatement of its received matter. Beyond these Gallicized and Americanized domestications, the old myths can scarcely be said to persevere in the theatre. New ones have re-placed them.

In fact, it is amazing that the pagan myths did not perish long ago. They ought to have died early in the Christian era. Yet Calderón the very Catholic, in Spain the most Catholic, can write a play like *La estatua de Prometeo* at the beginning of his seventh decade, *rendido al prolijo peso de los años,* bent under the burden of a great many years.

Technically, myth doubtless appeals to the creative artist because it combines the security of a relatively well-known subject with the possibility of variations upon a familiar theme. Myth is malleable. In discussing *Oedipus Rex,* Francis Fergusson observes that: "It is the way of myths that they generate whole progenies of elaborations and varying versions. They are so suggestive, seem to say so much, yet so mysteriously, that the mind cannot rest content with any single form, but must add, or interpret, or simplify—reduce to terms which the reason can accept."[4] Fergusson here seems to be speaking more from the artist's point of view than from the critic's, for in the fresh formulation of traditional matter the critic looks rather for a definitive individual stamp than for an entire range of possibilities. Even so, Fergusson's statement describes the Prometheus myth still better than it does the story of Oedipus, for Prometheus's history is, if possible, more cosmic than that of the king of Thebes.

The essence of the Prometheus myth is an account of how man obtained fire for his own uses. But this history of fire is nuclear to a complex of other narrations: a fable about creation with Prometheus fashioning the first man from water and clay; a tale about the appearance of the first of a new breed of women, Pandora; a related description of the fall of man; the rivalry between Prometheus and his brother Epimetheus. The cluster adds up to a whole that is not unlike the biblical genesis. Accordingly, Prometheus makes his literary debut in Hesiod's *Works and Days* and in the *Theogony*. Indeed, Pandora, as Hesiod's original and misogynist contribution, may be the first literary variation on the Prometheus theme.

Between Hesiod and Calderón, Prometheus's incarnations in literature are multiple, and the greatest of these surely is Aeschylus's *Prometheus Bound*. But, with one possible philosophical exception, to which I shall refer later, no previous formulation seems to have cast a spell on Calderón. He probably did not know Aeschylus's awe-inspiring play and would at all events have experienced great difficulty in adapting its static grandeurs to his dramaturgy of direct conflict and violent movement. In short, Calderón, in *La estatua de Prometeo,* makes the myth his own.

His Prometheus is first a political thinker who withdraws from society to formulate a more civilized plan of government than the semibarbarous system which obtains in the Caucasus.[5] He is unable to persuade his countrymen to accept his idea and again retreats into contemplation. There the image of Minerva, goddess of knowledge, *ciencias,* so passionately possesses him that, to fix and concentrate her image, he models a statue of her from clay and water, and colors and dresses it. His creation, unlike Yupanquí-Francisco's statue of the Virgin in *El aurora en Copacabana,*[6] is a dazzling success. And so Prometheus summons his brother and the Caucasians to see and worship Minerva.

Epimetheus, Prometheus's brother, is a sort of anarchist leader of the Caucasians whose entire legal system consists in punishing murder and theft. What Prometheus's superior plan may have been Calderón does not tell us. We learn only that Prometheus went to Syria and studied Chaldean astrology. Having mastered it, he returned to the Caucasus and attempted unsuccessfully to institute a government based on his new astrological wisdom. This his potential subjects refused to accept, thinking it a pretext for personal aggrandizement. Yet in their minimal way they do have a leader in Epimetheus, a battle-commander who organizes their movements. Accordingly, when Prometheus makes his summons, Epimetheus shapes the responsive Caucasians into an orderly troop: "No en desmandadas cuadrillas / vago ya el tropel discurra, / sino en seguimiento mio / a esta parte se reduzcan" (1: 2068).[7] (I won't have the crowd meandering about in straggling clusters. Come here and form up under my direction.)

Once the people have assembled, Epimetheus addresses them in a long and beautifully shaped expositional speech. Nearly all of Calderón's plays have at least one such extensive discourse. Its function is to effect a confluence, often turbulent, of the ill-starred past with the uncertain yet desperately hopeful present. In these historical harangues—which are long, long—time as a determining and tyrannical force begins to empty out, to exhaust itself, to relax its iron grip on destiny. In his exegesis, Prometheus rehearses the past of a pattern of conflict between him and his brother, for oppositeness defines their relations *ab ovo:*

de un parto nacimos yo	Epimetheus and I were born of a
y Epimeteo, sin duda	single delivery, doubtless so as to
para ejemplar de que puede	exemplify fate's power to bring two
haber estrella que influya	such divergent inclinations to bear
en un punto tan distantes	upon a single phenomenon that a
afectos que sea una cuna,	cradle could serve as one's first the-
en vez de primero abrigo,	ater of war rather than one's first
campaña de primer lucha. [1: 2068]	shelter.

Here there begins in *La estatua de Prometeo* that vital respiratory rhythm of expansion and contraction which inspires some of Calderón's greatest plays. Into the two children compressed in the same womb fate breathes a divergence of inclination that widely separates them: "en un punto tan distantes/afectos." Necessarily close, Prometheus and Epimetheus in their discrepancy nonetheless express a great range of human potentiality. Epimetheus, descending, explores bestiality. He is a prodigious hunter, and the strange sense of identity between hunter and hunted imbues him with animal qualities. But hunting is even so a pursuit, and with Epimetheus a passionate calling. He reminds one of Flaubert's St. Julian, whose enormous bloodlust is a purgation that prefaces sanctity. Prometheus, ascending, is man in pursuit of divinity, and his desire to know God semi-deifies him:

Este anhelo de saber,	It is this yearning to know which,
que es el que al hombre le ilustra	more than any other, ennobles man,

más que otro alguno (supuesto
que aquella distancia mucha
que hay del hombre al bruto, hay
del hombre al hombre, si junta
la conferencia tal vez
al que ignora y al que estudia).
[1: 2068]

for that great distance which separates man from beast also distinguishes the man who studies from
the man who does not, if for once
you bring them together for comparison.

Prometheus and Epimetheus, the rival siblings, thus represent a range of human response that extends from the tightest contractions of brotherly love— for this irresistible attraction does permanently bind them: "la voluntad que anuda / nuestros corazones" (1: 2068) (the love that splices our hearts to- gether)—to the broadest expansions of deep mutual aversion, from the bestial to the divine. The intermediate portion of the scale between their two extremes is the very large field of normal social behavior in man. Prometheus and Epi- metheus consequently tend to delimit and define society from their radical pos- tures. Both are beyond the pale yet influence the central mass by incursions across the borders. Aristotle, in his discussion of the importance of social par- ticipation, tends to banish the asocial: "Man is by nature a social animal; and an unsocial person who is unsocial naturally and not accidentally is either un- satisfactory or superhuman. . . . Society is a natural phenomenon and is prior to the individual. . . . And any one who is unable to live a common life or who is so self-sufficient that he has no need to do so is no member of Society, which means that he is either a beast or a god."[8] But Calderón's politics are poetics which creatively extend consciousness of the range of human social experience so that gods, men, and beasts all become partial modes of one another.

And Prometheus's poetics take the mute form of sculpture that seeks to concretize religious faith in the statue of Minerva, which he has assembled the people to behold and revere and for which they are to build and maintain a sumptuous temple. This is truly a *política de Dios* (politics divinely inspired) effected through art: "Llegad, pues, llegad: veréis / su efigie. Y pues mi cordura / ya no os da leyes sino / simulacros, sustituyan / a políticos con- sejos / sagrados ritos" (1: 2070). (Come close and you will see her effigy. And since my talent now bestows upon you images rather than laws, let sacred rites replace political recommendations.) Prometheus's ascent from the political to the religious is a success, for Epimetheus, correctly expressing the will of the multitude whom he roughly leads, agrees to worship Minerva and to construct her temple.

There next occurs a choreography of rhetoric, an incarnation of antithet- ical modes of speech into behavior. The figure is chiasmus. The antithesis is god as against beast. The chiasmus is the constant, dynamic shifting of the terms from place to place and from person to person, so that what began as relatively distinct opposition becomes a whole unpredictable field of conflict, "campaña de primer lucha."

The rhetorical terms start developing into interchangeable behavior when the beastly Epimetheus, at the sight of the statue, falls in love with its beauty. Accordingly, to the Promethean trajectory from human to superhuman, there is now added an imitative action progressing from subhuman to semidivine.

Beauty sways the beast, and the stage is set for the appearance of gods on earth and of men in heaven.

Prometheus's statue and Epimetheus's passion for it constitute the perfect invitation for Minerva to descend. They draw her down. Calderón's great stroke is the manner of her epiphany, for she first manifests herself as a destructive beast, "una fiera / . . . horriblemente sañuda" (1: 2071) (a wild beast on a terrifying rampage). The transference of divinity into animal form summons in Prometheus a descending response equal and opposite to Epimetheus's first look at heaven, since the studious brother now takes up arms to pursue the marauder. Epimetheus does likewise in the hope of offering the animal to Minerva's statue as its first sacrifice. But this time Prometheus is the more skillful hunter: "sabré por donde atajarla, / desmintiendo a quien murmura / que se embotan los aceros / en el corte de las plumas" (1: 2071). (I'll be able to head it off, disproving those slanderers who say that using the blade to sharpen quills gets it very dull.)

It is certainly true that Calderonian dramaturgy makes very sharp distinctions and oppositions. But these dualisms do not sustain themselves. They exist rather to blur and merge, bleeding the most hostile qualities onto each other. And so it is that while Epimetheus takes on some of Prometheus's theological coloration, Prometheus gets daubed with his brother's earthier stains as he plunges on after the threatening animal.

Contamination by contrariety is not limited to Prometheus. It extends even to Minerva, who in the process of appearing to her worshipper descends to the extreme animal depth of human nature, the raging beast that he pursues into the cave, where the sweetness of her voice stays his bow and its "ardientes flechas" (burning arrows). The goddess steps out of her animal skins to display her form and adornment as identical to those of Prometheus's statue. Calderón is vague about her dress, but it abounds in flowers meant to conceal the common clay from which he had shaped her image. Minerva's range is what is extraordinary, from deity to beast: "que lo que a un monstruo pregunta / me responde una deidad" (1: 207). (The question put to a monster is answered by a divinity.) The goddess, assuming the passionate modes of men, lures Prometheus to her altar, so that the methods of Venus are in no wise absent from the strategies of Minerva. Her relationship with Prometheus is an alternation between seduction and counterseduction.

I do not know whether it is possible to reconstruct the horoscope of Epimetheus and Prometheus; but at the moment of their birth, and probably at the moment of their conception, Mars and Venus surely were in conjunction. Consequently, their influence on the newborn brothers was passionate, their contribution "afectos," however distinct the field of each contributor. The native endowment with which we are dealing in this play is emotion. The means by which such emotion expresses itself may differ as much and as little as the career of arms differs from the career of letters. Yet we would woefully diminish the grandeur of the play and of much of Calderón's art if we did not recognize the passionate source and goal of Prometheus's rationality. Reason is a subservient instrument mediating as image between a natal inclination to and mature worship of superhuman truths. Prometheus's native proclivity is a desire to know the divine. That desire drives his intellect to ardent image-forming op-

erations. Because of his "anhelo de saber," Prometheus's mind exercises itself
in reasoning, the effect of which is to mirror and so is rightly called "especulación": "me di a la especulación / de causas y efectos, suma / dificultad, en que
toda / la filosofía se funda" (1: 2068). (I devoted myself to speculations about
cause and effect, an area of supreme difficulty, upon which all philosophy is
based.) And so, desiring to apprehend the divine, Prometheus's questing intellect becomes a Narcissus pool into which that single deity who motivated the
search comes at last to gaze and be reflected, doubly seductive as both the goal
and the image of desire. At the same time, Prometheus's very ardor is a counterseduction, drawing Minerva to him in delighted gratitude, *agradecida,* that
frame of mind which, in the completely secular *comedias,* every gallant strives
to cultivate in the psyche of his mistress so that love will later grow to full
bloom between them. Worship is a species of passion different from love only
in the degree of its elevation. After his political failure, then, Prometheus raises
his sights to the celestial hegemony of the Olympians and finds that the gods
share power among themselves in heaven and on earth.

In a kind of intuitive and dangerous monotheism, Prometheus chooses
one among the Olympians to revere above all others, because he too is grateful, *agradecido,* to his sovereign mistress Minerva. "Conque, obligado de
ver / cuánto en mí las distribuya, / liberal interior culto / más que a otra
deidad ninguna / (oféndanse o no se ofenden / las demás) rendí a la suya"
(1: 2069). (And so, grateful for her showering of knowledge upon me, I paid
her divinity fervent inner worship, more so than to any other gods, whether
they like it or not.) Prometheus, then, achieves this uneasy monotheism by
means of an intensification of more familiar literary styles of personal address.
At the outset, through astrological flux, Minerva draws him to her by implant-
ing a desire to know her, the closest parallel to which is sexual and biological.
The element of elevation, however, modifies this approach and makes not a relationship between man and woman but one between gallant and lady, sex sublimated into the courtly modes. Further elevation beyond this common literary
point makes of courtly address and its monomania a worshipful interaction between client and patron, Minerva a duchess, Prometheus her first minister, an
ambiguous love joining them. At her apogee, Minerva attains an ill-defined
supremacy, for as the mistress of every branch of knowledge, she approaches
omniscience, is a mode of omnipotence. Together, these qualities go far towards establishing a theology that is para-Christian, a *summa.*

And now we hear the questions put by other minds in quest of truth in
other plays of Calderón: St. Cyprian in *El mágico prodigioso,* so utterly persuaded by the idea of the unknown God's supremacy that the first element in
the definition which he ponders throughout the drama is: "Dios es una bondad
suma" (God is supreme goodness). Similarly and more nakedly in *La exaltación de la Cruz,* as Anastasio and Zacarías debate the respective merits of
Christianity and paganism, Anastasio doubts the existence of one supreme being: "Varias ciencias he estudiado; / varios libros he leído / y ni en ellas ni ellos
hallo / que pueda un dios ser posible / en la multitud de tantos / como las
gentes adoran."[9] (I have studied a number of fields; I have read numbers of
books. And in neither study nor books do I discern the possibility of a single
deity among the multitude of gods that the nations worship.) Zacarías majes-

tically replies: "Estudia / en el libro soberano / de la ciencia de las ciencias." (Study in the book of sovereign knowledge.) But this book is, we learn, a metaphor: "No es libro, / materialmente tomado / el nombre, sino un supuesto / tan grande, tan docto y sabio / que es capaz de todas ciencias" (1: 995). (It is not literally a book but rather a premise that is so great, learned, and wise that it subsumes all branches of knowledge.) And when Anastasio eagerly inquires, "¿Quién es, que ése voy buscando?" (What is that, for that I seek?), the reply naturally is "Cristo." In their next encounter, Zacarías, in a kind of *De los nombres de Cristo* of knowledge, glowingly lists God's *ciencias* as philosophy, jurisprudence, medicine, theology, mathematics, astrology, music, grammar, rhetoric, poetry, geometry, architecture, and painting. In Calderón's book, therefore, the Christian God is a scholastic unity embracing all mental multiplicity. Prometheus's fixation on Minerva as the fount of wisdom is a pagan and imperfect rehearsal of the Christianizing process of the plays properly classified as religious,[10] a pre-figuration of them, this of course well after their actual composition but spiritually anterior.

Another subtle mingling that points to the imperfections of paganism is the fusion, already discussed, in Prometheus's addresses to Minerva and reciprocally in her approximation to him of the purely carnal and secular with the sense of the divine. The Christian Godhead ultimately exempts the saved from the system of debits and credits in which we all trammel. God is the promoter of the system but he is not involved in it, for his circumstance is constantly to be giving—*liberal* in Calderón's lexicon—constantly to be owed but never owing. Accordingly, he can never be *agradecido,* gratefully cognizant of an obligation, since no human act, however sublime or grandiose, can remotely match his munificence. (I speak here descriptively, theologically.) Christ is surely a fisher of men, but no man can reciprocally enmesh him. He captures but is free of all bonds.

In contrast, Minerva ties herself to Prometheus in a covenanted relationship where the key word is precisely *agradecida:* "Yo soy, O Prometeo, / Minerva que a tu vida / no sólo agradecida / por tu estudioso empleo / mas por el ara en que arde / tu deseo" (1: 2072). (Prometheus, I am Minerva, and I am grateful for your existence not only because of its dedication to learning but also because your longing expresses itself in worship and sacrifice.) Yet the force that motivates the covenant is emotional rather than intellectual: "el ara en que arde tu deseo" (the altar on which your desire flames). Minerva's metaphor of Prometheus's quest for her also anticipates the fire that he will steal. But for now a goddess is the willing prisoner of his ardent spirit, "alma a quien todo un dios prisión ha sido."[11] Minerva abounds in Prometheus's sense. His idea of her captivates her. Therefore: "En aquel propio traje / que tu idea me copia / . . . / quiso mi amor que en busca tuya baje" (1: 2072). (Love impelled me to descend in search of you in the very clothing in which your imagination portrayed me.) Mind-fisher of the divine *nous,* Prometheus has netted himself a goddess who is his reciprocal in a chiastic interplay.

The next motion is ascendant as Minerva undertakes to reward Prometheus for his devotion with a gift from heaven which he must reconnoiter under her protection in order to make a proper choice. And, despite the flaws which increasingly emerge, the passion shared by Prometheus and Minerva is a harmonious and creative one. Responding to his persistent wooing, she assumes the forms his imagination has provided for her. She wears the characteristic dress with which he has clothed her. Minerva, then, impersonates; she speaks; she acts, *representa*. Her statue is the emotional and intellectual artifact that draws man to god and god to man. Drama is religion's great initial rite; and no one knew thaᴄ genesis better, presented it more clearly, than Calderón in *La estatua de Prometeo.*

But Minerva and Prometheus tell only half the story. Requited love is the first Edenic rhythm reaching from human to divine. Unrequited love is its equal and opposite complement. Replication is the central rite of requited love, destruction the liturgy of opponency. Accordingly, the patron-protégé relationship between Pallas and Epimetheus is the exact negative equivalent of the positive agreement between Minerva and Prometheus. Immediately after their departure, then, Epimetheus penetrates into the horrific cave where his brother found a goddess, and likewise encounters Pallas. She is the prototype of Boethius's *Fortuna,* divine when she lavishes benefits, subhuman when she snatches them away. Most mortals see her two faces consecutively. Epimetheus sees them simultaneously and is understandably confused: "¿Quién eres, bello prodigio / de tan encontradas señas / que tu voz dice deidad / y no deidad la aspereza / de tu semblante?" (1: 2074). (Who are you, lovely marvel so countersymbolizing yourself that your voice expresses divinity while your harsh expression denies it?)

The gods do not, of course, worship themselves. To be worshipped they require humans. And Prometheus's and Minerva's case is a happy one, for their aspirations to celebrate and to be celebrated harmoniously encounter each other in the statue, human mingling across its threshhold with the divine. Pallas's problem is far more complex, as her dual nature shows. To be worshipped, she must replicate disharmony and opposition. Inevitably, a portion of the oppugnancy that she propagates will be turned against her. This is exactly what occurs when she and her sister project in Prometheus and Epimetheus models of themselves, actors-out of their dominant propensities:

Y siendo así que de un parto
visteis las luces primeras
Prometeo y tú, imitando
nuestra fortuna en la vuestra
partimos los dos asuntos
trabada la competencia
de cuál mayor lustre,
mayor excelencia,
da al uno en las armas
que al otro en las ciencias.
A este efecto . . .
. . . .
te incliné a la caza bien
como imagen de la guerra
pero viendo cuán ingrato
al influjo que te alienta

And since you and Prometheus were born together, your fate imitating ours, we separated our two enterprises in a competition as to who could do more for one or the other either in warfare or wisdom. To this end . . . I gave you a taste for the hunt as the very image of war but, seeing that you are so ungrateful for the influence that inspires you as to dedicate sacrifices to a false and spiritless beauty. . . .

a una inanimada
fingida belleza
víctimas dediques. [1: 2074]

Thus Prometheus and Epimetheus embody dual and contrasting lines of relational descent, concordant where the enterprise is learning, dissonant where it is war. Moreover, opposition begets opposition in a multiplicate progression, because, as a personality cast in Pallas's likeness, Epimetheus reproduces not only her affinities but also her hostilities; and at least half of his connection with the goddess is aversion to the goddess counterbalanced by devotion to her sister.

When Pallas commands Epimetheus to destroy his brother's statue of Minerva, the reciprocal equivalence between love and hate, between the desire to worship the image and the obligation to obey the divine command, produces a perfect chiastic interlock of stasis, a kind of exactly balanced Calderonian subatomic emotional world: "expuesto a un sagrado ceño/ o a una dominante estrella, / obedecerla es el mismo/ riesgo que no obedecerla" (1: 2075). (With me helpless in the face of divine wrath or of a ruling passion, I run the same risk in obeying her as in not obeying her.) And Epimetheus precisely summarizes the process that has brought him to such a dilemma:

¿Quién habrá visto tan ciega Has there ever been such total confu-
confusión como buscar   sion as to be on the trail of one's
a un hermano y a una fiera brother and a beast and to find, in
y en vez de fiera y hermano the place of beast and brother, a god-
hallar deidad tan violenta   dess so unreasonable as to present
que se explique favorable   herself as a patroness in order to give
para declararse adversa? [1: 2075] injurious commands?

As important as the substance of Epimetheus's statement is its style, for the central figure is chiasmus, the *chi* interlock between *hermano* and *fiera*:

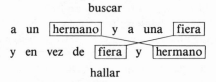

buscar

a un hermano y a una fiera

y en vez de fiera y hermano

hallar

Far from being a classicizing rhetorical ornament, this figure is a construct of basic interrelationships in the play: the affinities are diagonal lines of force, the aversions are horizontal fields of resistance. Indeed, the human siblings experience a connection to their goddess counterparts that parallels the quadripartite relations among the elements in the allegorical *La vida es sueño.* The play proper begins, as do many *comedias,* with a struggle, here among the four elements—earth, air, fire, and water—to ascertain which is supreme. Power, Wisdom, and Love witness their combat, observing: "¡Agua, Tierra, Fuego y Aire,/ qué contrariamente unidos/ y unidamente contrarios/ en lucha estáis divididos!" (3:1388).[12] (Water, Earth, Fire, and Air, with what hostile sympathy and what sympathetic hostility you are drawn up in combat!)

La vida's chiasmus is more adverbially elegant, more highly modal, than in *Prometeo,* but it is no less a fundamental structural principle, as Poder (Power), an aspect of the Trinity, shortly reveals. The elements make their obeisance to the triune god immediately upon recognizing him but he commands them not to desist from their "campal desafío," their challenge to one another on the field of honor. It is Poder whose voice commands and who explains:

convino que haya
cualidades en que uniros
y que haya cualidades
en que oponeros convino,
pues en una parte opuestos
y en otra parte benignos,
es fuerza que eslabonados,
cuando vaya a dividiros
el odio, os tenga el amor
y que amigos y enemigos
duréis conformes y opuestos
lo que duraren los siglos.

the solution was for there to be qualities that draw you together and qualities that keep you apart, since, with you elements hostile on the one hand and sympathetic on the other, it necessarily follows that when hatred is on the point of dividing you, love will keep you linked together and that as friendly enemies you will continue, quarreling and agreeing, for as long as time itself may last.

[3: 1388-89][13]

God's purpose is evident. He wishes to keep the physical entities that compose the world distinct and at the same time to bind them together until earth-time ends. The four elements as we find them in the allegorical *La vida es sueño* are a literary species of electromagnetic vector diagram, a complex field of force created by attractions and repulsions. Since these positive and negative impulses already have a psychological coloration, however, Calderón calling them hatred and love, "odio" and "amor," they easily transpose from the physical to the human scene, where chiasmus is an especially effective graph of their shifting positions, for the rhetorical figure depends on superposition for its effect, without which it would be simply antithesis. Superposition suggests hierarchy. It is precisely a striving for supremacy on the part of each of the elements that prefaces the intervention of God as true sovereign in the allegorical play. In *Prometeo,* chiasmus is an equally appropriate vehicle for expressing the compound-complex relationships among men, women, and the gods, but most particularly in the relationship between man and god.

Yet Epimetheus's response to command is notably different from that of the four elements. The elements humbly and unquestionably obey. Epimetheus dithers. Finally he decides to deceive Pallas. That such a possibility could even suggest itself to him shows that Pallas is far less absolute a deity than the god of *La vida es sueño,* even if she operates on the same structural principles as he. Her limited authority is one of Calderón's many attestations to the inferior rank which pagan divinities must assume in the Christian perspective even in the age of their unchallenged supremacy. Calderón never grossly Christianizes or moralizes in *Prometeo*; but the play's virtues readily translate to the Christian future, while its vices remain in the pagan past. So it is with trickery. Only a god who tricks could expect to be tricked. Such gods belong to classical antiquity.[14]

Hoodwinking the gods is indeed the mode of transition from Epimetheus's encounter with Pallas to Prometheus's promenade across the heavens in the company of Minerva. Their expedition is a shopping trip on which Prometheus is expected to choose the brightest bauble as a reward for his worship of wisdom. Inevitably, the richest, purest, and most dangerous jewel appeals to him, the sun itself, one of whose rays he would take. Apollo's descent was the great machine spectacle of *Prometeo* when it was performed for the Queen Mother, Mariana of Austria, widow of Philip IV. It is also the great physical and spiritual conjuncture of the play as an artistically unified conception. When Prometheus reaches out to steal fire from Apollo's declining chariot, all the opposing forces which have been infringing upon one another draw close in a moment of supreme poetic compression, man at his zenith, god at his nadir, so that they can—almost—touch. Calderón has carefully prepared this definitive encounter. The Caucasus mountains themselves are so high that they raise earth to heaven, or bring heaven down to earth: "¡Moradores de las altas / cumbres del Cáucaso, en cuya / cerviz inculta descansa / todo el orbe de la luna" (1: 2067). (Dwellers among the Caucasus's lofty peaks, which bear upon their uncivilized sierra neck all the weight of the lunar sphere. . . .) Apollo's goddess sisters have plunged to earth in meddlesome forays, and now Minerva has brought a man into the sacred precincts of heaven itself. The human and the divine are for the moment practically contiguous.

It is not precisely clear at what time of day *Prometeo* begins. But I would surmise that its action starts in inner time at noon, with the sun and the idea of divinity at their zenith. Now, as Act I draws to its close, the sun is just about to sink behind the mountains and plunge into the sea of night and death. This instant is perhaps Calderón's most numinous dramatic moment. Almost unfailingly, in whatever play, however light its tone, he marks sunset with an elegantly Gongoristic verbal fanfare which is a salute to its potentialities, even when he does not exploit them.

The quality of sunset which Calderón does most extensively exploit, when he is of a mind to, is its ambivalence, its interchangeability with sunrise. In the lighter plays he often applies this ambivalence to one of the common conceits of the period, that a lovely lady's appearance is like sunrise, her departure like sunset, the one a happy occurrence and the other an unhappy one. Consequently, in *Casa con dos puertas mala es de guardar,* Félix describes his first sight of Laura, his beloved, as both an afternoon and a morning event:

una tarde fue agradable	It was on a pleasant April afternoon.
del abril. Pero mal dije:	But no, I am wrong. It was at dawn.
al alba fue. No os espante	Don't be surprised that it happened
ser por la tarde y al alba,	in the afternoon and at dawn, be-
que con prestados celajes,	cause, if I remember rightly, on that
si bien me acuerdo, aquel día	day it dawned, with borrowed hues,
amaneció por la tarde. [2: 279]	in the afternoon.

More mournful is the encounter of Carlos with Diana in *De una causa, dos efectos*:

Entré, pues, esta tarde
en un jardín donde mi amor cobarde,
más a adorar que a merecer
  dispuesto,
el sol vio de Diana; mas tan presto
me despidió que la esperanza mía,
síncopa haciendo de la edad del día,
vió en un instante, un punto,
la aurora y el ocaso todo junto.
                    [2: 478]

I went this afternoon into a garden where my cowardly love, more fit to worship than to prosper, saw the sun that is Diana. But she sent me so immediately away that my hopes, curtailing the whole course of the day, saw dawn and dusk compressed together.

In the second example, the metaphor richly and ambiguously extends itself, for there to see one's lady is once again to hope that she will return one's love, i.e. *aurora,* and to have that hope dashed is a psychological sunset, *ocaso*. To experience hope and despair in rapid succession is so to foreshorten the normal expanse of day that sunrise and sunset seem to occur almost simultaneously, a marvelous poetic condensation, particularly when the fleeting hours of a single day symbolize the years—brief themselves—of human existence.

One great play of Calderón's is centrally organized around the dual sunrise-sunset perspective. *El príncipe constante* begins with a melancholy sunrise and ends with a triumphant one. The drama's first psychological dawning is that of the lovely and downcast princess Fénix. Her incipient moral sensibilities, despite all the promise of a new-born day, are gloomy because she realizes that dawn leads to dusk and dust. As a result, although her appearance is festive, "sale a este jardín / Fénix, a dar vanidad / al campo con su hermosura, / segunda aurora del prado" (1: 249) (Fenix is coming into this garden to make nature vain with her beauty, which is a second dawning over the meadows), her intimations of mortality—"Gran pena contigo lucha" (Great grief is in combat with you)—cast a pall even over the landscape. Thus when a servant suggests a soothing ride in a boat, "un barco sea / dorado carro de sol" (a boat can serve as the sun's golden chariot), the garden which she might leave for the water is imagined as gallantly but regretfully exclaiming, "Ya el sol en su centro esta; / muy breve ha sido este dia." (The sun is already in its watery grave; brief indeed has been this day.)

With Fénix, the extended metaphor is fundamentally the same as the life and death of hope symbolically expressed by courtly sunrise and sunset in *De una causa, dos efectos*. Her gaze is, however, longer and deeper as she sees past the moment to the end of day and senses nothing but night beyond. Moreover, in her case hope and despair are conjoined not in an emotional rise and plunge but in a profound psychological and moral oscillation, a disorder in which the manic and depressive are combined but with the depressive dominant. The technical basis for this splendid inner portrait is the difference and the similarity between the sun's first and last daily appearance, and Fénix is fatally rocked on a sea of spiritual fluctuation.

In contrast, Don Fernando, the captive Christian prince, has at least twice

Fénix's moral imagination. He sees the day staunchly through, as his counterpart weakly does, both of them grasping its significance, which Fernando magnificently propounds in one of the play's two central sonnets. In the first, Fernando expresses Fénix's primary intuition with dismaying cogency. His analogy is the flowers: "Estas que fueron pompa y alegría / despertando al albor de la mañana, / a la tarde serán lástima vana, / durmiendo en brazos de la noche fría . . ." (1: 266).[15] (They which, waking at the first white light of day, were all joyous ostentation will, at its end, be pitiful husks coldly sleeping in the arms of night. . . .) But where prince and princess truly draw apart is in their approach to night. Fénix, in her sonnet, sees it as a black translation of diurnal experience, the stars a sinister replacement for the innocent flowers: "si un día es el siglo de las flores, / una noche es la edad de las estrellas." (If one day is the time alloted to flowers, then one night is the span of stars.) She turns away from both night and day with horror and disgust.

Fernando, though he blesses the light of day, entrusts himself to night confidently, almost mystically. He knows that the fixed stars are permanently visible for the guidance of navigators and pilgrims and that God can at times be more easily found in the symbolic night of spiritual purgation and illumination. It is precisely this which San Juan de la Cruz tells us in his "Noche oscura":

En la noche dichosa
en secreto, que nadie me veía,
ni yo miraba cosa,
sin otra luz y guía
sino la que en el corazón ardía.
Aquésta me guiaba
más cierto que la luz del mediodía,
a donde me esperaba
quien yo bien me sabía,
en parte donde nadie parecía
¡Oh noche que guiaste,
oh noche amable más que el
    alborada![16]

Secretly, in blissful night, no one watching me and I watching nothing, without a light or guide, except for the one that was burning in my heart. It guided me more surely than the light of midday to where that person whom I well know was waiting for me in a place where no else was to be seen. Oh night that guided me, oh night more lovable than dawn . . .!

Aside from the erotic and ecstatic elements, this fragment's salient trait is the sense of absolute confidence in the guiding power of a beneficent darkness. Variants of *guiar* occur three times in ten verses, and night is apostrophized as essentially directive in the exclamation "¡O noche que guiaste!"

Roughly speaking, Fernando shares San Juan's view of night properly entered into. But an experience which for San Juan is sublime rehearsal actually occurs to Fernando, who dies as night is coming on, while Portuguese forces are landing to rescue him. Then the miracle occurs. The dead prince appears to the assembled Portuguese, with a flaming torch in his hand. He will guide the army to the walls of the city of Fez, there to ransom his body. In his guiding role, Fernando is a transfigured Christian Prometheus who applies stolen fire to transcendent uses: "con esta luciente / antorcha desasida del oriente / tu ejército arrogante / alumbrando he de ir siempre adelante" (1: 276). (I will con-

stantly light the feet of your valiant army with this blazing torch snatched from
the hand of the East.)

Victory, nonetheless, remains personal; Fernando explains to Alfonso that
he leads so that "llegues a Fez no a coronarte ahora / sino a librar mi ocaso en
el aurora." (You will reach Fez not to be crowned this time, but to redeem my
disappearance through dawn.) Faith is a sun that has guided Fernando through
the night of death and now his redemption is to be made visible to all, to those
of lesser faith or none. Fernando understandably strikes a jubilant note when
his task is done:

En el horror de la noche,
por sendas que nadie sabe,
te guié. Ya, con el sol
pardas nubes se deshacen.
Victorioso, gran Alfonso,
a Fez conmigo llegaste.
Este es el muro de Fez;
trata en él mi rescate. [1: 277]

Through the horrors of the night,
along paths known to no one, I have
guided you. Now dark clouds are dis-
persing with the light. With me you
have arrived victorious in Fez, Alfonso the Great. This is the city wall.
Parlay for my ransom here.

Clearly, the victory won is over night and death and only incidentally over opposing enemy troops. Calderón symbolically expresses it in the reciprocal of
sunrise and sunset with which *El príncipe* began. Then, with Fénix, death was
implicit in life, *ocaso* in *aurora.* Now life frees itself, by a heroic effort, from
the trammels of death, "a librar mi ocaso en el aurora."[17]

I do not believe it is an overinterpretation to see the whole structure of *El
príncipe constante* as a quadripartite chiasmus in which the antithesis of
Fénix's perspective, *aurora-ocaso,* comes to contrast with the antithesis of Fernando's perspective, *ocaso-aurora.* The day is hers but the night is his, as is the
triumph. And even though this brief survey of Calderón's use of a fundamental
opposition is far from exhaustive, one can see that the bipolar distinction between dawn and dusk ranges, in his poetic and dramatic practice, from a rather
conventional conceit through psychological depiction to deep character portrayal that becomes an organic artistic principle. The *aurora-ocaso* chiasmus is
a poetic analogue to the lines of force binding and separating the four elements,
a psychological and spiritual structuration paralleling their physical format.

So that when Apollo descends in *Prometeo,* he sings a wonderfully suggestive song: "No temas, no, descender, / bellísimo rosicler, / que si en todo es de
sentir / que nazca para morir, / tú mueres para nacer" (1: 2076). (Do not fear
the descent, loveliest roseate light, for if every living creature must regret that
birth is the path to death, you die in order to be reborn.) Here again, by implication, the contrast between sunrise and sunset appears; and the last three
verses constitute for Calderón's art on obsessive refrain. Wilson and Sage
reproduce slightly varying redactions from *La sibila de oriente, A tu prójimo
como a ti, Las manos blancas no ofenden, El gran duque de Gandía,* and a ten-
line poem composed for the celebrations of the canonization of St. Isidore.[18]

Like the two sonnets at the heart of *El príncipe constante,* Apollo's song
juxtaposes clashing points of view with remarkable compression, as strophe
and antistrophe. The tragic vision is the gloomy diurnal gaze that instantly

transposes the hopeful glow of birth to the red-verging-on-black hues of death. The anti-tragic view is the one that trustingly sees through the night to the dissolution of dawn which, in retrospect, redeem the depressions felt at dusk. Prometheus's is the anti-tragic vision. When Minerva offers him any of heaven's properties as her gift, he desires a ray of Apollo's light as a night sentinel and symbol of the illuminated spirit. In that desire he is a prototype of Don Fernando, who seeks not only personal but also a general public understanding of the divine:

Si yo pudiese llevar
un rayo suyo, que fuera
su actividad, aplicada
a combustible materia,
encendida lumbre que,
desmintiendo las tinieblas
de la noche en breve llama,
supliese del sol la ausencia. [1: 2076]

If I could take away one of its beams so that its properties, applied to combustible matter, might, defying night in concentrated flame, compensate for the absence of the sun. . . .

Apollo sings his song of hope and encouragement again, weaving its invitation to death and rebirth unwittingly yet effectively around the hesitant Prometheus. The key phrase is "No temas" (Fear not). Icarus-like, the bold spirit must brave the fatal plunge in order to emerge alive and transfigured. Prometheus detaches a blazing torch from Apollo's chariot and flies back to earth with it. The symbolism of his act is not difficult to perceive. Fire is essential to civilization. But the way to genuine culture is a spiritual route to the level of awareness on which Prometheus imperfectly but sublimely functions. The fire he steals is material; yet the benefit he strives to attain and distribute is knowledge so effective that it will light and comfort the knower through the long night of death and see him resplendently reborn at its end. Behind Minerva and Apollo is the Christian god. Prometheus reaches for him through them. Calderón, however, is a wonderfully subtle Catholic artist who deftly exposes the deficiencies of the precedent gods. They are not equal to the wholly gratuitous gift, to real grace. It does not occur to Apollo until much later that fire would have been a magnificent present to mankind. He bathes alone in his fire-bath of narcissistic self-glorification, more artist than ruler. Minerva gives gifts in recompense for adoration, an all-too-human goddess. And her gift is not really within her gift, so that Prometheus must steal the fire she has helped him understand. In so doing, he breaks one of the two laws in his brother's rude polity with the result that the gift, while remaining a great benefit, also becomes a scourge. Since they are predecessors, Calderón is reluctant greatly to impugn even the pagan gods. Consequently, their failings take human form, just as Prometheus's perceptions of the perfect assume a divine semblance in his statue of Minerva.

In Act I of *Prometeo,* men learn to know the gods largely in terms of their excellence. In Act II, this excellence comes to earth as both a creative and a destructive force. On the destructive side, the vices of the Olympians introduce themselves among men by means of the statue.

Epimetheus plans to steal it and hide it away where he can worship it in secret, thus partly obeying Pallas by preventing construction of a temple and the public cult of Minerva, but in essence disobeying his goddess by his devotion to her rival's image. When Merlín, the *gracioso,* or comical low-life character, objects that Pallas may learn of this, Epimetheus replies: "No lo sabrá, que la noche / siempre en sus sombras ampara / hurtos de amor" (1: 2078). (She won't find out because night always abets with its shades the thieveries of love.) Probably out of cowardice, Merlín presses on with his reservations: "Eso es dar / ignorancia en soberanas / deidades." (You are assuming ignorance in ruling deities.) Epimetheus's answer is devastating: "Esa objeción / pondrá alguno, pero es vana, / que deidad que tiene envidia, / ¿por qué no tendrá ignorancia?" (The objection might well be made, but it is groundless because why wouldn't a jealous deity also be an ignorant one?) The theme of Act II is contagion. The gods are fraternizing with mortals. Their weaknesses become known and are communicated to their worshipers, so that men come to form themselves into bands, factions, and parties like the Olympians, whose hegemony is partial, a "monarquía difusa."

But before Merlín and Epimetheus can reach the statue, Prometheus descends with his stolen torch and places it in the statue's hand. His idea is to present the gift of fire as Minerva's, so as to increase the fervor of her cult. When he leaves the grotto to summon the Caucasians to witness this new marvel, Merlín and Epimetheus move to seize the statue, but it has come to life through the animating influence of fire and wards them off with outraged cries.

Technically, the scene is one of Calderón's most effective: the would-be thieves stumbling toward the cave in the dark, the streaking comet of Prometheus's torch swooping down from the black sky, the image of the goddess flickering in the shadows, her screams as her abductors draw near, astonishment that she lives. Other Golden-Age dramatists achieve marvelous effects on occasion. The first scene of Tirso's *El burlador de Sevilla* is a masterpiece of stagecraft. But, along with his depth of conception, Calderón regularly offers the spectator dazzling visual experience, with or without the aid of properties and stage machinery. This was the aspect of his genius that Goethe, judging from his many years as director of the Weimar court theatre, so knowingly appreciated: "Technically and theatrically, Calderón is inexhaustibly great. . . . In Calderón . . . one finds the same dramatic perfection. His plays are altogether stageworthy; there is in them no element that was not introduced for a specific effect. Calderón is the genius with the greatest possible conscious control."[19]

One reason for the vividness of Calderón's technical effects is that they exist not for themselves alone but rather to serve an artistic goal. And statues had for Calderón personally a deep significance. In addition to the approximately 111 paintings which he willed to his heirs and which were appraised by Claudio Coello, he left some 13 statues, all of them on sacred subjects and, one assumes, relatively small. These the sculptor Juan de Yagüe appraised, and while their total value does not begin to approximate that of the paintings, especially the Italian ones, they seem to have been reasonably good.[20] Of course, ever since E. R. Curtius, Calderón's interest in art has been a well-known aspect of his work, especially among German scholars.[21] Most commentators have justifiably concerned themselves with Calderón and painting. Even when Helga Bauer writes a chapter on *La aurora en Copacabana,* in which Yupanquí fashions a rude statue of the Virgin which she miraculously perfects, the primary emphasis is on painting, and rightly so from a theoretical point of view, as well as from a theological one.[22] Yet, great as are the applications of painting to poetry, sculpture is uniquely suited to the drama and above all to Calderón's drama, which so often locates itself on the strategic frontiers of human experience, just as *Prometeo* is situated at the easternmost edge of the Greek-occidental world, on the border between heaven and earth.

For Calderón, the regions that border each other in sculpture are *naturaleza* and *arte,* nature and art. These, rather than immanent qualities, are powerful tendencies. Nature, the life-force, drives with irresistible logic towards death, converting the animate into the inanimate. Art defies the logic of biology and attempts miraculously to bring its subject-matter to life. *Naturaleza* and *arte* are thus reciprocal vectors, a relationship unforgettably expressed by Góngora in his funerary sonnet to the painter El Greco. The course of nature is a syllogism that concludes in death. Animate matter becomes mere matter. The gravity of natural experience, epitomized in the grave-stone, contrasts, in this sonnet, with the lightness and the near-immateriality of the painter's means—brush, canvas, wood. "Esta en forma elegante, o peregrino, / de pórfido luciente dura llave / el pincel niega al mundo más süave / que dio espiritu a leño, vida a lino." (Wayfarer, this harsh key, elegantly formed of polished porphyry, locks away from the world the most fluent brush that ever gave wood a soul or canvas life.)

The last six lines of the poem are a summation of El Greco's legacy and its effect upon his heirs. Nature has been willed Art by the painter, Art its complement and opposite, its improvement. Only death cannot be bettered. The result is an artistic one, to animate the material, to elicit emotion from the unfeeling. Dying is an ultimate kind of painting, in Góngora's superb tribute: "Yace el Griego. Heredó Naturaleza / arte, y el Arte, estudio; Iris, colores; / Febo, luces—si no sombras, Morfeo— / tanta urna, a pesar de su dureza, / lágrimas beba y cuantos suda olores / corteza funeral de árbol sabeo."[23] (Here lies El Greco. Nature has inherited Art, and Art, high technique; Iris, color; Phoebus, light; if not darkness, Morpheus. Despite its hardness, let so aggrieved an urn drink in tears and every balm that the funerary bark of the Sheban tree exudes.) Thus the sonnet celebrates the triumph of spirit over matter, of art over nature. Painting, as Helga Bauer stresses, is theoretically superior to sculpture because it relies less upon and is less conditioned by matter. Yet when man or woman is the artist's subject, the medium of sculpture strengthens the role of the physical, since flesh is after all the carapace of the soul during its sojourn on earth. Consequently, on several intense occasions, Calderón brings art and nature, soul and body, into conflictive interaction by means of the idea of the statue.

In *Casa con dos puertas mala es de guardar,* one of Calderón's masterpieces among his "lighter" plays, Félix describes his first vision of Laura in the gardens of the royal palace at Aranjuez. He has been hunting but feels drawn to the park. Entering it, he sees at a fountain either a woman or an image:

Estaba en la primer fuente
. . . .
una mujer recostada
en la siempre verde margen
de murta que la guarnece
como conefa o engaste
de esmeralda, a cuyo anillo
es toda el agua diamante,
tan divertida en mirar
su hermosura en el estanque
estaba que puse duda
sobre si es mujer o imagen,
porque, como ninfas bellas
de plata bruñida hacen
guarda a la fuente—tan vivas
que hay quien espere que hablen—
y ella miraba tan muerta
que no pudo esperar nadie
que se pudiese mover,
la Naturaleza al Arte
me pareció que decía:
"No blasones, no te alabes
de que lo muerto desmientes
con más fuerza en esta parte
que yo desmiento lo vivo,
pues, en lo contrario iguales,
sé hacer una estatua yo,
si hacer tú una mujer sabes:
O mira un alma sin vida
donde está con vida un jaspe.

[2: 279]

At the first fountain . . . there was a woman reclining in the evergreen margin of myrtle that adorns it like a band or setting of emeralds, to which circlet the water is one whole diamond. She was so absorbed in the pool's reflection of her beauty that I was perplexed as to whether she was a woman or a work of art, because lovely nymphs of burnished silver stand guard around the fountain and are so lifelike that one might expect them to speak, while she was gazing so lifelessly that no one could expect her to move. Thus it seemed to me that Nature was saying to Art: "Don't boast that you, Art, can countermand death more effectively here than I can countermand life, because, equal in opposite tendencies, if you know how to bring a woman to life from stone, I know how to turn a woman to stone. Behold a living soul inanimate among statues that are alive.

Calderón depicts here a moment of extraordinary conjuncture, during which a *coincidentia oppositorum* occurs. Working with living matter, nature moves it as close as possible to death without death actually taking place, while art, whose material is inanimate, so successfully counterfeits life that the statues of the nymphs are as nearly alive as Laura is nearly dead. It is at this moment that the two opposed forces are balanced in their contrasting tendencies. They are true reciprocals, vectors of each other with absolutely equal and opposite strengths. The long, elaborate, and artful speech of Félix might strike lovers of terser drama as otiose, but it does offer a glimpse of the inner design of Calderonian dramatic conflict. Like the elements, like siblings, like sunrise and sunset, nature and art are hostile complements, nature the death-force, art the life-force which strives to prevail over its twin. The adversaries are well matched, and it is no small wonder that art—the resurrectionary principle—should so frequently triumph in a multitude of the plays. Calderón wrote few tragedies. Yet, rightly understood, most of his plays are abortive tragedies, and

all the tragedies are abortive comedies.[24] That there should be so few clear tragedies suggests that Calderón improved nature with art: "Heredó Naturaleza / Arte. . . ." Unambiguous victory for one side or the other is a resolution
which he shuns, however, and the conclusions to his plays offer a fragile and
precarious balance for the victorious force.

One play preserves a perfect equilibrium up to the last line. In May of 1652
a superspectacle was performed in honor of Queen Mariana's birthday. The
play was *La fiera, el rayo y la piedra,* a tour de force in which three threads of
plot weave into a single strand. The central plot reflects Calderón's obsession
with the Segismundo pattern, although it is a Segismunda here, for the ill-fated
personage is female, a princess—Irífile—brought up in isolated imprisonment
by her father, who seeks to nullify her destiny. The side-pieces in this triptych
are the unhappy passions of Ifis for Anajarte and of Pygmalion for a statue in
Anajarte's garden. Anajarte is the living example of the might of Anteros, or
unrequited love, for she will love no man, no matter how passionate and persistent his addresses to her. Pygmalion represents the power of Eros or requited
love. He adores a statue and builds a temple for her. In the play's concluding
moments, Anajarte's living flesh, in accordance with the myth of Anaxarete,[25]
turns to marble just as Pygmalion's statue, in response to his ardor, comes
alive. Anteros triumphs in the death of Anajarte. Eros is supreme in the
statue's vivification. Each victory is won at the adversary's cost and so is a defeat for him. Consequently, both adversaries win and lose in perfectly equal
and opposite degrees, which is surely a consummate ambiguity, both an
"aurora en el ocaso" and an "ocaso en el aurora."

When the time comes for Minerva's statue to assume life as Pandora in *La
estatua de Prometeo,* its circumstances—blackest night—and its language resemble those of Fernando's reanimation at the end of *El príncipe constante.*
The prince's torch, "esta luciente / antorcha desasida del oriente," is Prometheus's stolen flame. Epimetheus, groping in the dark, witnesses with awe its
descent:

¿Ves en la alta
cumbre del Cáucaso un bello
nuevo esplendor cuya llama
no es relámpago que brilla
ni es exhalación que pasa
sino desasida estrella
del firmamento . . . ? [1: 2076]

Can you see, on the highest peak of
the Caucasus, a beautiful new splendor, the light of which is neither a
flash of lightning nor a passing
breath of fire but rather a star
snatched from the firmament . . . ?

But Fernando's torch is a form of religious art which transfigures him and
lights his way back across the border between life and death to an exemplary
personal triumph, whereas Prometheus's flame is a much more actively ambivalent force, introducing perplexity among men. Neither Prometheus nor Epimetheus yet knows, as Don Fernando has learned, that to approximate divine
knowledge is a paradox of fatal resurrection. Epimetheus, however, first confronts the problem as sensory experience when he attempts to draw near to Minerva's statue, alive now as Pandora. Her blazing hostility drives him away to

search for "quien me descifre el enigma / de una escultura animada / y un inanimado fuego / que con calidad contraria / abrasa como que hiela / y hiela como que abrasa" (1: 2080) (someone who can solve for me the riddle of a living statue and a lifeless flame that with opposing characteristics burns with the force of flame).

Pandora's emanations express the cooperative duality of a divinity that has come to reside among men. The gods fundamentally express their power by giving gifts and by taking them away. For men, life is the greatest gift, and divinity shows itself supreme in the bestowal and the repeal of earthly existence. Accordingly, the beams that Pandora's torch emits diffract into vivifying and annihilating rays that simultaneously shine to produce both a warming and a withering effect. These contrasting signals Epimetheus apprehends with his body but they act most sharply upon his mind, which is driven to solve the riddle that confronts him. And here the animal-like Epimetheus is not at all far from those other seekers of truth in Calderón's *comedias de santos* (conversion plays) who ponder mysteries. At the very beginning of *El mágico prodigioso* Cipriano eagerly attacks Pliny's definition of God with "misteriosas palabras" (mysterious words).[26] Eugenia, the Simone de Beauvoir of *El José de las mujeres,* applies her philosopher's wit to the arcana of its first two verses: "Nihil est idolum in mundo, / quia nullus est Deus nisi unus." ([Pagan] idols are as nothing in this world, for God is nothing but the One.) Crisanto, of *Los dos amantes del cielo,* has by chance come across the Gospel according to John and cannot fathom it. Muley Mahomet takes time out from war in *El gran príncipe de Fez* to wrestle with the difficulties of a passage from the Koran: "Del imperio de Satán / . . . solamente fueron / María y el Hijo suyo / tan divinamente exentos / que no pagaron el grande / tributo del universo" (1: 1366). (Mary and her Son alone were so divinely exempt from Satan's rule that they did not pay the world's ultimate tax.)

Through Pandora, Minerva has acted upon Epimetheus's body to bestir his mind, to draw his soul to herself. Epimetheus in his bewilderment is like Segismundo in *La vida es sueño,* exclaiming, while yet dressed in animal skins, chained, unenlightened: "Apurar, cielos, pretendo." (Heavens, I am trying to fathom why.) Sense, then, draws man to God as well as intellect. In their search, Epimetheus and Prometheus follow different routes to the same terminus. Their opposite styles expose the perfect economy of a play like *El mágico prodigioso* where, in its way, Cipriano's passionate sexual pursuit of the saintly Justina contributes as much to his salvation as do his ardent mental researches into the nature of God.

In *La estatua de Prometeo* Calderón illustrates a first encounter between men and gods. Its major result is the gift of fire and its accompanying gift of life to Pandora, Minerva's now human replica. But these bestowals, at first sight splendidly unalloyed, have on closer examination a lethal amalgam already apparent to the senses in the freezing component of the rays from Pandora's touch. And the gift itself is not really a pure gift, since Minerva has made it possible for Prometheus to steal from her brother Apollo rather than bestowing out of the plenary grace of her own possession. Such a gift involves donor, recipient, and other interested parties in a complicated, dangerous complicity that creates a partly criminal social contract. Guilt binds the parties as much as munificence. We are here, in short, in a social world not unlike that of Dostoyevsky's *Crime and Punishment;* and it is a stroke of genius for Calderón to perceive guilt as a fundamental social element from the beginning.

Theology, the passionate pursuit of knowledge as to the nature and identity of God, is for Calderón the prime intellectual impulse. Sexuality, the burning desire to possess what is most beautiful in another person, is similarly for him the prime physical impulse. These two major elements provide the basic currents in the temperament especially of Calderón's most significant male personages. They, however, are rarely drawn with equal strength to books and to women. One tendency is the stronger. Very often that is intellectual drive. But its predominance in a temperament, as we have seen with Cipriano, does not mean the eradication of the sexual and associated modes of physical expression in love, warfare, and hunting. It is true that in *La vida es sueño* Astolfo explains Basilio's childless state as the effect of the king's studies: "Basilio . . . más inclinado / a los estudios que dado / a mujeres, enviudó / sin hijos" (1: 506) (Basilio . . . more intent upon science than concerned with women, became a childless widower). Yet even here the mental does not suppress the physical; they coexist in relative strengths. And Astolfo speaks in ignorance of the existence of Segismundo, whose ill-starred presence Basilio reveals almost immediately after this statement. Segismundo, then, further attests to his father's physical reality, intensifying it and threatening it.

A not dissimilar son is Muley Mahomet, the protagonist of *El gran príncipe de Fez.* He first appears in a military encampment, as general of his father's army. But Muley's teacher Cide Hamet fears the consequences of his pupil's intellectual ardor: "Mucho temo / que este entendimiento tuyo / te quite el entendimiento" (1: 1365). And Muley confirms this fondness for speculation by disclosing that he fights for his father half-heartedly: "mi padre a quien obedezco, / bien que contra mi dictamen, / por inclinarme mi genio / más a la paz del estudio / que de la guerra al estruendo" (1: 1365) (my father whom I obey in disobedience to my own impulses, since my character is more suited to a studious calm than to the racket of war . . .). Thus Muley steals time from sleep to study and satisfy himself that "no embotan / a las plumas los aceros" (1: 1366) (the sword does not blunt the pen). Muley's words are the converse of Prometheus's when, in Act I of *La estatua,* he decides to hunt down the raging beast that threatens his people so as to prove that "[no] se embotan los aceros / en el corte de las plumas" (1: 2071) (the blade that sharpens the quill is not thereby dulled for war).

The *vita activa* and the *vita contemplativa* are thus in Calderón the two major modes of human address to the intellectual and physical challenges of existence. They clash as Prometheus and Epimetheus clash. But they complement each other as well. In fact, their progressive pattern of contrast and affinity creates a dynamic human construct that on the personal order is the equivalent of the chiastic interrelationships among the four elements on the phenomenological plane. *Armas* and *letras* are psychological concepts, like introversion and extroversion, which serve Calderón in establishing the dramatic economy of the individual himself and individuals as they address one another. *Armas* as against *letras* accordingly describes the temperament of humans like Prometheus and Prince Muley Mahomet as an energetic interaction among major pursuits, a dynamic disequilibrium. Their relative strengths also characterize the relationship between Prometheus and Epimetheus, the intellectual standing out against the sensorialist, the meditative mind taking its measure against the vigorous body.

The disposition to act and the disposition to think are, then, sibling tendencies in the Calderonian individual, as Prometheus, Muley, Don Fernando, and others clearly demonstrate. Calderón also individualizes this duality in the actual relationships between siblings. Just as one person is a compound of contrasting inclinations, so, very often in Calderón's plays of every description, pairs of brothers, sisters, cousins germane define themselves against each other in terms of their differences: *les frères ennemis.* Even more complex is the connection between brother and sister. But at all events the bond between siblings is the basic relationship in the theatre of Calderón and is a projection into separate but closely connected individuals of the dualism that for Calderón is fundamental to the single personality. Many great plays rest upon these configurations. In *El príncipe constante* there is a repressed rivalry between Prince Fernando and his brother, the King of Portugal. The younger princes have a less ample and glorious field of action open to them than the sovereign, but they attempt to emulate him through conquest in North Africa. From the beginning, the younger brothers' enterprise is ill-omened. Enrique falls as the Portuguese forces land. This misfortune begins the series of failed acts which, in a negative sense, constitute the play. For in *El príncipe constante* no effort succeeds. It is a drama of stasis. The Portuguese cannot gain ground in Africa. Neither can the King of Fez bring Fernando to exchange himself for Ceuta. King Alfonso's undertaking to ransom his nephew for any sum of money is likewise fruitless. Energy of the highest level and degree decays in frustration. Royal activity, even when directly applied, even when Alfonso acts as his own ambassador to Fez, is unavailing.

In so evenly matched a conflict, victory comes to the person who trains himself to convert the negative might of action into the positive force of contemplation. A noble or royal personage, schooled in the modes of profound analysis and of the shining deed, is best placed to appreciate the merits of both. A truly admirable prince like Muley Mahomet readily grasps the higher kinetic potential of *letras* and through immersion in these puts aside royal appurtenances so as to engage in and win the great battle of the soul. But Don Fernando, alone of Calderón's imposing figures struggling between the claims of inner demand and outer circumstance, consciously converts waning outward strength into an immutable and impregnable fortress of inwardness. The weaker he grows in body, the mightier he grows in spirit. In *El príncipe constante* action confesses its ultimate weakness and is converted into logos. With Fernando, then, from the time of his imprisonment, word is deed. In the rivalry between Fernando and his brother Duarte and nephew Alfonso, Fernando triumphs over his competitors by his superior address in governing the inner world of thought and meditation. The *discreto* overshadows the *valiente*. But the non-ruling prince's victory is even more complete. He literally cuts the ground from under his rival's feet by absorbing all possibilities for action into contemplation. The quickening of Fernando's spirit paralyzes the bodily will of all those who deal with him. They can do nothing to or for him. His logos is the sole possible sphere of action. It is for this reason that the only effective action in *El príncipe constante* is posthumous. After death, Fernando's spirit, free of and supreme over the body, can reanimate his mortal remains so that they can assume that sovereign role to which his spirit has steadily aspired but which the order of birth had, in the external sense, prevented. And in this temporary and miraculous reincarnation, the pen shows itself far mightier than the sword by inspiring, illuminating, and guiding it. Despite the blurring caused, unavoidably, by translation, Goethe's dramatic and critical instinct showed itself to be sure and penetrating in his predilection for the scene in which Fernando lights his nephew's army to the walls of Fez.[27] A greater triumph could scarcely be imagined. Sibling rivalry is its source, even though the death of Duarte and the accession of Alfonso mute the struggle between brothers.

The absorption of one brother by another takes its most extreme form in *De una causa, dos efectos,* a *comedia* encapsulated in serious political and dynastic problems. Its protagonists are the twin brothers Carlos and Fadrique. Such was the excitement of those attending at their birth that they forgot to identify the first-born. The siblings thus engage each other in terms of perfect equality. But at the beginning of the play Carlos is everything, a model of grace, learning, and deportment, while Fadrique is nothing, a lout who amuses himself by practicing cruelties upon his jester. The princes' father Federico purposes to end the long-standing hostility between his duchy of Mantua and the duchy of Milan by marrying one of his sons to Diana, the only child of its duke, Filiberto, who has himself suggested this accommodation. The difficulty is which son to choose for Diana. If the elder were known, he could remain to inherit Mantua, and the younger brother could be sent off to Diana and Milan. In his perplexity, Federico directs both princes to Milan, leaving the choice to Diana. *De una causa* thus takes the form of an *examen de maridos,* a play in which a highly-placed female must choose a husband from among several competing males. At first it would seem to be no contest. But love for Diana and competition for her with his brother bring alive and completely remake the oafish Fadrique into a model prince and courtier. His lightning transformation and its success with Diana put Carlos so much out of countenance that, shedding his intellectual, social, and physical attainments, he reverts to an even more pronounced brutishness than his brother had originally manifested. The brothers' roles are now completely reversed, and Diana appears to have no chance of making a rational decision. But before the official suit Carlos had presented himself *incognito* to Diana at a joust and ball, deeply impressing her. Trusting in her original response, Diana, pressed for time, chooses Carlos. So favored, he promptly regains his higher character and Fadrique proves the solidity of his own new achievements by accepting his defeat with real grace. This dry recital conveys nothing of the vitality and magnetically amusing interplay of fraternal forces that Calderón orchestrates in *De una causa, dos efectos.* There, hostile human forces progress in a disequilibrium that is consistently close to destruction, first for one and then for the other adversary, both of whom profoundly modify each other in their struggle. From that struggle Calderón realizes a net gain, for Carlos in his despair has learned to know the basal nature on which his more refined qualities rest, while Fadrique has attained to a culture to which he was indifferent and of which he was ignorant. In struggle and defeat, Fadrique has come alive, has triumphed as fully in the inner sense as Carlos has in the outer. Here, sibling rivalry very clearly is the whole stylish and stylized matrix for an extremely dynamic play.

Another variation on this theme is *En la vida todo es verdad y todo mentira,* a masterpiece of Calderón's high maturity, an elaboration on the Segismundo motif. Just as the novel aspect of *De una causa* was the untutored brother's rise to brilliance and Carlos's corresponding collapse into barbarism, so in the present play does Calderón multiply the complexities by presenting us with two heirs presumptive to the imperial diadem who both are and are not brethren. In *De una causa,* the *examen-de-maridos* format brought Carlos and Fadrique into a most dangerous and exhilarating rivalry. In *En la vida* an even more menacing scrutiny pits Leonido against Heraclio. Having usurped the empire from Mauricio, Focas many years later returns to his native Sicily. He hopes to find there the son he had fathered on a peasant girl and to establish him as his successor. It is also rumored that Mauricio's son Heraclio has grown up in concealment in Sicily. Focas, a ruthless man, aims to destroy Heraclio. But the two young men have been brought up in fraternal amity as noble savages by their tutor Astolfo. When Focas discovers them, Astolfo refuses to reveal which one is Leonido so as to save Heraclio's life. Focus then subjects the lads to a series of trials which are inconclusive, although they do disclose that Heraclio's character as a *discreto* is of higher potential than is Leonido's loyal brawn. Focas finally succeeds in identifying Leonido as his son. He then sends Astolfo and Heraclio to certain death by setting them adrift in a light boat on the stormy Mediterranean. They are saved, however, by the armada of Federico, Duke of Calabria, who plans to invade Sicily, and they join this successful expedition. Heraclio kills Focas and is acclaimed emperor. Leonido rallies to Heraclio as a faithful vassal. Heraclio marries Cintia, Queen of Sicily, and prepares to rule even more musingly and fearfully than Segismundo does in the last lines of *La vida es sueño.* The fresh and really sublime feature of the competition between brothers in *En la vida* is that, even though the young men are not blood brothers, Focas imposes a deadly struggle upon them of the type which so often characterizes kin in Calderón's drama and which they successfully overcome out of their true sense of brotherhood. The secondary sense of relatedness in them is far finer than the raw physical facts, which so often lead to a pitiless hostility.

Enmity *ab ovo* is not in Calderón restricted to brothers. Sisters mercilessly oppose each other, too. In the earlier plays, their theatre of action is often limited to love. Love, however, allows of a whole range of hostilities. In Act II of *De una causa, dos efectos* Fadrique excuses his arrogation to himself of his brother's achievements in these familiar terms: "Yo me quise atribuir / hoy, señora, los trofeos / de Carlos; que, como amor / es guerra y en guerra fueron / permitidos los ardides, / creí era bien usar dellos" (1: 481). (Today, my lady, I allocated to myself Carlos's booty, because, since love is war and trickery is allowed in warfare, I thought it appropriate to employ deceit.)

"Amor es guerra." The phrase is not merely a figure,[28] for, just as the accident of birth can deprive a younger brother of the glorious exercise of power, so also can it stand between a younger sister and her desires. In *No hay burlas con el amor,* the enemy is Doña Beatriz, the beautiful but monstrously affected older sister of Doña Leonor Enríquez. Leonor loves and is loved by Don Juan de Mendoza. But Don Juan is afraid to ask for Leonor in marriage because he does not want to cause in her father speculations as to how a young man unknown to him thinks he knows his daughter well enough to want to marry her. And if Juan asks for either daughter (very common among nobles at that time—think of Saint-Simon asking for *any one* of the Duc de Beauvillier's daughters), he will probably be given the elder, since the first-born should marry first. Thus the basic problem is purely mechanical. Calderón makes it individual by portraying Beatriz as a *précieuse ridicule* who appears to have convinced herself that learning is preferable to marriage. Worse from the point of view of convention, she is attempting to impose her celibacy on her sister: "Mariez-vous, ma soeur, à la philosophie!" The conflict of *No hay burlas con el amor* could hardly be clearer, or simpler: "no hay dos opuestos / tan contrarios como son / las dos hermanas haciendo / por instantes el estrado / la campaña de su duelo" (1: 498). (No two adversaries could be so hostile as the sisters are, making of their salon, minute by minute, a field of honor.)

Yet to this rather obvious situation Calderón adds a fresh dimension by masculinizing and externalizing a feminine and domestic problem. He also dramatizes an extremely conventional metaphor and in the process renews it by making the figure literal. Leonor and Beatriz fight a play-long duel. Leonor wins but Beatriz is only in a technical sense the loser. From this conversion of a metaphor to the dramatic letter, Calderón derives a good bit of humor, as when Inés urges her mistress Leonor to the attack on Beatriz with: "¡Santiago, cierra España! ¡A ella, a ella!" (1: 508). (St. James and Spain to the attack! After her, after her!) Nonetheless, this sibling rivalry, like the masculine one, remains cruel and dangerous, as Juan clearly recognizes: "que si hay envidia entre hermanos / es la más cruel envidia" (1: 511). (Sibling rivalry is the cruelest rivalry.) To save the situation, Calderón employs his customary maneuver of forcing a comic birth by Caesarian section, comedy emerging from a near-fatal tragic labor. Miraculously, then, Beatriz relents, albeit with a lingering Gongorism: "Mas desde aquí prometo / que calce mi conceto / a pesar de Saturno / vil zueco en vez de trágico coturno" (1: 513). (But I pledge that henceforth, despite Saturn, my mind shall be molded to the lowly sock in tragic buskin's lieu.)

But *Burlas* is more than a clever, amusing, and adroit play. It embodies a remarkable concept. Masculine outside hostilities invade privileged feminine inner space. Calderón has forged a link between dramatic exterior and interior dimensions. It is little short of a revelation: "también hay duelo en las damas" (Ladies duel, too), the title of a Calderón *comedia.*

In *Lances de amor y fortuna,* the ladies leave their accustomed domesticity, strike boldly out into the world of men's affairs, perturb, align, and pacify it. In this early play Aurora and Estela are sisters, the daughters of the deceased Count of Barcelona. Since they have no brother, Aurora, as the elder, would normally succeed. But Estela disputes her right to do so, claiming that Aurora was born before their father married their mother and so was illegitimate. Against the struggle between the sisters, a masculine competition also develops, and it is the principal action of the play. Rugero, a young nobleman, returns to Barcelona just as the factions supporting one sister or the other are forming. He falls in love with Aurora and joins her party, as does another *galán*, Lotario, for the same reason. Their rivalry for Aurora's favor, like that between Carlos and Fadrique over Diana, is the play's most important figure and replicates in the foreground the background of hostility between Aurora and Estela. Moreover, just as the two would-be countesses are, though politically opposed, very fond of each other, so are Rugero and Lotario excellent friends, though in love with the same woman. Accordingly, *Lances de amor y fortuna*, written early in Calderón's dramatic career, employs a strategy of fully developed chiastic formulation that practically amounts to his artistic signature. The play also boldly brings women out into the masculine open and allows them to be sovereign there. In the end, of course, Aurora and Estela compose their differences and Aurora and Rugero marry. But that convention should not be allowed to conceal the startling freshness of the emergence of women and the feminine in Calderonian drama.

The play which most artfully exploits a characteristic interweaving of affinity and oppugnancy, of brother and sister, of sister and sister, is perhaps *Auristela y Lisidante*. In the complexity and abstractness of its structure, this late work resembles a musical composition or lengthy mathematical formulation. There is emotion here. We mainly start and end with it. Yet the play's real beauty resides in its complicated architecture. With Calderón, opposition is both an emotion and an aesthetic. Rugero describes, very unfortunately for him, his first love to Aurora in precisely such terms: "Cejas grandes, ojos negros / que sobre la blanca tez / muestra que la oposición / es hermosura también" (1: 175). (Vivid brows and black eyes that, contrasting with white skin, show that oppositeness is also a form of beauty.)

The plot of *Auristela y Lisidante* is not novel. When Polidoro, the youthful king of Athens, dies in a duel, his twin sisters, Auristela and Clariana, quarrel over the succession. Forgetful attendants at their birth have again failed to identify the elder. Thus, like Carlos and Fadrique and Aurora and Estela, they advance apparently equal claims. Yet Calderón introduces fresh complexities into the familiar situation. The killer of Polidoro is Lisidante, Auristela's lover. Angry Athenians pursue him shortly after the death of their king. Lisidante and his servant abandon armor and clothing which his best friend Arsidas and *his* servant promptly find and put on. Arsidas is Clariana's lover. Lisidante's pursuers of course take Arsidas for Lisidante, and capture and imprison him. Nor is Lisidante able to make good his escape. A storm drives him ashore at Athens, where he remains in great perplexity over Arsidas.

While the men are detained in Athens, their sisters, fearing for them, raise armies which they themselves general. The crisis occurs when their two armies take positions at the city walls. A conference of all interested parties decides that it is best to resolve the issues by means of a series of duels. Consequently, in the play's final encounter, all its principal characters meet, completely armored and ready for battle, the women—Auristela, Clariana, Aurora, and Cintia—as well as the men—Lisidante, Arsidas, Milón and Licanoro. Their multiple duels resolve into a single contest between Lisidante and Arsidas. But before any fighting can occur, Lisidante yields to Arsidas. In the confessions and unmaskings that follow, every man and every woman gains a partner and a kingdom. To marry Lisidante, Auristela must renounce the throne of Athens but becomes the queen of Epirus. Union with Clariana makes Arsidas king of her city. Her sister Cintia marries Milón of Achaia, while Aurora accepts Licanoro of Macedonia.

These concluding human correlative structures result from an initial endowment of passion—the basic opposing forces of hatred and love, *odio y amor.* They repose in women just as forcefully as they do in men. Calderón's artistic strategy is to deploy hatred against love in a war of attrition that will exhaust enmity into conscious surrender so that it will subordinate itself to love and make offerings to it. To achieve the result, women must be introduced into the ranks, for their affective power—their strength—is equal to that of men. In the plays of Calderón, therefore, women act like men and men like women out of dramatic necessity. Women become generals and men, such as Achilles in *El monstruo de los jardines,* become ladies-in-waiting. And even though a play like *Auristela y Lisidante* may strike the late twentieth-century sensibility as silly or abstract, it is a not unworthy element in Calderón's remarkable dramatic discovery and exploitation of the female. His women, though less morose, are the Hedda Gablers of their age in that they reveal in art, with startling novelty, depths and dimensions of human nature not previously explored or shown. His dramatic elaboration of male and female derives not from a then nonexistent pychosexual science or from theories of society equally nonexistent, but from the difficulties and successes in giving life to the metaphor that "Amor es guerra," the paradoxical premise that combines hatred and love, man's sovereign passions, in one nuclear statement. On the human scene, siblings most nearly incarnate the polarities, at least according to Calderón, and a great many of his plays employ brothers and sisters to reveal the complex world of their sympathies and hostilities, usually with a view to producing peace for a while, as in *Auristela y Lisidante,* when Arsidas entreats his sister to accept Milón: "Y yo te ruego, porque / de un odio un amor se haga, / que des la mano a Milón" (2: 2052). (And I beg of you that you will make love out of hatred by marrying Milón.)

La estatua de Prometeo is, after the fact in some cases, the prototype or generic myth that prepares apparently quite distinct and non-mythological *comedias* such as *De una causa, dos efectos, En la vida todo es verdad y todo mentira, No hay burlas con el amor, Lances de amor y fortuna,* and *Auristela y Lisidante.* It examines more separately, but not altogether so, elements which, in works that do not focus on the problematics of the rise of paradox, are bonded together. *Prometeo* studies the forging of the links in that sympathetic contradiction which relates the human to the divine. It is Calderón's dramatic covenant. The fundamental confrontation there occurs between two families, one earthly and the other heavenly. The earthly family is rudely peaceful but vacuous. Prometheus most acutely senses that the Greeks of the Caucasus lack something essential. They are not completely human. They require passion. It is this absence of passion that makes it unnecessary for them to be governed. Desire creates the need for control, direction, and hierarchy. In the individual the reciprocal of desire is conscience, in the state the sovereign, in the cosmos

God. Desire might almost be said to create all three. Figuratively, then, Prometheus is mind in search of passion so that a universe of reciprocals may be created by his quest. Prometheus's mind is, fortunately for orthodoxy, a Platonist universalist one. Accordingly, the goddess he concretely fashions on earth closely conforms to the model resident in heaven. If God made man in his image, then, conversely, man will remake God in an approximation of the original.

There is in this play, however, one immense departure from orthodoxy. If it needs excuse in our time, let it be that Calderón's subject is pre- or para-Christian and so admits of departures from the dogmatic. A better explanation is that the Christian artist will inevitably find his faith and his art in conflict.[29] Even in the drama of Calderón, in so many ways miraculously attuned to post-Tridentine dogma, art occasionally, and here with great authority, asserts its claims against doctrine. The god of Calderonian secular drama is feminine, a goddess, a woman. She has much to do with the *Ewig-Weibliche* that subsumes Faust into itself at the end of Goethe's *Faust*. But in *Prometeo* the rhythm, the motion, of creation is mutual, and Prometheus's mind desiring desire, first draws Minerva itself: "Was wirt du tun, Gott, wenn ich sterbe? / Ich bin dein Krug (wenn ich zerscherbe)?"[30] (What are you going to do, God, when I die. I am your vessel. What if I shatter?) Then Minerva, the great mother mind, draws Prometheus to her: "Das Ewig-Weibliche / zieht uns hinan."[31] (The eternally feminine draws us onward and upward.) Furthermore, the fire that Minerva in heaven stealthily confers upon Prometheus has several senses. It is literal. It represents cookery and civilization. It also is the brand that will communicate the passions to a waiting humanity. Minerva surely intends the gift to be an unalloyed benefaction. But she is not alone. She belongs to a family of gods, among whom she stands in sharpest contrast to her sister Pallas, while Apollo, their brother, somewhat blandly mediates between the rival sisters. The three siblings doubtless amount to a kind of imperfect proto-trinity. The sisters, however, are its driving forces, reciprocals of each other. So Minerva cannot act alone; her deeds automatically implicate her sister. When Minerva replicates and incarnates herself among humans in the form of the statue fashioned by Prometheus, she also replicates and incarnates the converse of herself, Pallas. Calderón's genetics progress by the logic of contrast, of existence and nonexistence, of being and nothingness. The human counterpart is always less than the divine model because the human partly opposes the divine. Pandora resembles Minerva in her disposition to love, know, and preserve; but she departs from the creator of her soul in mingling these propensities with Pallas's pleasure in hatred, ignorance, and destruction. The sibling goddesses have incorporated their ruling passions into a single human: "Zwei Seelen wohnen, ach, in meiner Brust."[32] (Two souls, alas, inhabit my heart.) The genius of the system is that, like human sexual reproduction, it avoids replication, conferring on its product a variety of capacities or incapacities. Even more significantly, the encounter between the heavenly siblings and the earthly twins of the Caucasus demonstrates the essential reciprocal structure of *La estatua de Prometeo*. The two brothers here below face two sisters and a brother up above. Prometheus's foray into heaven brings to life on earth the form of a woman who mediates between the rival brothers much as Apollo mediates between Pallas and Minerva. Thus two men and a woman come to confront two women and a man. In this shifting, reflecting, loving-and-hating alignment, the key function comes to be Pandora's. She is, after all, the first woman.

Woman is Calderón's muse. Her ambiguities are the source of his almost wholly ambiguous dramatic art. She is, moreover, the mother of myth, the origin of those tales of love and rivalry which Calderón tells over and over again. Myth in Calderón is mythos, that primordial state of affairs from which the story develops. In *En la vida todo es verdad y todo mentira,* Astolfo catches sight of a woman in Act I. Her appearance in the wilderness where he lives in a cave with Leonido and Heraclio means their joint fall from the innocence of retreat into the historical world of perplexity and murderous hostility. Goodness and harmony are not altogether lost, however. They remain the major music but mix maddeningly with the new strains of discord. It is the same in *La estatua de Prometeo.* Pandora's coming to life is a marvelous gift which is celebrated in the repeated singing of the verses: "Quien triunfa para enseñanza / de que quien da ciencia da / voz al barro y luz al alma" (1: 2079). (She who triumphs in order to display that the person who bestows knowledge gives mute matter speech and light to the soul.) They are a mysterious answer to Epimetheus's question: "¿Quién, dioses, / nuevo espíritu la inflama, / nuevo aliento y nueva vida?" (1: 2079). (Who kindles within her, o gods, a new soul, new breath and life?)

Yet, like the contradictory beams of her torch, Pandora's persona diffracts into opposed elements, beauty the harmony, her voice—the very means of artistic expression—the dissonance. When Prometheus, immediately after Epimetheus, finds his statue of Minerva come to life as the woman Pandora, this new divine-plus-human expression is a symbol, an *écriture,* which he finds it most perplexing to interpret. What he sees conflicts with what he hears:

Otras dos y ambas
bien extrañas y bien nuevas
tú, al verte y oírte, causas:
una, que siendo tú más
favorecida, reparas
en que te conozca; y otra,
que vengas tan enojada
que desmientas divina
para castigarme humana.
¿Qué se hizo la harmonía,
qué se hizo la consonancia
de tu voz? [1: 2080]

Looking at you and listening to you produce two additional effects on me, both of them quite novel and odd. The first is surprise that you should wonder at my knowing you, when our worship of you has increased. The second is surprise that in anger you should abandon your divine nature in order to punish me in human form. What has become of the harmony and consonance of your voice?

After this interview, Prometheus and Epimetheus present the miracle of Pandora to their fellow Caucasians. As they all, in acceptance of her, repeat the musical phrase "Quien da ciencia . . .," the new dissonance moves from expression to action. Soldiers interrupt with cries of "¡Guerra, guerra! ¡Al arma, al arma!" Pandora explains the meaning of this fusion:

mezclar
horrores y voces blandas
jeroglífico es que diga
que pacífica esta llama
será halago, será alivio,
será gozo, será gracia
y, colérica, será
incendio, ira, estrago y rabia,
y así temed y adorad
al fuego cuando le esparza,
o afable o sañuda, a toda
la naturaleza humana
la estatua de Prometeo. [1: 2082]

Combining melody with the ghastly
is a mysterious symbol indicating
that in peace this flame will be a calm
breath of delight and grace but that,
as the instrument of wrath, it will
mean madness, arson, and destruction. And so, when the statue Prometheus made, either graciously or in
anger, diffuses fire to all humanity,
fear it and worship it.

Calderón, inventor of the *zarzuela,* combiner of immense synthetic and synaesthetic spectacles like *La fiera, el rayo y la piedra,* is a seventeenth-century Wagner whose art is rather a kind of composition than a purely verbal form of expression. With him the compound is the fundamental sub-unit, infrastructure. The thematic and rhythmic consequences of the metaphor that "amor es guerra" are a music that combines the diatonics of love with the chromatics and further inimical tones of ordered hostility. This strange new conceptual music, consisting in a pulsation that harmoniously asserts its independent conformity with God and the divine plan and yet closely accompanied by an equal and opposite dissonance, is so far from being a conceit or empty figure as to amount to a basic construct beaming throughout the dramatist's whole work a dual and ambivalent message, a yin and yang of creation never far from destruction, the first and second voices of the fugue. Calderón's companionable Manicheanism, fusing and triumphantly exploiting the forces of darkness and light, is, I would submit, nearer to the sources of his creativity than the doctrinal Catholicism which that creativity, in sympathy and distrust, so rewardingly draws upon. In art Calderón is a Manichean fusionist whose muse is a supreme goddess ambivalently drawing the strength of her omnipotence from the armies of both darkness and light. The commanding deities of those forces are her generals, between whom she mediates. The Manichee female, constant in the *obra,* emerges very clearly at times, as in, for example, *En la vida.* As previously mentioned, Astolfo there takes alarm when he catches sight of a woman in the wilderness in which he has raised Leonido and Heraclio. He mentions the event to his wards, and there follows a wonderfully fugal discussion in which Heraclio and Leonido are the contrasting voices of the dialogue, while Astolfo's function is creative mediation. The frequency of words connected with sound is highly significant. First, Heraclio regrets that Astolfo did not call him to see the woman, because

de cuantas cosas cuentas
que hay en el mundo, ninguna,
siempre que la nombras, llega
a igualar con el halago,
la caricia y la terneza

none of the things in the world that
you enumerate for us comes close to
the tenderness and caressing charm
with which one hears "woman" each
time you mention her. The soft

con que su nombre se escucha,
pues [su blando rumor] deja
segundo ruido en el alma
que, sin dar razón entera
de lo que quiere decir,
aun con la mitad deleita.

sound of her name stirs a second
rustling in the soul which, without altogether saying what it means, nonetheless delights with half a meaning.

But then Leonido thanks Astolfo for not exposing him to the awful vision, because

siempre que mujer dices
al oír su nombre tiembla
el corazón como que
de algun contrario se acuerda,
dejándome su sonido
no sé qué susto, qué pena
que acá en el alma parece
que, aun no sabida, atormenta.

whenever you say "woman," my
heart, as if recollecting some enemy,
trembles at the sound of her name,
whose echo resolves into an unclassi-
fiable alarm and hurt which, here in
my soul, even though unrecognized,
causes anguish.

Heraclio, however, is far too logical to allow Astolfo's declaration that both
reactions are right to pass unchallenged. The tutor then explains:

Como es cualquiera
mujer pintura a dos visos
que, vista a dos haces, muestra
de una parte una hermosura
y de otra parte una fiera
sin que se sepa en cuál puso
el arte más excelencia.
El más familiar amigo
de nuestra naturaleza
es y el enemigo más
familiar de la fe nuestra.
La media vida del alma
es tal vez, tal vez la media
muerte del alma. No hay
regalo, Heraclio, sin ella
y sin ella no hay, Leonido,
dolor ni ansia, de manera
que, mirada a entrambas luces,
hace bien el que la tema
y hace bien al que la estime.
Cuerdo es el que se fía de ella
y cuerdo el que desconfía
porque, en igual competencia
ella da la vida y mata.
Ella es la paz y la guerra,
la cura y la enfermedad,

It is because any woman is a painting
in two perspectives which, when seen
from two aspects, reveals on the one
hand a vision of loveliness, and on
the other one of savagery without
one's being able to decide in which
one art more greatly excelled.
Woman is our masculine nature's
most customary consort and the intimate enemy of our faith. At times
she half creates the soul, at others
half destroys it. Without her, Heraclio, there is no ease and without her,
Leonido, there is neither pain nor desire, so that, looking at her in both
lights, one does well to fear her and
one does well to esteem her. It is wise
to trust in her and wise to mistrust
her since, in equal measure, she gives
life and takes it away. She is peace
and war, healing and sickness, joy
and sorrow, the antidote and the poison, the calm and the storm and, to
sum it all up, the good and evil of
every situation because, as the arbi-
ter of good and evil, she both be-

la alegría y la tristeza,
la triaca y el veneno,
la quietud y la tormenta
y, para decirlo todo,
bien y mal de contingencias
que, árbitro del bien y el mal,
da el honor y da la afrenta,
que es cuanto hay que dar, de suerte
que, a imitación de la lengua
loable o nociva, no hay
cosa en el mundo que sea
tan mala como la mala,
tan buena como la buena. [1: 1116]

stows honor and administers the affront, in which two actions all giving consists, so that, like the tongue that exalts or slanders, nothing in the world is worse than an evil woman and nothing better than a good one.

It is more instructive to examine these three beautifully modulated passages from a functional than from a moral point of view. They are a synaesthesia. "Mujer" voices their tonic vibration, and the music of her name irradiates sympathetically to Heraclio's awakening soul, antipathetically to Leonido's. Mediating between them and merging their differences, Astolfo develops an image through recourse to the great visual art of portrait painting. But his is a very strange representation, constructed on both a dual perspective and a dual point of view, rather like Picasso drawings and paintings of the 1920s, with their multiple vantage points. The progression, which has been from sound to sight, does not stop there but moves to action, for woman is "árbitro del bien y el mal," mistress of circumstance, and so occasions good or ill fortune. As such, she is the fount of fable, of drama. The speeches of Heraclio, Leonido, and Astolfo—thesis, antithesis, and synthesis—provide a synaesthetic genesis of Calderonian drama in three stages: musical, visual, and mimetic. Indeed, as action, as drama, *En la vida todo es verdad y todo mentira* begins only after they are pronounced. It is then that *la mujer* acquires an individual name and face and that the events she inspires unfold.

Thus, in a very specific sense, woman is sovereign in the theatre of Calderón. The female who literally rules fascinates him, for she is both the vessel of immanence, "la quietud," and the lord of turbulence, "la tormenta," the *vita contemplativa* and the *vita activa* in a single personality. As "árbitro del bien y el mal" she also has the power to guide circumstance.

One great study in which woman magnificently guides events to catastrophe is *La hija del aire,* a portrait of hybris in two complete parts, two conjoining plays.[33] In them, Semíramis is a Segismundo who fulfills in letter and spirit her evil horoscope. She is also one of Calderón's most striking individuals in that she so completely combines in her hybrid character the most masculine modes and the most feminine, a monster of destruction and creation, murderess of her husband, mother of his son, yet a mother who reabsorbs her male offspring and rules as a man in his image. Semíramis's supreme moment occurs when, expecting the attack of Lidoro, king of Lidea, she exhibits her contempt for him and confidence in herself by preparing for battle with the utmost femininity: her ladies dress her hair to the accompaniment of music. But that intimate, feminine, and domestic music plays against the approaching crescendo of Lidoro's warlike trumpets and drums; mingling, these two qualities of sound characterize the bellicose female:

La gran Semíramis bella
que es por valiente y hermosa
el prodigio de los tiempos
y el monstruo de las historias,
en tanto que el rey de Lidia
sitio pone a Babilonia
a sus trompetas y cajas
quiere que voces respondan
y, confusas las unas y las otras,
estas suaves cuando aquellas roncas,
varias cláusulas hace
la cítara de amor, clarín de Marte.
[1: 752]

While the king of Lidia approaches to besiege Babylon, Semiramis the great and beautiful, who is the marvel of the age and the hybrid prodigy of the histories because of her courage and beauty, wishes to oppose other sounds to Lidoro's trumpets and drums so that, mingling, hers harmonic and his harsh, the lute of love and the bugle of Mars produce distinctive strains.

In her supremacy, Semíramis rules over all men, whom she encounters and employs and exploits in contrastive pairs. In the first play it is her initial lover, Menón, general of the armies, who loses the struggle for her with his king, Nino. In the second play it is a single man in two aspects: Arsidas, Semíramis's general, and Lidoro, the king of Lydia, whom Arsidas has been sent to conquer. He has been sent, then, to conquer himself. As Arsidas, he is bound in love and loyalty to his queen. As Lidoro, he is her bitter enemy. Here we have both the Heraclio and the Leonido response to woman in a single male:

¿Quién creerá que a un mismo
  tiempo
Arsidas contra Lidoro
se viese nombrado y, siendo
Lidoro y Arsidas yo,
en dos contrarios opuestos,
allí rey y aquí vasallo,
marchase contra mí mesmo? [1: 753]

Who would believe that at the same time that Arsidas found himself appointed a general to fight Lidoro, he, being both Lidoro and Arsidas, a king at home and a subject here, would divide himself into two opposing parts and march against himself?

The queen similarly exploits two separate personalities in the second play. They are her general Licas and her admiral Friso. Licas is loyal to Semíramis's son Ninías, while Friso steadfastly serves the queen. When Semíramis assumes the dress of her son and rules in his place, this conflict in loyalty assumes prodigiously complex proportions, such as Arsidas-Lidoro experiences in his several roles. It is, I think, abundantly clear, even after so brief an incursion into this very rich play, that Pandora and Astolfo's "woman" are Semíramis's ancestresses.[34]

They all have other descendants, as well. Passing from the mythical Pandora to the legendary Semíramis we encounter a semihistorical Madama Inés, the virile *Langräfin* of Hesse, in *Mujer, llora y vencerás,* and also the fully historical Christina of Sweden in the Cristerna of *Afectos de odio y amor,* both of them later plays intended primarily for a court public, no doubt. As *Mujer* begins, Madama Inés is superintending the mustering of her troops in anticipation of an attack by Federico, who is approaching with an army to free his brother Enrique, whom Inés holds prisoner. She so little fears her adversary that she continues the hunt which news of his arrival had interrupted. Inés's *nonchaloir* reminds one of her ladies of Semíramis's disdain for Lidoro: "De Semíramis, señora, / se cuenta que a una batalla / salió el peine en el cabello, / mostrando que no embaraza / el sobresalto al aseo" (2: 1412). (My lady, they say of Semíramis that she went into battle with her comb still in her hair, showing that a surprise attack need not disturb one's *toilette.*)

Clearly, Inés is even more masculine than Semíramis. She prefers the hunt to feminine adornment. But she does not greatly depart from her spiritual forebear in her management of men. Federico and Enrique are twin brothers and her cousins. Both have good claims to Inés's lands. Inés would rather rule alone; but, as Federico draws near, her subjects compel her to agree to choose one brother as her husband. The play now converts from warfare to the *examen-de-maridos* format, since Enrique and Federico are both in love with their enemy Inés. In their rivalry over her, they themselves become enemies and when Inés chooses the more warlike Enrique, Federico, realizing that her motive is predilection rather than politics, gathers an army and captures his brother and Inés in the *quinta* where they are honeymooning. When Inés sees Enrique lying apparently dead, she breaks down and weeps, and the spectacle is so affecting that it moves Federico to repentance. Enrique is of course not dead and can now enjoy his position and his union with a spouse who has triumphantly regained her femininity. Even so, Inés has maneuvered and exploited her cousins exactly as Semíramis used Menón and Nino, Licas and Friso, and the schizoid Lidoro-Arsidas. *Mujer llora y vencerás* is, moreover, a most perfect literal incarnation of the notion that "amor es guerra."

But *Afectos de odio y amor* is not far behind in that respect. Its subject is a fantastically difficult love affair between Casimiro, grand-duke of Muscovy, and Cristerna, newly-crowned queen of Sweden. Not only are the states of Sweden and Muscovy hereditary enemies but also Casimiro has killed in battle Adolfo, Cristerna's father. To get revenge, she has offered her hand in marriage to the noble who will kill or capture Casimiro. There are details which are more or less "historical" here: the death of the king in the battle of Lützen (1623), Christina's notorious fondness for learning and the hunt, her aversion to marriage.[35] But the "historical" Christina is a convenient actuality on which Calderón restructures his obsession with the sovereign female. His Cristerna is the ultimate evolution of the type; and he develops her to such an extreme that the whole subject matter of his art is in danger of disappearing as the new queen, in her first appearance, reviews the laws which she is about to promulgate in Sweden. Cristerna's code completely rehabilitates women and corresponds with amazing exactness to present-day programs seeking perfect equality between woman and man. Equal access to power is, Cristerna most astutely realizes, the guarantor of women's rights. Thus, even though the Salic law has never been enacted in Sweden, the queen bans it so that no one will ever attempt to exclude women from command. Moreover, she anathematizes the whole concept of female inferiority:

. . . a voz de pregón y a son de trompas y cajas se dé por traidor a toda la naturaleza humana al primer legislador que aborreció las entrañas tanto en que anduvo que quiso del mayor honor privarlas. [2: 1761]	To the accompaniment of the executioner's shouts, trumpets, and drums let that first law-giver, who so loathed the womb in which he took shape that he wished to deprive women of the highest office, be denounced as a traitor to all mankind.

Her second edict throws all public life open to women:

Y porque vean los hombres que, si se atrasan las mujeres en valor e ingenio, ellos son la causa, pues ellos son quien las quitan, de miedo, libros y espadas, dispone que la mujer que se aplicare, inclinada al estudio de las letras o al manejo de las armas, sea admitida a los puestos públicos, siendo en su patria capaz del honor que en guerra y paz más al hombre ensalza. [2: 1762]	And in order that men may realize that, if women fall behind them in courage and intellect, they are themselves responsible, since men, from fear, deprive women of books and swords, the law provides that any woman who develops her talent for learning or warfare will be appointed to public office and will be eligible in her country for those honors which most grace man in peace and war.

Cristerna's defense of this law employs unassailable logic: "Pues lidien y estudien, que / ser valientes y ser sabias / es acción del alma y no es / hombre ni mujer el alma" (2: 1762). (Women ought, then, both to fight and to become learned, because courage and wisdom are spiritual properties and the soul is neither male nor female.)

The final two edicts are the most erosive of Calderón's and other dramatists' basic material. The first abolishes dueling. Here again the reasoning is powerful: "que se borren / duelos, que notan de infamia / al marido que sin culpa / desdichado es por desgracia" (2: 1762). (Duels are abolished, for they brand with infamy the guiltless husband who is unfortunate in the choice of a wife.) The queen then exposes the fundamental paradox of the honor situation:

Hombre, si por ser inútil la mujer no la fías nada, ¿como todo se lo fías, puesto que el honor la encargas? ¡Bueno es que quieras que no	Men, if you entrust women with nothing because they are untrustworthy, how is it that you entrust everything to them, since you give your honor into their keeping? It is

tenga ingenio o valor para
darte honra por sí y por sí
los tenga para quitarla!
¡O pueda darla o no pueda
perderla! [2: 1762]

absurd to insist that women in themselves have neither intellect nor courage and yet to find that they have these sufficiently to destroy the very honor they were unable in themselves to bestow. Woman can either bestow honor or is incapable of destroying it.

And finally, Cristerna abolishes the romantic intrigue that is an essential narrative part of most of Calderón's nonallegorical plays:

. . . la que desigualmente
se casare enamorada
en desdoro de su sangre,
lustre, honor, crédito y fama
sea comprendida en pena
capital, sin que le valga
de amor la necia disculpa. [2: 1762]

Capital punishment is provided for any woman who marries out of her station for love to the detriment of her breeding, standing, honor, solidity, and good name. A pleading of love cannot mitigate the severity of the sentence.

The Queen's new dispensation pushes through that fertile field of ambiguities and complexities, with the dualistic female figure at its center, which is the locus itself of Calderonian dramatic art, and into a sexless paradise of perfect equality. There woman becomes whole again. Cristerna's legislative vision is the habitat of a triumphant female inwardness, which is the answer to Eugenia's anguished appeal in *El José de las mujures:*

¡Oh nunca mi vanidad,
viendo que los hombres son
por armas y letras dueños
del ingenio y del valor,
me hubiera puesto en aquesta
estudiosa obligación
de darles a entender cuanto
más capaz, más superior
es una mujer el día
que, entregada a la lección,
de los libros, mejor que ellos
obran, discurre veloz! [1: 407]

Since men by means of weapons and of learning are sovereign in the spheres of intellect and courage, I wish that my pride had never compelled me to show them the superior ability of the woman who, once she puts her mind to her books, grasps with much greater promptness than men display.

Cristerna's laws also completely restore woman to the full exercise of public functions. Her fighting female is the perfected version of Semíramis and of Madama Inés, ruling without alloy over the outer world of action. Gone now is the comb in the elaborate coiffure, and gone too are the tears that purchase victory at the terrible price of a retreat into the stultifying conventions of a traditional femininity, that allness and nothingness of which Cristerna so bitterly and tellingly complains. In fact, the queen of Sweden's idea removes all the barriers between inwardness and outwardness, femininity and masculinity, impression and expression. Since talent and courage are psychological traits that are independent of sex, she allows them to flow unimpeded into the minds and bodies of those men and women who abound in such qualities, there to take the form of significant achievement—intellectual, physical, or both. But it is not only audacity that makes Cristerna's construct startling. Upon emerging from the mist one can begin to make out its form, extent, and location. Similarly, with the queen's legal leap into another social world, one can see what she has left behind. It is the whole mythic mass that goes to make up Calderón's secular drama.

As we have seen, woman is at the heart of this myth. Her central endowment is the power to move men inwardly, especially as to the emotions connected with honor, and outwardly, particularly in connection with deeds relating to honor, dueling above all. The key to the dynamic structure of acts and feelings resulting from "honor" is sexual differentiation. Men have their role and women theirs. One of Calderón's boldest and most original dramatic strokes is to confuse, combine, and reverse traditional sexual roles. We have seen many examples of this technique, which is a psychology as well as an *ars poetica*. But the logic of an art that breaks down the barriers between masculine and feminine leads inexorably to a world in which no real difference between male and female can be defended or even permitted. This world is, precisely, Cristerna's legal paradise. Yet it is also a new world, another world, where Calderón has no clear and familiar forms and outlines to confuse and blur. Consequently, it remains a vision and not a site where the artist yet dares to function. Thus *Afectos de odio y amor* amounts to a falling away from the perfection of its primary objective. It is a regression to exactly those conflicts of love and honor which Cristerna had meant to abolish and without with Calderón's plays are inconceivable. We emerge from the myth only to revert to it.

The dynamic of the play is Calderón's characteristically comedic desire to convert hatred into love. To achieve this, Casimiro faces overwhelming obstacles, and in the overcoming of them *Afectos* closely resembles *La hija del aire*, for he has to contend not only with Cristerna's understandable hatred but also with other illustrious rivals, as the action proceeds to the *examen-de-maridos* situation, greatly favored by Calderón because it so strongly presents woman as the ruling and motivating force. The solution is worked out in a *reprise* of the Arsidas-Lidoro duplication of *La hija del aire.* Casimiro enlists as a common soldier in Cristerna's army and wins her admiration and affection. When, in response to a challenge, he appears as Grand-Duke Casimiro at her court, the queen is torn between love for the soldier and hatred for the duke. Love wins and forces her back into the old order, in contrast with Semíramis, who remains sovereign to the tragic last:

Y pues que mis vanidades	And since my pride surrenders on
se dan a partido, puedes,	terms, you, Lesbia, may erase free-
Lesbia, borrar de aquel libro	dom from that book. Let the world
las exenciones. Estése	be again as it was and let it be known
el mundo como se estaba	that women are born subject to men,
y sepan que las mujeres	because, in feminine feelings when-

vasallas del hombre nacen,
pues en sus afectos, siempre
que el odio y al amor compiten,
es el amor el que vence.[2: 1796]

ever hatred and love compete, love is
always the winner.

Yet even this conscious relapse into the *ancien régime* retains a rich interchange of ironic ambiguities. Women may well be born enfiefed to men, but Casimiro has won Cristerna's love by willingly subjecting himself to her. She is, furthermore, a reigning monarch and a formidable campaigner whose goal is not the day's battle but ultimate victory. How it can best be achieved is a technique which Cristerna learns from Casimiro. Surrender is his strategy, a paradoxical one which nonetheless brings him honorably to her bed. There, more intimately, the struggle continues; but this time it is Cristerna who fashions triumph from apparent submission. Her seeming recumbency terminates in an absolutely erect conquering shout: "es el amor el que vence." Even grammatical gender lends it support to her huzzah and its wonderful ambivalence. Cristerna thus completes and returns to a progression that begins with Pandora, mother of all our dubieties.

Once the Caucasians of *La estatua de Prometeo* begin to worship Pandora, the whole mechanism of Calderón's craft starts functioning. The twin goddesses Pallas and Minerva have endowed their creature with their own attractions and aversions, *odio y amor*. And so, after both Prometheus and Epimetheus have worshipped Minerva, both must deal with her incomplete counterpart Pandora. She, however, applies half of her emotional heritage to Prometheus, half to Epimetheus. She warms to the man who formed her statue but is cold to his brother. Yet Epimetheus immediately presses his claims while Prometheus hangs back. The fact is that Prometheus cannot transfer his feelings for Minerva to Pandora. Nonetheless, Pandora's very presence kindles an intellectual dispute between the brothers, which quickly involves the emotions. Pandora intervenes, successfully for the moment: "No más, que no es bien que a duelo / pase de la voluntad / la luz del entendimiento" (1: 2085). (Stop. An intellectual debate shouldn't degenerate into a battle of the emotions.) But Pandora then proceeds to open the urn which Pallas has given her. That act releases dissension in full strength. Discord next appears, to pronounce a cosmic curse on mankind, but it aims most immediately at Prometheus and Epimetheus who, in punishment for their misdirected affections, are to love without return and to be loved without being able to return:

El sacrilegio del culto
y del culto el sacrilegio
con tan discordantes hados
como que tú, Epimeteo
amarás aborrecido.
Tú, al contrario, Prometeo,
aborrecerás amado
y todos en bandos puestos
arderéis en duras lides. [1: 2086]

The crime of worship and the crime that comes from worship [produce] discordant destinies. You, Epimetheus, will love a woman who loathes you, while you Prometheus will loathe the woman who loves you; and all of you, split into factions, will burn in bitter strife.

Epimetheus loves Pandora who loves Prometheus who loves Minerva. On the human scale, this chain of unrequited passions brings to mind the pastoral novel or the *feuilleton.* Calderón's unique structural principle, however, pairs each attraction with a repulsion: Epimetheus loves Pandora and is loathed by her. She loves Prometheus and is loathed by him. *Odio* is not, then, a sin of absence or omission but rather an almost positive countervailing force, a basic architectonic element which Calderón deploys with near-scientific dispassion, even though hatred is itself a passion in scholastic psychology. Hatred, or violent aversion, forms bonds between humans that approximate the linking strength of love. In *La estatua de Prometeo,* hatred and love contribute the basic inflow of energy that shapes its human vectogram. This is the same configuration that aligns the physical world, or, as earlier in the play, the human genetic schema.

The difference here is that the cosmos and human conception are a prologue or *loa* to the human drama of conflict between the psychological properties of violent attraction and violent aversion—*afectos de odio y amor*—which Prometheus, Epimetheus, and Pandora are primordially enacting. Woman again displays the highest potential for conversion, because, in the stasis which the equilibrium of attraction and antipathy brings about, she moves blindly but brilliantly in the direction of love and reconciliation. Love attracts more powerfully than hatred can repel. So Pandora, heeding Epimetheus's sacrificially dispassionate command, pursues Prometheus:

Epim: Ve tras él aborrecida,
no tras mí amada.
Pand: Eso intento
porque tengo por menor
dolor, menor sentimiento,
aborrecida y amada
seguir entre ambos extremos
al que amo aborrecida
que no al que amada aborrezco.
[1: 2086]

Epim: Pursue him who loathes you
and not me you love you.
Pand: That is my intention, because
when one man loves you and another
loathes you, I feel that in choosing
between the two extremes, it is less
hurtful to pursue the one you love
unrequited than to take up with the
one whose love you cannot return.

The pursuit of requited love in an emotional and physical and spiritual world where love and hate function in nearly equal strength is the fundamental impulse of Calderón's *comedia,* a great unbalancing force that breaks the impasse between the Manichean antagonists and tumbles them into decisive conflict from which love barely but usually[36] emerges triumphant. This is Rosaura's role in *La vida es sueño,* and it is no accident that the drama begins with her, ends with her.[37] Rosaura is both an active and a passive principle, a vessel of reconciliation to the extent that she loves, a vial of potent wrath to the extent that she hates.[38] Her deepest use however, is as the agent through whom God, at least the God of Calderón's *comedia,* effects a tolerable resolution. She submits to him and, through her, he causes the counsels of love to prevail. Like Rosaura, Pandora is both the human source of strife among men and its remedy, *el veneno y la triaca,* the poison and the antidote.

And yet the salutary pursuit of love leaves behind it a wake of hatred and destruction. Requited love is a progress that throws up its own bow wave of terrible obstacles. This unavoidable hatred is love's reciprocal, one that incites men to perform the second of honor's two main rituals, the duel. If we recall that *duelo*'s etymon is *duellum,* an archaic variant of *bellum,* war, then the sense of "amor es guerra" becomes complete. In the secular religion of Calderón's *comedia,*[39] men and women seek primarily the perfect communion of a love that is equal between them. But women and men almost never love perfectly when they are loved. Such imperfection creates in the unrequited lover, usually but not always male, a tide of rage and frustration that threatens to overwhelm the whole frail vessel of the play. Thus "amor es duelo," a phenomenon by means of which the frustrated lover seeks the relief of indirect revenge upon the lady through the maiming or murder of the man she favors, or appears to favor. Epimetheus is in Calderón's artistic canon the first man to experience these evil promptings, and he responds to them with a wondering intensity:

. . . no sé que especie de ira qué género de veneno, qué linaje de rencor ha introducido en mi pecho, no tanto el que a mí me deje cuanto el que vaya siguiendo a otro, que de su desaire me vengara en él primero que en ella. ¿Quién introdujo tan ilustre ley al duelo; tan bárbara al pundonor como ser en un desprecio la dama de quien me agravio y el galán de quien me vengo? [1: 2087]	I don't know what sort of wrath, what kind of poison, what species of rancor she [Pandora] has inaugurated in my emotions, so that I would want to get revenge for her disinclination to me on him [Prometheus] rather than on her, not so much out of resentment that she would leave me as that she would leave me for somebody else. Who first established so illustrious a rule in duelling, and such a barbarous one in the male code that, in a slight, I should take offense at the lady and get revenge on the gallant?

So it is that the primary office of adoration, failing of equal response, engenders a second and almost as powerful rite of revenge. The harmonic of creation gives voice to the dissonance of destruction, which is the echo of an unachieved perfection. The pursuit of perfection is, accordingly, an entropy, might in deterioration. To reverse the tendency to chaos, a fresh application of energy is needed. In *La estatua de Prometeo,* this renewing force comes from an appeal to Jupiter which Minerva successfully submits. Until she breaks out of Pallas's restraining grasp, Prometheus's sublime, energy-giving act expends itself in dispersed hostilities which are meant to terminate in his and Pandora's sacrificial extinction in the very fire which he has brought to earth. This is the natural tendency of the play, a tendency to degrade and deteriorate. It expresses itself musically in the duet which Prometheus and Pandora sing, or, rather, which they declaim and which the music, most significantly, picks up in an echoing reprise:

Prom. y Pand.:	¡Ay de quien vio . . .	Take pity on him who has seen
Música:	¡Ay de quien vio . . .	
Los dos:	. . . el bien convertido en mal	good changed into evil
Música:	. . . el bien convertido en mal	
Los dos:	. . . y el mal en peor!	and evil into greater evil.
Música:	. . . y el mal en peor!	

[1: 2096]

In *La estatua de Prometeo* the struggle between a striving for perfection and its decomposed reciprocal takes a properly mythological form. Apollo, unable to decide between Pallas's attacks on Prometheus and Minerva's defense of him, abandons the decision to his rival sisters. They organize the Caucasians into two factions, devoted exclusively to Minerva or to Pallas. These are preparing for a battle in which Prometheus expects to be killed and in which Pandora plans to fall at his side. But Discord tries to win a cheaper victory for Pallas by pretending to have been sent by Jupiter to the Caucasians to announce the condemnation and sacrifice of Prometheus and Pandora. At Jupiter's apparent command, the factions merge for the purpose of arresting and executing the guilty pair. As we have seen, however, Minerva fights free of Pallas and successfully appeals to Jove. Apollo himself appears with Pandora's and Prometheus's pardon "porque nunca niega / piedades un dios" (1: 2096) (because a god never withholds mercy). His light dispels the mists of hatred. Pallas and Discord disappear. Prometheus and Epimetheus regain their affection for each other, and Prometheus loses his aversion to Pandora. They immediately marry and the play ends with a chorus in counterpoint to its tragic voice, so nearly successful: "¡Felice quien vio / el mal convertido en bien / y el bien en mejor!" (1: 2097). (Blessed is he who has seen evil changed to good, and good to a greater good!)

But *La estatua de Prometeo* escapes its classicizing confines at the close of Act II in Epimetheus's poisoned and tormented speech exploring man's first experience of jealousy and the desire for revenge. Its vocabulary is exclusively that of the *comedia de capa y espada* (cloak and sword play): *vengara, ley, duelo, pundonor, agravio, dama, galán.* Here, the play's major characters lose their mythological stature (which they recapture in Act III) and assume the proportions of standard figures in Calderón's popular stage successes of the 1630s. From this point, affairs could easily whirl off to a troubled and exciting conclusion like that of *El galán fantasma* or, more easily still, like that of *Afectos de odio y amor,* which *La estatua de Prometeo* so significantly resembles. What links the mythological play to the comedy of manners is their common preoccupation with problems centering about the female.

The contemporaneousness of this central conflict in the mythological play with the major preoccupation of Calderón's lighter comedies of entertainment—what we vaguely call honor—suggests a genetic relationship, in Calde-

rón's mind, between myth and mythos. As shaped by Calderón's art, the ready-
made material of classical fable slowly is transformed into the essential matter
of contemporary, that is to say, seventeenth-century, drama. Calderonian
mythology yields essentially the honor myth. In chronological fact, of course,
the honor myth precedes its supposed progenitor. Calderón had written many a
play for the *corrales* before he composed his first mythological *comedia, El
mayor encanto, amor,* of 1635. Yet the really suggestive connection is the one
Calderón clearly makes in *La estatua* between the fable of Prometheus and the
wrath of Epimetheus that springs from impulses that any theatre-goer would
have recognized as perfectly present-day (with him). *La estatua de Prometeo* is
thus in a theoretic and dramaturgical sense, though not so in fact, the progenitor of all Calderón's secular plays in which at the last evil is just barely
changed into good, and thus of his entire comedic production. It is a reconstruction of the ascension of his *comedia.*

If the observation is exact, then perhaps its most significant critical result
would be to show the usefulness of reassessing the nature of Calderón's art, in
large part, at least. That art does not immediately and directly derive from
Christian theology. The matter of *La estatua de Prometeo* is pre-Christian, although the play itself is unimaginable outside a Christian context. Great dramatic and other art also precedes the entrance of Christianity into history. *La
estatua* traces its lineage back to Aeschylus's *Prometheus Bound* (479-78
B.C.?), the only survivor of his Prometheus trilogy. Aeschylus's play, in fact,
tells us much about the essential theme of Calderón's drama. Prometheus's
great deed is to act against God with the lesser multiples of Apollo, Pallas, and
Discord. Calderón shields us from Aeschylus's awful oneness. Yet the party
most nearly interested is lofty "Jupiter" himself, an essential element of whose
sphere Prometheus has stolen. At the end of *La estatua,* a Christianizing Jove
pardons the malefactor, for no humanly very clear reason. But the deed that
creates the artistic space in which the play comes to life is the sublime leap into
heaven and the arrogation of its most precious and perilous material. Genet-
ically, then, this play and many others like it come into being because man
splendidly opposes himself to God, or the gods, or a god. And the benefits to
mankind are so important that the offended deity is at least constrained to forgive. Prometheus is thus unbound and himself becomes a semi-deity through
civilization and art. Obviously God, however named, is deeply implicated in
these proceedings. They challenge him. But the tacit assumption of most *calde-
ronistas* that Don Pedro's theatre celebrates in plenitude, à la Claudel, the divine order of the universe, needs to be challenged and, I believe, revised.

No one could seriously question, on the other hand, the affirmative theological commitment of the *autos sacramentales,* which this study does not directly scrutinize. Yet even there the presence of so many nakedly mythic subjects should give pause to any categorical assertion that Calderón's drama
serves Christian doctrine merely with a simple and direct reverence. Consider
several of the *autos sacramentales alegóricos: El divino Jasón, Psiquis y
Cupido, Los encantos de la culpa, El sacro Parnaso, El verdadero dios Pan,
Fortunas de Andrómeda y Perseo* and *El divino Orfeo.* Although only seven
plays out of about seventy in the allegorical group, these mythological adapta-

tions span nearly all of Calderón's career in the field, and the mythological *auto* recurs with a fair regularity. What I am suggesting is that we abandon the notion that the *autos* are catechism and doctrine in dramatic rhyme. This is the fundamental assumption of A. A. Parker's lonely and most intelligent and valuable book.[40] One reason that no companion volumes have joined Parker's may be that art *de fide propaganda* has a chilling effect on the aesthetic and critical sensibility, whatever the critic's posture of belief. If Calderón is doctrine, where is there room for self-sufficient creation? Even in the extreme case of the allegorical theatre, however, art as itself, though hardly for its own sake, has in the mythological a distinct matter and theme. Even though art is an *ancilla* to dogma, and one that serves well, to do so she must be a person apart, but not always a perfectly obedient person. Indeed, one aspect of art's service to morals and dogma is a creative disobedience in which the *non serviam* fashions a counter-world to the sublime idiocy of omnipotence. The counter-world threatens, challenges, and activates the inertness of supremacy. Because of it, God bestirs himself and intervenes, drastically or beneficently, in human affairs. The Promethean challenger brings God to life in the mortal and historical sense.

Calderón's dramatic art, in the *comedias* and even in the *autos,* I would venture to say, challenges the smugness of a providentially ordered universe in the full expectation of a massive and annihilating response. Before the play begins, God is not so much dead as sleeping. Art awakens him to wrath and he lays about him with many a heavy blow. But the incredible power behind divine aggression is so inconceivably great that it generates its own contrasting principle of mercy and forgiveness. And, after all, even the most threatening of men is a puny adversary to God, who therefore more often—much more often—spares than destroys. Kings, too, have much of this self-converting absoluteness. In *El príncipe constante* Don Fernando speaks *en connaissance de cause* when he makes his wonderfully detached plea for mercy to the King of Fez: "Rey te llamé y, aunque seas / de otra ley, es tan augusta / de los reyes la deidad, / tan fuerte y absoluta, / que engendra ánimo piadoso" (1: 273). (I called you king, and even though you profess a different religion, the divinity of a king is so exalted, so strong and absolute, that it engenders a disposition to mercy.) Fernando's appeal is in the nature of a final formality before the condemned man goes to his inevitable execution. It is nonetheless spoken with fervor, not for the prince's own sake—he prefers to die—but for the soul of the King of Fez. The king is unmoved, unlike "Jupiter" in *La estatua,* and Fernando soon expires. His tragedy is a partial and ambiguous one.

But there are in Calderón's *obra* a few plays that result in the annihilation of the challenger. They constitute his tiny corpus of tragedies, a core of really only three plays, to which I would hesitate to add *La hija del aire* and *Las tres justicias en una.* At all events, however one defines the genre, Calderón wrote extraordinarily few tragedies, particularly in view of his deeply serious cast of mind. Taken as a whole, the function of tragedy in the *obra* in general is to serve as an earnest of God's readiness to destroy on rare occasion. He would prefer to bring his opponents around, to convert them. But he can and does obliterate them. The risk the challenger takes is real. He can perish. The tragedies are thus a kind of real presence that makes the comedies grimly rather than light-heartedly playful.[41] It is a part of the essential critical hypothesis of *La dama duende,* for example, to believe that the quarreling among its three male protagonists can lead at any time to death. Calderón's comedy is not the perhaps more familiar and certainly more comfortable world of *marivaudage* in which even the most frightening capers and gymnastics are shielded from the ultimate by a kind of comedic safety net. Death defines Calderonian comedy. The tragedies assure the reliability of this definition. Consequently, the challenger cannot lightly defy the order he opposes. He risks death.

Physical death is also a constant presence in the *comedias* as a result of duelling. Occasionally, the death of the comedic spirit occurs. In *Para vencer amor, querer vencerle,* love dies. César and Margarita are noble cousins who at the death of their uncle advance nearly equal claims to rule his dukedom of Ferrara. They are meant to marry and govern together. César loves Margarita. But Margarita loathes him. In the fashion of Tirso's *Palabras y plumas,* César does every possible and impossible thing to win his cousin's love. When, despite every conceivable *fineza,* Margarita remains adamantly cold, César deliberately murders his love for her and marries another woman. The play ends with Margarita ignominiously destitute. Its plot is not unlike that of *El médico de su honra* in the assassination of love and a new marriage consequent upon it.

A possible theoretical mythological model for Calderón's tragedies is *Los tres mayores prodigios,* of 1636, which is itself prodigious in the brilliant clearness of its fusion of three myths around a central miscarriage of love. The play's motion is pursuit. The centaur Nessus has abducted Hercules' beloved wife (yes, wife) Deianira. To find her, Hercules calls upon his friends Jason and Theseus. The three heroes will search the entire world for her. In the course of their part of the search, in Acts I and II, Jason and Theseus each have their greatest adventure, with Medea and the Minotaur respectively. From these dangers they emerge triumphant to join forces with Hercules in Act III, when he finds Nessus and his wife. Deianira has stoutly resisted all of her abductor's advances. Yet Hercules, when he recovers her, considers her spoiled for his use, spares her life, but sends her away from him. It is then that Deianira decides to use Nessus's poisoned shirt to win back her husband's love. When Hercules, in his agony, immolates himself, Deianira follows him in death. Fundamentally, *Los tres mayores prodigios* is a mythological tragedy of honor; and its plot resembles that of *El pintor de su deshonra,* especially in the abduction of Serafina and her faithfulness to her pursuing husband. It and other of Calderón's mythological dramas, which as a group lean far more heavily to the tragic than do his other plays, guarantee the awful seriousness of *La estatua de Prometeo* and invest Prometheus himself with a genuinely heroic quality. Like Theseus and Jason, he survives. But he might have perished in a Herculean agony, in fact came very close to doing so. Calderonian comedy is tragedy-haunted; and his characters believe in the ghosts that harass, even though they do not often destroy them.

Perhaps the most important lesson that *La estatua de Prometeo* can teach us is that Calderón's art is heterodox. Two different kinds of cosmic consciousness are its basic ingredients. The first is the passive, womblike, enveloping consciousness of God's hold on the universe, fixing man in his mysterious place on earth. The second is man's challenging awareness that he has a terrible destiny. The genetic event in the work of art that is Calderonian drama is an act of defiance of God's imprisoning system. The defiance can be intellectual or it can be physical, a crime. In either case, the challenge takes the essential form of a theft, a usurpation, of divine powers. To steal from God is to impinge upon him, to try to eclipse him. It is, above all, to enter into a relationship of struggle with him. The system that the challenger constructs in opposition to God is the play, the work of art, over which the challenger's consciousness presides, just as God's presides over the universe. Man can be absolutely sovereign within himself. In response, God of course can crudely annihilate his opponent. As we have seen, he does this on occasion. But the far more rewarding tactic is for God to break into and puncture the individual hermetic system so as to convert it to his rule, to bring the dissident to heel. God's countertactic, thus, is usually to invade, undermine, and overmaster his adversary's consciousness indirectly, by means of an agent, who may be unaware of his or her mission. At the termination of this unequal contest we are left with a subdued antagonist whom God the protagonist has put in his place, converted, so that he keeps that place more or less willingly. But Calderón's antagonists are nearly all noble, lordly, and proud. They rule naturally. And the chances that they or others like them will assert their independence again soon are very good. Consequently death is the only permanent resolution in Calderón.

La estatua de Prometeo fairly well exemplifies the abstract model just proposed. The structure of *La vida es sueño* may make the pattern of stimulus and response clearer still. Its situation is, however, brilliantly complex. Yet the key to this play, so often discussed at the cost of others of Calderón's rewarding works, is Basilio, king of Poland, a sovereign personality. Basilio sends out to those who witness him two differing signals, a physical and an intellectual one. The physical icon of himself beams out a message of submission. The king is old and bent—"rendido al prolijo peso" (1: 507). Like all mortal men, he must submit to the operations of time, and die. The song the prisoners sing at the beginning of *El príncipe constante* beautifully states this general law which even a ruler must obey: "Al peso de los años / lo eminente se rinde, / que a lo fácil del tiempo / no hay conquista difícil" (1: 249). (Eminence must yield to the burden of the passing years, for the operations of time make any conquest easy.)

This constant, crushing pressure of time is the God-presence in the play. It directs Basilio to a certain and tragic destiny—his own death—from which he cannot escape. But though enslaved in body, Basilio creatively rebels in the spirit. He strikes out against the real enemy, which is time, and seeks to master it, dominate it, conquer it. With his astrology, Basilio is the sublime thief of time, and time is the protagonist against which he struggles:[42] "contra el tiempo y olvido / los pinceles de Timantes, / los mármoles de Lisipo, / en el ámbito del orbe / me aclaman el gran Basilio" (1: 507). (In defiance of time and oblivion, Timante's brush and Lysippus's chisel acclaim me, throughout the breadth of the world, as Basilio the Great.)

Thus Basilio takes the characteristically Calderonian adversary stance, "contra el tiempo y olvido." The posture is complex, but its main components are a rebellion against the law that prescribes death as the one and universal penalty, and a corollary desire to transcend time, to overreach it. At root the will to reach beyond one's allotted span of years is a long-recognized force leading to achievement in the arts: "Exegi monumentum aere perennius."[43] And it is indeed art in the form of Timantes's painting and Lysippus's sculpture that projects Basilio into a future that his body will not last long enough to know.

Yet Basilio the Great is not only the subject of art. He is himself an artist working in the social and political sphere. The government of Poland is his subject. His aim is to determine who shall rule the kingdom after his death so that it will be wisely and virtuously administered. Accordingly, the living state becomes for Basilio a work of art, but not quite in Burckhardt's sense.[44] In a literal sense, rather. Art, however, gives existence to that which previously had none. Basilio's problem is that Poland already has a king, has entered into time, has a historical past as well as a future that will sooner or later be out of his hands. Consequently, if Basilio is to achieve a measure of timelessness for himself, he must deprive Poland of its right to history. As a Christian monarch, he nonetheless knows that God has entered human time as historical Christianity and that since the coming of Christ history has been a divine property with a providential purpose in both tragedy and triumph. Basilio's quarrel, then, is with God. The king has cast the son's horoscope and does not like what he sees there, what God has in mind for the future of the throne and of Poland. As a result he seeks to countermand those disagreeable orders by depriving his son of a life in time and Poland of its ordained succession. He disposes that Segismundo's cousins Astolfo and Estrella shall marry and so fuse their competing claims in joint rule. Segismundo is not to be allowed to exist. His prison is a life-long womb from which he is meant never to emerge, thus never to be born.[45]

Poland, just before *La vida es sueño* begins, is a state hermetically sealed off from history and time, whose ruler has made it his spiritual mortuary in which his sovereign idea and dispensation will never decay, even though the body turns to dust. Basilio's political artistry thus forms of the state a kind of mausoleum where succeeding sovereigns will be the keepers of the sarcophagus, guardians of an arrangement that outlives the arranger's mortal part. The only doubtful element in this truly Pharaonic scheme appears to be the identity of the keeper. Will he be of the direct or of the collateral descent?

Looking down the biological perspective of the life of Segismundo, his only son, his only child, his only direct succession, Basilio sees the future as a grim one, for others, for Poland, for the flock in his keeping:

Segismundo sería	Segismundo would become the most
el hombre más atrevido,	uncontrollable man, the cruellest
el príncipe más cruel,	prince, and the most pitiless mon-
y el monarca más impío,	arch, who would divide his kingdom
por quien su reino vendría	into factions and make it a school for
a ser parcial y diviso,	treachery and an academy for all the
escuela de traiciones	vices
y academia de los vicios [1: 508]	

Yet the essence of the tragic vision is personal. Basilio sees the son cruelly harrowing *him,* the aged, great, kind, learned, venerable, and virtuous father:

y él, de su furor llevado,	and he, in the midst of his stunning
entre asombros y delitos,	crimes, on the crest of his passions,
había de poner en mí	was destined to tread me down and I
las plantas, y yo rendido	was destined to find myself prostrate
a sus pies me había de ver	before him (how it grieves me to say
(¡con qué congoja lo digo!)	this!) with my venerable locks a car-
siendo alfombra de sus plantas	pet for his feet.
las canas del rostro mio. [1: 508]	

Segismundo's horoscope, as Act III shows, does have objective validity. It comes true literally. But Basilio's anticipation of it has an equally great subjective importance for the king. The scene of his humiliation is a kind of Rohrschach test that reveals his inner states of mind. And what dominates Basilio's apparently scientific, dispassionate, orderly, reasonable, and benevolent intellect is a terrible dread. The king immensely fears (¡con qué congoja lo digo!) to die. In the normal flow of events, Segismundo, as Basilio's son and heir, would be the witness to and the beneficiary of his father's demise. The strong young man rises as his aged parent sinks to the tomb. These are the usual operations of time: "Al peso de los años / lo eminente se rinde." Like Basilio himself, the child is to the parent an ambivalent icon, symbolizing at the same time the parent's continuance and his extinction. Yet Basilio can take no comfort in the idea of partly living on through another. He dwells with such horror on the message of extinction that he makes his son the agent of death rather than the witness to it. Quite simply, Basilio "fails" the test; he misinterprets the scene placed before him, for it is a scene rather than a blot. The king cannot face a future world in which he is not supreme. He therefore suppresses that being, his son, who in time would rise to replace him on the throne. This is a terrible aggression, a terrible usurpation, and Basilio's conscience is, with reason, deeply troubled. But the royal response is not the salutary one of opening the sealed chamber of horrors and of taking one's chances, with trust in the ultimate goodness of God. The king decides, rather, to give both God and his son a second chance, in the hope that one or the other will have changed his mind:

Quiero examinar si el cielo	I mean to determine whether heav-
. . . .	en . . . has relented, or at least re-
o se mitiga o se templa	laxed, and might not, if successfully
por lo menos y, vencido	resisted with strength and prudence,
con valor y con prudencia	change its mind, because man can
se desdice, porque el hombre	master the stars
predomina en las estrellas [1: 511]	

And Basilio carries his experiment out under strictly controlled laboratory conditions. Segismundo arrives at the palace and leaves it in a drugged coma so that his recollection of the experience will have a dreamlike and unreal quality. Believing that the discovery of himself as heir-apparent to the throne of Poland was a vision and not fact, he will, reasons his father, not despair at returning to the nonexistence of prison. At the palace Segismundo of course conducts himself with the savagery that confirms Basilio's reading of the future; and the king returns the prince to his cell, tranquil in the conviction that he has done his Christian best.

Segismundo's behavior is certainly indefensible, certainly reprehensible. His murder of the injudicious second servant is hugely shocking and doubtless derives in part from the well-known barbarities of Ivan the Terrible, from whom Segismundo and Basilio both partly descend.[46] And yet, even though death and dishonor at the prince's hands threaten successively Clotaldo, Astolfo, the second servant, Estrella, and Rosaura, the real focus of Segismundo's rage is his father. Every accusation he makes against Basilio is tragically well-founded. At the core of their disastrous relationship is the father's denial of the son. They have never met as humans bonded by flesh and blood. This non-meeting recurs when Basilio, arriving just after Segismundo has hurled the servant to his death, refuses the prince a first parental embrace. Basilio's explanation is a confession. He is afraid: "tengo miedo a tus brazos." (Your arms frighten me.) Segismundo is Basilio's future and that future holds death in store. The king turns away from it with loathing and dread. This fresh denial elicits a fresh outburst:

Sin ellos me podré estar
como he estado aquí,
que un padre que contra mí
tanto rigor sabe usar
que con condición ingrata
de su lado me desvía,
como a una fiera me cría
y como a un monstruo me trata
y mi muerte solicita,
de poca importancia fue
que los brazos no me dé
cuando el ser de hombre me quita
[1: 515]

I can go on doing without your love because, when one has been robbed of his humanity, the refusal of an embrace has very little significance in a father who treats me so harshly that he can, in his unlovingness, keep me apart from him and bring me up like an animal and treat me like a monster and wish for my death

The truth of the accusation and of the ones that follow it seems to me unassailable. Segismundo is a non-being. Basilio's denial is a denial of his reality. The prince's actions at court amount to a desperately hostile search for that lost reality. But the rigidly controlled nature of Segismundo's day at court precludes any ultimate encounter. Servants and protectors constantly intervene between the prince and his victims. He has no time to ponder the awful severity of his sentences, to reverse them. And let us remember that in the first major encounter of *La vida es sueño* Rosaura faces death at Segismundo's hands, submits, and is reprieved. There are no submissions in Act II. Its encounters are summarized by Basilio's interview with Segismundo, which is all fear, flight, denunciation, and denial. The murder of the second servant is, then, a kind of monstrously triumphant self-assertion and the only real action in the second act. Segismundo annihilates that meddling paternal intervention which robs his consciousness of objectivity by keeping from him decisions of life and death. Segismundo cannot possibly be a man or a prince until his actions carry through to their ultimate consequences. He cannot be real until he can truly condemn and truly pardon. The murder of the second servant destroys Basilio's rigid asepsis and makes later deeds of clemency, on behalf of the same major personages, meaningful. Segismundo can kill. And he can be merciful. The whole sense of government, of the self and of the state, is for Calderón tied up with the wonderful and for us frightening interplay of *rigor* and *piedad,* which must be seen as modalities of each other, in the fashion of *armas y letras.*[47]

But, above all, Act II of *La vida es sueño* gives the measure of Basilio's imperial mind. It has searched the future and found a dread event, a beast in the jungle. Poland consequently is a kingdom constructed to counter, to ward off, to circumvent its ruler's fated harrowing by his son. Basilio's is the artistic temperament that anticipates its disappearance from the human scene and in compensation seeks to build a monument to and of the spirit that will long remind following generations of his brief and glorious span on earth. His kingdom is in essence a vision that obsessively fixes on tragedy in the hope of preventing tragedy. It comes into metaphysical and social being in response to God's assertion of his supremacy, which it challenges. The drift from orthodox to heterodox, from doctrinal to artistic, is subtle yet immense, and centers about a major posture or figure of the play, man in relation to his fate. The fundamental question is: Who fabricates destiny? Whose artistry is sovereign?

Where it concerns Segismundo, Basilio's reply is perfectly orthodox: "el hado más esquivo, / la inclinación más violenta, / el planeta más impío / sólo el albedrío inclinan; / no fuerzan el albedrío" (1: 508). (By even the most importunate fate, the most unnatural disposition, the most pitiless horoscope, the will is bent rather than compelled.) The evil propensities that frequently assail the Christian draw him away from God, if he heeds them. He can overcome such temptations, no matter how strong they are. No man is irretrievably condemned to evil, especially when evil opposes the providential plan. In choosing the good, man obeys. In choosing evil, he disobeys, freely.

But the problem that Basilio confronts is that of an apparently foreordained evil: Segismundo's rule and his own humiliation. Here the king is unsubtle, even confused. Misfortune is ambiguous. Good can come from it. To impede certain catastrophes would be to interfere with the workings of providence. Here, of course, we are dangerously close to Leibniz, but Calderón is a Leibnizian tragedian. Ours is the worst of all possible worlds, from which nevertheless a tolerable though temporary edifice can be riskily constructed.

I suppose that tragedy has to be simple-minded. It operates so with King Basilio. When he looks to the future, he sees it as unalloyed disaster and thus tries to prevent it. His posture, though it springs from a dogmatically sound understanding of the operations of free will, is heterodox because it opposes the King of Poland to God. God has his uses for coming events. Basilio doesn't want them to occur. Basilio, in explaining his enterprise, uses unequivocal terms: "determiné de encerrar / la fiera que había nacido / por ver si el sabio tenía / en las estrellas dominio" (1: 508). (I determined to imprison the beast that had just been born in order to see whether the learned man could prevail against the stars.) "El sabio" is Basilio. "Las estrellas" are an aspect of God, his plan. Basilio wishes to thwart it. The result is a glorious but hugely unequal struggle. For two-thirds of *La vida es sueño,* however, Basilio maintains his hegemony. Calderón has a penchant for losers: *La gran Cenobia, La hija del aire.* And it is especially the language used to describe man's control over his fate that imbues it with a heterodox hostility: "en las estrellas *dominio.*" The real question is that of the Christian conscience governing itself, the inner struggle. When Basilio talks directly of Segismundo, the focus is better, but the terminology is still militant: "aunque su inclinación / le dicte sus precipicios, / quizá no le *vencerán*" (1: 508) (even though his temperament may prescribe to him its pitfalls, perhaps they will not overwhelm him); "el hombre / *predomina* en las estrellas" (1: 511-12) (man prevails against the stars); "Si magnánimo *se vence,* / reinará" (1: 512) (If great in spirit he overcomes himself, he shall rule); "*vencerás* las estrellas / porque es posible *vencella* / a un magnánimo varón" (1: 513) (you will prevail against the stars, because it is possible for the man of splendid spirit to prevail against them). In sum, when Basilio addresses himself to the future, his basic posture is dogmatically correct; but its inner content is hostile and full of contrary and heterodox intent. Man's theoretical freedom to fabricate a fate in close conformity with providence becomes in his hands an instrument of challenge, a time-defying counterstructure built to glorify him and the supremacy of his spirit.

In Basilio's struggle with God, Segismundo is a pawn. If the son gives the lie to his father's prognostications, he will be confirming the judiciousness of the king's doubt as to whether one should unreservedly believe in predictions. If Segismundo behaves as foretold, Basilio will be justified in his apprehensions and countermeasures. It thus appears that the father has taken up all of the son's options and left him no room for independent judgment. This preclusion of the exercise of free choice, together with Basilio's insulation of Segismundo from the enduring consequences of his acts, constitutes the prince's well-founded case against his father for tyranny. Basilio has created a world in conformity with his own dread vision and has forced Segismundo to inhabit it. Like many heterodoxies, like many heresies, the cosmos in Basilio's mind closely resembles the universe to which it is opposed. The two main features of this artistic Arianism are its determination and its replacement of God with the king. Otherwise, Poland does not greatly differ from the traditionally Catholic moral empire from which Basilio has caused it to secede, in the fashion of England under Henry VIII, so that the sovereign might become the head of the church. Basilio is a Caesaro-papist to the greater glory of himself. He is also a schismatic who needs to be returned to his former vassalage, a monarch to whom the formula of *cuius regio, eius religio* will not lastingly apply. Indeed, it is not by accident that *La vida es sueño* is set in Poland, whose nobility largely accepted Protestantism while the ordinary people remained Catholic. The papal nuncio's great diplomatic skills notably assisted the country's return to Roman spiritual hegemony. The rhythm of *La vida es sueño* is similarly one of withdrawal and return, of separation from established historical process and a re-engagement with it, a dying and a quickening. Basilio's entombed idea of death and disaster is the pyramid that crushingly dominates Acts I and II. Act III destroys the sepulcher.

In the reconquest of Poland, Rosaura is the nuncio and Segismundo the revolutionary agent. Despite her masculine garb and the desperate energy associated with it, Rosaura's role is fundamentally a passive one. She is in God's hands: "yo, sin más camino / que el que me dan las leyes del destino" (1: 501). (I, with no other direction than that decreed by fate.) She is a mission needing to be carried out, by Clotaldo and, when he fails her, by Segismundo, successfully. What Rosaura really means, then, is what she means to Segismundo. Rosaura makes Segismundo real by providing him with a field of moral decision and its consequent action where the inner conscience and the outer deed have genuine and lasting importance. At their first encounter, when all boundaries and distances are minimal because of the prince's life-long sequestration, Rosaura strays into Segismundo's tiny radius of action, the distance that his powerful arms can reach; strays into the death zone as randomly as the bullet that finds her companion Clarín in Act III. Now for once, in this miniature compass, Segismundo briefly enjoys the absolute power of death and life that is his by inheritance; and he means to use it to kill Rosaura, because she has witnessed his shame: "Sólo porque me has oído, / entre mis membrudos brazos / te tengo de hacer pedazos" (1: 503). (Just because you have overheard me, I mean to crush you in my powerful arms.) Rosaura's response is one of instant submission—no evasions, flights, horoscopes, or new dynastic arrangements: "Si has nacido humano, / baste el postrarme / a tus pies para librarme" (1: 503). (If you were born a human, throwing myself at your feet should be enough to save me.) It is, and this moment begins the human rebirth of the prince. Its essential condition is the unfettered exercise of judgment and action. The reason Basilio's experiment in Act II fails is that he has merely expanded and gilded his son's confinement. Every encounter there is the opposite of Rosaura's first meeting with Segismundo. No one walks into his effective sphere of action. Basilio recoils from his heir in horror: "y aunque en amorosos lazos / ceñir tu cuello pensé, / sin ellos me volveré, / que tengo miedo a tus brazos" (1: 515). (And although I had thought to weave loving bonds about your neck, I will leave without them, because I fear your arms.)

The second sight of Rosaura, now Astrea, helps to create in Segismundo a sense of the past, of a powerful yet merciful background in historic time that is essential to his reconstitution. Rosaura helps to return Segismundo to the past and the future, to the finite and to the things that endure beyond the finite: "Sólo a una mujer amaba; / que fue verdad, creo yo, / en que todo se acabó / y esto solo no acaba" (1: 522). (The only person I loved was a woman; that, I think, was true, since all the rest of it stopped and it was the only thing that didn't.) Segismundo needs time and its concomitant awareness of what entities perish and what things last to reconstruct himself as a fully functioning person. Rosaura gives the clue. She reveals the operations and uses of time. He grasps and improves upon them.

In *La vida es sueño* time favors Segismundo and is Basilio's greatest enemy. It may bring the king humiliation and will bring him death. But his father's death will see Segismundo seated on the throne. If the past was Basilio's, the future is Segismundo's. In bringing down the obstacles that block the future, the prince is self-serving but also assists in freeing events so that they may conform to the providential plan. Working against his father in a way that might appear to be disobedient and immoral, Segismundo challenges Basilio's plan, which is itself a challenge to God's. The heir-apparent thus becomes a self-serving agent of the divine in the complex interplay of defiance and counter-defiance that structures the play.[48] Its primordial mode reflects Christian Catholic dogma and doctrine. Before *La vida es sueño* comes into being, an uncreated cosmos of perfect obedience *is*. Pure dogma is the play's *loa*, its field theory of relativity. Then, like hell, it leaps into both physical and metaphysical being at the moment when Basilio's mind, probing Segismundo's future, rebels at what it interprets as the significance of that future. The king's countermaneuver is to assert his own authority over time, to fabricate it more to his liking, to remake it in his own image. This sovereign artistic impulse is an aggression, a usurpation. Thus the essential creative act is theft, like Prometheus's theft of fire. It possesses man of godliness while putting him in undoubted opposition to God. To regain the ground lost, God uses agents to subvert the kingdom, whether it be a single mind or a whole nation like Poland, that has seceded from him. These agents restore it and themselves to obedience. But though counterrevolutionaries, the agents are themselves sovereign personalities and can at any instant yield to the artistic temptation to create an absolutely independent and self-perpetuating state. Segismundo, in his own way, could so easily repeat his father's mistake, and very likely will.

A departure from orthodoxy consequently is, if the preceding discussion has any validity at all, of absolutely fundamental and crucial importance to the life and function of Calderonian drama. To rise up in rebellion against the mandates of governing powers, paternal and divine, is an essential role which man constantly creates for himself, in contradistinction to the part that God or one's father would have one passively play. In this sense, though an oversimplification, it might help to say that the pressures towards paternalistic conformism are the medieval dogmatic continuum in Calderón's theatre, while the irrepressible urge of the gifted man to fashion his own fate constitutes a Renaissance corollary. Both impulses are required. They engage each other so as to give voice to the contrapuntal melody of struggle that always informs Calderón's plays. Disobedience, there, can be original, creative, and can ultimately be reconciled to the world harmonic. It is no accident that most of the protagonists of the dramas of conversion find themselves at terrible odds with their parents. It is so with Eusebio in *La devoción de la Cruz,* with Cipriano in *El mágico prodigioso,* with Eugenia in *El José de las mujeres,* with Crisanto in *Los dos amantes del cielo,* and with Muley Mahomet in *El gran príncipe de Fez.* For all of these except Eusebio, martyrdom is an act of defiance of their earthly father but obviously is extremely welcome to the heavenly one; and these multiple martyrdoms resemble Segismundo's armed revolt against Basilio in Act III of *La vida es sueño.* There, when events come to their resolution, the product of the father's and of the son's disobedience is renewal for them both: "Hijo, que tan noble acción / otra vez en mis entrañas / te engendra . . ." (1: 533). (My son—for so noble a deed renews the siring of you in my vitals. . . .)

These fresh parts are, however, new wine in old bottles, since the predicted form of their mutual disaster has taken place exactly as foreseen. It is the meaning and content of the event which are original and unexpected. There is a given role, but one must improvise its sense as richly and humanely as possible, a formidable but far from impossible task in Calderonian drama. Thus, in Calderón's greatest plays, role is dual, ambiguous. On the one hand, God imposes the part that each man and woman must take; and every role, therefore, has the reality of that mandate. At the same time, this God-given role lasts only as long as fleeting life itself, to fade out along with earthly existence. On the other hand, God does not decree the meaning of the role that he distributes. Its interpretation is left to the individual actor, to devise for evil or for good. Naturally, God favors the virtuous interpretation of role and, in the *autos,* quite shamelessly prompts, to no avail in many cases. At all events, the individual's interpretation, whether for good or for evil, has consequences that outlast the role itself, that in fact determine the soul's place in eternity. Calderón combines the approach to acting of Stanislavsky—complete identification with role—with that of Diderot—distance from role for the sake of control.[49] If he does not accept his princely mission, Segismundo will remain incomplete and will disobey God, who has destined him for it. If he is unable to view his royal condition with detachment, as one who at death will cast his costume aside, he will lose that control which principally makes him a virtuous prince.

As an actor, Segismundo triumphs by believing in his destiny with sufficient strength to undertake to carry it out, while at the same time holding his spiritual consciousness apart from public posture. He remains a private individual judging his own public actions. This ultimate Segismundo is a highly theatrical personality. Yet the dispute about the applicability of Abel's[50] notion of metatheatre to Calderón's plays is at best unsubtle, for in the Stanislavsky portion of Calderón's technique we have a solidly dogmatic stance. Segismundo *is* his role. In the Diderot corollary, we have, however, a Renaissance augmentation of the individual. Improvisation, detachment, self-consciousness and control are here as vital to Segismundo as they were to Cesare Borgia. O'Connor and Reichenberger have falsified the issue by seeing a *bien-pensant* orthodoxy as the major Calderonian idea of role. Their detractors have similarly exaggerated the Hamlet-like qualities of Calderonian and other Golden-Age protagonists.[51] Both senses are necessary if the private person is to become a successful public performer. The believer is the foil of the doubter, and the doubter the foil of the believer.

With such stipulations in mind, one can, I am convinced, find a true sense of role as Abel understands the term. It takes on, in Calderón, the peculiar coloration of disobedience, and though the revolt may collapse, its enduring effect on the individual undertaking it is to revive and renew him. Playing the disobedient part has made him more, if not entirely, real. It might also be said that man's struggle with God in Calderón makes God more real, at least to his prime antagonist and perceiver, man.

Two seemingly random utterances in *La estatua de Prometeo* necessitate discussion of a more traditional and perhaps more apologetical kind than the foregoing excursus. The first is Merlín's stale joke in Act I concerning the whereabouts of Prometheus, who has disappeared in pursuit of a dangerous wild animal. Merlín's humor, like that of most of Calderón's *graciosos,* is singularly unfunny, a *frialdad.* When all the Caucasians are wondering what has become of Prometheus, Merlin conjectures that the beast has carried him off to cook him and serve him as the main course to its dinner guests. Challenged to give his reasons for so bizarre a notion, Merlín explains: "De que sin duda / sería gran plato en su mesa, / porque el que crudo sabía / tanto, forzoso es que sepa / más o cocido o asado" (1: 2075). (Because he would surely be the *pièce de résistance,* since somebody who already knew so much raw would have to know more stewed or roasted.)

The second is Prometheus's aside in Act II when he has just asked Pandora, come to life only a few instants previously, who she is. Pandora gropes for a reply until a mysterious chorus responds for her: "Que quien dé las ciencias, da / voz al barro y luz al alma." (The giver of knowledge also gives speech to clay and light to the soul.) Prometheus musingly repeats the refrain to himself and then comments: "¡Ah moralidad envuelta / en fabulosa enseñanza, / qué de cosas que me dices!" (1: 2081). (Ah moral cloaked in fabled doctrine, how suggestive you are to me!)

Calderón's *La estatua de Prometeo* is probably his finest mythological play and ranks with his best dramas of any category. In analyzing it, I have not knowingly used any special precautions or unusual technique. Rather, I have tried to show how rewarding it is to see *La estatua* in the light of many of Calderón's other works. My assumption has been that a mythological drama presents the viewer or reader with no extraordinary critical difficulty. Indeed, this lengthy examination has aimed to show that *La estatua de Prometeo,* if not a monomyth, is a master myth in Calderón's theatre. My special sense of myth has been that of *mythos,* or a ready-made plot which is obsessively used over and over again, with many variations. A play on a subject drawn from Greek mythology, however, offends and discourages many a modern sensibility. Consequently, some account should be given of the tradition in which Calderón is operating, so that his very great success in it may be clear.

The main contemporary problem with the mythological is our unwillingness to lend it credence. In present-day speech, myth, wherever it occurs, suggests a living legend of falsity. Moreover, many Greek and Roman legends are associated with that very disparate set of beliefs which Christianity came to replace. Thus Greco-Roman mythology appears in the Christian perspective as historically discredited and lifeless. Even though one may not be a believer, such a natural Christian bias may throw up obstacles to the appreciation of a work like *La estatua de Prometeo.* Yet, while the play is independently viable, Calderón does provide the key to its official justification in Prometheus's remark quoted above. It will be the basis for a brief look at the Prometheus myth in literature and the Christian handling of that myth. Merlín's silly joke, on the other hand, suggests a connection between Calderón's play and more or less contemporary interpretations of myth from the anthropological and structuralist point of view. In these final considerations, as the notes will show, I shall be relying heavily on secondary sources.

It seems that myth, like epic, comes in both primitive and cultivated guises. There is Ovid and there are collections like Claude Lévi-Strauss's three-volume compilation of South American material in *Les Mythologiques.*[52] Prometheus, though probably of "primitive" stock,[53] comes down to us entirely from literary and cultivated sources. Hesiod twice writes of him, in the *Theogony,* a work on the origins and epochs of the gods, and in the moral-didactic

Works and Days. These two accounts provide a fairly full history, but are at times puzzling and contradictory.[54] The great dramatic avatar is of course Aeschylus's *Prometheus Bound,* written perhaps in 479 or 478 B.C. and thought to be the first in a trilogy of which the succeeding *Prometheus Unbound* and *Prometheus the Fire-Bearer* have been lost.[55] After Aeschylus and until the Christian era there are numerous mentions of Prometheus in classical literature but no literary, moral, or philosophical treatment of him on anything approaching the scale of *Prometheus Bound.*[56] Despite the cosmic dimensions of his story, Prometheus did not greatly appeal to the Greco-Latin imagination and one would have expected him to disappear along with the more favored members of his company at the time of the triumph of Christianity. That the figures and narrations constituting what we so vaguely call classical mythology did not perish from mind in the Middle Ages and were revived in the Renaissance is a hugely vexed question and an undeniable truth admirably studied by Jean Seznec and learnedly supplemented by D. C. Allen,[57] among others.

Even in antiquity, one reason that myth survived was that it soon came to be read allegorically, that is, as consistently meaning something other than the "literal" story. This is the Euhemeristic tradition;[58] and Prometheus's remark in *La estatua de Prometeo* about there being a moral to this fabulous bit of doctrine puts Calderón's play, apologetically speaking, squarely in that tradition. It is far from being a comfortable tradition, for the almost unanswerable challenge to the Euhemeristic cast of mind is its deviousness. Surely God and Christianity had revealed themselves with sufficient clarity to have no need of a host of indirect epiphanies. To this the allegorizers of paganism would, I believe, readily accede but would counter with the historical problem. Christ chose a time to appear. Before that time, only the spiritually alert could properly interpret the signs pointing to what was to come. Like certain famous persons in the Old Testament, pagan forces and tales could be seen as prefiguring Christ. The figural habit of mind reinforces the Euhemeristic. Thus the famous phrase of Tertullian: "verus Prometheus Deus omnipotens blasphemiis lancinatur."[59] (Blasphemers attack with the proposition that Prometheus really is God Almighty.)

Raymond Trousson destroys the received idea that the identification of Christ with Prometheus was common in the Patristics and sagely limits the range of Tertullian's apparently somewhat reckless statement.[60] But even if Christianizing allegorizers did not trouble to assimilate Prometheus into their world view, they quickly went to work on the great monuments of pagan literature. D.C. Allen writes: "Clement of Alexandria, Augustine, the orthodox, and the heretical saw in the *Odyssey* not only an account of Christian progress but also something reminiscent of the life of Christ. By the fifth century the relationship between the two heroes is so well established that Maximus can use the adventure with the Sirens as a pulpit *exemplum:* Christ tied Himself to the cross as Odysseus did to the mast to avoid the 'desires of pleasure' in order that 'all men might be saved from shipwreck in this world' " (pp. 65-66).

When to this formula is added Allen's further observation that "the search for biblical faces in the gallery of pagan gods and heroes was one of the numerous Christian obsessions of the Renaissance, an obsession that does not fade out even when the sun of the Enlightenment rises" (pp. 90-91), I think we have the fundamental external justification not only for the mythological *El golfo de las sirenas* and the openly allegorical *Los encantos de la culpa* but also for the entire corpus of Calderón's mythological and mythico-sacramental plays. They rejoin a very old and very respectable tradition, in which pagan myth survives because it is haunted by Christianity, however distasteful both Christianity and myth may be to the post-Enlightenment sensibility. And even though Prometheus did not receive a great deal of this kind of interpretative attention in late antiquity or the Middle Ages, he did come to be specially favored by the Renaissance.

The matter of Calderón's sources for *La estatua de Prometeo* is not difficult. Beginning with Boccaccio's *De genealogia deorum gentilium,* numerous manuals and dictionaries of classical mythology had been written and had spread all over Europe. Trousson writes of the many editions in several languages of Boccaccio's *Genealogy,* as well as the wide distribution of the manuals of Comes, Cartari, and Gyraldi, adding that even if Calderón had not perused such works, he would inevitably have been acquainted with their common interpretative idea, that of Christian moral truth contained in the allegory, the " 'vérité cachée' sous l'allégorie" (p. 168). Indeed, the French phrase is remarkably close to Prometheus's "¡Ah moralidad envuelta / en fabulosa enseñanza!" Trousson also mentions Pérez de Moya's *Philosophia secreta* and Fray Baltasar de la Victoria's *Teatro de los dioses de la gentilidad* as Calderón's most probable Spanish informants.

In addition, Calderón seems to have found in Marsilio Ficino's interpretations of Prometheus a style of mind sympathetic to his own. Trousson's summation of Ficino's view in his commentary on Plato's *Protagoras* and elsewhere reveals a familiar but less complex figure. The Florentine philosopher interprets Prometheus as the man endowed with the higher faculties that devise the technical means necessary to insure human subsistence, whereas Epimetheus is a natural man. Both brothers have the disadvantage of not being pure spirit but rather spirit entrapped in matter, so that man finds himself on the borderland between matter and spirit, a decided superiority in this world which human beings dominate, yet a source of torment for the mortal who, like Prometheus, would unite himself with the divine. The painful resistance of matter to the soul's aspirations is symbolized by Prometheus's bonds to the rock, a situation that moves Ficino to describe the bound man as most wretched: "infelicissimus ille Prometheus" (Trousson, pp. 101-02).

While fighting shy of a simple Christian allegory in *La estatua de Prometeo,*[61] Trousson sees in the play not only certain remarkable affinities with *Prometheus Bound* but also a kind of *summa* of the Prometheus myth, at least in its philosophical elements. Calderón, in his view, has extended and completed the Renaissance idea of Prometheus: "His Prometheus's thirst for wisdom is modified by reflection and a sensible cast of mind." The Calderonian hero continues a tradition twenty-two centuries old which he epitomizes in a peculiarly Renaissance fashion, so that the play is "the masterful conclusion to a line of thought which had steadily been growing richer from the fourteenth to the seventeenth century and which in that conclusion expresses a new understanding of humanity" (pp. 176-77). This remarkably learned and sound appreciation settles the problem of pre-Christian myth in the Christian context by finding justification in the intellectual and artistic success of the amalgam. The demonstration is helpful and perhaps even convincing, certainly as allowable as my assumption and attempt to demonstrate that *La estatua de Prometeo* is conceptually and dramatically coherent. To these conclusions other speculations may perhaps be usefully added.

Greco-Roman myth is peculiarly difficult to define. Intelligent, learned and sensitive efforts to do so are quite disappointing, as with Robert Graves in the *Greek Myths* or, in a more conventional vein, G. S. Kirk's *Myth*.[62] One reason for this waywardness is that, in contrast to primitive fable, the occidental material comes to us exclusively in literary form; and mythological narration quite often has a creative quality. The *Metamorphoses* of Ovid is the best-known example of such traditional tales in the service of literary art. Ovid there attempts to order through art a huge narrative inheritance. Thus, in western myth, the fusion of literature with myth is simply undeniable and has caused another difficulty. This occurs when students of myth try to separate it from belief, especially from religion or ritual. G. S. Kirk succeeds rather well in adducing examples from primitive sources in which myth apparently is related neither to rite nor to religion, but his treatment of Greece is not persuasive. Even when a story like that of Oedipus does not directly involve any god, as Kirk maintains, it craves acceptance from the mind of the reader or other audience. In the West, myths are familiar tales that want to be believed and which have come to be at last partly accepted through long repetition. Belief, as we know, is a tremendously nuanced and complex type of response. Consider the range of Judeo-Christian reaction to the Old and New Testaments. There, every permutation of acceptance is bewilderingly displayed and yet we can grossly term this panorama "belief." An almost equal horizon of response to classical myth is theoretically possible and doubtless occurred. But the great difference between biblical and classical myth is that the Bible, while containing many powerful and beautiful passages, is not a primary literary document, as Ovid is. We do not take the Gospels to be exercises in literary art. Classical myth, on the other hand, is identified with expertly fashioned language, Greek or Latin. Ancient fable is, then, woven into oneness with the prestige of the artful old tongues, especially the Latin. In such artifice there is a rhetoric of appeal, a glamour in the etymological sense of that word, which can be seen as something distinct from the substance of the mythical narration but which fundamentally is the narration itself. Ovid rehearses the old tales with a diction of such elegance and eloquence that the actors in them return to life and once again command belief. No longer well trained in the sublimities even of the Latin, we can scarcely detect today the force of its verbal fascination. In the Middle Ages and the Renaissance it was the mother tongue of the mind and *letras humanas* could bewitch the most austere intellect. Such seductive language, to whose charms the learned and the artistic have grown cold because of ignorance, added enormously to the credibility of myth.

The ancients and even the remoter moderns knew this and were uneasy about the allurements of the classical materials in any program of Christian education. But even early in the Christian era, the old and especially Latin literature had already become so familiar a companion to the converted mind that it was not destined to abandon it until after the eighteenth century. Myth had in particular irreplaceable attractions and it continued to coexist in a kind of sym-biotic hostility to the faith. By rediscovering in depth above all the beauty—verbal, pictorial, and plastic—of the ancient world, the Renaissance restored the full power of the classical beguilements and sought to guide them to a Christian goal. In the arts of the Renaissance, this Christian redirection of the classical, in all the appeal of its beauty, is a tremendous challenge that is not al-ways successfully met. One great Spanish poem does, however, beautifully ef-fect the transition. This is Fray Luis de León's "Noche serena."

The poem takes the form of an impassioned oration which, by eloquently making an invidious comparison between heaven and earth, tries to convince its audience of the emptiness of temporalities and of the plenitude of eternity. Fray Luis's basic struggle is against the lures of earthly pleasure. To nullify them, he artfully deploys all the attractions of beauty and art. And so his apos-trophe to heaven begins with a reference to its *antique* grandeur and beauty; it is an abode in the past from which the soul has fallen into a dark and narrow prison. The key word is "templo": "Morada de grandeza / templo de claridad y hermosura, / el alma que a tu alteza / nació, ¿qué desventura / la tiene en esta cárcel baja, escura?" (What misfortune confines the soul that was born equal to your elevation, oh abode of greatness, temple of brightness and beauty, to this vile and dark prison?) Within a temple one expects to find its god; but Fray Luis's sanctuary is more, a pantheon composed, surprisingly, of the pagan gods arranged hierarchically to lead the thirsting eye to the *supremo dios,* who presides over them all:

> la luna cómo mueve
> la plateada rueda, y va en pos della
> la luz do el saber llueve,
> y la graciosa estrella
> de amor la sigue reluciente y bella
>   y cómo otro camino
> prosigue el sanguinoso Marte airado
> y el Júpiter benino,
> de mil bienes cercado,
> serena el cielo con su rayo amado
>   Rodéase en la cumbre
> Saturno, padre de los siglos de oro;
> tras él la muchedumbre
> del reluciente coro
> su luz va repartiendo, y su tesoro.

how the moon rotates her silver-sheathed disc, succeeded by the light that showers wisdom down, which in gleaming loveliness the gracious star of love follows upon, and how Mars's blood-thirsty scowl takes a new course; and kindly Jove, in the midst of a thousand blessings, paci-fies the heavens with his bolts of love. At the summit Saturn turns, sire of the centuries of gold; above him the hosts of the shimmering choir share their treasury of lights.

The function of the pagan pantheon is clear. It progressively delights the eye upwards, like a vertical *cour d'honneur* or *grande allée* of splendid statu-ary, so that the real goal and sanctum may be reached without pause or fatigue. Yet there they are, all the greatest gods of classical antiquity, tamed, domesti-cated as to the exercise of independent power, but if anything augmented in majestic beauty. The old gods usher the dazzled soul to the new heaven where *agape* replaces *eros* but does not obliterate all memory of him because *agape* supplants rather than destroys: "aquí asentado / en rico y alto asiento / está el

Amor sagrado, / de glorias y deleites rodeado. . . ."[63] (Here is sacred love seated on a rich and lofty chair, surrounded by supremacy and delight. . . .)

Still, the new paradise is not fundamentally a pagan one. Fray Luis translates that great and beguiling contemporary myth—the pastoral—to the Empyrean in fulfillment of his promise to the reader of spiritual repletion. At best, even in literature, the pastoral mode had only interstitial reality. In the *Quijote,* for example, pastoral moments are rare nuclei, wondrous enclaves that exist in wilderness well off the road. They are all the more delicious for their nondirectional isolation, but the reader leaves the *Quijote* with his appetite for the pastoral whetted rather than appeased. Fray Luis's own appetite for the true pastoral is dolorously expressed early in the poem, in phrases reminiscent of the eclogues of Garcilaso: "el amor y la pena / despiertan en mi pecho un ansia ardiente; / despiden larga vena / los ojos hechos fuente. . . ." (Love and grief awaken a burning desire in my heart; my eyes—a spring—abundantly flow. . . .) To staunch this flow, he feeds the spiritually concupiscent eye with a vision of glory *a lo pastoril:*

¡Oh campos verdaderos!	Oh landscape of truth!
¡Oh prados con verdad frescos y amenos!	Oh meadows truly cool and delightful!
¡Requísimos mineros!	Oh richly sunken shafts, hidden valleys a thousand-fold blest!
¡Oh deleitosos senos,	
repuestos valles de mil bienes llenos!	

Here the enclave has flowered out into a vast and lovely landscape, but Fray Luis has not abandoned the delicious sense of wonder and containment that accompanied the discovery of the earthly pastoral pocket. Heaven, in addition to its vistas of light, has matrices of enfoldment, *mineros, senos, repuestos valles* into which the soul can be, like Dionysos, resewn and born again at full term, refreshed. In such alcoves, the soul does indeed return to its womb. Yet the most captivating promise that Fray Luis makes is the general, abstract, and immaterial one of unfailing, unceasing beauty in the form of light: "Inmensa hermosura / aquí se muestra toda y resplandece / clarísima luz pura / que jamás anochece; / eterna primavera aquí florece." (Boundless beauty here reveals itself entire and light of the most brilliant purity, which never dims, beams resplendent. Here spring flowers eternal.)

Now that our sensibilities no longer respond, without training, to the charms of classical myth and its associated verbal beauties, and still less to the blandishments of the pastoral, "Noche serena" has lost, in the immediate sense, much of its rhetorical force. But reconstruction of its modes of persuasion is a kind of miniature history of the Christian involvement with myth. As art, myth predisposes its audience to acceptance and to at least the limited and provisional form of belief which we concede to a work of literature, especially to the poem. Deeper forms of conmitment are more than theoretically possible. Unable because of historical accident to obliterate this competitor, Christianity responds by denaturing—the Euhemeristic approach—and by trying to appropriate the beauty and appeal of the pagan stories. That undertaking recognizes the possibility of believing in myth and underscores its attractions. Thus, in

combatting myth, Christianity guarantees its survival, and not until the eighteenth century does its appeal really begin to fade, along with that of Christianity itself. Both Seznec and Allen are somewhat scandalized by this long cohab-
itation, which, however, strikes me as a perfectly comprehensible union,
though one of hostility. At the last, Christianity tames myth and puts it in a
pantheon-museum, of surpassing beauty, which beauty is meant to draw the
beholder to the Christian God.

Calderón doubtless used myth because to do so was traditional and because its materials lay accessible in the public domain of art. But in the seventeenth century myth as the subject of literature had special properties. Everyone thought he knew that myths were made up. In his dictionary, Covarrubias
regularly prefaces his retelling of a story such as that of Icarus (and his taking
the trouble to do so is itself significant) with the phrase: "Fingen los
poetas . . ." (the poets would have it that . . .). Yet those same fictitious tales
continued, after centuries, to be vivid and current and attractive. Myth could
give the creative artist—*poeta, Dichter*—special assistance. Its substance was
readily granted to be nonfactual, but its form and history, paradoxically perhaps, predisposed the public to acceptance of a limited kind, they judging myth
to be false in one sense, true in another. And this is precisely the hypothesis that
is essential to the existence in the public mind of the creative work of literary
art. The matter of literature probably is not factual, or historical, or if so is
much altered; but nonfactual art—fiction, *Dichtung*—can convey a valuable
impression of truth. The larger, deeper forms of fiction which have long since
been widely accepted throughout Europe, were just getting under way in Spain
in the seventeenth century. Cervantes undoubtedly created the novel there. But
the greatest form of fiction in the Golden Age was theatre. Even in the hands of
so aristocratic a practitioner of the drama as Calderón, plays had to follow
popular taste. They were, however, extremely vulnerable to censure and even to
suppression because they were "made up" and so, in naive judgments, untrue.
Curiously, myth gets around much of this problem by being patently false and
yet having a history, admittedly round-about, of involvement with at least
"moral" truth. This is, of course, only a tactical advantage, but it derives from
the fact that mythic narration is an excellent abstract model for the kind of interaction between the artist in fiction and his public necessary to the metaphysical existence of the work of art. For as long as it had appeal, myth was the
metaphysics of especially poetic fiction, in drama and verse. Consequently,
when myth formed the basis of a narration in the new dramatic fiction, the fab-
rication was less open to the kind of ingenuously moralizing attack we find the
Canon making in Chapter 47 of the First Part of the *Quijote*. Cultivated people
understood the tacit contract between themselves and the mythological subject.
Their part in nonmythological dramatic fiction was far less clear.

On the example of Fray Luis's "Noche serena," a further explanation of
the role of myth in *La estatua de Prometeo* is possible. The poem draws its
reader along on a voyage from the sublunary to the Empyrean. In addition to a
steady increase in beauty and majesty as the soul rises, the poem posits an important Western religious truth. The Greco-Roman mythological pantheon rehearses man's earlier and less rewarding experiences in the pursuit of the
knowledge of God. Now that, in Fray Luis's poem, the one true Christian God

is known, his predecessors have been corrected and harmonized. They, in the aftermath, concord with Christ: "otro camino / prosique el sanguinoso Marte airado." (Mars's bloodthirsty scowl takes a new course.) And they are imagistically present in the final sublime recuperation because they represent stages on the path to that perfect sense of the divine which the last two stanzas of the poem portray as so infinitely desirable. Since they are mileposts along the way to knowledge of perfection, they partake of it, not in their own right but as a witness to the soul's true goal.

Calderón's Prometheus is the first man to undertake a voyage into the space of Christian divinity. Man, in such a perspective, stands on the frontier between the human and the divine: "coelestium et terrestrium vinculum et nodus."[64] (A link and bond between heaven and earth.) Prometheus crosses this frontier and inaugurates the process that will culminate in the vision of "Noche serena." Prometheus is thus, historically speaking, Calderón's first personage. For in Calderón a person becomes a character in a drama when he perceives his lack of oneness, his hybrid nature. Segismundo comes alive and becomes an actor when he can declare, in Act II of *La vida es sueño:* "Pero ya informado estoy / de quién soy y sé quién soy: / un compuesto de hombre y fiera" (1: 576). (But now my eyes are opened as to who I am and I know who I am: a composite of man and beast.) Once in possession of such knowledge, the potential actor must decide on a role in which either one or the other of the fundamental aspects of his nature will predominate. It is the same with Prometheus. He is a hybrid of the human and the divine and, knowing this, he chooses to explore and reveal the divine, at great human cost: "infelicissimus ille Prometheus."

Anthropologists would call Prometheus a culture hero. Calderón himself is not at all far from the anthropological, because one of his major dramatic preoccupations is the relationship between the savage and the civilized, between nature and culture, or, in the special baroque view, between nature and art. Critics have lost sight of the fact that perception of one's feral nature is a primary discovery and apprehension in his plays. Savagery frequently assumes in them the guise of the utmost refinement. In Act II of *La vida es sueño,* for example, Segismundo puts on and takes off courtly speech as easily as he dons and doffs court costume; but the nature covered by gorgeous cloth and glittering words is ferocious and, for the time, unchanged by its outer integuments. *La estatua de Prometeo* manifestly deals, in a collective sense, with the rise from a lower to a higher order of civilization, since the Caucasians in it appear as semibarbarians who are brought to a realization of a better social order by Prometheus's deeds. But, like Freud, Calderón is keenly aware of the price that culture exacts. In rising to new levels of awareness, the Greek Caucasians develop deep new hatreds. A competition of cults develops. Men prepare to die in the fight over their recently discovered beliefs. Merlín's absurd joke—that the wild beast stole Prometheus in order to cook and serve him to its waiting dinner guests as a marvel of wisdom, increased in the cooking—prefigures the sacrificial cost of greater attainments in social organization and knowledge and relates these to the art of cooking, which cannot have existed among the Caucasians at the moment when Merlín speaks, since they do not yet have fire. Even so, Prometheus is a victim to the advance which he has effected, to the encounter which he has brought on; and Merlín's joke, though unfunny, is symbolically true.

This linking of civilization with cooking, then, strangely resonates in sympathy with certain findings of Claude Lévi-Strauss as to the nature and structure of primitive myth among South American Indians. I take this happenstance to be a product of Calderón's genius, of his deep understanding of the primitive personality that suffuses the most highly civilized one, and I do not plan to pursue the parallel further than to point it out. Nonetheless, Lévi-Strauss's abstract of the purpose of primitive myth—"to construct a model by which the contradictions in men's view of the world can be mediated"[65]—strikingly resembles the binary polarity of Calderón's theatre, which in its permutations I have called "Manichaean fusionist." G. S. Kirk, while challenging and disallowing many of Lévi-Strauss's assertions, does readily grant to him a triumph of interpretation with the polar opposites of life and death, nature and culture: "One of Lévi-Strauss's most brilliant successes is to have shown the dominant position of the second of these pairs (nature and culture) in the thought and imagination of the central Brazilian Indians and their neighbors. Many, perhaps most, of their myths are concerned directly or indirectly with this problem, and Lévi-Strauss has shown conclusively that the contrast between the raw and the cooked is the model through which the problem is most commonly stated, and fire, cooking and natural processes of corruption the means by which it is elucidated" (p. 79).

In Act I of *La vida es sueño,* Estrella admonishes Astolfo for appearing before her with the insignia of both life and death, as a warrior and a lover, for in Calderón literally "amor es guerra": "Y advertid que es baja acción, / que sólo a una fiera toca, / madre de engaño y traición, / el halagar con la boca / y matar con la intención" (1: 506). (And take notice that it is a vile deed, one leading to deceit and treachery consistent only with a savage beast, to flatter with the lips while murdering with the mind.) Just as Claude Lévi-Strauss in *La Pensée sauvage* revealed to long-"civilized" Westerners the rigor, patience, richness of structure, and meticulous detail in the observations of nature made by their less advanced brethren, so Calderón reveals the contiguousness, the kinship, the reciprocities, and the sympathies in man of his two great opposed polar modes of nature and culture, of savagery and civilization. Calderón's portrait of man, despite its limited political and socioeconomic range, is a far profounder one than has been understood. It is a pantheon in which all the earlier stages of consciousness and development are preserved in their original and independent strength.

PART II

THE IDIOMS OF SILENCE

Cervantes, Honor, and
No hay cosa como callar

"entiéndame quien entiende
los idiomas del silencio."

Fuego de Dios en el querer bien (2: 1259)

Characters in Calderón's *comedias* mention other authors—Garcilaso and Boscán, Góngora, Mira de Amescua, Lope de Vega. But the writer most often alluded to is Cervantes. The following pages undertake to demonstrate that Calderón in his drama truly succeeds to the fictional inheritance of Cervantes. Of this Cervantine inheritance, the richest mass is a concept which has bedevilled the critics: honor. In dealing with honor, I put aside the traditional efforts to explain it in favor of a psychological approach. Cervantes' great discovery was that honor communicatively yokes the male to the female and the female to the male. Consequently, the man who has under his protection a woman—sister, wife, or mistress—whose conduct can either destroy or preserve him, surveys the mysterious inner world of the female with extraordinary attention and solicitude, taking on in the process many traits of mind and behavior customarily labelled feminine. Conversely, the woman who must work against masculine aggression if she is to have some say in her own destiny, as a result of her study of a sometimes beloved adversary comes to understand and assume ideas and actions that are usually labelled masculine. Honor thus permits Cervantes to explore male and female in terms of each other and to diminish the conventional distinctions between them.

His discovery of the feminine—for he focuses on woman—is especially enlightening. It is this Cervantine progress away from maleness and into femaleness which Calderón brilliantly exploits for the theatre. The many references to Cervantes in Calderón's plays and, much more, the invited presence of his fiction in *No hay cosa como callar,* in *El alcalde de Zalamea,* and elsewhere, disclose the deep congeniality of their two spirits. The fundamental sympathy is in their understanding of honor as a means of seeing man and woman in new perspectives. Accordingly, although both certainly deplored extremes, they adhered to the tenets of honor as to an artistically essential construct. This construct will now be studied as theme and variation in Cervantes and Calderón.

About twenty of Calderón's plays have references to the author of the *Quijote* and the *Novelas ejemplares,* and it is precisely these works that are most often cited, above all Don Quijote himself.[1] The situation that most readily calls for a Cervantine comparison is one in a light play in which the Sancho-like servant marvels at his master's alacrity in getting himself into high-minded scrapes. Generally a lady in distress has asked for the unknown gentleman's protection, which he has unhesitatingly proffered. The servant then, not surprisingly, marvels at his master's imprudence and qualifies him as quixotic. So it is that in *Mañana será otro día,* when Beatriz successfully calls upon Don Fernando, whom she does not know, to help her escape from the constables surrounding her, Fernando's servant Roque captures the essence of his deed with the phrase: "Enquijotóse mi amo." (My master's quixotified himself.) The phrase is a wonder, for it verbalizes a whole book and compresses its legend into an act. Nor is the characteristic set of circumstances in which works of Cervantes appear less remarkable: Don Quijote's own experience is recapitulated. A book translates itself into action. This action, quintessentially male— public and involving honor—, pledges the male to the female in her own condition, private and risking dishonor. Here we have a central Calderonian encounter between the fundamental modes of female and male and with the spirit of Cervantes not infrequently presiding over it.

Calderón does not employ only Don Quijote, of course. His characters lead complicated and implausible lives, as they are themselves well aware, so that when they undertake to give an account of themselves, they call especially upon the witness of the *Novelas ejemplares.* In *Casa con dos puertas,* Lisardo, after epitomizing his whole biography, prefaces his description of a mysterious dalliance with the observation that: "todo esto / ya vuestra amistad lo sabe, / pero importa haberlo dicho / para que de aquí se enlace / la más extraña novela / de amor que escribió Cervantes" (2: 282). (You already know all this as my friend, but it helps to have said it out so that I can connect it up with the wildest tale of love that Cervantes ever wrote.) Similarly in *Los empeños de un acaso,* of which the very title suggests a fundamentally quixotic situation, Hernando, Don Juan's servant, parodies his master's idea of love in a *gracioso*'s caricature, so frequent in Calderón: "Quisiera una dama yo / extravagante y sujeto / capaz de novela, porque / es mi amor tan novelero / que me le escribió Cervantes" (2: 1045). (My lady would have to be a capricious creature and a fit subject for a novel [tale], because my love is so novelistic that Cervantes wrote it out for me.)

El celoso extremeño appears vividly in *Antes que todo es mi dama.* Beatriz advises Laura not to admit her lover Don Félix into the house with:

Ya sabes que es mi señor	You know how extremely Extrema-
tan extremeño de amor	duran my master is about love, so
que, aun sin saber lo que pasa,	that, though not even aware of
vive con recelos tales	what's going on, he lives under such
que es una copia, un traslado,	awful apprehensions that he is an
bien y fielmente sacado	exact replica of the jealous Car-
del celoso Carrizales. [2: 879]	rizales.

Act II of *El escondido y la tapada* begins with Mosquito's pessimistic assessment that:

Esta es la casa, sin duda,	This, without a doubt, is the house
que aquel famoso extremeño	that the famous Extremaduran Car-
Carrizales fabricó	rizales built to the scale of his jeal-
a medida de sus celos,	ousy, since there isn't a door or win-
pues no hay puerta ni ventana,	dow, storeroom, court, or hole that a
guarda, patio ni agujero	mosquito could get out of, let me tell
por donde salga un mosquito,	you.
dígalo yo. [2: 686]	

El licenciado Vidriera does splendid service in a humorous exchange between servants. Simón is denouncing the bad points of Isabel in the hope of winning Inés. Under the impression that he is talking to Inés, he is in fact addressing Isabel, whom he accuses of wearing a glass eye. Simón then offers Isabel-Inés a diamond, which she calls glass: "¿Fué desperdicio / de alguno que se le quiebra / a esa mi señora doña / Licenciada Vidriera?" (2: 1523). (Is it a sliver from one of my lady Licenciada Vidriera's that got broken?) The humor collapses in my clumsy version, but it is brilliant and adroit, especially in the shift from the glass eye to the jewel to the glass-eyed lady named Vidriera. Another amusing application is that made by the servant Ginés, in *La niña de Gómez Arias:* "Ya los caballos, señor, / atados quedan, con harta / queja de los tres, diciendo / en rocinantes palabras / que ¿por qué, siendo los locos / nosotros, a ellos los atan?" (1: 805). (I've tied the horses up, sir, much to the dissatisfaction of all three, who in nag-language ask why they should be the ones put under restraint, when we're the crazy ones.) Horse speech here is "rocinantes palabras," those of Don Quijote's nag Rocinante, that most literary of mounts.

But the presence of Cervantes among Calderón's obsessions does not make itself known through direct citation alone. After all, Calderón is the author of the regretted, lost *Los disparates de don Quijote.*[2] Its ghost and Cervantes' haunt several other plays. Cosme, in *La dama duende,* calls his chivalrous master a "don Quijote de la legua," of which I take the meaning to be that Don Manuel is a kind of third-rate, theatrical knight, one suited to those less fortunate companies of players in seventeenth-century Spain which were not permitted to perform within a league of major cities: "¡Qué bien merecido tiene / mi amo lo que se lleva, / porque no se meta a ser / don Quijote de la legua!" (2: 241). (How richly my master deserved what he got, as a lesson not to set himself up as some kind of bastard Don Quixote.)

But Cosme's comparison does not express the truly quixotic quality of *La dama duende.* The real likeness is to be found in the protagonist's situation. Don Manuel is the house guest in Madrid of his old friend, Don Juan de Toledo. The same house shelters Juan's recently widowed sister, Angela, a lovely young woman who has come to Madrid to try to straighten out her deceased husband's tangled customs accounts with the government. Like Pedro Crespo in *El alcalde de Zalamea,* Juan means to keep the attractive female and the ardent male apart. To do so, he seals Angela's quarters off from the rest of the house by placing against her door a kind of *vitrine, alacena,* used to display fine objects of crystal. Angela is thus compelled to come and go by the street door that gives access to her rooms. Of course she is not supposed to come and go much; but her widowhood and impetuous nature turn her dangerously outward and she falls into the habit of engaging in flirtatious repartee with intrigued gallants in public places. Angela goes about *tapada,* all wrapped in a cloak, except for an eye or two. When, by chance, her younger brother, Don Luis, joins the group of males with whom his sister is bantering, Angela flees at the first opportunity. But Don Luis is so intrigued with the witty lady that he resolutely follows her; and Angela, in desperation, appeals to a strange gentleman, none other than Don Manuel, to stop Luis in his pursuit. Manuel does romantically interpose himself and ends up in a sword fight with Luis, which the appearance of Don Juan stops before much blood is shed. When Angela learns that her protector is the family's guest, the plot turns inward, and remains so. For Angela's servant discovers that the concealed door is not really blocked off and that it, together with the *alacena,* can easily be opened and shut. Angela can thus slip into and out of Don Manuel's room. And here is where her conscious pursuit and persecution of Manuel begin. His situation as a guest assailed by mysterious females is mightily reminiscent of the *Quijote,* of Maritornes at the inn, of the Princess Micomicona, but most of all of the series of females who harass Don Quijote at the ducal establishment in the Second Part of the *Quijote*. The duchess herself is Don Quijote's prime *dama duende* there; but the most ghostly, metaphysical, and obsessive female presence in the Second Part is Dulcinea's. In the *Quijote*, it is the materialist philosopher Sancho Panza who corroborates the reality of Dulcinea's ideal existence by alleging to have delivered his master's letter to her and by further alleging to have found her in a debased form of a *labradora*, a peasant girl, when sent on a mission to her in the first scenes of the Second Part. Thereafter, this ghostly female haunts knight and squire until Don Quixote lies on his death bed.

When Doña Angela moves decisively into Manuel's private sphere, she leaves a letter for him. It is written in normal seventeenth-century Spanish but has the tragic tone characteristic of even the lightest of Calderón's honor plays: "el secreto importa, porque el día que lo sepa alguno de los amigos, perderé yo el honor y la vida" (2: 248). (Secrecy is essential, because the minute any one of your friends finds things out, my life and honor are forfeit.) To soothe the sting of that contingency Don Manuel replies in the humorous mockery of a style adapted to reconstructed romances of chivalry, such as we find coming from Don Quixote's memory and mind.[3] Manuel's cleverly archaic parody is an antidote to tragedy and characterizes its author as a shrewd and patient realist, in obvious contrast to the model of his style. But the original, for all these distinct proceedings, clearly is the *Quijote* and the point is underscored by Angela's strenuous efforts to dupe Manuel into believing her a very great lady through an interview conducted late at night and in a high and mysterious manner. The deceptions practiced on Don Quijote in the ducal residence are once again not distant from Calderón's play. Like Don Quixote, Manuel, drawn inside from his customary male world of action, must contend with a female antagonist on her own domestic ground, where she can maneuver much more adroitly than he. "Amor es guerra." But here, also, the resemblance ends, because Angela seeks a real victory over Manuel, the capitulation of marriage; and, more by luck than art, she gets it.

Of the plays that cite Cervantes, *La dama duende* is probably the one most completely possessed by his spirit. Others show an episodic connection. *El astrólogo fingido* is, for Calderón, an uncharacteristically satirical and Italianate play. Don Diego professes to have studied astrology with Giambattista Della Porta, the most famous practitioner of that art in his day:[4] "Llegué a Napoles, adonde / por mi dicha conocí / a Porta, de quien la fama / contaba alabanzas mil" (2: 142). (I reached Naples, where I had the good fortune to meet [Della] Porta, whose reputation consisted of a wealth of praise.) But Della Porta was also a dramatist;[5] and it is his kind of mocking mood that infuses Calderón's play, in which Diego turns the betrayals of a mistress's confidence in a servant into a reputation for omniscience that he uses unfairly in his rivalry with Don Juan for the love of María. As the play ends, all of Diego's deceits return to accuse him, and losing María, he abjures astrology. One of his accusers is Otáñez, an *escudero*, or poor gentleman attendant, a standard butt of literary humor in seventeenth-century Spain. Otáñez's complaint, however, is not romantic. He has saved some money on which to retire in his old age to "la montaña," his native place in the north. Fearing highwaymen and wishing to spare himself the cost and trouble of the journey, Otáñez has asked Don Diego to send him home by magic. Otáñez is then blindfolded, placed astride a bench to which he is painfully tied, and sent in his credulous imagination off into the air. This is a simpler version of the elaborate *Clavileño* hoax in the Second Part of the *Quijote*. A. Julián Valbuena calls it "la huella cervantina más concreta en Calderón" (2: 128). Perhaps. But the spirit of the play as a whole is not Cervantine.

Another play with a touch of Cervantes is *No siempre lo peor es cierto*. Don Carlos loves Leonor. But when he comes to court her he finds another man in her house and seriously wounds him. His suspicions aroused, he does not immediately marry Leonor after their flight together from her house. That she has left her father's house under compromising circumstances puts her life in danger, so that Carlos is bound to protect her. But the stranger fills him with jealous doubt, and he will not give himself to Leonor until it is satisfied. So, chastely and silently at the begining of the play, the wretched lovers travel from Madrid to Valencia, where Carlos entrusts Leonor to his cousin Juan. Carlos plans to go off to the Italian wars and get himself killed. His and Leonor's painful progress—Carlos scarcely spoke: "desde Madrid aquí, / . . . juraros puedo / que no la hablé dos palabras" (2: 1457) (I swear that between here and Madrid I didn't say two words to her)—brings to mind the sighing silences of Luscinda and Don Fernando as they travel together, she his prisoner, in the Sierra-Morena chapters of the *Quijote*. The difference is that, in *No siempre lo peor es cierto,* Leonor is finally shown to be innocent of any complicity in her other lover's presence. She and Carlos therefore marry. But Luscinda and Fernando must give themselves to the lovers—Cardenio and Dorotea—to whom they had made previous and binding pledges.

One play demonstrates a major congruence between the two authors. The resemblance of Calderón's *No hay cosa como callar* to Cervantes' tale *La fuerza de la sangre* has not escaped at least one critic,[6] even though Calderón does not mention Cervantes at all in that work. The immediate similarity is plot. In both works, a wealthy and idle young man rapes a lovely young noblewoman whom, ultimately and not unwillingly, he is brought to marry. Thematically, the tale and the play are distinct. With Cervantes, the major mechanism in putting matters right is kinship. For a child has been born to his Leocadia; and when the boy, Luisico, is injured near his paternal grandparents' house and taken there for help, Luisico's face so reminds the grandparents of the boy's father Rodolfo that they are irresistibly drawn to him: *la fuerza de la sangre.* This spiritual anagnorisis prepares the way for physical confirmations of the truth. After raping the unconscious Leocadia in his bedroom, Rodolfo locked her in to go off and take counsel with his friends. During his absence Leocadia stole a small silver crucifix from the room and she produces it seven years after the event, when the moment is opportune for substantiating her allegations. Rodolfo's mother, Doña Estefanía, already two-thirds persuaded as to her son's responsibility, now is utterly convinced and proceeds to prepare a matrimonial trap for Rodolfo. She baits it with the extremely appetizing Leocadia, and the victim is taken, willingly. There thus emerges another sense of *la fuerza de la sangre*. The phrase at first suggests the appeal for recognition of the kinship tie. But when Leocadia, in alliance with Rodolfo's parents, brings the self-indulgent young man to nuptial heel, one discerns Cervantes' appreciation of the *power* of the family.

This well-developed sense of the family is absent from Calderón's play, the theme of which is extraordinary; the eloquence of silence. Silence is a secondary motif in many a Calderón play, especially since most characters, from the low-born *gracioso* to the noble Doña Mencía in *El médico de su honra,* do not know how to observe it. Doña Leonor of *No hay cosa como callar* does. But her total isolation in her misfortune makes her a heroic sufferer, whereas Leocadia is immediately restored to the family from whom she has been torn and they protect and nurture her until that fortunate accident befalls her son and permits her to take a public role once again. Calderón's Leonor has a brother but no parent and she dares not tell her brother what has happened. In her assailant's father, Don Pedro, she has a protector. When a fire in her house has driven Leonor to take shelter with Don Pedro, the young woman is so uneasy that Don Pedro makes her a general pledge: "Quedaos aquí y yo os ofrezco / del menor inconveniente / de esto os resulte haceros / satisfecha" (2: 1010). (Stay here and I promise to allay even the slightest suspicion that may arise from your doing so.) Since Leonor is uncertain of the identity of the man in question, she silently bides her time until she has proof. Then Don Pedro, like the gentleman he is, keeps his word. Thus in *No hay cosa* we have only a partial set of family groups, in contrast to the full ones in *La fuerza de la sangre.* It is true that Leocadia's father and Rodolfo's mother are the more striking parents. Doña Estefanía is perhaps the most vigorous portrait of a mother in all of Golden-Age literature. But the complete families are there, contributing to the theme of family power. With Calderón the brother is an obstacle but, when the time comes, the father does help.

Neither Leocadia nor Leonor knows who her attacker is, and it becomes the object of their lives to learn the identity of the men who have robbed them of their honor. Leocadia's major clue is the luxurious crucifix, small but made of solid silver. The object itself suggests both the woman's martyrdom and its opulent conclusion. Leonor's evidence is rather more complex. It too is a cross, but a cross on the scallop-shell insigne of the Order of Santiago, which hung from a bejewelled ribbon about the neck of Leonor's assailant. When she seized it, the clasp parted, leaving her in possession of a puzzle which becomes more perplexing when she discovers the portrait of a lady inside the ornament or *venera.* This mute object has great evocative power, is a poetry of silence and an objectification of Leonor's own voiceless dilemma. Accordingly, she speaks to and for the *venera* in this extraordinary conversation:

no vi la hora de verme sola para preguntarle a este testigo quién fuese su dueño y cuando pensé que debiera responderme: "Noble es, conocer sabrá la obligación que te tiene". no sólo (¡ay de mí!) es aquesto	I couldn't wait to be alone to ask this witness who its owner was and when I imagined that its reply would be: "He is noble and will admit his obligation to you," not only did it tell me that but also clearly the opposite: "He is noble but so treacherous that you are not the only one he

lo que me dice y me advierte
mas tan al contrario es
que me dice claramente:
"Noble es, pero tan traidor
que no a ti sola te ofende".
Y es verdad, pues un retrato
que la venera contiene
me da a entender que no he sido
yo la sola (¡oh traidor aleve!)
la quejosa. ¡Oh muda imagen,
dime quién es y quién eres,
que yo por las dos
tomaré y. . . . [2: 1014]

has offended." And it's true, because a portrait in the insigne gives
me to understand that I am not the
only one (oh monster of deceit!)
with cause for complaint. Oh silent
image, tell me who he is and who you
are and I will act for both of us
and. . . .

The *venera*, then, is a typically ambiguous Calderonian symbol, simultaneously testifying to its wearer's nobility and his ignoble conduct. Under Philip
IV, the *hábito* of the Order of Santiago was a much-coveted honor. The recipient had to prove his nobility, and a background investigation was conducted to
verify the candidate's claims. Calderón himself was awarded the *hábito* in
1637, but not without difficulty. The problem was that his father and grandfather had been *escribanos,* or notaries, a calling considered inconsistent with
nobility. Pope Urban VII granted a dispensation from this presumed deroga-
tion and Calderón was received into the order in April of 1637.[7] That Calderón
attached great importance to this distinction is shown by his constant identification of himself in terms of Santiago in every legal document concerning himself after 1637.[8] One late *comedia, Cada uno para sí,* indirectly reflects Calderón's difficulties and success with this ultimate trial of noble blood. There,
Don Carlos appears to have been secretly denounced as not really noble at a
time when, flushed with his victorious participation in the siege of Barcelona
(the city surrendered October 13, 1652), he has been nominated for Santiago:
"un hábito con que / su majestad, que los cielos / guarden, honró mis servi-
cios" (2: 1666) (the order of Santiago with which the King, whom Heaven keep,
rewarded my services). Carlos's antagonist in the play is Enrique, also a Knight
of Santiago, who, like Don Juan in *No hay cosa como callar,* first appears
"con hábito de Santiago." The novel feature of *Cada uno* is that Enrique is
charged with carrying out his enemy Carlos's background investigation. He
discharges his duty with perfect impartiality and completely to the credit of
Carlos. That deed dissolves their enmity and permits the play to close harmoniously. But *Cada uno para sí* shows, as Calderón himself learned, that nobility
is a precarious possession.

Moreover, knighthood in Santiago was not purely honorific. Philip IV
called all the knights of the several orders to service at the beginning of the revolt of the Catalans.[9] Calderón answered the summons on May 28, 1640, in
Madrid, served with the royal army in the field in Catalonia, and was lightly
wounded in the hand. Calderón's brother Joseph, a professional soldier, was
killed in battle in the same campaign on June 23, 1645. Santiago was not an
award to be taken lightly.

And finally, the evaluation of Calderón's property after his death shows that, in addition to being a collector of religious painting and statuary, he was something of a connoisseur of *veneras.* He left five of them, one fairly costly.[10]

Clearly, Calderón attached great importance to the knighthood in Santiago, and in *No hay cosa como callar,* probably written late in 1639, two years after his induction into the Order, its insigne plays a major role as it passes from Marcela's possession (she is the original donor), to Don Juan's, to Leonor's, back to Marcela's, and finally and triumphantly into Leonor's avenging hands. The silver crucifix in *La fuerza de la sangre* has a more modest function. It remains with Leocadia to prepare the ultimate scene of recognition to which Cervantes is devoted. It is something like the birthmark beneath Preciosa's nipple which her mother uncovers with such unseemly haste in *La gitanilla.* Nonetheless, in each work a precious object, of high symbolic intensity, plays a major part.

In addition, each such object is a painful reminder to its possessor of the scene of her dishonor. Leocadia and Leonor come to their definitive encounters by different routes, but both of them are violent progressions that feature an abrupt transition from the public to the private sphere. The sixteen-year-old Leocadia is slowly walking home on a clear night with her parents, her young brother, and a servant after they have all spent some time along the river or in the country outside Toledo. They encounter Rodolfo and his four companions. Rodolfo is a very different person from Don Juan in *No hay cosa como callar.* One supposes that Don Juan is rich enough to dally with relative ease in Madrid, but Calderón gives us no impression of overwhelming wealth. Rodolfo is very rich indeed and can afford to indulge himself. He is a consumer, a man of appetites, and Cervantes defines him by his possessions: "Hasta veynte y dos [años] tendria un caballero de aquella ciudad, a quien la riqueza, la sangre ilustre, la inclinacion torcida, la libertad demasiada y las compañias libres le hazian hazer cosas y tener atrevimiento que desdezian de su calidad y le davan renombre de atrevido."[11] (About twenty-two years of age was a gentleman of that city, whose wealth, illustrious lineage, perverse tendencies, excessive liberty, and unsuitable associations caused him to do things and take risks out of keeping with his nobility and which gave him a reputation for insolent derring-do.) "Riqueza" comes first in the contrastive list.

Rodolfo and his comrades, when they meet Leocadia's family, cover their faces and scrutinize and catalogue the physical attractions of the three women—mother, daughter, and servant—before them. Leocadia's aged father can do no more than verbally chastise the young men for their lewd and insolent remarks. It is in this context that Leocadia's beauty so impresses itself on Rodolfo that he feels he must possess her. With lightning speed, abetted by his friends, Rodolfo abducts Leocadia, who conveniently faints as she is carried off to Rodolfo's room in his father's house.

Here, another stage property becomes highly significant. Rodolfo's bedroom is a kind of bachelor's *pied-à-terre* set apart from the rest of his father's house. He can come and go without being heard entirely at his own liberty because "tenia de su estancia la llave y las de todo el quarto, inadvertencia de padres que quieren tener sus hijos recogidos." (He had the key to his room and to all the adjoining ones, an oversight on the part of parents who are trying to keep their children home.)

Don Juan's room in *his* father's house in *No hay cosa como callar* has the same strategic location. The father, Don Pedro, mentions this fact to Leonor, who is unsure about spending the night at a neighbor's: "este cuarto es, donde entrasteis, / tan apartado y tan lejos / del mío que nadie tiene / que hacer en él" (2: 1010). (The room that you were in is so far and set apart from mine that nobody has any occasion to be in it.) But—*¡o inadvertencia de padres!*—Don Pedro does not think it necessary to mention that the room is normally occupied by his son, Don Juan, who has obediently gone off to fight the battle of Fuenterrabía. Even so, Don Pedro gives Leonor his master key and she locks herself in. And there she would have been safe if two servants had not been forgetful. Don Juan's Barzoque forgot to pack his master's army papers, and Don Pedro's Celio forgot to ask Barzoque for his key, which opens both the street door and the bedroom door. So when Don Juan and Barzoque return for the papers, they naturally decide to enter the house through the door that gives direct access to the bedroom, in order not to wake everyone up. In the tale and in the play, the indulged son has the key to his own room, and the room is relatively isolated. Thus the parents, the father in particular, more or less unwittingly connive in their sons' misdeeds.

Of the two rooms, Cervantes' is the more extraordinary, so hauntingly detailed that it could almost provide the elements for an O'Neill stage setting, wonderfully vivid to the mind fervid for fiction but nearly impossible to bring physically into being, the novel defying the theatre. That Cervantes constructed Rodolfo's bedchamber as theatre clearly emerges from the manner of Leocadia's description of it to her parents: "Dixoles lo que avia visto en el teatro donde se representó la tragedia de su desventura" (p. 125). (She told them what she had seen in the theater where the tragedy of her disgrace was performed.)

Leocadia is raped in darkness and pleads with Rodolfo in darkness. The interview between him and her is as explicit as the censor would permit until our time. Only when Rodolfo leaves, after vainly attempting a second sexual attack, do the physical features of her surroundings become distinct. In their luxury, they nourish fantasy; but Cervantes both creates and curbs the night-wandering mind. Rodolfo and Leocadia are extremely sensible people who act with firmness on the most unbridled occasions. For example, Rodolfo, while he is racing home with the unconscious Leocadia, though sensing that she is unconscious, still takes the precaution of blindfolding her so that she will not be able to remember their route or his house. He blindfolds her again when he decides to conduct her to the church, so that she can find her way home from it. He then addresses to her the only words he speaks during their time together; but he alters his voice and uses a mixture of Castilian and Portuguese. The two epithets "sagaz y astuto" (p. 117) fit Rodolfo extremely well.

Leocadia, however, is still more perspicacious. Despite her precarious situation, she reconnoiters and inventories the room in which Rodolfo has left her. At first she feels her way about but then discovers a window and draws its curtain. Bright moonlight enters now. Leocadia perceives the colors in the damask hangings, the princely elegance of Rodolfo's gilt bed; she counts chairs and tables, makes note of the position of the door, remarks a number of pictures but cannot make out their subjects, studies the great and richly draped window which, looking out on a garden, bars her escape with a grille, as the garden does with its high walls. The meaning of the chamber is evident. Rodolfo is inordinately rich. It is then that Leocadia appropriates the crucifix: "no por devocion ni por hurto sino llevada de un discreto designio suyo" (p. 124) (for neither a pious nor a possessive motive but rather acting in accordance with a clever plan of hers). She thereupon puts the window back as it was and returns to the bed (of her shame) to await the night's outcome.

Perhaps the most powerful poetic process in *La fuerza de la sangre* is the series of human faces that fatally impress themselves on the souls of those who behold them. The moment of vision with carnal eyes is inflammatory. But the extinction of that prime vision, for it to be even more brightly reborn against memory's dark background—the literal *chiaroscuro* of the tale—is more potent still. Leocadia's beauty is a flame that burns more brilliantly for being snuffed out: "la mucha hermosura del rostro que avia visto Rodolfo que era de Leocadia . . . comenzo de tal manera a imprimirsele en la memoria que le llevo tras si la voluntad y desperto en el un desseo de gozarla" (p. 116). (Leocadia's great beauty of face began so to imprint itself upon his memory that memory swept the emotions along with it and there welled up in him the desire to possess her.) This is not love at first sight but love in aftersight.

Similarly, when Rodolfo's father is moved to pick up and take into his house the seriously injured Luisico, the path is from memory to the emotion of love. The child's face brings to this grandfather's mind the image of Rodolfo, now seven years absent in Italy; and the love for the son is transferred to the grandson: "quando vio al niño caydo y atropellado, le parecio que avia visto el rostro de un hijo suyo a quien el queria tiernamente y que esto le movio a tomarle en sus braços y a traerle a su casa" (p. 131). (When he saw the child knocked down and trampled it seemed to him that he had seen the face of a son of his whom he dearly loved and that this had moved him to take the child up in his arms and carry him to his house.)

The final confrontation comes about as a result of the "discreto designio" of Estefanía, Rodolfo's mother. In order to impress Leocadia's beauty as powerfully as possible upon her son's mind, Estefanía treats Leocadia with brilliantly artistic Italianate painterliness. Here, surely, is the subject of one of those paintings which Leocadia was not able to discern in the darkness of Rodolfo's shuttered room, something like "The Bridal Feast" (an imaginary subject). Rodolfo himself will have seen and remembered similar works from his long sojourn in Italy, which has transformed him from a "mozo inexperimentado" into a connoisseur of fine food and women. The feast is on the table to celebrate the prodigal son's return, and it must have been a splendid one in view of Rodolfo's tastes and appetites and of his parents' wealth. But Estefanía's master stroke is to progress from salivation to a splendid nourishment for the beauty-hungered eye. She serves Leocadia up as the banquet's visual *pièce-de-résistance*:

Poco tardó en salir Leocadia y dar de si la mas improvisa y mas hermosa muestra que pudo dar jamas compuesta y natural hermo-

sura. Venia vestida, por ser invierno, de una saya entera de terciopelo negro llovido de botones de oro y perlas, cintura y collar de diamantes; sus mismos cabellos, que eran luengos y no demasiadamente rubios, le servian de adorno y tocas, cuya invencion de lazos y rizos y vislumbres de diamantes que con ellos se entretexan, turbavan la luz de los ojos que los miravan. Era Leocadia de gentil disposicion y brio; traia de la mano a su hijo y delante della venian dos donzellas alumbrandola con dos velas de cera en dos candeleros de plata. [pp. 140-41]

Leocadia was not slow to emerge and make of herself the most lovely and unexpected display within the power of natural and artificial beauty. Since it was winter, she approached clad in a long-skirted tunic of black velvet picked out with gold and pearl buttons, and wearing a diamond necklace and girdle. Her own hair, long and not too blonde, dressed in waves and curls interwoven with diamonds that half gleamed through, was a natural *coiffure* which dazzled the eyes that sought it out. Noble were the bearing and manner of Leocadia. She led her son by the hand, while in advance of her came two maidens lighting her with a pair of waxen candles in silver sticks.

This is an incomparable portrait. In its calculated play of darkness and light, it descriptively and visually subsumes the main narrative process of *La fuerza de la sangre,* which is a flash of revelation followed by a burrowing into the subconscious of the beholder of the image, seen in a moment of illumination and then extinguished, only to emerge again. These areas of inner awareness Cervantes calls "memoria" and "voluntad." In Leocadia they are, partly through circumstance, intensely active; in Rodolfo they are intermittent. The carefully prepared vision of Leocadia is designed to assault the insulated citadel of Rodolfo's inner life. It is the riposte to his aggression on Leocadia. In the foreground is the blaze that lights the festive table. Then, from the darkness of the background steps Leocadia, clothed in brilliant blackness set off by shimmers of light. Her hair, which the poet usually would have had outshining all possible competition—"oro bruñido al sol relumbra en vano"[12]—is not excessively blonde, so that the interplay between its gleams and those of the jewels and ornaments set in it may be more subtly complementary. Yet these effects are all secondary to the miraculous beauty of Leocadia's face, illuminated in this masterful mixture of nature and art by the candles in the silver candleholders that the accompanying maidens bear. At the table, seated opposite each other, Rodolfo and Leocadia with their eyes consume each other. But, once again, Leocadia flickers out in a fainting fit like the one she experienced when Rodolfo abducted and raped her. When Rodolfo learns that the swooning and perhaps moribund beauty is his destined bride, in his most terrible act of appetite he virtually consumes Leocadia's soul; Rodolfo could rape Leocadia when she was unconscious; he virtually repeats the deed as she seems to lie dying, a kind of spiritual rape: "llevado de su moroso y encendido deseo, y quitandole el nombre de esposo todos los estorvos que la honestidad y decencia del lugar le podian poner, se abalanço al rostro de Leocadia, y, juntando su voca con la de ella, estava como esperando que se le saliesse el alma para darle acogida en la

suya" (pp. 143-44). (Carried away by burning sexual desire and with his bridegroom's status removing every obstacle that the decency and decorum of his home might impose, he hovered over Leocadia's face and, joining his mouth to hers, seemed to be waiting for her soul to come out so as to make room for his.)

Leocadia herself is quite well aware of the similarity, and the essential difference, between her first and second swoons: "cuando yo recorde y bolvi en mi de otro desmayo, me halle, senor, en vuestros bracos sin honra; pero yo lo doy por bien empleado, pues al bolver del que aora he tenido, ansimismo me halle en los bracos de entonces, pero honrada" (p. 145). (When I regained consciousness after an earlier fainting fit, I found myself in your arms, dishonored; but I consider it all to have been worthwhile, because, in coming out of this present faint, I once again found myself in the arms of the same man, but honorably.) So the *chiaroscuro* continues. Leocadia and Rodolfo marry quickly in a blaze of light. For Rodolfo there is a fresh vision: "Viose Rodolfo a si mismo en el espejo del rostro de su hijo" (p. 146). (Rodolfo saw himself in the mirror of his son's face.) But the most vivid scene is the final one, which Cervantes must of course blot out but which is perhaps no less luminous for that. Rodolfo cannot much enjoy the wedding feast "tan grande era el deseo de verse a solas con su querida esposa" (p. 146) (so great was his desire to see himself alone with his beloved wife). Thus Cervantes covers Rodolfo's and Leocadia's lovemaking with a decent darkness that in no wise inhibits the imagination: "Fueronse a acostar todos, quedó la casa sepultada en silencio" (p. 146). (Everybody went to bed and the house remained buried in silence.)

Yet the most arresting photograph of *La fuerza de la sangre* is that pale image of Rodolfo's room which Leocadia commits to anguished memory until it is blotted out by a new blaze of technically licit sensuality. By means of its luxurious detail, Cervantes has fashioned a novel theatre of the suffering inner mind, and this is where Leocadia most truly performs, in dimness and silence.[13]

One of the most startling effects of Cervantes' new novelistic drama is the speed with which his prose moves from the outer landscape to the inner one. It requires only four longish paragraphs to shift from the moonlit family procession trudging home to the muffled luxury of Rodolfo's shuttered apartment. This much is the physical modification. Its spiritual corollary is a heightened awareness of the ways of public and private life. After being raped, Leocadia psychologically closets herself in the mournful memory of her misfortune. She never quits the scene of her dishonor because her mind haunts it. She is traumatized. Leocadia's father wisely does not attempt to conjure away the event itself, but he does try to mitigate its severity with a classically judicious speech of consolation. His words are a balm, a therapy. The family have been discussing Leocadia's plan to entrap her assailant into identifying himself with the lure of the silver crucifix. But her father sees too many uncertainties in the scheme and rejects it. He does, however, advise her to hold fast to the cross:

lo que has de hazer, hija, es guardarla y encomendarte a ella, que pues ella fue testigo de tu desgracia, permitira que haya juez que buelva por tu justicia. Y advierte, hija, que mas lastima una onza de deshonra publica, que una arroba de infamia secreta, y pues puedes vivir honrada con Dios en publico, no te pene de estar deshonrada en secreto. La verdadera deshonra esta en el pecado y la verdadera honra en la virtud; con el dicho, con el deseo y con la obra se ofende a Dios, y pues tu, ni en dicho, ni en pensamiento, ni en hecho le has ofendido, tente por honrada, que yo por tal te tendre, sin que jamas te mire sino como verdadero padre tuyo. [pp. 126-27]

what you should do, daughter, is to keep and commend yourself to it because, as a witness to your misfortune, it will provide a judge to seek justice for you. And remember, daughter, that an ounce of public dishonor does more harm than a hundredweight of secret shame and since you can live honorably in public with God, do not be disturbed by secret dishonor. Sin is true dishonor and goodness true honor. One offends God in speech, by intent, and through actions. And since you have offended him neither by word, thought, nor deed, consider yourself to be honorable, as I consider you to be and will never cease to be anything but a father to you.

"Con estas prudentes razones consoló su padre a Leocadia." (Leocadia's father consoled her with these wise words.) And his is the language of the confessional, of the sublimated parent. And yet these thoughts, which so notably contrast with the sense of obligation common in Calderón, though high-minded and soothing, remain null.[14] Leocadia's encounter with Rodolfo has brought about the girl's total eclipse. If her father's ideas had been as valid for the public as for the private sphere, she might have resumed what little outer life she had. But Leocadia burrows in: "se reduxo a cubrir la cabeza, como dizen, y a vivir recogidamente debaxo del amparo de sus padres" (p. 127). (She resigned herself to covering her head, as they say, and to living quietly under her parents' protection.) Of course, her pregnancy and the birth of Luis make further precautions necessary. Cervantes, nonetheless, draws a desolating portrait of secrecy. Rodolfo adds to the sense of annihilation and withdrawal by going off to Italy in total forgetfulness of his misdeed: "se fue con tan poca memoria de lo que con Leocadia le avia sucedido, como si nunca huviera passado" (p. 128). (He left with as little recollection of what had happened between him and Leocadia as if it had never occurred.) The memory was all Leocadia's. She inhabited it and it possessed her until Luisico's accident set in train the series of events that roused her from that long metaphorical swoon which was her life from the time she was raped without her consent until the time she came to be legally raped, with her consent. In *La fuerza de la sangre* Cervantes probes the secret of this psychological ecliptic and makes it dazzlingly public, giving expression to that "silencio, en el qual no quedará la verdad deste cuento" (p. 146) (silence which the truth of this tale will not keep). Cervantes' tale is, then, a kind of dramatic poem of the inner consciousness which gives voice to the inexpressible. Its path of development is lineal. Rodolfo feels an overwhelming desire for Leocadia and satisfies it as directly as possible. For the rest of the story, Leocadia must live with the consequences of his attack.

Calderón, in *No hay cosa como callar,* constructs a rather more complicated architecture. His play uses inner and outer space as skillfully and as variously as a great builder uses solid and void. The basic element of his technique is to displace his personages from their normal habitat. For the Golden-Age male the "normal" area was public: war, sport, family business, government. In Calderón's plays all these activities are represented by the road and the street, especially the street. Women were conveniently relegated to domesticity: the house, the room. All dramatists must grapple with social norms. Calderón accepts these very Spanish and nearly exclusive identifications of the female with the inner sphere and the male with the outer sphere so as to fashion variations upon them.

Thus Marcela, mistress of Calderón's inconstant Don Juan, pursues her unreliable lover with a masculine firmness and publicity. He is himself in pursuit of Leonor, whose beauty he has glimpsed at mass. Marcela's appearance intercepts Don Juan's attempt to follow Leonor and learn her address and name. There, in the street, Marcela and Juan indulge in a lovers' quarrel equivalent to those in English well-made plays of a generation or two ago. The difference is that this one occurs not on living-room sofas placed back to back but completely in the open. As Don Juan admonishes Marcela: "Mira que estás en la calle; / no des voces. Esas quejas / suenan en casa mejor. / Vete, por tu vida, a ella, / que voy tras ti" (2: 1004). (Remember that you're in the street. Don't shout. This kind of recrimination sounds better inside. For God's sake, go on home and I'll be right along after you.) All of this is quite amusing, of course, and Calderón is wonderful at repartee, particularly in the plays of this period. For example, *Mañana será otro día* revolves around a quarrel and a lawsuit between Don Luis de Ayala and his son Don Juan de Leyva. In the course of their dispute over an inheritance of entailed property (*mayorazgo*), when the father finds the son on a surprise visit to his sister in the family house in Madrid, he exclaims: "No creyera / ser vos, porque no pensaba / que los Leyvas se dignasen / de visitar los Ayalas" (2: 772). (I would never have thought it was you because I had no idea that the Leyvas condescended to call upon the Ayalas.) This bit of Wildean wit flashes out against a sombre background, however. Juan, before his father's appearance, nearly killed his sister because of her compromising conduct. The sister, Beatriz, is able to explain her behavior and so escapes, but very narrowly.

Similarly, Juan and Marcela's scrap leads *No hay cosa como callar* into much less light-hearted themes. One realizes the near-scandalous quality of Marcela's conduct when Don Juan's father, coming upon the contumacious pair, almost reprimands his son for the scene he and the lady are making. But, of course, the piquancy of their verbal duel comes from its publicity and Marcela's daring displacement from the "recato" and "prudencia" of domesticity. Moreover, that same displacement provides the means by which the action of the play shifts from private to public events. Don Juan's father, Don Pedro, has come to fetch his son away to war, and not to a distant one in Flanders or Peru. The French are attacking Spain on her very borders, and Don Juan returns to active service to fight the battle of Fuenterrabía,[15] almost the last Hapsburg victory. Castile's men and resources were nearly exhausted, and each major engagement produced a governmental paroxysm. Don Juan's readiness to take up arms again exemplifies Olivares' view of the battle as a supreme test.[16] In urging his son to his duty, Don Pedro is likewise exemplary:

es menester salir, hoy
que no es justo, estando puesta
pena de traidor a quien,
habiendo servido, deja
de salir, que, comprendido
tú en el bando, te detengas
ni un instante. [2: 1004]

You must leave today, because, since
you come under the ruling that declares any veteran who fails to rejoin
the army a traitor, it wouldn't be
right for you to delay even for an instant.

Interesting and saddening as the historical circumstances are, their significance is not in themselves alone but rather in their contribution to the work of
art. Don Pedro's discovery of Marcela and Don Juan is a conjuncture between
public and private that reveals the fundamental structure of *No hay cosa como
callar,* which focuses on public events from a personal perspective and on the
personal world with the light of publicity. To some degree, all drama must expose the inner human processes to public view; but Calderón exploits relations
between inner and outer with such skilled and inspired obsessiveness that it
seems plausible to conclude that the connection between, say, individual emotion and history is a major mode of his drama. Only a poet convinced that
"amor es guerra" could persuasively move us from a lovers' quarrel to a great
and historic battle.

But in Calderón's art there is a principle of correspondence between the individual microcosm and the collective macrocosm. If man is at war with himself, it cannot surprise us to find him at war with his fellows. Yet it is startling
and revealing to pass abruptly and without any preparatory line of argument
from private to international conflict. Still, when the two kinds of conflict are
thus poetically juxtaposed, they form a conjuncture that improves our understanding of the ways of each form of hostility because we see them as connected, not logically but as image, *Gestalt.*

This need of Calderón's to place apparently opposed functions side by
side imposes upon him compounds of plot. Dramatic technique in the seventeenth century could not allow nonlineality or plotlessness. But simple line development does not afford a great deal of opportunity for multiple juxtapo-
sitions. And the progression from confrontation to confrontation, juxtaposition to juxtaposition, opposition to opposition is Calderón's real method of
artistic advance, through a dialogue of shifting contrasted images. One basic
meaning of *La vida es sueño,* for example, is that constructed by the three encounters between Rosaura and Segismundo, one in each act of the play. In each
of these they speak revealingly to and of each other as human metaphors im-
probably but dazzlingly combined. They are body and soul images that gain in
meaning each time they meet, just as Clarín delivers up his real meaning only in
the final encounter with Basilio. What brings Rosaura and Segismundo together is plot—his the primary, hers the secondary, if you will. But the real plot
of *La vida es sueño* is a progressive revelation achieved through imagistic juxtaposition in well-calculated sequence. This real plot is nonanecdotal, nonlogical
(but reducible to logical statement), poetic. To achieve its effect, however, it relies on the conventional notion of plot, or rather on plot and subplot and sub-
subplot. A wealth of line development provides innumerable possibilities for

intersection. Don Pedro, in *No hay cosa como callar,* is a vector in pursuit of his son; Don Juan is one in pursuit of an unknown beauty (Leonor); Marcela is another in pursuit of Don Juan. They come together as a cluster of images. Behind their meeting is logic: history, duty, a tale of love. Even so, the meeting makes poetic sense in itself as voices in conflict, pulling Don Juan away.[17]

But Don Juan does not depart directly, lineally, as Rodolfo departs for Italy in *La fuerza de la sangre.* Another thread of plot, with its associated images, intervenes. Between Leonor and Diego, sister and brother, the displacement is now neatly balanced, as it was not between Don Juan and Marcela. For Diego is rigidly house-bound while Leonor, *tapada,* moves about Madrid with masculine ease. The explanation for this inversion is an unhappy one. While gambling, Diego had quarreled inconsequentially with another man. He and two friends followed and fought with Diego. In this unequal contest Diego's life was saved by the assistance of an unknown *caballero.* The two then attacked the three, gravely wounding one of them. The fight began drawing a crowd, and Diego sought sanctuary in the church of San Jorge. At nightfall he removed to the ambassador's residence in which he has been given asylum and where Leonor visits him. As long as it remains uncertain whether the wounded man will live or die, Diego does not, for fear of arrest, dare to leave the ambassador's. If the man dies, Diego plans to flee so as to escape prosecution and Leonor will go to live in a convent, not as a nun but simply as a resident. This plan is an extreme form of the "normal" male and female habitat, for in it Diego will be expelled from all inwardness and domesticity, while Leonor will remain cloistered, each exiled from the complementary mode of the other.

This bit of infraplot is not secondary but essential, for it explains Leonor and her unprotected situation, allows Don Juan to catch a second glimpse of her, and is the basis for many further intersections and confrontations. There is also autobiographical echo here, for Calderón himself and his brothers ran into very serious difficulties when, in 1621, they got into a sword fight in which Nicolás de Velasco was killed. The brothers took asylum in the Austrian embassy, but had to pay the dead man's family a 600-ducat settlement. To raise that sum, they had to sell their father's notarial practice. On another occasion, Calderón himself set the law on the actor Pedro Villegas, who had seriously wounded one of the Calderón brothers. Villegas took refuge in the convent of the Trinitarian nuns, but the police pursuing him did not respect the convent's immunity. They searched the whole place without finding Villegas, creating something of a scandal and angering Lope de Vega, whose daughter Marcela was one of the nuns.[18]

Diego escaped into the church of San Jorge, not into a nunnery, but he did receive asylum in an unspecified embassy. The point is not that *No hay cosa como callar* is autobiographical but rather that events in his earlier years reinforced Calderón's preoccupation with violent transitions from public to private, from the clash of swords in the street to the quietness of the sanctuary or of the residential room. And the infraplot of *No hay cosa* just discussed patterns itself on sudden displacements from and exaggerated returns to the normal habitat. It is a detail faithfully reproducing the major architecture of outwardness and inwardness that characterizes the play as a whole.

Moreover, it prepares the spectator for the play's major occurrence, which depends upon the dislocation of Juan and Leonor. At first, when Don Juan dutifully goes off to serve the king, he does not forget Leonor as Rodolfo forgets Leocadia. Indeed, he bears her image away with him: "Ignorado amor, perdona / si antes de saber quién seas / me ausento de ti, que no / será tu olvido mi ausencia" (2: 1005). (Unknown love, forgive me if I leave before finding out who you are, because my absence will not mean forgetting you.) This is the first step into the emotive and psychological for Don Juan. It is conventional for the beloved so to impress herself on the consciousness of the lover. Leonor's history is far less conventional. She is living with her maid in quarters opposite the house of Don Juan's father. In her misfortune, the link between intimate concealment and general knowledge, like that between Juan's and Marcela's dispute and the battle of Fuenterrabía, is a metaphor, fire. But this metaphor is curious in that it changes its nature as it moves from the public to the private world. Fire breaks out in Leonor's rooms and drives her into the street "medio vestida," half-clothed, half-naked, a hybrid creature, semi-"decent," semi-sexual. From the street she takes refuge in Don Pedro's house. He, as we have seen, persuades Leonor to spend the night in Don Juan's room. When Barzoque and Don Juan return they find Leonor sitting up with a light on, but asleep. She awakes and Don Juan prepares to rape her. Her final protest is "¡Piedad, cielos, / y no permitais que venga / a dar de un fuego a otro fuego!" (2: 1012). (God have mercy. He cannot let me escape one fire only to be destroyed in another!) Thus does that objective phenomenon of fire, which drove Leonor from her home into the street, acquire metaphoric subjective value—the fire of Don Juan's sensuality, destructive of Leonor's honor.

In cities like Madrid fire was both a terrible and commonplace happening. But Calderón, so city-centered in his less serious plays of the 1620s and 1630s, rarely uses it. When he does so, the outburst is portentous. The fire most like Leonor's and Juan's is the one that takes place in *El pintor de su deshonra*. In that play, however, the subject is the problem of an unequal marriage between an older man,[19] Don Juan Roca, and a very young woman, Serafina. Aside from the fact that Serafina had loved the youthful Don Alvaro, whom at the play's beginning she believes lost at sea, Don Juan has long felt a disinclination to marriage, which he at last undertakes for dynastic reasons, *por razón de estado:* "aunque siempre fui / poco inclinado al amor, / de mis deudos persuadido / de mis amigos forzado, / traté de tomar estado" (1: 868). (Although I have never felt very much drawn to love, urged by my relatives, constrained by my friends, I did attempt matrimony.)

Don Juan Roca's temperament is, consequently, his flaw as a husband. His cool and studious character does not make him a completely vigilant guardian of his blazingly beautiful wife, whom he appreciates aesthetically but not so much sensually. Indeed, his relatives and friends occupy the first place in his affections. Temperament, then, becomes here a question of temperature. The *gracioso* Juanete, in commenting on his master's wedding, tells a story to illustrate how badly Don Juan Roca and Serafina blend. A Madrileño on the banks of the Manzanares invites a stranger to share his meal and gives his guest very cold chicken and very hot wine. Finding both food and drink extreme, he slyly dips the chicken in the wine, despairingly. Juanete then applies the anecdote to the newlyweds:

me han dado moza novia y desposado no mozo, con que habrá sido fuerza juntarlos al fiel, porque, él cano, ella donzella, o él la refresque a ella o ella le caliente a él. [1: 870]	Here I have a youthful bride and a bridegroom that is not, so the thing they should have done would have been to balance one off the other so that, with her just a girl and him a greybeard, either he would have cooled her down or she would have heated him up.

The blending did not and does not occur. When Alvaro, not drowned after all, returns to Serafina, he is unable to renounce her and exploits her distempered marriage to gain admittance to her house in Barcelona. In a tragic adaptation of perhaps his most characteristic comic device of the twenties and thirties, Calderón has the husband return as the lover is pleading his lost cause, just as in the lighter play the father or brother comes home at the worst possible moment.[20] Serafina has had nothing to do with bringing Alvaro into her house, but upon her husband's return she knows a moment of ultimate fear. Though blameless, she is not equal to revealing her lover's presence in the darkened house. Consequently, with supreme art she plays the loving and devoted wife to draw Don Juan away so that Alvaro can escape from his place of concealment. She is nearly successful. But the *gracioso* Juanete brushes against Alvaro as he is making his way out, and Juanete gives the alarm. Don Juan's suspicions are thus aroused, and Serafina's torment continues.

It continues in public now, for Don Juan has come bursting back with the news that those same "parientes y amigos" around whom his life revolves have arranged to honor Serafina on the occasion of festivities in the streets of Barcelona by inviting her to take part in them, disguised, as they will be, and then to a banquet at the country place of Don Diego de Cardona.[21] During these celebrations Alvaro again addresses Serafina, who this time succeeds in convincing him that she cannot desert her husband. Alvaro is about to embark when fire breaks out in Cardona's *quinta*. Don Juan rushes in to save Serafina. He brings her out alive but unconscious. Then, leaving his wife under the care of her lover in the guise of a sailor, Juan plunges back to rescue "deudos, parientes y amigos." Don Alvaro cannot resist profiting by this almost miraculous piece of good fortune and carries Serafina off with him to the ship, which immediately sets sail.

Don Juan Roca has helped to save all the gathered guests of his clan, but he has lost Serafina. And honor, for Calderón, is far superior to life. But blame is not now a useful critical canon. What we see here in Don Juan Roca is defeat—lack of ardor. More subtly, what we perceive in the smothered and smouldering unconscious of Serafina is a tragic blaze of passion—unexpressed, unacted upon—but moving and with a silent poetry compelling events that appear to be beyond desire and control. The fire in *El pintor de su deshonra* is both an objective phenomenon and a doubly psychological construct that takes the temperature of the two principal characters.[22] Their readings are the reverse of those of Don Juan and Leonor in *No hay cosa como callar*. But in each case fire is the means of admittance to that private world which Bruce Wardropper has so well called "the unconscious mind."[23]

Among Calderón's tragedies of honor, *A secreto agravio, secreta venganza* is the least enigmatic. Leonor has excellent intentions. She means to dismiss her importunate lover Don Luis, returned, like Alvaro of *El pintor de su deshonra,* from the dead. But, despite the extremely impressionable and suspicious nature of her Portuguese husband, Don Lope de Almeida, events combine to defeat a resolution which she recognizes as necessary to the preservation of both her own life and that of her lover, Don Luis. Like *No hay cosa como callar, A secreto agravio,* as a result of its Leonor's failure, becomes a poem expressing the silent and unspeakable agony of the protagonist, Don Lope. That Portuguese nobleman's marriage by proxy to a Castilian gentlewoman is another union of irreconcilable opposites which reveals a disordered, distempered cosmos not yet ruled by any harmonizing principle. Accordingly, the very elements act in a chaos of murderous hostility. Don Lope is an anti-artist who wishes forever to stifle the injury done him, and he dispatches Don Luis and Leonor in elementally different ways so as to erase their connection and efface their crime (of intent). Don Luis dies drowned and Leonor perishes by fire, again in a *quinta* on the water's edge. Some contiguities are ineradicable. But Don Lope's nonaccidental fire is a horrendous statement susceptible of two interpretations. The offical public reading which Don Lope gives is that Leonor has died, untarnished, in a tragic accident. The private sense, deciphered for King Sebastian by Lope's intimate friend Don Juan, is that the fire was a contrivance to conceal Lope's infamy from the world at large. The hideous irony is that Don Lope's obsession with the integrity of the intimacy of his married life results in nothing less than a monumental disclosure. Don Lope is the Herostratos[24] of honor who, by immolating his disgrace, gives it lasting publicity. It is perhaps for this reason that King Sebastian refers to Don Lope's deed as "el caso más notable / que la antigüedad celebra" (1: 453) (as remarkable an occurrence as those in the annals of antiquity). Here, even more eloquently and painfully, fire symbolizes a public and private passion, simultaneously. Don Lope is an unsuccessful yet horribly sublime Leocadia.

For Leonor in *No hay cosa como callar,* many more weapons are available than for the tongue-tied protagonists of Calderón's three great tragedies of honor. A sense of the irremediable governs Don Guitierre of *El médico de su honra,* Don Lope of *A secreto agravio, secreta venganza,* and Don Juan of *El pintor de su deshonra.* Leonor's goal is to put things right. The comedic consciousness feels that time is on its side: *Dar tiempo al tiempo,* "give things time to work themselves out," while much of tragic awareness comes from the realization that time has run out. Cervantes, in *La fuerza de la sangre,* is simply prodigal with time and allows seven years for a solution to be found. Indeed, even though Rodolfo and Leocadia are somewhat past their prime, he nearly thirty and she about twenty-three when they at last marry, Cervantes portrays them as still very youthful. Time clearly does favor them.

In addition to the benefactions of time, Leonor of *No hay cosa* possesses power over both silence and speech. This power derives from a sense of timing, of knowing when to keep silent and when to speak. Her most unusual gift, however, is the ability to master simultaneously both silence and speech, to speak and act through silence. Here her procedure is rather like that of a symbolist poet who trains himself to talk so precisely around the image he wishes to evoke that, once he has closed the circle of circumlocution, it brilliantly blooms. So, in the safety of her private thoughts, Leonor ponders the problem of how to express the injury done to her: "¿Qué frase habrá más decente / que lo refiera? Ninguna, / porque la más elocuente / es la que sin decir nada, / el más rústico la entiende" (2: 1014). (What phrase is the most suitable for expressing it? Not a one, because the most eloquent utterance is the one which, saying nothing, permits the least-lettered to understand.)

Leonor's sense of the power of nonutterance helps her to avoid grave mistakes of utterance. During the two months of private grief that follow the fire, she resists the temptation to confide in her servant Juana. Even more, she so guards herself that Juana is not even able to surmise the nature of her mistress's trouble. Thus when Leonor's brother questions the girl, she can offer no explanation: "Tú que debías / saber (como [que] siempre acompañada / de ti está, aún más amiga que criada) / la causa de que nace su tristeza / ¿también la ignoras?" (2: 1012). (You mean to tell me that you, who are always with her and are even more her friend than her servant, don't know why she's so depressed?)

Calderón's age stereotyped women as clannish among themselves and incurably garrulous. Leonor comes to life by departing from these lifeless conventions. And her unusual strength of character is all the more notable in comparison with the ill-fated heroines of the tragedies of honor, who become deeply and dangerously involved with their servants. In the honor tragedies the great and misleading temptation for the critic is to blame. One cannot really blame Doña Mencía in *El médico de su honra* for complicity with her servant Jacinta. Jacinta is a slave and Prince Enrique promises her freedom in exchange for allowing access to her mistress. When Enrique's presence, more or less unbidden, brings crisis upon Mencía, she uses Jacinta to help her deceive Gutierre, her husband. As matters go more and more badly for Mencía, she comes increasingly to rely upon Coquín and Jacinta. Indeed, it is they who unwillingly deliver her up to her husband for execution, Coquín by conveying Enrique's message, Jacinta by attempting to inform Mencía of Gutierre's return when she is composing the fatal letter to the prince. But before Gutierre takes his revenge, he dismisses all the servants, and Mencía dies alone.

In *A secreto agravio, secreta venganza,* the relationship between Leonor and her servant Sirena is one of such uninhibited intimacy that it is the servant who must warn her mistress as to the gravity of her expression of grief over her marriage to Don Lope: "¿Qué dices, señora? Advierte en tu peligro, y tu honor" (1: 429). (What are you saying, my lady? Consider the danger, and your honor.) Leonor reproaches the girl for her coldness: "tú, ¿que me calle me aconsejas?" (Do you, of all people, advise me to keep quiet?) Sirena must resign herself to hearing the confession. Later, she takes an active part in Leonor's undoing by carrying messages between the lovers and introducing Luis into Don Lope's house. She no doubt would have carried the letter Leonor wrote to Don Luis, bidding him come and collect her love after Don Lope's departure with Sebastian for Africa. But Luis drowns and Leonor burns before this can be consummated.

Serafina, of *El pintor de su deshonra,* is more discreet than Leonor about unburdening herself to servants, but pours her heart out to her friend Porcia in much the same way as Leonor did to Sirena, for practically the same reasons. And even though she has driven her servant Flora out of hearing for her initial confession, Flora plays the same role as Jacinta and Sirena in the misfortunes of *her* mistress. She carries messages and lets the fatal man into the house. Since the third act shifts the play from Barcelona to Naples, Flora has no further part to play, and it is a piteously solitary Serafina whom we encounter there.

An important element in the tragic mechanism operative in the three tragedies of honor is that their heroines undertake to exercise a kind of control that is no longer applicable to their circumstances. In comedies and before marriage, multiple suitors are manipulated by words; and messages, speeches, and nonverbal forms of communication such as dress and disguise superabound. There, the word is the deed and men whose primary means of expression is action are rather at a loss. As Saint-Simon says of the consummate courtier: "Il savait parler le langage des dames."[25] Thus in the premarital world of comic courtship, woman rules as mistress of the logos. Everything depends on her word and the whole action tends to utterance climaxing in the binding question and affirmative response. In courtship, woman has the power of refusal; and it is immense, even though its goal is to create an acceptance.

But Calderón's tragic women have crossed over into another realm of discourse. This is the silent male world of marriage. For Mencía the transition is mainly temporal. She has left the past world associated with Enrique for the isolated kingdom of Gutierre. Leonor and Serafina, however, literally leave their native lands for new marital domains where another language is spoken. Leonor, married by proxy to Lope in Castile, has just arrived in Portugal at the moment of her first appearance in *A secreto agravio.* Serafina exchanges Naples for Barcelona on the occasion of her marriage to Don Juan in *El pintor de su deshonra.* For both women there is a significant pause intermediate between the old and the new environment. Leonor halts to rest and volubly grieve before Lope comes to fetch her home over three leagues of water, while Serafina extends the past into the present with a stop at Gaeta, accompanied by her father, before she proceeds to Barcelona with Don Juan.

These women, obsessed with vanished lovers, do not trouble to learn the silent speech of their new lands. In the past, when they were unmarried, conversation and encounter, though controlled and even discouraged, were the essential means of guiding events towards the licit and socially desirable goal of marriage. After marriage, any communication with the lover becomes criminal conversation,[26] for the logos of courtship is dead and the word powerless before the awful force of deed. At the beginning of each tragedy, its heroine engages in such a criminal conversation with her lover, lost and now returned. Except in Serafina's case, the interview is conducted in the presence of the new husband and the lovers convey their meaning in a verbal game of double allusion. Basically, these dialogues are lovers' quarrels at which, as we have seen, Calderón excels, because they give him an opportunity to show the sexes as equal in at least this kind of conflict. In fact, of course, the woman has the upper hand, since she shines with words and the man may not use his best weapon, the sword, against her, although he may, and does, use it against his rivals and so indirectly against her.

In a comedy, public quarreling may be an effective way for the woman to bring the man around, and it elicits no more than a half-hearted admonishment, because of its unseemliness, from Don Pedro in *No hay cosa como callar*. But in the other world of marriage, so rarely explored in Calderón, it is a monstrous thing. The reason is that in marriage the male dominates by the deeds, and words no longer have their courtship power of control, which dissolved itself in the lady's utterance of acceptance. The tragic heroines, however, carry over into their marriages the now baseless conviction that they can order their lives and the contradiction of husband and lover with the same triumphant manipulation of speech that brings so many unwed females safely home to a desirable and legal union. This persuasion is more than forlorn; it is terribly dangerous, because when speech is used up action becomes the only possible form of expression. Once the cloud of the lover has passed over the marriages in these three tragic plays, conversation between husband and wife virtually ceases. The husband, torn between courtship-love, where words could placate rivalries, and honor, where appearance is the speechless mime, returns to the simulacrum of love before he resolves to avenge his honor. He acts before he acts. And his wife is reassured, feeling that her verbal tactics have worked. They have, rather, only made the deed inevitable. And the deed is that the husband takes up arms against his wife in an ultimate recourse to the sword which, in the world of comedy, is totally disbarred. All protestations are unavailing now and Mencía's pathetic cries of "¡Inocente muero!" (I die innocent!) are the death-rattle of the cruelly displaced spirit of comedy throttled by the deed of death which, in its inadaptability, it has helped to bring on. In Calderonian tragedy the logos of conflict, for Calderón almost tantamount to the logos of art, dies. That may be why Calderón wrote so few tragedies. For him they are anti-art, comedy deprived of speech and run amok.

Leonor, then, owes her salvation to the fact that she can manfully master the weapon of silence, just as womanfully she can manipulate the arms of speech; but in the last two acts of *No hay cosa como callar,* they are in abeyance. In *El médico de su honra,* for example, the great symbols of the speechless male world are the dagger and the sword. They literally are Mencía's undoing. For when Don Arias and Don Gutierre unsheathe their swords in the presence of King Pedro the Cruel, he punishes them with a summary imprisonment which creates the opportunity for Enrique's stealthy visit to Mencía. She heroically conceals the prince's presence, only to give herself away when she catches sight of the dagger concealed beneath her husband's cloak. Gutierre is able to confirm the suspicions to which his wife's terror has given rise at the sight of the dagger by comparing it with Prince Enrique's sword. They match. And, finally, when the enraged King Pedro confronts his half-brother with the evidence of his misbehavior—the same dagger—in his perplexity Enrique wounds the king as he takes back his weapon. Pedro's response is wildly disproportionate to the injury, just as Mencía's was to the mere glimpse of the dagger; and the resultant hostility between the royal brothers determines Enrique to leave without the king's permission. That decision causes Mencía to write the final, fatal letter to Enrique, never completed, never delivered, crushed in the utterance.

A bond between Pedro and Mencía is their losing way with speech. Each would wish to inhabit a world where words are supreme and arms totally banished, the palace and the noble house. Pedro attempts to manipulate conversation with feminine wiles more characteristic of the *comedia de capa y espada* than appropriate to his grim palace in Seville. These stagemanaged declarations regularly go awry. For example, when Leonor, Gutierre's first love, applies to the king for sufficient dowry to love in a convent, Pedro revives her quarrel with Gutierre by promising her total redress. After he has heard Leonor's story, the king hides her and requires Gutierre's explanation in her hearing. Gutierre's account puts Leonor in a questionable light. She comes forth to defend herself; and Enrique's friend, Don Arias, explains how he came to leap from a window in Leonor's house, thus creating baseless suspicion in Gutierre and so ruining the proposed marriage between Leonor and Gutierre. Far from being the clarifying kind of declarations with which the typical Calderonian *comedia* ends, these speeches make mischief because it is too late for them; and indeed they yield in silent terror to arms, the swords that imprison both Gutierre and Arias and set in train Mencía's tragedy. But the disastrous outcome of this first interview does not prevent King Pedro from contriving a second one like it. It is the culminating conversation between him and his brother Enrique. Don Gutierre, at the king's bidding, listens to it concealed. Pedro's idea is that his examination of Enrique will reveal the prince's blameworthy attentions to Mencía and her virtuous deafness to them. To his dismay, Enrique tries to justify his conduct by ambiguously alleging that the lady was not averse to him. To prevent further damage, the king tries to impose silence on his brother. Enrique defends himself more warmly still with explanations even more damaging to Mencía. Deeply disturbed, the king so conducts the remainder of their conversation that it ends with the unintentional but grimly prophetic dagger wound. Communication between the brothers has degenerated into words of chaos, the elements of speech arrayed against one another in hostility; and the king's echoing adjuration to the prince: "¡Callad; callad!" (Hold your tongue; hold your tongue!) has the same powerless pathos as Mencía's "¡Inocente muero!" The mismanaged logos has turned against both sovereign and lady, and the dagger puts an end to their perversions of the word. The silence of death remains.

In *No hay cosa como callar* the action takes a tragic turn when Don Juan buckles on his sword. The difference is that, unlike Gutierre reaching for his weapon in the presence of the king, or Don Lope preparing to accompany Sebastian on a mission of disaster, Don Juan, in obeying his father and King Phillip IV, shows a fundamentally amenable and docile spirit. He recognizes the sovereignty which his elders exercise over him. Above all, he is nowhere touched in the dominions of honor, that kingdom of the mind and imagination over which Gutierre and his brethren absolutely rule, exempt from any intercession on the part of their temporal sovereign.

But, as Don Juan obediently sets out for Fuenterrabía, external honor satisfied, inward honor vacant, the spirit of honor settles into his deserted realm as Leonor prepares to spend the night in his room. Even though the ruler, Don Juan, is absent, Leonor feels that she can abide with security because of a more important male presence and pledge, those of Don Juan's father, acting *in loco filii*. There can be no doubt that Leonor's occupation of the young man's quarters in his physical absence, but lingering presence as a function of his recollection of her, is a psychic event, *the* psychic event in Don Juan's totally superficial existence. By accidents that Calderón would certainly compute as design, the young woman physically and spiritually moves into the young man's marital and psychic emptiness. Without Don Juan's knowledge, the borders of that emptiness have been inviolably ringed about with the magic incantation, the words pledging honor more powerfully than any force. Unconsciously, Don Juan has been possessed in this profound and serious sense, just as in an ephemeral and corporal sense he is impressed with Leonor's beauty: "¡O, qué feliz fuera yo / si, como a Madrid me vuelvo / a buscar unos papeles, / volviera alegre y contento / a buscar una hermosura / que dentro del alma tengo!" (2: 1011). (Since I am going back to Madrid to fetch some papers, how happily I would be going if, joyous and pleased, I were returning to fetch a lovely that I have, contained, within my soul.)

Thus Don Juan is "dos veces cautivado"[27] (twice possessed), consciously and unconsciously. On both levels there are strong bonds between him and Leonor; but obviously the deeper and more lasting connection is the unconscious one. As Don Juan gazes down upon the sleeping Leonor alone (for Barzoque has fled the scene of what he considers to be a demonic possession) he mentally paces the frontier between consciousness and unconsciousness. On the simplest level he is wakeful while Leonor sleeps. But the improbability of her being there causes him to doubt his senses, so that he concludes their attachment to be a duet of modes of the unconscious, she sleeping and he dreaming. In this astonishing meditation, Juan at least reconnoiters, if he does not cross into, the new kingdom of nonrational states of awareness, in which his experience is the dream of her sleep:

si de ser inmortal	If sleep is a clear indication that the
el alma es clara señal	soul is immortal and if I gave you
el sueño y yo te la dí,	mine, it follows that, although it is
cierto es que, aunque anime en mí	the source of my consciousness, in
en ti vive; y así, cuando	you it abides, and so, while you
duermes tu, estoy soñando	sleep, I am in a delirium. Thus, oh
yo, con que ser puede (¡ay Dios!)	God, is it possible for the two of us
con un alma estar los dos,	to share a single soul, you sleeping
tú durmiendo y yo soñando.	and I dreaming!

[2: 1012]

Much of the matter here is traditional, of course. In seventeenth-century Spain, the soul was a concept of multiple consciousness, after Aristotle.[28] It had three levels of awareness: vegetative, intellectual, and theological *(alma vegetativa, racional y angelical).* The *alma vegetativa* is the seat of sensation, and all living things, from the lowest to the highest, possess it. The rational and theological functions are man's alone. The scene between Juan and Leonor rests upon the vegetative and the rational, although, insofar as honor is an awareness intermediate between the rational and the theological,[29] the theological soul is indirectly present by implication. The other principal convention, source of so many poetic conceits, is that when one falls in love he conveys his soul to the beloved through the eyes, although he does not quite lose it himself.[30] Just what the lover remains in possession of and what precisely the beloved has got is never, to my knowledge, made really clear; but the thing that each one retains is obviously less than entire. The souls of lovers are thus displaced and to some degree diminished in the displacement, although the diminution whets the appetite for a return to integrity and is in fact love. The novel content of Don Juan's dialogue with his silent partner is precisely its invasion of nonconscious levels of cognition. Leonor's noncognizance contaminates Don Juan's own wakefulness. The marches of the borderland between consciousness and unconsciousness so greatly expand that the whole dominion of the one is coterminous with the other, a single capital—*alma*—ruling the two realms.

The soul is asexual and as easily inhabits the female as the male body. For a moment, then, Don Juan has left all sexuality behind to approach an area of pure and unincorporate psychology where there is neither male nor female, only waking and sleep. For both Juan and Leonor to arrive at this zero point has required a great and largely unwilled journey away from the customary. Leonor's brother's scrape has freed her masculine psyche by confining and feminizing him. Fire has also driven her out into the open. When she retreats from it, her withdrawal is not into a conventlike inner space but rather into a ringed masculine confine, the word-fortress of Don Pedro, the vacant citadel of Don Juan's room. For Don Juan himself, the outward journey to Fuenterrabía has been contradictory, a function of the differing modes of memory and forgetfulness, Juan's recollection of Leonor, Barzoque's forgetting the papers. Still, the servant's omission serves. Juan and Barzoque return as ghosts of themselves, the departed and permanently dismissed. They accordingly come back with a minimum of fleshly reality and are momentarily much more of the spirit than of the body. Master and servant respond to the apparition of Leonor similarly but distinctly, Barzoque seeing ghosts, Juan sensing the presence of the immaterial soul in its subconscious and unconscious states and these awakening in his own awareness sympathetic sensations.

One reason for this surprising sympathy in a person as insensitive as Don Juan is that, Leonor's soul having entered his spirit, she possesses him and is naturally attuned to her own emanations. Just as her body has been displaced into an alien masculine site, so her soul, unknown to her, has emigrated into a strange masculine spirit. To it her own ghostly remnant responds. The encounter between Leonor and Juan is, then, the gathering of many ghosts; and Barzoque was not far wrong when he fled before them. There is, in Don Juan, a similar quailing before the engagements of the spirit. The first two visions of Leonor began the quickening of his inner life. Now, with the beloved image before him both in body and in mind, its gestation has come to term and, for an instant, we are in the presence of that true marriage of minds which Cervantes so wonderfully sustains, without physical consummation, between Periandro and Auristela in the *Persiles*. It has come about by means of a near-total interchange between Juan and Leonor of the traits of their respective sexual habits, her inwardness for his outwardness, his silence for her speech, his deed for her emotion.

It is significant above all that in the nonwakeful portion of their interview, Juan speaks while Leonor is, of course, voiceless. In the same ghostly situation of her undoing, Leocadia, in *La fuerza de la sangre,* remains unconscious throughout most of her abduction and all of her violation, and so cannot speak. But after the event, she most eloquently gives voice, astonishing even herself. Rape has brought her to a precocious maturity and she resists and bargains with Rodolfo by means of a rhetoric that has the ideal balance between nobility of impression and nobility of expression. But Rodolfo fights back with silence, so much so that Leocadia doubts the reality of the situation much as, in the flickering light of his room Don Juan does: "con las manos procuraba desengañarse si era fantasma o sombre la que con ella estaba" (p. 119). (She tried with her hands to disprove to herself that the presence with her was a ghost or shade.) Silence is the companion to darkness in Rodolfo's tactic of oblivion and he maintains it until he utters the few words of Portuguese with which he takes leave of Leocadia. Thus, between them, word is the woman's and silence the man's, in the main, at least.

Between Don Juan and Leonor, Calderón varies the pattern by conceding utterance first to Don Juan, with all the psychological implications that attend on speech. But at the conclusion of his dialogue with silence in the form of Leonor, Don Juan shows that he is far from being completely possessed and tamed, by drawing his sword against Leonor. I am aware of the amusing phallic implications of the phrase; but, in the light of the tragedies of honor, I would rather underline the literalness of the statement. Cervantes bears it out. His Leocadia begs Rodolfo to kill her, using persuasive military metaphors: ". . . te ruego que ya que has triunfado de mi fama, triunfes también de mi vida; quítamela al momento, que no es bien que la tenga la que no tiene honra; mira que el rigor de la crueldad que has usado conmigo se templará con la piedad que usaras en matarme, y así, en un mismo punto, vendrás a ser cruel y piadoso" (p. 119). (Now that you have triumphed over my reputation, I beg you also to triumph over my existence. End it at once, because it is not right for a dishonored woman to go on living. If you do this, the harshness of your cruelty to me will be tempered by your compassion in killing me; and thus, simultaneously, you will be cruel and merciful.) This is the voice of dishonor pleading for the surcease of total silence, the deadly male gift. Having reached the farthest possible frontier in psychic interchange, Don Juan recoils from dream and begins to reshape his masculine identity in the form of an act of aggression against Leonor. Accordingly, he wakes her. Yet even though both of them are now awake, dream is very close, for each has just emerged from his own. Don Juan feels safe in the dream-bound reality of his bedroom, into which, he believes, the adverse and spoiling forces of obligation cannot penetrate: "Y puesto que sueños son / las dichas y los contentos / soñémoslos de una vez" (2: 1012). (And since happiness and pleasure are dream-stuff, let us dream them this one time.)

In the brief struggle that ensues, the customary modes of female and male increasingly speak their own idiom. Leonor regains her voice and uses it with unavailing eloquence. Juan intends to commit the deed of rape in a triumph of silence. Their duel is the fundamental and tragic conflict between logos and action. This time, action brutally strangles all utterance. Juan uses speech against speech: "Es en vano / disuadirme de mi intento." (It's useless to try to dissuade me from what I mean to do.) Finally, Leonor attempts weaponed shouts, but Juan can throttle them too: "Al viento / daré voces." "Taparéte yo / la boca." (I will scream into the air. I will stop up your mouth.) Juan's suffocation of Leonor gives insight into another dimension of Calderonian tragedy. Their case is provisional, to be sure. They are not married. And Juan's deed lacks the cruel artistic intent that characterizes Calderón's great murderers of their wives. Like Rodolfo, Juan possesses Leonor in a sudden seizure: "me ofendiste por accidente" (p. 121), as Leocadia puts it to her ravisher. (You assaulted me in a fit of passion.) Nonetheless, the essential attributes are there, the basic figures of utterance and taciturnity. Calderón's tragic heroines are *outspoken,* too easily give voice, represent to an extreme the modes of expression. To combat these dangers their husbands fall more and more deeply into the prison of silence and emerge from their fortress for a last foray which imposes everlasting dumbness upon their wives. The beautiful irony is that they fashion their monuments to speechlessness with such terribly supreme art that tongueless action itself is transformed into a manner of expression that proclaims what they had tried to suppress: *El secreto a voces.* Art triumphs, but at an unaffordable price. Close as the situation in *No hay cosa como callar* is to the tragic mode, it is still not altogether tragic because the murder remains metaphorical. Juan has obliterated Leonor's honor, but not her life, even though to both Leocadia and Leonor life without honor has no meaning or value, except hope. For honor can, in these cases, be healed, restored, revived. Both women, then, artistically nurture a commitment to resurrection which the truly tragic heroines cannot entertain. Their only hope, as Gutierre makes clear to Mencía,[31] lies beyond the grave.

In *La vida es sueño,* silence and speech similarly condition the relationship between Rosaura and Segismundo. In their first encounter, highly ambiguous sexually (for Rosaura is androgynous, and Segismundo, too)[32] the word is with Segismundo; and he gives full-throated utterance to the perplexities of a being who, though he has a mighty potential for action, finds himself restricted by force to pure inner life, to painful reflection and meditation. Just as Rosaura is about to tell her story, Clotaldo breaks in on the conversation and arrests Rosaura and Clarín. Segismundo once again is master of the word, *le langage des dames,* in their second dialogue, at the royal palace. But in his purpose, word is corollary to deed, for he means to enjoy Rosaura sexually and believes that courtly address will be a seduction to that goal. When language fails he resorts to brute force and is prevented from raping Rosaura only by Clotaldo's unexpected intervention. Segismundo's behavior renders Rosaura speechless, and her essential part in their conversation is eloquent silence: "Respóndate retórico el silencio; / cuando tan torpe la razón se halla, / mejor habla, señor, quien mejor calla" (1: 516). (Eloquent silence will be my reply because silence is the best speaker when the mind is tongue-tied.) Rosaura finds her voice and Segismundo loses his in their third encounter, on the field of battle. With high implausibility but great poetic precision, she confronts him in the thick of the fight, for if "amor es guerra," the male must ultimately decide whether or not to wield the sword against the female. And Rosaura is a female who has persistently eluded and thwarted the love which she has wakened in Segismundo. Rosaura's frustrations are of a different kind with respect to him, for ever since her first interrupted discourse she has longed to unburden herself to Segismundo, in whom she has recognized an *âme soeur*. She now proceeds to make her confession in a magnificent speech, in a play full of magnificent speeches. Its essential rhetoric is the persuasiveness of the dual manner, female emotivity and masculine force. Rosaura summarizes her plea in a beautifully bipartite anaphora of masculine and feminine modes in collaboration:

Mujer vengo a persuadirte
al remedio de mi honra
y varón vengo a alentarte
a que cobres tu corona.
Mujer vengo a enternecerte
cuando a tus plantas me ponga
y varón vengo a servirte
cuando a tus gentes socarra.
Mujer vengo a que me valgas
en mi agravio y mi congoja
y varón vengo a valerte
con mi acero y mi persona.
Y así piensa que si hoy
como a mujer me enamoras,
como varón te daré
la muerte en defensa honrosa
de mi honor, porque he de ser,
en su conquista amorosa,
mujer para darte quejas,
varón para ganar honras. [1: 529-30]

I confront you as a woman to persuade you to take up the cause of my honor, as a man to incite you to regain your crown. I confront you as a woman to play upon your emotions by throwing myself at your feet, as a man to serve you by joining your forces. I confront as a woman to seek your support in my outrage and affliction, as a man to second you with my sword and my self. Consider, therefore, that if you make love to the woman, the man will kill you in worthy defense of her honor because, as a conquistador of love I am resolved to be a woman in burdening you with her quarrel, to be a man in pursuit of high renown.

Word and deed, in Rosaura's astonishing speech, occupy their proper spheres. Word is handmaiden to deed: "Mujer vengo a persuadirte," and the passage between them is immediate, harmonious. But in her passion Rosaura has reached, like Leonor in the troubled sleep that follows affliction, a Platonically undifferentiated zero degree of sexuality. Her one soul presides over two distinct incorporations, the female logos and the male kinesis. This is a play in which Rosaura performs the two leading roles, a "normal" and an "abnormal" one. Yet Calderón preserves Rosaura from a charge of abnormalaity that would have, in his time, ruined her credibility by making the abnormal role a temporary and rhetorical enactment. Having no man to help her, Rosaura must, for a time, take the man's part. But she creates the part in order to be replaced in it. The male role that she conceives is a rhetorical act, fusion of word and deed, designed to entice and persuade some suitable man to take it up in her behalf. Just previous to her plea, Clotaldo has definitively failed her in that respect and she turns to the only possible remaining male. In Segismundo she finds her man. But their relationship is deeper than sex and deeper than marriage. They are *almas gemelas,* twin souls, a perfect Periandro and Auristela, a perfect Teágenes and Cariclea. The problem is that, while Rosaura has sounded these spiritual depths of Segismundo's being, he has not yet realized a sufficiently perfected consciousness to probe them himself. Sexuality still powerfully conditions his concept of Rosaura. The miracle of her return to him is like the miracle of Leonor's presence in Don Juan's bedroom, an invitation to pleasure made acceptable by the unreality of its circumstances.

Segismundo's response to Rosaura is promising, for he silently withdraws into himself to ponder the situation. And his long following speech is the mental, inner corollary to Rosaura's exhaustingly lengthy declaration. Sex still very much colors Segismundo's thoughts; and his first impulse is precisely Don Juan's, to rape the relatively helpless Rosaura. Some of the essential language is nearly identical. Don Juan thinks: "Y puesto que sueños son / las dichas y los contentos / soñémoslos de una vez" while Segismundo reflects: "Esto es sueño; y pues lo es, / soñemos dichas agora, / que después serán pesares" (1: 530). (This is a dream, and since it is one, let us now dream the pleasure that later will be pain.) But that deeper consciousness which at the beginning Rosaura has implanted in Segismundo now begins to function. At this point, Rosaura achieves success, for she ceases to be his goal and becomes instead his inspiration, precisely what her rhetorical strategy had envisaged, a feminine logos directing a male kinesis. Accordingly, Segismundo's whole strength turns to heroic action: "¡Vive Dios! que de su honra / he de ser conquistador / antes que de mi corona" (1: 530). (Great God, I am determined to reconquer her honor even before my crown!)

Nonetheless, the temptation of Rosaura's beauty remains so great that Segismundo will entrust himself to only a few and, for Rosaura, ambiguous words. In them, though, the antithesis of Leocadia's appeal to Rodolfo revives in redeemed form. To show Rosaura the ultimate mercy, Segismundo must turn away from her now: "Rosaura, al honor le importa, / por ser piadoso contigo, / ser cruel contigo agora" (1: 530). (Rosaura, honor dictates my being cruel to you now so that I can be compassionate towards you later.) Yet the really important aspects of Segismundo's parting address is that in it speech yields to action, logos to kinesis: "No te responde mi voz / porque mi honor te responda; / no te hablo porque quiero / que te hablen por mí mis obras" (1: 530). (My voice does not answer you so that my honor can answer you. I don't speak to you, because I want my deeds to speak to you for me.) To be sure, action is, as Segismundo makes clear, a continuation of speech by other means, semiotics *avant la lettre.* Yet each has its homeland and proper residence. The relationship between Rosaura and Segismundo describes the emigration, conflict, concordat, and repatriation of her feminine logos and his masculine kinesis. The brilliant ambiguity of their resolution is that each is most at home in the other. Rosaura inspiring Segismundo, he protecting her. Home is exile in the beloved other. And the great and sacrificial change in Segismundo is that the hostility he felt towards Rosaura for her invasion of his privacy and for her thwarting of his love has now been converted to zeal for her spiritual well-being. The sword he had raised against her is raised against her enemies. The conflict moves from the inner to the outer world.

In *No hay cosa como callar,* enmity, that between Don Juan and Marcela, is at first intimate. Then, with the call to arms at Fuenterrabía, the hostilities take on the familiar form of war. But at Don Juan's unexpected return to Madrid they again assume domestic manners, a Fuenterrabía among lovers and within the family. The central and enduring confrontation is, of course, that of Leonor with Don Juan. When rehearsing her disgrace two months after the event, Leonor presents it in terms of a battle between two opponents, one brave and the other cowardly, except that the weaker fighter in this dishonorable combat draws to herself much of the strength of the ostensibly stronger. During the assault, Leonor, like Leocadia, had entirely collapsed into unconsciousness; but that passing extinction has only caused all her faculties now to blaze with a most painful brightness as she relives the engagement:

Volví del desmayo cuando
el que (aquí el dolor se aumente)
más osado estuvo, más
cobarde la espalda vuelve.
¡Oh infames lides del amor
donde el cobarde es valiente,
pues el vencido se queda
mirando huir al que vence!
Más animosa yo entonces
(propia acción de los que tienen
poco valor, alentarse
en sintiendo que los temen)
por conocer mi enemigo
quise (¡ay de mí!) detenerle. [2: 1014]

I regained consciousness just at the moment when (here grief grows keener) my intrepid assailant was showing his back. Oh ignoble engagements of love, in which the coward is brave, since he remains defeated on the field watching the victor in flight. Growing more spirited I then (and it is typical of the fainthearted to pluck up their courage when they feel they are feared) tried to detain my enemy so that I could know him.

Before the rape, a psychic interchange occurs in which Don Juan becomes spiritually alive when Leonor's active consciousness takes possession of his vacant inner being. The rape itself is a brutal reaction against this new and rich unfolding of dormant awarenesses. Abruptly awakened, Leonor loses consciousness in horror at the aggression against her person. Don Juan's intent is to obliterate, and he does efface all involvement with Leonor, to his entire satisfaction. But for Leonor the psychic interchange is permanent, marital; and it energizes her faint spiritual resources with vigorous new masculine infusions. She becomes intrepid just when Don Juan puts aside the sword. He becomes weak and loquacious when she has grown silent and strong. She attacks and he defends. Their struggle is the central subject of Acts II and III. It is a struggle for possession, and the texture of the last two-thirds of *No hay cosa como cal-*

lar is a pattern of theme and variation on having and having not. The basic theme is that Leonor has been dishonored. But since she, like Leocadia, has had absolutely no part in the rape, her loss of honor is cruel and baseless social judgment. Leonor, however, has no kind father to speak such soothing words; and her conduct after the rape is nothing less than heroic. For two months she locks herself up in a purgative convent of the self. As we have seen, with a self-dominion denied her tragic sisters, she confides in no friend or servant and banishes all males from her presence, including her brother and the man she loves, Don Luis. All of this is a lengthy vigil of the spirit, a purification before she sets out on her quest, a masculinization of the feminine.

In her bereaved state, Leonor's sole material weapon is the *venera* that she tore from Don Juan's neck. It identifies her assailant and, in its association with pilgrimage to the shrine of Santiago de Compostela, suggests just such a quest as Leonor's for the redress of an unspeakable grievance, a silent embassy. Indeed, possession of the *venera* by a series of dispossessed lovers, beginning and ending with Leonor, is the major motif of the last two acts of *No hay cosa como callar*. Luck is with Leonor from the start, for a convenient carriage accident at her door, involving Marcela, acquaints her with the original of the portrait in the *venera*. But when, with great courage, she goes *tapada* to Marcela's house in order to learn Don Juan's identity, her plan miscarries because her brother, to whom she dare not reveal herself, pays a surprise call on Marcela. Leonor surrenders the *venera,* only promptly to regain it when Marcela returns the call and insists on showing that she attaches no importance to the first recipient of the ornament by giving it now to Don Diego. As he and Marcela courteously quarrel about the gift, Leonor steals it. It remains in her possession until a new round of duels, like that at the beginning of the play, delivers her enemy Don Juan into her hands and she confronts him with the evidence. But it looks as if silence is to remain the only remedy for Leonor and Juan until he doubts Leonor's purity and a final convulsive twist of plot brings Don Juan's father to her house. Leonor asks Don Pedro to honor his word. He is willing to do so, even against his son. Now, with her enemy at bay, the time has come for Leonor to speak. In such circumstances the word is far more destructive than the sword; and logos triumphs over kinesis, female over male. Nonetheless, speech held in reserve has now become so potent that to threaten it is sufficient. Don Juan quails at the prospect of Leonor's tirade, forbids further utterance, and surrenders his hand to her: "Esta es mi mano, Leonor." (Here is my hand, Leonor.) Out of surrender, then, comes ultimate victory for symbolic gesture, for civilized action. Word has tamed the deed so that it may safely perform. Silence reigns, and the remaining dispossessed lovers are mutely heard resigning themselves to its rule with the supremely ambivalent phrase "No hay cosa como callar." (Silence works best.)

On their tortuous way to the altar, Cervantes has once again touched Leonor and Don Juan. Just as Don Manuel in *La dama duende* defended himself against supernatural and dishonorable interpretations of the mysterious presence in his rooms by a humorous adaptation of the archaic speech of the romance of chivalry, so Don Juan, while describing his strange experience to Don Luis, likens it to an erotic episode in a chivalric novel. Luis is astonished at

Juan for being so incurious as to the explanation for the event. But assumed indifference is Don Juan's defense, because he knows that he bears a heavy responsibility and seeks to shirk it through a literary composition:

> En mi vida fuí
> curioso y antes quisiera
> no preguntarlo jamás
> ni que nadie me llegara
> a decirlo, que estimara
> el no saber della más
> porque estoy ya muy cansado
> de saber cómo se llama
> y dónde vive mi dama,
> qué porte tiene y qué estado,
> y así sólo me desvela
> pensar que lo he de saber,
> porque me muero por ser
> caballero de novela
> y que se cuente de mí
> que una infanta me adoró
> encantada, de quien yo
> no supe más. [2: 1019]

> I was never in my life curious, and
> I'd rather never ask or have anyone
> tell me, because I'd be glad to hear
> no more about her, since I'm fed up
> with trying to find out what my lady
> friend's name is and where she lives
> and what her manner and circum-
> stances are, and so the only thing
> that bothers me is the thought that
> I'm going to learn those things, be-
> cause I want desperately to be a
> knight in a novel and for it to be said
> of me that an enchanted princess,
> whom I never knew anything more
> about, adored me.

The tactic, so opposed to Leonor's tenacious silence, does not work. One reason is that, while thinking he is unburdening himself to a friend, Don Juan is delivering himself up to his enemy, an event of frequent occurrence in a whole cycle of early plays, such as *Nadie fíe su secreto*.[33] Don Juan does not know that Don Luis is in love with Leonor and she with him. Also it is, more literally, this ill-advised and distorted confession to Luis which puts Juan completely in Leonor's power. For when her brother questions Juan about his strange language to his sister, Don Luis at once grasps the situation and turns against his friend. Don Juan understands perfectly: "¿Eso es haberos yo dicho / mi secreto?" (2: 1036). (Is this because I told you my secret?) The answer is yes, and Don Juan is confronted not with a capricious princess but with the powerful and vengeful woman whom he had tried so desperately to avoid. Against her, language, even that of Cervantes, is an insufficient protection.

Along with her masculine resolve, Leonor herself takes on a chivalric coloration of action corresponding inversely to Don Juan's garrulity. Leonor confronts her enemy Marcela disguised, *tapada*. Marcela objects on the grounds of the laws governing challenges—*También hay duelo en las damas*: "si es desafío, no quiero / daros ventaja y es cierto / que en vos sera acción indina / tirar detrás de cortina / estando yo en descubierto" (2: 1021). (If this is a duel, I don't want to give you any advantage; and it would be an action unworthy of you to shoot from behind a curtain while I was exposed in the open.) Leonor bases her reply on the laws governing knight-errantry. She is an *aventurero* and so is permitted a disguise:

la que siguió tan bien la metáfora, no dudo que sepa también que pudo entrar de rebozo quien aventurero es, y así descubrirme yo no quiero, pues la ley de aventurero me comprende. . . . [2: 1021]	I don't doubt that someone who so clearly grasped the allegory could fail to know that an unknown chal- lenger may enter the lists disguised; and so, since I am covered by the rul- ing concerning unknown challengers, I do not wish to show my face. . . .

And if it seems to be straining a point to ascribe to Cervantes all of Calderón's allusions to knight-errantry or *novela,* the evidence shows that, in Calderón's mind, these phenomena were absolutely associated with Cervantes: "la más extraña novela / de amor que escribió Cervantes" and "es mi amor tan novelero / que me escribió Cervantes."[34]

Between two such immense talents as Calderón and Cervantes there can, of course, be no question of petty theft or slavish imitation. Certain functions in one range of Cervantes' art confirmed intuitions and techniques already alive in Calderón's sensibility. As between *La fuerza de la sangre* and *No hay cosa como callar,* parallels in the two plans of operation produce remarkably distinct tactics. For example, though their destinies are similar, Leocadia and Leonor attain their goals in widely divergent ways. Leocadia's rehabilitation comes about as a result of her passive resistance to the idea of permanent outrage. Though the deed has been done, her idea of herself refuses to admit the enduring implications of "dishonor." In her neo-Platonic microcosm, then, an act of violence burst in upon a frugal but harmonious economy. Rape is equivalent to the irruption of wild and savage men into the pacific and female-dominated imaginary realm of the pastoral novel, as it occurs in the *Diana,* for one example. Violence emanating from the male, under those circumstances, challenges the governing principle of a philosophically idealist psychology and society. Will it, China-like, absorb and reform the barbarian invader? At first, in *La fuerza de la sangre,* the barbarous Rodolfo is expelled, but not back to Scythia. Rather, he is expatriated to Italy, motherland of Renaissance neo-Platonism and academy for the refinement of even the grossest appetites and tastes. Rodolfo's schooling there is perilously long, but it is exactly sufficient. It is a schooling in taste.

Before raping Leocadia, Rodolfo has consented to his father's proposal that he should give his Spanish nobility an Italian finish by sojourning for some time in Italy. His tour will take him to Barcelona, Genoa, Rome, and Naples. But the real attraction is Italian food, and associated pleasures, of which Rodolfo and his travelling companions have heard an excellent report from returning Spanish soldiers: "el, con dos de sus camaradas, se partio luego, goloso de lo que avia oydo dezir a algunos soldados de la abundancia de las hosterias de Italia y Francia, de la libertad que en los alojamientos tenian los españoles. Sonavale bien aquel *Eco le buoni polastri, picioni, presuto et salcicie*" (p. 128). (With two of his comrades he soon departed, hungry for the plenty of the hostels of Italy and France and for the freedom from constraint which Spaniards

lodging in them enjoyed, as he had heard from a number of soldiers. *Eco le buoni polastri, picioni, presuto et salcicie* sounded very good to him.) In this description so like the much more ambitious program pursued by the far less sensual protagonist of *El licenciado Vidriera,*[35] the key word is *goloso.* Rodolfo is a man of appetites. Italy will satisfy and refine them.

Rodolfo's taste for beauty was of course what impelled him to abduct and rape Leocadia in the first place: "la mucha hermosura del rostro que avia visto Rodolfo" (p. 116) (the great beauty of the face that Rodolfo had seen). The change operated in it by the seven Italian years is that he has become a collector and a connoisseur of female beauty rather than a savage consumer of it. No really great distance has been travelled; but it is the distance between rape and marriage, between dishonor and honor, between a perpetuity of silent suffering and the possibility of speaking, at last. Thus, when Rodolfo's parents recall him from Italy to be married, they shape the image of the bride in entire conformity with their son's desires. Their summons does not fail to excite Rodolfo; and he departs almost immediately, driven by a sexual appetite analogous to his previous hunger for the plentiful pleasure of Italy.

Doña Estefanía makes sure that her son has no craving for spiritual or intellectual attributes when, alone with Rodolfo, she places before him the portrait of an unattractive woman, whose lack of beauty is compensated for by her moral character. She is noble, intelligent, and tolerably rich. The mother assures the son that this is the wife for him and that the verbal and painted descriptions are her authentic portrait. After close scrutiny, Rodolfo rejects this woman because her ugliness will make it impossible for him to experience that "justo y devido deleyte que los casados gozan" (p. 139) (licit pleasure which by right belongs to married couples). Without such enjoyment, he will not find the marriage bond tolerable and subtly threatens his mother that he will be a bad and unfaithful husband. Adroitly terminating his appeal with a catalogue of what suitors seek—rank, intelligence, wealth, or beauty—Rodolfo asserts that he has sufficient social standing and wealth to be content and that wit in a woman interests him not at all.[36] His wants are perfectly clear: "la hermosura busco, la belleza quiero." (I seek beauty, I require loveliness.)

Far from being disconcerted, Doña Estefanía is delighted with her son's confession, for she can now proceed to serve Leocadia to Rodolfo at the banquet, certain that he will want to devour her matrimonially. In addition, the mother is a far more discerning artist than her son is a connoisseur. He studies images with carnal eyes only. She reads inner character. Leocadia's real beauty is her intelligence and high resolve. The outer loveliness can and will disappear. That is what happens to Isabela in *La española inglesa,* poisoned by a jealous rival and left, after having been incredibly beautiful, "un monstruo de fealdad" (a monster of ugliness). But her faithful suitor Recaredo is no Rodolfo. In a majestic and perfectly neo-Platonic speech, Recaredo, even though his parents have found another wife for him, renews his pledge to Isabela: "desde el punto que te quise, fue con otro amor de aquel que tiene su fin y paradero en el cumplimiento del sensual apetito, que puesto que tu corporal hermosura me cautivó los sentidos, tus infinitas virtudes me aprisionaron el alma de manera que, si hermosa te quise, fea te adoro, y para confirmar esta verdad, dame esa

mano" (p. 49). (From the beginning I have loved you with another love than that which takes as its goal the satisfaction of sexual appetite, for, even though your bodily beauty captivated my senses, the infinity of your virtues imprisoned my soul, so that, if I loved you when you were beautiful, I worship you now that you are ugly, and, in confirmation of this truth, give me your hand.)

It is Doña Estefanía's *designio,* however, to make of Rodolfo at least a partial Recaredo. Even Recaredo achieved his pure love only with considerable fuel from the "sensual apetito." He first loved Isabela when she was beautiful and his love, having achieved a firm spiritual base, is then equal to the banishment of external beauty (which in the course of events returns to Isabela in *La española inglesa*). The portrait shown Rodolfo is surely Leocadia's in her spiritual character.[37] The mother's strategy is to guide sensuality to spiritual goals, since she has satisfied herself that Rodolfo has no moral or intellectual wants. At the banquet, then, in her bewilderment, Leocadia falters and faints. While she is unconscious, Rodolfo possesses himself, in a pneumos-rape, of her "soul." This is the sensual soul of sensation, of beauty. But it also is the soul of wit, of thought. It is even, and especially in the matrimonial context, the *alma angelical*.[38] Thus Rodolfo's basal appetite, in satisfying itself, provides his consciousness with the necessary richer nutrients, ingested from without, to be sure, but entering all the same into the structure of his own being permanently. Therefore Rodolfo will not allow Leocadia, after she has recovered from her second swoon, to break out of his grasp: "no es bien que puneys por apartaros de los braços de aquel que os tiene en el alma" (p. 144). (It is not right for you to struggle to release yourself from the arms of the person who possesses your soul.) Despite Rodolfo's indifference to the higher human functions, Leocadia brings him these, in addition to her dowry of beauty. Cervantes at least suggests that thought and theology may find a place in Rodolfo's awareness. Nonetheless, in *La fuerza de la sangre,* the most powerful portrait is that of the man governed and ruled by his appetites. When virtuous women undertake to channel these, they may be made to serve civilized ends. But the blood of the house of Rodolfo, though Christian and noble, throbs with a sensual imperative that will not be denied.

Calderón's Don Juan is a sensualist too, but one of a far less primitive sort. Where Rodolfo is passionate, Don Juan is susceptible. The most recent love, with him, is the satisfying and enduring one. Barzoque deftly characterizes his master: "Como en siendo cara nueva, / siempre es superior, que en ti / la mejor es la postrera" (2: 1001). (A new face is always preferable because, as far as you're concerned, the most recent girl is the best.) The real reason for this ability to disentangle himself from women easily is that Don Juan, like Zorrilla's Tenorio, has never loved a woman genuinely: "no hay mujer que me deba / cuidado de cuatro días" (2: 1001). (I've never been seriously involved with a woman for as long as four days.) And Don Juan has in part been prevented from loving genuinely because he looks upon women with the painter's eye, as a connoisseur or dilettante seeking absolute female perfection. Such perfection is not to be found in a single female but rather in a composite portrait of the finest features of many women, a universal comprehending every particular. In Leonor, Don Juan believes he has found the faultless face:

la naturaleza así,
viendo las varias bellezas
que hasta entonces hizo, todas
las enmendó, sabia y diestra,
borrando désta el defeto
y la imperfección de aquélla
hasta que en limpio sacó
una hermosura tan bella
que, más que todas divina
y más que todas perfeta
fue una impresión sin errata
y un traslado sin enmienda. [2: 1001]

and so nature, scrutinizing the beauties which up until that point it had produced, in her knowledge and skill, corrected them all, erasing the flaw of this one and the imperfection of that one until she had edited in final form a beauty of such loveliness that, divine and perfect beyond all others, it was a printing without errata and a version unretouched.

Calderón bases this fervid speech on the notation of nature as an artist that is at the same time the very mind of beauty desirous of expressing perfectly its thought. This, "sabia y diestra," in the form of Leonor, it succeeds in doing without blemish, so that she becomes absolute art, both as published poetry, "impresión sin errata," and effortlessly exact protraiture, "traslado sin enmienda." The protagonist of *No hay cosa como callar* thus resembles the Don Juan Roca of *El pintor de su deshonra* who, while passionate in the pursuit of knowledge and art, only weakly inclines to woman. He acquires his wife Serafina as one would acquire a remarkable portrait. But when he himself tries to paint her, he fails. Her flawless beauty is beyond his skill. What Don Juan Roca does paint, then, is the fatal blemish in high masculine intelligence and matchless female loveliness. His life and Serafina's become the satanic portrait, the picture of Dorian Grey. Similarly, the Don Juan of *No hay cosa* fails the test of Leonor's beauty and must give utterance to his own facile and forgetful sensuality as well as to his moral cowardice. He paints his own flaws.

Fortunately, the nontragic Don Juan is vulnerable. He has a conscience. He cannot forget Leonor as Rodolfo forgets Leocadia. Indeed, Leonor becomes for him "material," subject matter fit to be turned into art. And so, from her story he fashions a narrative very much to the satisfaction of his friend Don Luis, who exclaims: "En toda mi vida he estado, / don Juan, más entretenido / que este rato que os he oido" (2: 1019). (Never in my life, Don Juan, have I been so entertained as when listening to you just now!) Leonor's catastrophe has been converted into a *novela* which its creator and public can dispassionately enjoy. Art is, for the two Don Juans, a defense against a life of pledge and obligation. Yet in *No hay cosa como callar* Don Juan and Don Luis are far more than author and reader. They are involved. Luis loves Leonor as Juan ought to love, and is to be cruelly deprived of her, owing to his friend's mistake. Juan bears a heavy burden of responsibility, of which he cannot all that easily discharge himself. When Luis asks concerning the nocturnal beauty: "qué porte tenía?" Juan is constrained to reply: "tal que, si algo en este estado / me hubiera de dar cuidado, / su ofendido honor sería" (2: 1019). (What was her bearing? Such that if anything were capable of bothering me such as I am, it would be her offended honor.) Thus he is not yet dead to a woman's need for integrity. He can, potentially, feel for woman as living subject rather than artistic object. And that surely is, where Don Juan is concerned, one major theme of the play, the transformation of artistic and sexual object into human subject. Juan's punishment derives from the same experience with Marcela, who starts out by being an amusing plaything, a "dama de respeto que, / sin estorbar, divierta" (2: 1002) (a lady to whom one pays attention and who, without getting in one's way, amuses one). The game turns serious, however, when Juan learns that another man takes a deep interest in his toy. Juan then falls in love with Marcela; his is a highly urbanized and social kind of love, an *amour vanité,* as Stendhal would call it. This engagement precedes and prepares his engagement with Leonor. And just as she must innocently pay for her assailant's mistake by renouncing her first and (as Calderón repeatedly insists)[39] most enduring love, so Juan must renounce Marcela almost immediately after he has realized that he is so profoundly committed to her. An ending less satisfactory to the primordial impulses of the contracting and noncontracting parties than that of *No hay cosa como callar* could scarcely be imagined within the framework of comedy, a framework that the play itself comes so close to shattering. Despite his shifting artistic fancy, Don Juan discovers his first love, only to have to lose her to Leonor, in whom he must abide.

Clearly, there are great differences between the overwhelmingly sensual and relatively uncivilized Rodolfo and Don Juan, connoisseur, soldier, and wit of Madrid. But there is a real kinship between them, as well. They are both discriminating sensualists, rather after the pattern of Charles Swann, so that they see in lovely women the achievement of a supremely natural painter who, instead of moving away from the model's flesh to the appetizing but unattainable canvas, restores art to the living form, which can be completely possessed and then forgotten, just as the well-trained eye takes in and enjoys one picture, only to pass on to the pleasures of the next. Rodolfo and his companions, at the beginning of *La fuerza de la sangre,* scrutinize the women of Leocadia's little returning family party in precisely this lascivious-objective way, devouring them with libido-lighted eyes. Less erotically but still quite sexually, Calderón also moves from pictures to bodies. Don Juan's speech in celebration of Leonor's beauty provides the master mold from which all the particular forms of the women in the play emerge. And Marcela's portrait in the *venera* that Leonor possesses comes to life in the second act of *No hay cosa como callar.* Art works into life by means of a Pygmalion process[40] which, catalyzed by "love," converts the beautiful object into a human subject. This much is certainly common to both men and to both works. Also common to Don Juan and Rodolfo is their "feminization" in the exact sense that their minds and consciousnesses are vacant premises which the women they assail come to haunt and to occupy. Similarly and agonizingly, the men haunt the women because of the great injury they have done them. This reciprocal "masculinization" is, however, far more active and pronounced in Leonor than in Leocadia. Calderón develops his female protagonist in terms of a conflictive construct that decidedly bears his peculiar hallmark.

Despite this greater and more symmetrical elaboration in Calderón, Cervantes made the initial discovery. It is simply portentous. In transferring his major creative activity from the public stage to the privacies of prose fiction,

Cervantes creates and discovers, discovers and creates a whole new universe of the silent yet ceaselessly articulate human psyche. He breaks into this world violently. Before him, the inner "teatro donde se representó la tragedia de su desventura" had never clearly found its voice. With elaborations and adaptations of genius, Calderón integrates Cervantes' new theatre into his own stage. But in Cervantes' prose fiction the art has taken a decisive step. What will be the novel haunts, occupies, and possesses the inner sphere as decisively and as irrevocably as Leocadia and Leonor take up their mandates over Juan and Rodolfo. In this fresh field of knowledge, Calderón is a great scientist. He fashions its corresponding principle. He explores and describes manifold mysterious passages between the inner and the outer worlds. Even so, Cervantes is its original genius, its Columbus, its Einstein. Where he placed the novel—within—there it remains.

On the inward voyage the great question appears not to have been philosophy or psychology so much as literary technique. Bergson's great premise—that deep inwardness gives perceptions their validity[41]—now strikes the reader as obvious, but to utter it with assurance would have been impossible without the event of Freud's self-analysis. And for that self-analysis to occur, a technique of penetration into the infraconscious zone was indispensable. This was the analysis of dreams, an avenue leading from the conscious and external paths of memory—the dream recollected—into the nonconscious realm of the forces that form the dream. Dream analysis is Freud's principle of correspondence between the waking and the nonwaking world. Lacking Freud's kind of technique, Cervantes' and Calderón's actors burst violently into the feminized zone of psychological awareness; but the very violence of *La fuerza de la sangre* and of *No hay cosa como callar* is accompanied by a sacrilegious awe, for the intruders, like Prometheus in *La estatua de Prometeo*, realize that they have blundered into the forbidden precincts of the portentous new cult of the psychological self. Theirs is a sacred violence that founds a new artistic religion which conforms to but spiritually draws apart from the inherited faith.[42]

Cervantes' great technical discovery, above all in the *Quijote*, is the literary fecundity of drawing apart, of leaving the known roads and routes for unexplored byways. Don Quijote is of course a hero who is " on the road" in quite a conventional sense, for he has missions, goals, and destinations that draw him on throughout both parts of the book. But he is also "on the road" in the adventurous sense of Kerouac, voyaging in search of spiritual profits, graces, favors, *mercedes.* Don Quijote serves *a merced* on his quest, while Sancho would serve *a salario* (on wages) on his. The master's pursuit of nonmaterial reward, psychological recompense, is what forces him off the high road of convention and sanity into the trackless areas of the human mind. In these regions, woman is Psyche; she draws and dominates.[43]

Don Quijote's early deviation from the rectilinear in the first *salida,* when he spends a calamitous night at an inn, shows that the world off the road is mind-space into which the knight thinks himself. Matter is notably resistant there, nonetheless, for the inn does not readily adapt itself to the form of a silvered castle or the innkeeper to the demeanor of a castellan, even though—and the accomplishment is Don Quijote's first important victory over recalcitrant subject matter—he does succeed in compelling the innkeeper to dub him

knight. Of the same order but far more complete is Don Quijote's achievement
with the two women whom he encounters upon turning in at the inn. They are
"fallen" women, of the venal sisterhood, "destas que llaman *del partido*" (p.
60). Their first reaction to the knight is convulsive, helpless laughter. But his
virile spirit possesses them with all the incantations of a redemptive rhetoric. It
provisionally raises them to the status of those "tan altas doncellas" (p. 61)
(maidens most noble) whom Don Quijote had originally perceived in their
forms. His courtly address is a fresh and novel garment that, in the end, they
willingly though hesitantly put on, like actresses trying on the costumes for an
unaccustomed role which they had first thought absurd but now see as being invested with rich possibilities and yet still fall back into the sense of its absurdity. Don Quijote, however, firmly guides them into his verbal realm. The first
girl is called la Tolosa and is from Toledo. This early feminine articulation
sounds curiously like Dulcinea del *Toboso*. The second girl is called la Molinera. The knight asks them both to assume the honorific *don* and to call themselves Doña Toloso and Doña Molinera. They promise to adopt his names and
he departs, offering services and *mercedes*.

Once his back is turned, his vision no doubt dissolves. The *doncellas* resume their corrupted form, with much laughter. The very basis of the incident's
humor, the disparity between a peasant prostitute and a noble maiden, makes
the knight's construct untenable. But Don Quijote is a masterful stage-
manager. While under his spell the actors believe in the roles he assigns them
and perform them passably well. About the production there is, moreover, a
quality of gratuitousness, of grace, which moves the actors to interpret their
parts without any expectation of reward. The innkeeper, to his grief, does not
get paid. Generally in the *Quijote* men take less promptly to their destined
parts, like the innkeeper; but once they do think their way into a role it is with a
tenacity that can match Don Quijote's own, as with Sansón Carrasco. Yet
women are figures of a more ostensible metaphysic. They are the original actresses in the drama of fall and redemption. Though Don Quijote's projection
of his logos onto la Tolosa and la Molinera is absurd as actuality, these women
are potential Magdalens, and Don Quijote the magician capable of releasing
their pure and poetic spirits from the trammels of the coarse fleshly form that
disguises their essence. The events at the inn in the first *salida* could easily be
recast as a poem that probably would not have been unconvincing to a seventeenth-century Spanish reader.[44] What happens to Don Quijote is a parody of
such a poem only because of the provisional nature of the conversion, an artistic rather than a spiritual one. But, like God in human theological history, Don
Quijote has found in woman a great subject because she is matter less resistant
to mind. Overriding all contradictions he can fashion her flesh into his word
and then submit to his own creation. Woman made logos thus comes to rule the
new psychological dimension that Cervantes creates off the road in the *Quijote,*
whether poetically or parodically is not easy to determine. The two modes alternate and collaborate, one reason why there is a fair amount of verse in the
Quijote. At all events, woman is more yielding and woman represents inwardness, so that she is the key to techniques of approach and penetration.

Yet if woman is Don Quijote's most rewarding means of metaphysical expression, he still lacks a definitive personal source for the logos with which he

clothes her and others. From the beginning, the *Quijote* is a book originating in other books rather than in classical inspiration. The difficulty with purely literary sources is that the book springing from them has a diminished author and authority. The problem with Don Quijote as protagonist is the fashioning of his individual authority. Man cannot live by citation alone. Indeed, Cervantes himself has mock difficulty in mustering the conventional array of texts that should preface *his* book. The apparent solution is to convert things and books into functions of Don Quijote's mind. Quijote himself begins the process by exchanging land for books: "vendio muchas hanegas de tierra de sembradura para comprar libros de cavallerias en que leer" (p. 50). (He sold many rods of arable land so as to buy books of chivalry to read.) The company of Don Quijote's housekeeper, niece, priest, and barber completes the transformation of the physical into the metaphysical by removing and burning nearly all the books in his library and then by blocking off the door to the library itself. Their common goal is exorcism. The books have produced Don Quijote's aberrant behavior. If they are gone, it will cease. But the real effect of their act is to implant indelibly in their subject's superbly receptive and retentive mind the vanished and now sacred texts, of which he is the vessel, the logomachos, and, in a sense, the author because *the* authority. At their hands the heretical literary flesh that they condemn and burn reverts to disembodied inspiration: "entraron dentro [en la libreria] todos, y la ama con ellos, y hallaron mas de cien cuerpos de libros grandes muy bien enquadernados, y otros pequeños" (p. 95). (They all went in [to the library], the housekeeper too, and they found over a hundred texts [bodies] of big, wellbound books plus other little ones.) The inspiration that they have released through the flame of destruction takes up permanent residence in Don Quijote's mind and he thus becomes the keeper and treasurer if not the absolute author of the chivalric logos. Sacrificially, flesh is made word.[45]

In the *Quijote* woman poses the problem of direction. Crudely stated, woman when fleshed has a vulgar destination at variance with the ideal epiphany towards which Don Quijote's mind directs her ghostly, doppelgänging sister. La Tolosa and la Molinera are picaresquely on the hustle from imperial Toledo to mercantile Seville, *the* port of embarkation for both Indies and all aspirations to traffic. The dilapidated knight summons their giggling souls to a different encounter. Its crazy charm briefly beguiles them and for a moment they are indeed "rameras damas," prostitute ladies. But they resume their journey when he resumes his. For a while, they have been on the same pilgrimage.

But Don Quijote's second progress leads him off the road to the feminine psychological center, a destination which, throughout the *Quijote,* eludes him and which at the last he renounces when he renounces the whole undertaking that constitutes his book and all that we know of him. For Alonso Quijano el Bueno is an unrecorded person, the truly "false" Quijote, and not Avellaneda's, who is simply another Don Quijote and fully supportive of Cervantes' original. The physical journey is as well, then, a mental journey. Though at times both proceed for a while in company, the mental voyage has an autonomy that the physical one has not. Money, food, and even rest are essential to it, while its companion is self-creating and self-destroying, a kinetic essence that thinks its existence and its nonexistence. Don Quijote's philosophy, however, is a kind of godhead logos that cannot be supreme unless it additionally relates every contingent existence to its own essence in motion, through either sympathy or hostility or permutations of these. And the knight is indeed a logos blest, for he never encounters that Nietzchean toppler of the divine—apathy.

Don Quijote's two great concerns are thus to find his own direction and to change that of others. For him, names are essences that contain a polar magnetism. Like any founder of a faith he must nonetheless first deal with a vulgar actuality that moves in a sense contrary to his own sublime intention. In short, to set his enterprise in motion he is compelled to convert, to rename, to baptize. His doing so is shown to be a process of artistic rather than religious manufacture by the initial unawareness of the person being baptized. So it is with Aldonza Lorenzo: "una moça labradora de muy buen parecer, de quien el un tiempo anduvo enamorado, aunque, segun se entiende, ella jamas lo supo ni se dio cata dello" (p. 56) (a very good-looking peasant girl with whom he had been in love for a while, although apparently she never found it out or became aware of it). Here Don Quijote treats the girl's person as pure "material," rather as Scott and Zelda Fitzgerlad considered their own lives as "material."[46] Yet when it comes to the refashioning of the girl's name, Don Quijote attempts to effect a genuine conversion in which the original substance merges with the new elevation: "Llamavase Aldonça Lorenço, y a esta le parecio ser bien darle titulo de señora de sus pensamientos; y, buscandole nombre que no desdixesse mucho del suyo, y que tirasse y se encaminasse al de princesa y gran señora, vino a llamarla *Dulzinea del Toboso,* porque era natural del Toboso" (p. 56). (Her name was Aldonza Lorenzo, and to him it seemed a good idea to confer upon her the title of mistress of his mind; and, seeking a name not widely at variance with her own but which would redirect itself towards one suitable for a princess and great lady, he came to call her *Dulzinea del Toboso,* because she was a native of Toboso.)

Dulcinea's two main reasons for existence in this converted philosophical sense are to serve as Don Quijote's goal and as the goal of those whom he wins over to his ways, either by word or by the force of arms. Accordingly, he imagines that he needs Dulcinea in order to send to her the defeated giant Caraculiambro. In the mind of the knight the poetry of the name has an irresistible magnetic attraction. Unfortunately for him, a number of other human consciousnesses are nonferrous and will not be drawn by the magic of Dulcinea's name. This is the condition of the galley-slaves who, led by Ginés de Pasamonte, will not be converted and turn against their liberator because he wishes to deflect them in his mistress's mythic direction. Dulcinea is a decided failure as a psychic model drawing upon all others. Nonetheless, Don Quijote's basic method for achieving feminine depth remains unchanged. He continues to create the lady from the tramp. His success seems to be a function of the degree of grossness of the primary material. Maritornes, the deformed servant girl at a later inn, is of far too recalcitrant a stuff to forward even as temporary a comic illusion as the two prostitutes helped to form at the first inn. Sancho's reincarnation of Dulcinea in Part II as an ugly and foul-smelling peasant girl so weights Don Quijote's mental functions that he is unable to liberate her spirit from Sancho's matter, to his deepening and understandable melancholy. The knight's Aldonza was at least good looking. But, among the failures, there is an occasional success, even a string of successes. With these, the basic element remains relatively humble. Don Quijote's most remarkable women are not noble ladies but rather *labradoras* (female commoners) refined.

Marcela and Dorotea are, in Part I, quixotic cynosures. For them both, material abundance paradoxically makes possible the peregrination from ordinary occupation to metaphysical pursuits. Marcela's evolution is startling. Wealth sets her free: "en nuestra aldea huvo un labrador, aun mas rico que el padre de Grisostomo, el qual se llamava Guillermo, y al qual dio Dios, amen de las muchas y grandes riquezas, una hija de cuyo parto murio su madre, que fue la mas honrada muger que huvo en todos estos contornos" (p. 159). (In our village there once was a farmer called Guillermo even richer than Grisostomo's father, and one to whom God gave, in addition to great and various wealth, a daughter, in giving birth to whom her mother, who was the most virtuous woman anywhere in these parts, died.) When Guillermo *el rico* himself dies of grief, Marcela grows up in the custody of her uncle, a locally beneficed priest who, when his ward reaches marriageable age, does not compel her to accept any of the parties to whom he inclines but rather gives her time to make her own choice. At that point Marcela slips away from bourgeois trammels and sets up as a shepherdess, roaming the countryside with a freedom as total as her abstinence from any suggestion of sexual contact with men who, drawn by her beauty, moan and pant behind nearly every bush and tree. This is her physical genealogy, one that by the very excess of its materialities propels Marcela into the domain of the nonphysical. There, she and Don Quijote meet, for he is her spiritual father, her author. It is obviously true that, before Don Quijote, Marcela has a physical being in the wardship of her parents, her uncle, and the church. But this she abjures to take up a new mode of existence, a *vita nuova,* which is both independent and enormously, fatally attractive to men.

In the creation of this, a Christian and erotico-spiritual person, Don Quijote quits the road and thinks Minerva-Marcela into being. The context of her creation is suggestive because it allows us to see art as a luxury product, dependent upon the previous satisfaction of need: before encountering goatherds who receive them kindly and feed them well, Sancho and his master have dined meagerly. Don Quijote accepts their frugal meal in good part; Sancho of course does not. Both, however, gladly take the far more substantial nourishment that the goatherds have to offer. After the meat course, acorns and cheese are set out, not to speak of wine in abundance. It is then that the acorns remind Don Quijote of the mythological Golden Age, so that his share in its collective memory stirs him to fashion a beautiful Renaissance discourse on the subject. Its purpose is to explain himself, his presence. The essential matter of this discourse is women and rape. The knight justifies his existence by explaining that, in the present degenerate times, men want to rape unprotected women and that his job is to prevent them from doing so. In the Golden Age, women were free to roam with impunity. In the present Iron Age, Don Quijote must protect women, even though they are provocative. The real theme, then, of the Marcela episode is rape—repressed, frustrated if you will, but nonetheless rape.

In his speech Don Quijote displays a brilliant command of homiletics, for he modulates from the common context—food—by degrees to his chosen subject. Nature, he declares, willingly dispensed in that golden past what men now toil to achieve. And he personifies Nature in the Golden Age as a complaisant cornucopia of a *magna mater,* freely giving then what is now taken by main force: "aun no se avia atrevido la pesada reja del corbo arado a abrir ni visitar las entrañas piadosas de nuestra primera madre, que ella, sin ser forzada, ofrecia por todas las partes de su fertil y espacioso seno lo que pudiesse hartar, sustentar y deleytar a los hijos que entonces la posseian" (p. 148). (The weighty colter [*reja*] of the curved plow had not yet presumed to pierce or to penetrate the compassionate inner depths of our first mother, for she, without any threat of violation, proffered from every surface of her fertile and expansive breast that which was susceptible of satisfying, nourishing, and regaling the sons of man who possessed her then.) Here Cervantes' imagery is boldly sexual. Preagricultural Nature gladly yielded to any male. Now she must be raped, "forzada." The progression from food to agriculture to sex is completed when Don Quijote describes how young and appetizing Golden-Age females were able to wander at their will, even though scantily dressed by seventeenth-century Spanish standards. After a detour into the conceits of present-day dress and language and into the associated need for a penal system, the knight returns to the gravamen of his argument: "Las donzellas y la honestidad andavan, como tengo dicho, por donde quiera, sola y señera, sin temor que la agena desemboltura le menoscabassen, y su perdicion nacia de su gusto y propia voluntad" (p. 149). (As I have said, maidens and chastity went where they would, alone and unescorted, having no fear that moral relaxation and lascivious goals belonging to another would tarnish them, and their downfall came of their own will and desire.)

Of course, even though women in the Golden Age could freely choose and though the vision of their uncorrupted condition animates Don Quijote as if it were his muse, men and women both have fallen and are the sexual prisoners of the Fall. Cervantes wonderfully suggests sexual incarceration by means of the ambivalence of the Spanish for colter, *reja.* Its second meaning in the Autoridades dictionary, for example, is the familiar one of iron bars placed, most particularly, at a window for security and defense. In addition, as everyone knows, the *reja* is the traditional trysting place for lovers in Spanish literature and symbolizes their accommodation to and partial triumph over a system of powerful restraints placed between men and women.

Don Quijote chooses to emphasize the futility of all such physical restraints, but now with a shift to the classical blunder of the labyrinth, in his near-final declaration: "Y agora, en estos nuestros detestables siglos, no esta segura ninguna, aunque la oculte y cierre otro nuevo laberinto como el de Creta; porque alli, por los resquicios, o por el aire, con el zelo de la maldita solicitud, se les entra la amorosa pestilencia y les haze dar con todo su recogimiento al traste" (p. 149). (But now, in these despicable times of ours, not a single maiden is secure even though a modern labyrinth, like the Cretan one, were to hide her and shut her in. Because, even there, the plague of sexual love, pushing through the cracks or borne upon the air, by means of the damnable persistence of the male in rut reaches them and brings all virtuous resolve down.) Thus Don Quijote, whose major function is to protect maidens, "defender las donzellas."

From the speech we learn that the knight's major commitment is to female virtue. Once it was secure. Now neither inflexible resolve nor the most total reclusion can preserve it, and Don Quijote offers himself as the redeemer in the circumstances. Readers of Cervantes will also rediscover in this speech a major portion of his creative program, the uncorrupted pastoral world of the *Galatea* as well as those later realms of conflict between purity and passion, such as *El celoso estremeño*. Indeed, the plot of that exemplary novel is neatly traced out in the abstract now here. But the major mythic phenomena, worlds pre- and post-lapsarian, are arranged in interpenetrating sequence. One is tempted to say theological sequence. But I find myself restrained from using the adjective by the absence of a master crime for the master myth, although the latent crime may be the attempt of humans to hide from fate, and criminality is certainly suggested by Don Quijote's discussion of the disagreeable need for a system of laws. Nonetheless, culpability has in this myth no commanding presence like that which it imposes on Calderón's *La estatua de Prometeo*. Cervantes' fable shows women, and men, as half-fallen, half-redeemed. Nature before the Fall figures as a cosmically sinless prostitute, while maidens may or may not choose "perdición," as their judgment dictates.

Like Calderón's version of Prometheus, however, Don Quijote's reconstruction of the Golden Age terminates in a meditation on honor, a despairing one in contrast to the outraged resignation of Calderonian males enmeshed in its exigencies. Woman lies at the heart of honor by virtue of her propensity to fall into sexual love before and outside of marriage. Consequently her jealous male protectors shut her away in a world of domesticity and unwilling inwardness symbolized by the *reja*. But Don Quijote's females before the Fall had the same freedom as men and occupied no peculiarly bounded space. Then men and women were, in fact, sexually undifferentiated except for purely biological differences. Neither could the rigid social code that finds its extreme artistic expression in honor have governed relations between the sexes in the Golden Age, for, like Nature herself, women gave themselves freely, or did not; but in no event was force necessary.

The Fall, Don Quijote's myth tells us, means psychological differentiation and reclusion for the female behind the window bars of her prison house. Her world is now almost exclusively the interior one, while the male, disbarred from her space, occupies the far broader field of action that lies outside her window. Yet each longs to regain the world that she or he has lost. In her shadowy precincts—new labyrinth—the female exercises over the male a richly compounded fascination, erotic, mystic, and spiritual. At the same time the open male outside domain summons the shuttered female to its freedoms. In short, the male psyche longs to recapture its moiety of femaleness, while the female soul yearns to repossess its lost portion of maleness. In this respect, Don Quijote's myth resembles Aristophanes' explanation of sexual love in the *Symposium*. Humans were originally, in his droll reconstruction, binary units of male and female, male and male, female and female. When, like the giants, these first humans attacked Olympus, Zeus severed them as one would Siamese twins, so as to weaken but not totally destroy them. Once severed, they longed to return to their primary attachment, and that longing explains both heterosexual and homosexual love. There are many warnings in the *Symposium* itself that Aristophanes, the comic poet, may be slyly poking fun at his auditors. But serious or comic, and I believe it to be both, Aristophanes' discourse on love amounts to a new mythic formulation of sexuality. Bisexuality is its prime construct. But a theological crime brought about the punishment and diminishment that is sexual severance, psychosexual differentiation. Deprived of their other half, humans long to return to it. Of course, Aristophanes insists upon the superiority of male homosexuality, an impossible idea for Cervantes or Don Quijote. Similarly, the redemptive solution to both sexual myths—for both put humans in the impossible situation of wanting to return to circumstances that have vanished—is something on the order of marriage. In ideal marriage the male has free access to the inner feminine world through his wife, while she can live more adventurously through her husband. But this is vicarious. It is not free. Don Quijote's mind is intent on perfect freedom. Woman must emerge unfettered. Consequently his mind reinvents shepherdesses in absolute security. Marriage pales to invisibility in the comparison, especially for the female. As a Golden-Age shepherdess she enjoyed a liberty of movement unattainable for an upper-class Spanish woman of the seventeenth century.

Now, if Don Quijote is to have any real reason for continued existence, woman contemporary with him must be set free so that he can defend her. Socratically, Platonically, his mind retrieves the unsevered and undiminished female from the past. Intellectually and emotionally, he authors her. The miracle is, nonetheless, that a living woman appears and occupies physically the metaphysical dimensions of Don Quijote's recollection. This is Marcela, his greatest success.

To be sure, as noted earlier, Marcela does have a good biological origin. Her progress, however, is away from the physical. Her parents die. She rejects marriage. Finally, she becomes precisely that shepherdess whom Don Quijote had in mind. She creates her second ideal nature precisely to his specifications. Marcela is an actress who unerringly and quite independently anticipates in Don Quijote her Stanislavsky, the creator and director of her role. Theirs is an unconsciously perfect collaboration. It strangely resembles the relationship between Prometheus and Minerva in Calderón's *La estatua de Prometeo,* for, just as Prometheus discovers the divine idea of Minerva for the human mindscape so that she is reciprocally drawn to him as he was drawn to her, so Don Quijote's Platonic idea of perfect original woman draws into itself a specific formulation of that woman, Marcela, who in turn draws Don Quijote and the goatherds and Vivaldo and his followers like pilgrims to an irresistible shrine. In many respects Don Quijote's defense of Marcela seems inconsistent. In the conversation with Vivaldo en route to Grisóstomo's burial, he tenaciously defends the essential coupling through love of knight with lady. But then, when Marcela interrupts the ceremony to defend her sexual indifference to Grisóstomo and indeed to all men, he springs to her aid.

One overriding explanation is that Marcela's appearance is a miracle, an epiphany, word made flesh and deed. Don Quijote's mission strikes all who encounter him (Vivaldo, for example) as madness; and he himself does not fail to sense their incredulity, voiceless in the case of the goatherds, ironically articulate as an expression of Vivaldo's more educated disbelief. Marcela, however, vindicates Don Quijote, who has canonized his main purpose as the protection of innocent maidens. In Marcela one such appears and he defends her. The mad idea takes on another's flesh and actually performs. Don Quijote, mad or sane, therefore exists.

But the inconsistency remains. In a world of males panting to be in some sense joined to her or to other women, Don Quijote chief among them in his mystic connection with Dulcinea, Marcela rejects all men, all want. There, I think, *is* the explanation. Marcela wants for nothing. She is autonomous, self-sufficient, divine. The marvelous vision of perfect disinterestedness in Marcela, however, intensifies in her beholders the sense of their own imperfection, lack, and longing. The more they gaze upon her freedom and independence, the more they suffer from the awareness of their own incompleteness, which they wish to end by joining themselves to her. The Marcela episode deals, then, with appetite on a great many levels, beginning with the physical and ending with the theological. Its main action takes place, nonetheless, at an elevation half-way between eating and godthirsting, at the sexual mean. There, sexual desire measures the distance from and the distance to God. Men and women can calculate their remoteness from their origins by a new law. Desire increases in intensity as God recedes, or man recedes from him. As desire increases in intensity, it also grows in violence and craft. The male attempts to reconstruct his originally harmonious nature by reckless, cunning, and lawless invasions of the sacred precincts of the female temple. In these, wittingly or unwittingly, she half connives: "la maldita solicitud." Despite such incursions, men and women are condemned to separateness and unsatisfied longing. Though madly metaphysical, Don Quijote's commitment to Dulcinea partakes of the same cursed condition, he in open confinement, she cloistered to the point of invisibility. The knight, though, is a male measuring his distance to God rather than from him. He longs for an end to longing. The attraction of Marcela is precisely that she has ceased to long, or never began. She is semidivine in that sense of individual surcease. But in an active sense she fails of divinity by being unable to give satisfaction. Rather, she incites desire while unequal to its accommodation. The contrast between Marcela and all-yielding Nature in Don Quijote's recollection of the Golden Age could not be greater.

This "unnatural" Marcela is Grisóstomo's undoing. Indeed, his most unusual trait is the fact that he comes undone, is unmade, commits suicide. And suicide is sufficiently rare in Spanish letters for the event to have caused some controversy among critics over its exact sense.[47] With Grisóstomo, the "golden-mouthed" Chrysostom, it is useful to remember that we are dealing with a converted nature, like Marcela's, although Grisóstomo is of higher social standing while somewhat less rich than she: "el muerto era un hijodalgo rico" (p. 156) (the deceased was a rich gentleman) and also a gentleman with a rich and curious background, for he had studied for many years at Salamanca and had returned to his native place with a reputation for great learning. Astrology was his most striking attainment in the opinion of Pedro, Don Quijote's informant, and his skill so great in estimating the agricultural outlook that those who took his advice, his father and his friends, grew rich from it. To Grisóstomo's learning, some of it extremely practical, must be added another significant skill, that of composing verses: "Grisóstomo . . . fue grande hombre de componer coplas; tanto, que el hazia los villancicos para la noche del Nacimiento del Señor y los autos para el Dia de Dios, que los representavan los moços de nuestro pueblo, y todos dezian que eran por el cabo" (pp. 157-58). (Grisóstomo was a great versifier, so much so that he wrote all the skits for Christmas Eve and Corpus Christi, which the youths of our town acted out, and everybody said that they were really good.)

Nonetheless, with the appearance of Marcela, Grisóstomo's life takes a new turn and his art acquires a new inspiration and subject. From Christian creative enterprise, nativity plays and Corpus Christi allegories, he reverts to the classicizing role in life and in art, for he and his friend Ambrosio assume the dress of shepherds, while Grisóstomo adopts the golden-mouthed diction of Virgil's *Bucolics*. This, then, is a reconversion, an ambiguous artistic apostasy, the most important feature of which is play-acting, role-playing, theatricality. The names Ambrosio and Grisóstomo, calling to mind the great saints and doctors Ambrose and Chrysostom, who lived and worked for the fuller conversion of lingering pagan antiquity to Christian *communitas* in the fourth century, suggest that what has developed from paganism can return to it. This artistic return is conjugated with Don Quijote's mental return to the Golden Age at the beginning of the episode, where, upon one's first learning of Grisóstomo's death and manner of burial, the a-Christian nature of the arrangements is strikingly commented upon: "mando en su testamento que le enterassen en el campo, como si fuera moro. . . . Y también mando otras cosas, tales, que los abades del pueblo dizen que no se han de cumplir, ni es bien que se cumplan, porque parecen de gentiles" (p. 155). (He directed in his will that he be buried out in the open country, as if he were a Mohammedan. . . . And he also directed other things of such a nature that the village authorities say they won't be carried out, nor is it proper that they should be because they appear to be pagan.)

Grisóstomo was both poet and dramatist, probably a poet before he took up the theatre. Of all verbal artists, poets probably are the least dependent upon others, while dramatists must rely very heavily on others for the performance of their plays. In addition, the dramatist of the Renaissance and of Cervantes' time had to contend, directly or indirectly, with the authority of the state and, above all, church, where Western drama may have originated. Since in Golden-Age Spain all dramatists were poets, the technical term for dramatic author being *poeta,* a real potential for conflict between the private poetic vision of the dramatist and the public requirements for theatre on the part of the authorities existed and was variously and deeply experienced. Artists, even the most sincerely reverential and orthodox, are imperious as to their art and seek to assert its independence in every way. Grisóstomo is an artist whose abstraction into his art leads him into heterodoxy for the sake of creative freedom. He moves away from church-sponsored modes of expression into the more personal idiom of verse. Now, there are at least two forms of supreme self-assertion in art, and they are creation *and* destruction. Writers bring people into existence and they remove them from this world. In that they are like God. But only *like,* for art creates and destroys metaphysically. Grisóstomo, however, does not leave drama completely behind when for Marcela he takes up classicizing pastoral verse. Although he no longer practices the drama, he is an actor in the play of his adoration for Marcela. As a shepherd he plunges into that *Literarisierung des Lebens* so often and so rightly seen as deeply characteristic of the Marcela-Grisóstomo episode in particular and of the *Quijote* in general. Or better, *die Theatraliesierung des Lebens,* for Marcela and Grisóstomo are compounded persons, sufficiently commonplace as *labradora rica* and *hijodalgo rico* to gain admittance into ordinary literature as undoubted and unselfconscious individuals, yet drawing away from the first biological role into a second artistic and metaphysical one. It is the pertinacious practice of the second role that makes of them actress and actor.

In their theatrical world, art is another religion distinct from the Catholic Christianity from which it has retreated into an apparent autonomy. There, Marcela is muse, Psyche, and divinity ruling over the creative eros of every male who by change of costume enters her realm, the Green Cabinet,[48] outer space psychologized into closed and inner confine. Unlike the Christian God's, however, her divinity is unyielding, and artists such as Grisóstomo immortalize it without any hope of return or recompense: "su vida, a la qual dio fin una pastora, a quien el procurava eternizar para que viviera en la memoria de las gentes, qual lo pudieran mostrar bien essos papales que estais mirando" (p. 177). (His life, ended by a shepherdess whom, as these papers before you could readily show, he strove to make immortal so that she might live on in the memory of the nations.) Acting, then, is a metaphor for such service to such a mistress.

And the former composer of *autos* has not lost his taste for allegory. Grisóstomo's dedication to Marcela signifies his consecration to art, to poetry. Marcela is beauty, not beauty leading to a Christian consummation but entirely self-sufficient, attracting but not attracted, moving but unmoved, stimulating but not satisfying. She is analogous to Baudelaire's representation of art as *idée fixe* in the sonnet "La Beauté": "Et mon sein, où chacun s'est meurtri tour à tour, / Est fait pour inspirer au poète un amour / Eternel et muet ainsi que la matière."[49] (And my breast where each in turn has lacerated himself is designed to inspire in the poet love as lasting and mute as matter itself.) In his unrewarded service, the poet's effusions take on a sacrificial character. Grisóstomo is very nearly a *poète maudit,* an artist whose loyal worship of beauty wins him hell rather than heaven: "Venga, que es tiempo ya, del hondo abismo Tantalo con su sed, Sisifo venga con el peso terrible de su canto; Ticio traya su buitre, y ansi mismo con su rueda Egion no se dentenga, ni las hermanas que trabajan tanto. . . . Y el portero infernal de los tres rostros, con otras mil quimeras y mil monstros, lleven el doloroso contrapunto" (p. 183). (Now it is time for Tantalus to appear from the abyss with his thirst, Sisyphus with the fearful weight of his song; let Tityus bring his vulture, closely followed by Ixion's wheel and the sisters who do so mightily travail. . . . And let the dreary counterpoint be sustained by hell's three-headed gateman together with a host of monsters and hallucinations.) The conjunction of so many renowned inhabitants of Hades—Tantalus, Sisyphus, Tityus, Ixion, and Cerberus, its representative body—in Grisóstomo's "Canción desesperada" as posthumously read by Ambrosio further directs the enterprise away from Christian contexts into a pagan and classical preserve which, because it preceded historical Christianity, can by regression win independence from it, a temporal secession into autonomy.

Even here, acting does not disappear. The dramatic genre most difficult to cultivate in a Christian context is antique tragedy. It is also the drama's most prestigious, most seductive form. The Christian artist in the theatre seeking greater control over his work during the Renaissance very often responds to the spell of tragedy. With it Juan del Enzina, for example, at last unfetters his muse in *Plácida y Victoriano,* where love gains absolute dominion and both kills and resurrects. In art, to give life and to take it away constitute a declaration of independence from the moral and social establishment, a dangerous one in Spain. Similarly, Grisóstomo asserts his artistic autarchy by taking his own life. With him suicide amounts to a manifesto: "puso fin a la tragedia de su miserable vida" (pp. 176-77). (He put an end to the tragedy of his life of wretchedness.) But his is an act which one must read ambivalently, a tragedy in the human sense, a triumph in the artistic. Indeed, the absence of disease, age, ugliness, and decay from Grisóstomo's remains suggests a consummation rather than wickedness: "vieron cubierto de flores un cuerpo muerto, vestido como pastor, de edad, al parecer, de treinta años; y, aunque muerto, mostrava que vivo avia sido de rostro hermoso y de disposicion gallarda" (p. 176). (They saw, covered with flowers, a dead body dressed as a shepherd, apparently about 30 years old and which, though dead, showed that in life he had been handsome and well-formed.) Beauty lingers here, and Grisóstomo has done himself in handsomely, "with vine leaves in his hair," as Ejlert Lovborg should have done. Hedda Gabler, at the opposite secular end of the long dramatic *allée,* could only have rejoiced and approved.

Grisóstomo is, nevertheless, two persons compounded, student along with actor-shepherd: "murio esta manana aquel famoso pastor estudiante llamado Grisóstomo" (p. 155). (This morning that acclaimed shepherd student called Grisóstomo died.) "Famoso" is a curious adjective here. It obviously means "widely known." But in the Golden Age, if one had immediately to apply that adjective to a noun, the reflex would be to make it modify *comedia,* or play, *any* play as the word was used in Cervantes' time. Its definition in the Autoridades dictionary confirms the inclination to associate *famoso* with *comedia:* "FAMÓSO, SA. adj: Lo que tiene fama y nombre en la acepción común, tomandose tanto en buena como en mala parte: y asi se dice, Comedia famósa, libelo famóso." Its qualification of Grisóstomo in his shepherd's function subtly but deeply intensifies his theatrical character.

It is, I believe, in his theatrical character, one half the compound, that Grisóstomo commits suicide. His doing so one might almost call a Renaissance dramatic convention, as with, for example, Juan del Enzina in Spain in his twelfth and fourteenth *églogas.* And, more than dramatic convention, it is as well an allegorical representation of the poet's career of unrewarded sacrifice in the service of art, a pure, perfect, and utterly indifferent mistress, Marcela. I do not believe, however, that the well-schooled student can have so completely divorced himself from the teachings of the church as to have killed himself. The shepherd-actor's death would have easily sufficed. There is no evidence for the conjecture; but I would guess that, after Marcela has spoken and disappeared, drawing Don Quijote after her, Grisóstomo rises up from his bier and, dressing himself again as a student, buries his shepherd's costume along with the poems and the books. The *pellico,* or shepherd's tunic of skins, was the fundamental and simplest of stage costumes. In sum, Grisóstomo's suicide is an enormously complex *burla,* or highly theatrical deceit. In support of the view, I would adduce the only other suicide in the *Quijote,* that of Basilio in the chapters on, ironically, Camacho's wedding. The two men, poor Basilio and rich Camacho, both love Quiteria. But Camacho uses his wealth to secure her as his bride. At their wedding feast, but before the wedding itself, Basilio appears to commit suicide by impaling himself. Before he confesses, he asks to be married to Quiteria as the consolation of his final moment. Quiteria agrees, and they are married. But Basilio is not wounded at all. The narrow blade has transfixed a cleverly concealed tube, not his body. Quiteria confirms that she has freely married Basilio, and the lovers go off to Basilio's village to spend the first days of their honeymoon with Don Quijote. Tragedy has a pompously operatic potential that can readily convert it into parody, as with the tale of Pyramus and Thisbe, for example. Basilio's suicidal version of tragedy remakes his play into a comedy, at least for Quiteria and him. Nor is parody absent from Grisóstomo's death on stage. Even so, his dying is convincing if partial. The shepherd perishes. The student lives on, unseen, like Marcela *disparue.*

In addition, Don Quijote himself in his role as knight errant and aberrant knight might be likened to an actor who obliterates his ordinary physical nature in the metaphysical passion for perfect identity with the role that he creates. In the assumption of that role, the indispensable first step is a change of name. The second step is an absolute pledge to femaleness. Such a pledge as the one to Dulcinea brings her knight into conflict with the moral establishment, for though our time (the seventeenth century) may be detestable, it has in Spanish eyes the advantage over classical antiquity of at least being Christian. The female muse of chivalry and poetry alike, however, provokes in her followers a longing for a total freedom in which to practice their related professions. A basic part of that freedom is unencumbered access to women such as one finds in the Renaissance pastoral novel. But not in Renaissance Spanish life, where woman is cloistered behind the bars of her window, so that craft and violence are often necessary to reach her. The appearance of Marcela is an intellectual anachronism combining total freedom and total frustration, for all the males contemporary with her have unhindered access to Marcela, but her "virtue" is perfect and she will yield to no man. Marcela is an iron maiden in this our Iron Age, the prisoner of her own chastity. She prefigures the transmogrified Dulcinea of Part II, the ghostly captive whom Don Quijote never succeeds in releasing. Thus the knight fails in his major undertaking and is also defeated in combat, so that he must return home the prisoner of his promise not to engage in knight errantry. Until the end of the *Quijote* one generally forgets that Don Quijote, like Grisóstomo, is two people, *hidalgo* and *caballero,* the *hidalgo* the man, the *caballero* the actor. At the close of the first stage of Don Quijote's final illness, there is a classic palinode in which Don Quijote abjures his former chivalric self and reverts to the name Alonso Quijano, until that time unknown to the reader. Don Quijote dies first as a knight errant. That death is a voluntary one, a suicide of the metaphysical personage. Physical death then promptly supervenes, and Quijano makes a very Christian end. Grisóstomo's suicide prepares the actor's paganizing demise but not the Christian's exemplary departure. It nonetheless may be the ultimate *burla,* the final role.

Together with its introduction in the form of the encounter with the goat-herds, the Marcela-Grisóstomo episode amounts to a myth of degenerescence concerning the relations between the sexes, once characterized by freedom, wholeness, and perfect choice, now in a state of separation and violent longing in which the male attempts to repossess himself of femaleness by rape, the female to repossess herself of maleness by betrayal. The cloistered female psyche yearns to break out, the excluded male psyche to break in. The word that best describes this state of affairs is honor. Though often ghastly indeed, honor for Cervantes is forgivable because even its calamities betray a profound desire for a better psychosexual world. We briefly glimpse such a world, during the Marcela-Grisóstomo chapters, in a collaboration between Don Quijote on the male side and Marcela on the female. He penetrates her sphere without violence and she emerges into his without crime. In a sexually undifferentiated pastoral space they meet, independent, autonomous, androgynous. But the balance, an asexual one, does not, cannot hold. Marcela disappears, like Albertine, and never returns. Even so, the detour from the highroad into her dominion consti-tutes the first great psychological adventure in prose fiction, the first time that a novelist really masters inner space. As in the relationship between Don Quijote and Marcela, it is hard to say whether Cervantes discovers or invents this new world. Nonetheless, and to her peril, woman characterizes and dom-inates it, woman, to be sure, in part released by the male mind. "Das Ewig-Weibliche / zieht uns *hinein!*" (The eternal feminine draws us *in!*)

Marcela and her constituents preface a second great incursion. Don Quijote and Sancho, fearing the Santa Hermandad, or country police, take ref-uge in the wildest parts of the Sierra-Morena mountains. This region then im-mediately becomes another Green Cabinet, but trackless and labyrinthine and thickly populated with individuals who are in themselves a whole living and suffering literature. The personages who make their appearance there are liter-ary *objets trouvés,* instantaneously convertible into delightfully unhappy and elegant narrative, life as close to books as is possible.

Fear drives the knight into that region. He has freed a group of galley slaves and readily allows that the Hermandad will not be slow in pursuing him and Sancho. The episode of the galley slaves itself serves as a preface to the rich vein of literature that Cervantes will mine in the extensive Sierra-Morena chap-ters. Don Quijote requires each condemned man to tell his story. None is edify-ing. But each recital looks forward to and is the burlesque counterpart of the noble tales told almost without interruption in the succeeding chapters. The contrapuntal contrast between the lives of the galley slaves and the lives of the elevated personages at large in the Sierra Morena—parallel lives juxtaposed not temporally or horizontally as between Greek and Roman[50] but juxtaposed ver-tically at distinct but complementary levels of discourse—greatly resembles that rich and puzzling variance in the *Novelas ejemplares* between noble and ig-noble experience.

In one galley slave the ignoble and the noble are, however, wonderfully combined. Like several other men interrogated, he is not equal to speaking for himself. But his appearance is eloquent: "era un hombre de venerable rostro, con una barba blanca que le passava del pecho" (p. 304). (He was a man of venerable mien, whose white beard overflowed his chest.) He goes to the galleys for having been an *alcahuete,* procurer, a calling well represented in older Spanish literature. He has also been convicted of sorcery, the classic adjunct to procuring. Don Quijote opines unexpectedly on these two activities, denouncing sorcery but delivering himself of an amazing apologia for the trade of sexual go-between:

> por solamente el alcahuete limpio no mercia el yr a vogar en las galeras, sino a mandallas y a ser general dellas, porque no es assi como quiera el oficio de alcahuete; que es oficio de discretos y necessarissimo en la republica bien ordenada, y que no le devia exercer sino gente muy bien nacida, y aun avia de aver veedor y examinador de los tales, como le ay de los demas oficios, con numero deputado y conocido, como corredores de lonja, y desta manera se escusarian muchos males que se causan por andar este oficio y exercicio entre gente idiota y de poco entendimiento. [1: 304]

> Simply as an unadulterated pimp he didn't deserve being sent to row in the galleys but rather should set their course and be their commandant, because the pimp's job is not properly understood, for it calls for people with their wits about them and is vital to the well-run state, and it should be filled only by people of good breeding, for whom there even ought to be inspectors and examiners, as there are for other trades with a fixed and known number, as with stockbrokers, and in that wise would be avoided many an ill caused by the trade's being plied by mindless, highly limited people

The irony of the declaration is probably as impenetrable as its panting parataxis. But it functions in a fairly straightforward manner.

As preface, Don Quijote's address on pimping announces that subsequent events will fundamentally deal with disordered sexuality in noble lives. Among the four extensive personal histories related in the Sierra Morena, Don Fernando's provides the most vital impetus. He represents "la maldita solicitud," sexual appetite that thrives on obstacles. Where Dorotea is concerned, he is a new Loaysa in a reprise of *El celoso extremeño.* Where Luscinda is involved, he is another eager Lotario who goes farther than seducing his best friend's wife. He eclipses Cardenio by almost marrying his intended bride. This base and ignoble potential in a duke's carefully trained second son comes as less of a surprise after one has experienced the venerable manner of a common pimp.

The pimp himself has other apparently ill-assorted qualities. He is notably lachrymose and, in common with a number of his brethren, full of pity for himself. The tendency to tears upsets one's conventional notion of exaggerated masculinity in such a person. His "feminine" subjectivity suggests that these are lyrico-pastoral tears, very much in the manner of Garcilaso's grieving shepherds,[51] and that their flow will be resumed and increased by Cardenio, who is, after all, the reincarnation of Salicio and Nemoroso: "Salid, sin duelo, lágrimas, corriendo."[52] In short, a near-burlesque feminine sensibility in the procurer foreshadows the emergence of a psyche in men like Cardenio and the reciprocal appearance of virile courage in women like Dorotea, whose life is parallel with Cardenio's.

Don Quijote's desire to organize and control pimps on a good economic basis is also very curious and revealing. The fact is that the knight easily imagines himself in the pimp's role, exaltedly no doubt; but he intervenes quite as much in the lives of such as La Tolosa and Maritornes as he does in those of Marcela and Luscinda. Even when the function of the go-between rises to the dignity of broker, as when the knight proposes a pimps' guild along the lines of the stockbrokers', it still involves an ignoble commitment to the market. The broker makes a market, merchandises his human wares. This is what Don Quijote has in mind when he says there should be *veedores,* or market inspectors, for pimps. Sex is a commodity that, despite all, will be bought and sold. The state should regulate the sex market in the persons of its principal brokers and dignify them through selection and a sound organization. The four tales that go to make up the bulk of the narrative material in the Sierra-Morena chapters basically involve the finding of a socially acceptable sexual outlet. Fernando's inordinate appetite upsets the economic system. Don Quijote's more or less involuntary intrusion into the frustrations of Cardenio, Dorotea, Fernando, and Luscinda breaks their unhappy impasse precisely by making a market, by finding a buyer for the seller and a seller for the buyer. Don Quijote acts as marriage broker and noble pimp.

Of the many boundaries crossed and recrossed in the Sierra Morena, that between the noble and the non-noble is probably the most important. As we have seen, sex drives even the highest-born person to the lowest form of treachery, while the incompleteness that history has imposed on women and men compels them often to pass with violence the frontier between realms tabooed as exclusively female or male, the wrong side of the *reja* as the case may be. The key person for most of these transits is Dorotea, placed like some modern capital on a strategic border, for she looks out closely upon the great divide between *villano* and *hidalgo,* simple and gentle. Like Marcela, she is a *labradora rica,* rich commoner, and one of Cervantes' most original characterizations. As a *labradora,* she has highly ambiguous social standing, for, despite their birth, her parents have near-princely wealth and their life is indistinguishable on the material plane from that of the upper nobility: "Ellos, en fin, son labradores, gente llana, sin mexcla de alguna raza mal sonante, y, como suele dezirse, christianos viejos ranciosos, pero tan ricos, que su riqueza y magnifico trato les va poco a poco adquiriendo nombre de hidalgos, y aun de cavalleros" (p. 13). (In fine they are commoners, untitled, without a drop of Jewish or Moorish blood in their veins, and, as the saying goes, aged mellow in their Christianity, but so wealthy that their wealth and splendid state gradually are obtaining for them the reputation of being quality and even nobility.) This is satisfactory social progress, but not rapid enough to prevent Dorotea's misfortunes. Her explanation is that her lack of rank emboldened Fernando to love and leave rather than marry her: "mis padres, humildes en linage, pero tan ricos, que si los bienes de la naturaleza ygualaran a los de su fortuna, ni ellos tuvieran mas que dessear, ni yo temiera verme en la desdicha en que me veo" (p. 13). (. . . my parents, of humble birth but so rich that if their rank equaled their fortune they would have nothing further to wish for, nor would I have any reason to fear finding myself in the unhappy situation in which I do find myself.)

On the extreme upper limit of non-aristocratic society, Dorotea is near the safety of high rank and, at the same time, far from it. When the duke's second son Fernando sees and falls passionately in love with her, his addresses openly envisage seduction rather than marriage. Fernando, scaling his assault to her wealth and defenses, nonetheless considers Dorotea as a caprice to be indulged and forgotten, an attitude encouraged by her apparent social standing. He sees the escapade as a *pastourelle,* a knight seducing and light-heartedly abandoning the pretty country maid who has briefly caught his fancy. But Dorotea has been trained to behave like most of the lovely young aristocratic ladies one reads about in books or sees at the *comedia.* A great marriage is her and her parents' goal, one that will permit them all definitively to cross over into the world of nobility and thus absolutely to consolidate their social position. Dorotea is an actress who hopes to play her assumed role so well, *labradora* impersonating lady, that it will become her authentic part. The crisis comes when Fernando importunes her sexually instead of seeking her hand in marriage. For her to yield to him would mean her family's losing all hope of bringing their inner nature into harmony with outward appearance, of becoming in fact what they seem to be—noble. Of course, the transition from non-noble to noble status is far more complex than any mere recital. Theoretically, one can only be born noble. Exceptionally, males could be ennobled as a result of some extraordinary feat of arms. For the female, the sole route to an assured place in society was marriage. And this is Dorotea's path, made extremely difficult for her by Don Fernando's manifest desire to seduce her but not to marry her.

The seriousness of the social and moral consequences of Dorotea's yielding to Fernando deepens the gravity of his attentions, makes of them a *caso de honor* comparable to a lover's pursuit of another man's wife. Consequently, even though Dorotea is not married, Fernando lays siege to her after the fashion of Loaysa in *El celoso extremeño.* This is another example of "la maldita solicitud." Indeed, the phrase recurs: "los [ojos] del amor . . . me vieron, puestos en la solicitud de Don Fernando" (p. 15). (Don Fernando looked upon me with the eyes of love, pleading the cause of his desire.) The difference, however, is that this time we encounter no Carrizales. There is in Dorotea's family circumstances an absence of that aggressive maleness always present in Calderón in the form of the irrepressible father or brother. Dorotea's father is like Leocadia's in *La fuerza de la sangre* or even Carrizales in *El celoso extremeño,* essentially helpless. Even so, her parents resemble Leocadia's rather than Carrizales the obsessed, for they wrongly or rightly put all their trust in their daughter: "Dezianne mis padres que en sola mi virtud y bondad dexavan y depositavan su honra y fama" (p. 16). (My parents repeatedly told me that they entrusted their good name and reputation exclusively to my virtue and goodness.) They were banking on her. Despite this wise and humane disposition, Dorotea lived a life of retirement from the world of men very much like that imposed by Carrizales on his young wife: "passando mi vida en tantas ocupaciones y en un encerramiento tal, que al de un monastero pudiera compararse, sin ser vista, a mi parecer, de otra persona alguna que de los criados de casa, porque los dias que yva a missa era tan de mañana, y tan acompañada de mi madre y de otras criadas, y yo tan cubierta y recatada, que apenas vian mis ojos mas tierra de aquella donde ponia los pies" (p. 15) (spending my life amongst so many occupations and in such seclusion that mine might be likened to that of a religious house, seen, as far as I knew, by nobody except the household servants, because, whenever I went to mass it was so closely accompanied by my mother and female servants, with me all wrapped up and shrinking, that I hardly saw any more of the world than that part of it where I put my feet). Thus there is an absence of maleness in this conventional world, with the exception of Dorotea's father. And she is an only child, with no brother.

In the circumstances, Dorotea responds by developing masculine characteristics in addition to her feminine ways. Not only does she rule over her parents' hearts but also is mistress of their household and landed wealth. She calculates. She keeps the accounts. She has overcome the greatest imposed feminine disability—she is good at arithmetic: "Y, del mismo modo que yo era señora de sus ánimos, ansi lo era de su hazienda. Por mi se recebian y despedian los criados. La razon y cuenta de lo que se sembrava y cogia passavan por mi mano: los molinos de azeyte, los lagares del vino, el numero del ganado mayor y menor, el de las colmenas" (p. 14). (And, just as I was the mistress of their hearts, so I was mistress of their estate. I hired and fired the servants. I determined and kept account of sowing and reaping, of the output of the oil and wine presses, of the heads of cattle and sheep, of the number of beehives.) For all that, Dorotea does not give over feminine pursuits. When she tires of the masculine role, she turns to the feminine—sewing, embroidering, weaving, playing the harp, and even reading "algun libro devoto" (some religious book).

But here she fails to mention another major occupation, reading romances of chivalry so extensively that, when called upon to take up the role of afflicted maiden so as to lure Don Quijote back to his village, she interprets her part to perfection, even to having the right dress and jewels at hand: "ella avia leydo muchos libros de cavallerias y sabia bien el estilo que tenian las donzellas cuytadas quando pedian sus dones a los andantes cavalleros" (p. 34). (She had read many romances of chivalry and was well acquainted with the mode of address adopted by afflicted maidens when petitioning knights errant.) Dorotea's history is a succession of impersonations based on the figure of the "donzella cuytada" but given virile intellectual depth by her bold and calculating mind, her much-admired *discreción*.

Her real afflictions begin when Don Fernando unexpectedly looms up before her in the privacy of her own bedroom. The scene is of capital importance for the *Quijote* and for all later prose fiction, because, with it, the novel enters the bedroom, never really to leave it again, especially in our time. It is also one of the funniest scenes in the *Quijote,* whether intentionally or not I truly do not know. On the stage, its humor would be inescapable and irresistible, because Dorotea plays it uninterruptedly in the arms of Don Fernando, who imprisons her in his embrace upon first appearing, "tomandome entre sus braços" (p. 18) (taking me in his arms), and releases her only after she accepts his many assurances that he will marry her. One can only assume the end of the embrace. (Dorotea and Fernando will need their hands to make love.) But it is one of the earliest, longest, and most compelling in prose fiction.

Moreover, Don Fernando's actions are tantamount to rape. His invasion of Dorotea's privacy, after a lengthy barrage of persuasion, prefigures sexual penetration by force. Dorotea resists: "Conmigo no han de ser ningun efecto tus fuerças" (p. 19). (Your compulsions will be unavailing with me.) But she has taken the measure of her opponent and defines him in terms of violent, compulsive strength: "hacerme fuerça," "con tanta fuerça." Yet Dorotea herself is strong. For one thing, she doesn't faint, as both Leocadia and Leonor do. After a brief spell of confusion, she finds her tongue and uses it before the deed as eloquently as Leocadia does after the fact. And in the duel between Fernando's desire and Dorotea's ambition we readers witness a comic confrontation between male kinesis and female logos in which the logos triumphs by surrendering on terms. At the same time, Fernando exhibits a pretty wonderful way with words himself. It is his words, marching into the sacred compound of honor and marriage, that incline Dorotea, rather than Fernando's comeliness and strength. Reciprocally, Dorotea shows remarkable endurance. Besieged, she neither faints nor succumbs unconditionally. She knows her price. And here the comparison between regulating pimps and regulating stock and produce markets comes back to mind.

Dorotea knows the marriage market and realizes that she cannot reach her goal by deception. If she fails to state the whole case, her union would be invalid. So she points out all the objections to so unequal a match as that between a *labradora*, even a very rich one, and a duke's son. Fernando and Dorotea are haggling, she in earnest, he using any means to bring her to bed. Later, Dorotea understands his motives: "Todas estas razones . . . no fueron parte para que el dexasse de seguir su intento, bien ansi como el que no piensa pagar, que, al concertar la barata, no repara en inconvenientes" (p. 21). (None of my objections was equal to dissuading him from his purpose, just as the person who has no intention of paying does not, when the bad bargain is closed, heed its disadvantages.) Even so, Dorotea's commercial imagery (*barata* is clearly related to barter, although the old-French etymon, like the Spanish form, has the additional sense of deceitful exchange) places the struggle between her and Fernando at its most naked level. Her price for sex is high—a great and unequal marriage. He is willing to pay in promises but not in specie. She, in a calculated soliloquy worthy of Noel Coward, allows herself to be beguiled by the advantages of so splendid a match and to be discouraged by the difficulties of explaining to her parents Fernando's presence in her chamber. So Dorotea yields, after casting up all possible accounts. Not for nothing has she been the *mayordoma* of her parents' estate. Furthermore, cloistered though her life within the confines of her parents' property may have been, those daily contacts with "mayorales," "capatazes," and "journaleros" (foremen, overseers, and day laborers) on the estate itself must have taught her much about the male and made her feel easy in his presence. For her victories over the opposite sex come in a series of four, the first encounter with Fernando, the involvement with a male servant from her father's house, her months of employment by the cattle-raiser, and the final confrontation with Fernando.

The theme of all these meetings with the male is the problematics of mixing high and low, in the artistic as well as in the social sense, because, when the duke transforms himself into a shepherd, it is difficult to reconcile the martial epic style with the pseudo-humble pastoral. In their special fields both Juan del

Enzina and Garcilaso struggled with this challenge, and now Cervantes takes it up again in prose fiction. His solution is to turn the knight away from the epic highroad inward into the pastoral *locus amoenus* (ideally pleasant spot in nature). But Cervantes' Arcadia, though outside the city walls and far from police and roads, is private, enclosed. The Sierra Morena, by seventeenth-century Spanish standards, is practically a nudist camp. Everyone feels inclined to undress there—Cardenio, Don Quijote, Dorotea. The Green Cabinet becomes a bedroom, a place for naked physical and psychic display. This is a new Arcadia, transformed by open reference to purely sexual desire and to sexual intercourse into a battlefield, and contrasting sharply with the pacific nature of the earlier pastoral, achieved in large part through repression and sublimation. The ducal shepherd cannot leave the style of strife behind him. He challenges his mistress aggressively with all the weapons of love and art. Such is Grisóstomo. But Marcela belongs to an older order in which the swain knew his place, knew that he could hope neither to seduce nor to marry Diana, for those were not the rules of the game. Diana-Marcela will not, therefore, respond in any way to the erotic male. But Diana-Dorotea traffics in both seduction and marriage. Just as she has exchange value, so do they. She hopes to convert the one into the other. Marcela has a hundred men in her bedroom and refuses to countenance the advances of any of them, while Dorotea yields to a single, powerful seducer. This is the true sequel, the real *Diana enamorada*.

Thus the original Diana refuses battle where her successor openly engages in it. In the first skirmish, Dorotea wins a dubious paper victory. The second results in the total defeat of the male, Dorotea's servant. But his experience provides a variation on the theme of high versus low and of the sexualization of the pastoral. In a sense, it is Dorotea who first seduces the servant, for she unwisely tells him her whole story: "al qual descubri toda mi desventura" (p. 25) (to whom I exposed all my misfortunes). This is a kind of psychological undress and reveals Dorotea's vulnerability. If one man has slept with her, then another may hope to do so. But the servant knows and keeps his place for as long as he accompanies his mistress, against his better judgment, in the urban social world. Even so, in the city itself the crier mistakenly publishes that Dorotea fled her parents' house at the instance of her servant. The thought of such a misalliance provokes her wrath and shame, he being "subjeto tan baxo y tan indigno de mis buenos pensamientos" (p. 28) (so base and unworthy an object of my fancies). But if a *labradora* may hope to marry a duke's second son, may not a servant elope with his mistress?

At all events, once mistress and servant reach the Sierra Morena, the servant hopes to enjoy the same privileges that Fernando did: "mi buen criado, hasta entonces fiel y seguro, assi como me vio en esta soledad, incitado de su mesma vellaqueria antes que de mi hermosura, quiso aprovecharse de la ocasion que, a su parecer, estos yermos le ofrecian" (p. 28). (My good servant who, up until that point, had remained faithful and trustworthy, as soon as he saw me in uninhabited country, aroused by his own vileness rather than my beauty, tried to take advantage of the opportunity provided, as he thought, by these wilds.) The social distinctions that Dorotea had hoped to overcome in her bedroom now disappear from the mind of her companion in the Sierra Morena and she must again deal with rape. This time she summarily condemns the rapist by pushing him over a cliff, easily, even though she is not physically strong: "con mis pocas fuerças y con poco trabajo, di con el por un derrumbadero, donde le dexe, no se si muerto o si vivo" (p. 28). (With my small strength and with small trouble, I pushed him over a cliff and left him, I don't know whether dead or alive.) And that is the end of the presumptuous servant. But not the end of Dorotea's troubles with the sexual aspirations of the base-born. For she next takes service with a cattle-drover. Although she has been in male costume since leaving her parents' house and avoids close contact with the *ganadero,* he learns that she is female and also tries to rape her. This time, she runs away from unwelcome male attentions and is giving voice to her despair, as well as bathing her feet, when Cardenio, Sancho, the priest, and the barber discover her.

Indeed, the whole process that originates in Don Quijote's mind with Golden-Age woman resurrected dis-covers the female. Dorotea might be in her own bathroom when the four men stalk her. She is only modestly and minutely naked, of course. She has pulled up her leggings to wash her feet and later throws back her hood to reveal her magnificent hair. But the feet, emerging from the water with the white perfection of *objets trouvés,* exert a sexual fascination which it is hardly necessary to have Dr. Freud explain: "los pies, que eran tales, que no parecian sinos dos pedaços de blanco cristal que entre las otras piedras del arroyo se avian nacido. Suspendioles la blancura y belleza de los pies" (p. 8). (. . . the feet, which were such that they resembled nothing so much as double white crystals spontaneously generated among the other rocks of the stream. The whiteness and beauty of the feet made them catch their breath.) The hair confirms the suspicion of femaleness to which the feet have given rise. The real erotic quality of gold-blonde hair glimmering in the sun is such a poetic commonplace as to require no justification here in prose fiction. But it does deepen discovery: "Lo que vuestro trage, señora, nos niega, vuestros cabellos nos descubren" (p. 11). (Your hair, my lady, reveals to us what your clothes conceal.)

With Sancho, Cardenio, the barber, and the priest, Dorotea is of course safe from attempts to penetrate her physically, but this restraint is counterbalanced by a spiritual or psychological avidity that is insatiably possessive. As she has to her servant and to the *ganadero,* Dorotea now will discover her intimate history to four male strangers, introducing them into her bedchamber, making them witness her and Fernando's acts of sexual love, communicating to them her most private calculations. Except for the secondary matter of explicit detail, art's invasion of human privacy has not gone any deeper than this immense, powerful thrust into every retreat of feminine psychological inwardness. But to make the results of the exploration known, the poles of maleness and femaleness have had to draw together from their frozen extremes. Moved by desire towards the female, the male, like Fernando, has had to learn the speaking part of a new role in which he must eloquently voice—pleading, laughing, and weeping—his need. The aroused male must clothe himself with a feminine cloak of words, *en travesti verbal.* Moved by desire towards the male, the female, like Dorotea, especially when seeking redress, must armor her vulnerability with silent and powerful action, array herself with deeds. In the Sierra Morena, the servant pleads; Dorotea executes. His first weapon is words, hers strength. The male, yearning for the female, acquires at least a superficial femaleness, while the female in the same search acquires a certain maleness. Their relationship of desire is also mistrustful and hostile. But man and woman do meet, and in a new region—the borderland between the outer male world and the inner female one. Just as Dorotea assumes male attire in order to move more freely about in the masculine open, so men tend to put on women's clothes to approach them. Thus, on their unknowing way to Dorotea, two of the four men who find her have actually worn female costume: the priest and the barber, clumsily and unconvincingly, have tricked themselves out as women to play the part of the maiden in distress whose job it will be to get Don Quijote home. And of course Dorotea remains dressed as a *labradora* until, shortly after the meeting, she arrays herself in gown and jewels to play the Princess Micomicona, restoring male-female relations to their original, extreme, and false positions. But as Micomicona, Dorotea will enjoy a certain revenge upon the male by possessing Don Quijote himself, as Marcela did Grisóstomo and Don Quijote, too.

Thus in the prose fiction of Cervantes that taught Calderón the most, in the *Quijote* and the *Novelas ejemplares,* the basic pattern reveals two fundamental postures between man and woman. The first structures itself around a woman who spiritually obsesses and possesses a man. The second shows the man physically in possession of the woman but more or less strongly trying to rid himself of her once desire is satisfied. The first arrangement is the more traditional, because the male, usually afflicted by his inability to own the female who has totally occupied his soul, does so easily make the ritual gestures of neo-Platonism in art. He is possessed but does not—yet—possess.

In three of the first four *Novelas ejemplares* the elusive female, governing her lover with her spirit but resolutely denying him her body until the inevitable nuptial *finale,* dominates the scene. Preciosa, of *La gitanilla,* so rules the heart of Andrés that he remains faithful to her through a long novitiate and even to the doors of death. Ricardo's obsession throughout *El amante liberal* with lovely and unattainable Leonisa persists during the course of what amounts to a miniature Byzantine novel, packed with battles, storms, abductions, and shipwrecks. Their history occurs on the shifting borderlands and seas between Christianity and Islam and repeats itself Atlantically along the sea and land frontiers between Catholic and Protestant Europe in *La española inglesa,* where the haunting bond between Recaredo and Isabel survives, almost literally, every vicissitude. Recaredo is by far the more haunted of the two. And all three males, despite the poetic, pastoral traditions by means of which they so easily express their unhappiness, form really a new breed, or half-breed, of feminized, sensitized men whose often lachrymose emotions in no way derogate from or impede the most virile and heroic actions. They are feminized but not effeminate.

With *La fuerza de la sangre,* the dominant role reverses and the male becomes the forgetful possessor and the female a dispossessed victim, haunted by the memory of her voluntary or involuntary dishonor. The solution is for her to cover all losses with marriage; and, as we have seen, this is what occurs between Leonor and Rodolfo. *El celoso extremeño* terribly intensifies the problematics of possession, for Carrizales, having squandered a fortune in his youth, arduously recovers it in the Indies and returns home to consummate his identification with property through marriage to an extremely young girl. Not equal to her sexually, he strives to secure her against any other male and through his insane exertions provokes the very event he had wanted most to avoid. Here the theme is richly ironic and complex. Marriage is the problem rather than the solution, and marriage conceived of as ownership reveals itself to be monstrous and tragic, the most complete perversion of possession. *La ilustre fregona,* playing upon a characteristically Cervantine combination of the elevated with the base, delightfully complicates sexual role within the architecture of owning another. The tale shows a high-born lad in lowly disguise, Avendaño, captivated by Costanza, a servant at an inn, much as if she were Marcela and he Grisóstomo, neo-Platonic love in the servants' hall. But when the story reaches its inevitable anagnorisis, the narrative reverts to the sexually dominant male who, in an access of lust, raped a great lady whom he had gone to visit and whom he found sleeping the siesta unattended. The servant Costanza is of course the daughter of that lady and her assailant, Don Diego de Carriazo. Thus does *La ilustre fregona* combine the female-dominant pattern of *El amante liberal* with the male-dominant motifs of *La fuerza de la sangre,* but the first is more powerful than the second, although the fact that Don Diego absolutely escapes the consequences of his deed and is even rewarded for it, is an anarchical counterstatement to all the calls to order that marriage makes.

Las dos donzellas is a subtle duplication, with variations, of the structure of *La fuerza de la sangre.* Its governing male figure, Marco Antonio, has wronged two women, Teodosia and Leocadia. Teodosia's experience was very much like Dorotea's. She succumbed, against her better judgment. Leocadia would also have succumbed to Marco Antonio, but he did not appear at the assignation in the course of which she was to have become his. Similarly, he vanished from Teodosia. Both women set out, disguised as men, in search of their lover, and of course they meet and join forces. They find him in Barcelona, gravely wounded, and in a false deathbed scene he recognizes Teodosia as his wife. Leocadia must content herself with Teodosia's brother, Rafael. *La señora Cornelia* also tells the by-now familiar story of seduction to the accompaniment of promises of marriage, but this time in the world of the highest Italian aristocracy and with the female lover as eager for sex as the male, the male as eager for marriage as the female. Immensely complicated but largely external obstacles keep the lovers apart and it is clear that a balance has at last been struck. Though temporarily ill-starred, Cornelia Bentivogli and the Duke of Ferrara are psychological equals, her physical nature as urgent as his spiritual demands. Their marriage is indeed a consummation. *El casamiento engañoso* also portrays man and woman as equal in calculation, emptiness, and treachery. It closes, with appropriate irony, the long and rich analysis of sexual role and change in sexual role that is a major theme of all the *Novelas ejemplares* except *Rinconete y Cortadillo, El licenciado Vidriera* and *El coloquio de los perros.* Moreover, in their perspective, the Marcela and the Sierra-Morena sections of the *Quijote* look very much like variations on a similar theme. With Marcela we have the female dominant as in *La española inglesa,* who even bears the same name, Isabel, as the reigning English sovereign, Elizabeth. With the Sierra-Morena chapters, the oppresive male returns, especially in Don Fernando; but he summons his equal and opposite in Dorotea, who defeats and tames him. She undergoes a penultimate metamorphosis as Micomicona, submissive afflicted female in dire need of the knight's stalwart arm. Her last transformation, unwitnessed by readers of the *Quijote,* transposes her into the part of Fernando's wife and manageress, *mayordoma.* With Fernando and Dorotea, the progression is from the near-rape of initial events to the near-equality of the episode's final actions, a development not unlike that of the *Novelas* themselves, even to the ironic touches of *El casamiento engañoso* and its absolute and mutual calculation. From the spiritual extreme of bodiless female dominance to its polar opposite of mindless male dominance, Cervantes creates and explores a whole new inward psychological universe. The crude but essential instrument for penetrating this novel environment is the phenomenon of rape, together with near-rape and surrogates for rape, such as marriage.

Similarly, violent collision between the external world of action and the internal world of thought and consciousness is a major, one is tempted to say *the* major, event in a majority of Calderón's secular plays. If man's principal sphere is deeds and woman's is awareness, it follows that male and female will frequently encounter each other in hostile engagements between their respective realms. One way in which powerful men frequently make incursions into the territory of women is to appear armed with the intent to rape and so to seize physically from the female that condition, virginity, which should have for her the highest spiritual value. Rapes occur frequently in Calderón, but structures growing out of the threat of rape take form even more often than that fundamental act of violence perpetrated by man against woman.

Amor, honor y poder is the earliest play known to have been written by Calderón. It mainly concerns itself with the imperious desire of England's King Edward III to possess sexually his noble and beauteous subject Estela. Arrayed against his gaining satisfaction in this way are Estela's very considerable self-possession, her rank, her brother's objections, her father's position as Edward's first minister. But only a trick prevents Edward from having his way with Estela in the first place. Next her brother Enrico intervenes and, in a marvelous scene in which he pretends to mistake the living monarch for a statue, upbraids the supposed statue for the malefactions of its original. The stratagem so enrages Edward that he strikes Enrico. Enrico wounds Teobaldo as a substitute for the sovereign whom he may not assault, but is tried and condemned to death by his own father for *lèse-majesté.* The only person who can now save Enrico is his sister, but Enrico well knows what the price will be and forbids Estela to intervene. Disobeying her brother, she nonetheless intercedes with Edward, who makes his conditions for pardon clear. Dagger in hand, Estela launches into a long and brilliantly operatic speech which shows her to be an earlier and more adamant Tosca, ready to let her brother die and to kill herself before yielding to the king. Estela's impassioned demonstration converts Edward. Transformed, he himself marries Estela and permits the *infanta* Flérida to marry Enrico. Clearly, in this conclusion, two kingdoms have merged, after prolonged siege, into a single and now peaceful empire that includes both value and energy, static and dynamic modes. The king's avowed intent to rape Estela and her success in frustrating him are the principal means of effecting this desirable fusion of opposites.

The sovereign's persistent efforts to rape one of his beautiful and noble female subjects take sensational form in *El galán fantasma,* perhaps the most exciting, technically adroit, and stageworthy of Calderón's lighter *comedias.* Astolfo and the reigning Duke of Saxony both court Julia, who loves Astolfo but does not know how to discourage the duke. Astolfo bursts in on them after the duke has been admitted to Julia's house as Astolfo, and the duke apparently kills Astolfo in the ensuing duel. But Astolfo is not dead. His father has allowed people to believe him dead while having him nursed back to health in secret. Once Astolfo is well, his thoughts immediately return to Julia, and he remembers a tunnel connecting the house where he has been recovering to Julia's garden. Its exit into the garden has been covered over, but Astolfo forces his way up through the sod just as Julia is walking in the garden. The vision of her dead lover rising up out of the depths of the earth provokes screaming and fainting from her, total desertion from the servants. The duke, *rondando,* leaps over the wall to Julia's defense but refuses to believe in ghosts when she explains. He does, however, see and attempt to seize his opportunity. He is alone with Julia. As he is about to rape her, Astolfo again plays the ghost, moaning and putting out the light. Now the duke summons the servants and investigates, only to discover Astolfo's best friend Carlos. Angry and frustrated, the duke retires. His final effort is abduction. It miscarries when the duke's henchmen make off with Laura, Astolfo's sister, rather than Julia. In the inevitable final confrontation, the duke is brought to sanction the marriage of Astolfo and Julia, but he banishes them from Saxony. This conclusion is far from harmonious and may partly be explained by the action's taking place in the Protestant heartland of Europe. But *El galán fantasma* portrays the most obsessed ruler in Calderón's entire gallery and his near-monstrous character helps to make the play one of Calderón's most extraordinary, very far indeed from the delicate balance of conflicting forces that constitute, for example, *La dama duende,* to which the title of the Saxon play might falsely suggest a close parallel.

The basic ingredients of *Amigo, amante y leal* very much resemble those of *El galán fantasma.* Alexander, Prince of Parma, powerfully desires Aurora, who loves another, lesser man. In pursuit of her, Alexander contrives many of the same stratagems, including a runaway that will make raping Aurora possible. At the last the prince desists so that the customary marriage may take place.

Calderón's biblical *Los cabellos de Absalón,* the third act of which was written by Tirso, of course has the main lines of its plot laid out by the source. But the play profoundly explores a major theme in Calderonian drama, the love-hate relationship between father, David, and son, Absalom. It features strikingly drawn characters among the king's sons: the cautious Solomon, Absalom a heroic narcissist, and Ammon, moody and passionate. Ammon overwhelmingly desires his half-sister Tamar. He rapes her. But the minute he has raped her, he loathes her. Absalom's tragedy stems from this incest-rape. As it unfolds, Calderón delineates with the utmost skill a house divided, with rape expressive of the terrible failings of the ruling dynasty. The work is, then, not far in theme from *Amor, honor y poder.* Both link public and private life.

Accordingly, if rape is a temptation of the politically and socially power-ful, then the greater the power, the more rape affects the course of events. In several mythological plays, this guiding influence is particularly apparent. Nar-ciso's unhappy history in *Eco y Narciso* seems to originate from his conception and birth after the abduction and rape of his mother by Cefiro. In *El hijo del sol, Faetón,* Calderón characteristically modifies the myth of Phaeton when his young man drives the horses and sun-chariot of his father Apollo very well un-til, from the heights, he witnesses the attempt of Epafo to abduct and rape Thetis. Then immense jealousy causes him to swerve abruptly from the ap-pointed course, scorching the earth. Perseus, of the *Fortunas de Andrómeda y Perseo,* fashions a similar background into heroic triumphs of love. He is the son of Jupiter and Danae, Jupiter having forced himself upon the lady in the form of a golden shower, *lluvia de oro.*

Achilles, in *El monstruo de los jardines,* is born as a result of the rape of Thetis by Peleus. His mother is an astrologer and foresees Achilles' death at Troy. To prevent it, she brings the boy up in a cave from which he has never emerged. But music lures him out and he is discovered. In a final effort to keep her son hidden until the Greeks leave for Troy, Thetis sends Achilles, disguised as the woman Astrea, to the court of Deidamia on Gnidus. There by day he performs the duties of a lady-in-waiting but at night reverts to the male role and makes love to Deidamia, fruitlessly:

Monstruo, pues, de dos especies	Thus as a hybrid creature combining
tu dama de día y de noche	two strains, your lady by day and
tu galán, no te merece	your lover by night, neither as lady
mi amor de galán ni dama	nor as lover do my addresses draw
ni favores ni desdenes,	any response from you, neither
pues ni dama me despides,	scowls nor smiles, nor do you dismiss
ni galán me favoreces. [1: 2010]	the lady or encourage the lover.

It is wily Ulysses who brings Astrea-Achilles to step into his destined hero's part. When he proffers an assortment of jewels and weapons to Deidamia's ladies, Astrea lovingly tries the swords. But before Achilles departs with Ulysses to glory and death, he marries Deidamia.

The essential matter of this remarkable play is traditional.[53] Calderón marvelously adapts the received plot to his own psycho-mythic structures, the inner timeless womb of the cave as against the heroic outside world of history and disaster. For this clash, rape is the prime event. But the real revelation is the feminine aspect of even the most heroic personality. In addition to his re-nown, Achilles acquires psychological depth through Calderón and so becomes a *monstruo,* a person fully participating in the two major dimensions of human experience.

Christian myth provides the material for a contrapuntal play, *El José de las mujeres,* in which the maleness of the female protagonist contrasts with Achilles' femaleness. For Eugenia, the female Joseph of the title, is a thoroughly emancipated—one would now say liberated—woman, lovely and learned, a professor at the University of Alexandria in Egypt, whose imperial prefect is her father Filipo. A text of Paul which has come into Eugenia's hands overwhelmingly engages her mind and sets her on the way to Christianity. Her father's position makes a dangerous conflict inevitable. Eugenia runs off to study Christianity in a cave with Eleno, a venerable anchorite. When he is arrested, she, disguised as a man, takes refuge with Melancia, Eugenia's old intellectual and sexual rival. Melancia falls in love with Eugenia and offers herself to the person she takes to be a man. When Eugenia rejects Melancia's advances, Melancia denounces her to the authorities as a rapist! The accusation is not difficult to disprove but disproving it means that Eugenia must reveal her identity. She also reveals her Christianity, is beheaded, and rises a saint to heaven. Rape in *El José de las mujeres* is a decidedly minor feature but one of much characterological complexity, showing principally how a woman's virile mind can lead her to a heroic apotheosis, although hardly to biological maleness. Yet Eugenia's psychological maleness seems the confirmation of Circe's declaration in *El mayor encanto, amor* that

las mujeres, cuando tal vez aplicar se han visto a las letras o a las armas los hombres han excedido. Y así ellos envidiosos viendo agudo nuestro ingenio, porque no fuera el dominio todo nuestro, nos vedaron las espadas y los libros. [1: 1516]	when on occasion women have been known to devote themselves to learn- ing or to weapons, they have sur- passed men. And so men, perceiving our dauntless spirit and our penetrat- ing wit, out of jealousy forbade us weapons and books in order that the control of all things might not pass into our hands.

Eugenia leads a small battalion of men—her father and brothers—into martyrdom, thus adding martial prowess to her mental achievements and realizing in a Christian way Circe's pagan program. Since she had already recuperated a fair portion of her heritage before undergoing Christian influence, no violent incursion of the male into her consciousness is needed, although one might say that Christ comes totally to possess her, the most self-possessed of women, that this is spiritual rape not enormously distant from Rodolfo's inhalation of the immaterial essence of the inanimate Leocadia towards the end of *La fuerza de la sangre*. In Calderón, rape, as I hope this rapid little survey of a variety of its manifestations will have shown, always has a spiritual goal or potential and often has a spiritual actuality. But at the same time it moves through a considerable scale of refinement, from the relatively gross appetite of Edward in *Amor, honor y poder* to the total spirituality, absolutely excluding the physical, in *El José de las mujeres*.

And even when rape is not directly in question, its surrogates perform very nearly the same functions. Most of the light *comedias* of the 1620s and 1630s feature one or several irruptions of the male into the female world. The domestic interior most often represents woman's realm. Consequently, the house, and above all the house entered by force or stealth, provides of itself a major dramatic situation: *Casa con dos puertas mala es de guardar*. But another space, the garden, occupies a region intermediate between the house and the street. The garden is semipublic and therefore all the more dangerously communicable, admitting men to domestic intimacy, releasing bold or desperate women to the public glare. Accordingly, women counterbalance male effrontery in breaking in on them by themselves bursting out into the streets. Of course, a strange male presence within is just as great a shock to that decorum against which Calderón constantly plays as is a lady openly walking the streets. Therefore the man hides or is hidden and the woman goes forth *tapada* or *rebozada*. These persistent phenomena, not themselves social but forming a high unconventional relief against a conventional social background, consciously trace Calderón's dramatic signature in the *comedias* written before 1640. So it is that Alonso comments, in Act II of *No hay burlas con el amor:* "¿Es comedia de don Pedro / Calderón, donde ha de haber por fuerza amante escondido / o rebozada mujer?" (1: 514). (Is this a play of Don Pedro Calderón's, where a hidden lover and a muffled-up woman are absolutely *de rigueur?*) The formula is in fact so definitive that it comes to occupy a whole play, *El escondido y la tapada,* which carries role reversal to its ultimate limits, at least in works intended for the *corrales* of Madrid.

With the palace play, as we have already seen in *El monstruo de los jardines,* inversion reaches psychological depths from which dramas appealing to a wider audience were disbarred. Technique is the psychology of Calderón's more popular drama. To complete the basic formula, however, one corollary is needed—the interruption of the irruption by the male responsible for domestic tranquillity, a father or a brother. Such a person's ill-timed return constitutes the second part of Calderón's basic plot mechanism, and that he was proudly aware of the fact is shown by the statement of Isabel, a servant, in Act II of *La desdicha de la voz:* "debe de ser comedia ésta / sin duda de don Pedro Calderón, / que hermano o padre siempre / vienen a mal tiempo y ahora / vienen ambos juntos" (1: 938). (This just has to be a play of Don Pedro Calderón's, where the father or the brother always returns at the wrong time, and now they're both returning together.)

The fundamental plot is already in place with *De un castigo, tres venganzas,* a play that Hilborn dates 1628.[54] Its action occurs at the court of Charles, Duke of Burgundy. This sovereign presence places the work in a category that is distinct from that of the purest comedies, in which political rulers invisibly sustain events and circumscribe them, as in *La dama duende,* but do not personally participate in the plot. When the ruler does enter into the flow of occurrence, his doing so adds another and deeper dimension. Even so, pure comedy and the politically shadowed play are very close. It can be quite instructive, then, to compare them.

In *De un castigo,* the occasion for wanted and unwanted male incursions upon the female is darkly political. The Duke of Saxony warns the Duke of Burgundy that the Burgundian court harbors a traitor close to its duke. Charles suspects four of his courtiers, the elderly Manfredo, the mature Clotaldo and the youthful Federico and Enrique. Enrique is the duke's nephew. Federico and Enrique quarrel and duel. As a result of it and of Duke Charles's suspicions, Federico is exiled, Manfredo banished from court, and Enrique placed under house arrest.

Now the action shifts from the court to the bedroom of Flor, Manfredo's daughter. Enrique's beloved, Laura, has arranged to meet him at Flor's house. Flor is herself in love with Federico. And Clotaldo, the duke's minister, greatly desires Flor. All three variously ardent males disastrously intrude upon Flor. Enrique arrives first, and of course inopportunely, and so must hide in the bedroom. Clotaldo discovers him there when he swings in from the balcony, having bribed the servants to admit him to the grounds. Clotaldo murders Enrique, leaving it to Flor to attempt an explanation for the body in her room. She tells her father that Enrique tried to rape her and that she killed him in defense. But Federico has quit his exile just in time to return and witness Clotaldo's departure from Flor's room by way of the balcony. His suspicions are therefore cruelly aroused. Even worse, chance causes the chest containing Enrique's body to be discovered in Federico's possession and he is naturally suspected of murder. It takes Federico's apparent death, an attack by *bandoleros* on the duke, and Clotaldo's fatal wounding and dying confession to clear up all the obscurities in this black thriller of a play, the essential mechanism of which is nonetheless a minor invasion *en masse* of the crucial female by the male, in an atmosphere of violation and rape.

In many of the lighter *comedias,* women respond to masculine invasion of their sacred precincts by bold excursions out into the world of men, a course of action not developed in *De un castigo.* Even so, in a majority of the *comedias* of complication, the genesis of the drama is male violence breaking in upon the seemingly sheltered female. *Bien vengas, mal, si vienes solo* mounts invasions on at least three fronts. Don Juan loves and courts María, the sister of his friend Luis, and has nightly conversations with her at her window. During one of these, a jealous rejected suitor of María's attacks Don Juan but is killed by him in the resultant duel. With the police closing in, Juan must run off without any explanation from María.

María, whose very difficult brother is her guardian, entrusts Juan's portrait and letters to her friend Doña Ana. But Ana has in Don Diego a lover every bit as jealous and irascible as María's brother. And of course he walks in upon her at the very moment when she has María's mementos in her hands. The third major development is Juan's request for sanctuary in the house of his old friend, Don Bernardo. Don Bernardo is Ana's father and he undertakes to harbor Juan without his daughter's knowledge. The ensuing complications are simply incredible but lead to a final confrontation and to the inevitable marriage of the principals.

The feminine interior assumes the proportions of *genre* painting in *Fuego de Dios en el querer bien* and in *¿Cuál es mayor perfección? Fuego de Dios,* in addition, features a supremely clever female, Angela, who uses all her actress's wiles and wit to get and keep her man. He is Don Juan de Toledo, engaged to Angela's new friend Beatriz but unable to marry her because his father is financially embarrassed and because of her removal from Toledo to Madrid. Beatriz is Angela's new friend because Angela's brother, Don Alvaro de Acuña, has rescued her from the insolences of a band of callow males who frightened her when she was promenading along the Manzanares. Don Alvaro has fallen in love with Beatriz and eagerly encourages their friendship, since it affords him an opportunity of seeing her. Beatriz arrives while Alvaro is off on an errand.

The two women engage in a rather catty first interview until Diego breaks in upon them. He hopes to attract Beatriz by pretending to return a jewel that he alleges he has found in her coach. Beatriz understands at once; but Angela, in her first sally of wit, claims the ornament as hers to punish Diego. Then, formulistically, Alvaro returns. Diego must hide. Beatriz leaves, abandoning to Angela the problem of Diego in her bedroom. Unsuspecting, Alvaro settles down to compose, with many sighs, a letter. As he writes, the clash of swords is heard from the street; and directly the door bursts open to admit a young man and his servant. It is Don Juan de Toldeo, who has just killed an assailant in the street. After amazed greetings and explanations, Alvaro goes into his sister's quarters and discovers Diego. They fight and Diego falls, in appearance mortally wounded. Alvaro is preparing to turn upon his sister when peace officers in pursuit of Juan break in. Angela tells them that Diego, rather than Juan, is their man. They are convinced, examine Diego, and discover that he is unconscious rather than dead. Before going off to fetch a confessor and a doctor, the constables entrust Diego to Don Alvaro's care. Angela's inspired lie has prevented sorry circumstances from becoming far worse; and Angela has also begun to love Juan, who protected her from her brother. The first act of Calderón's *Fuego de Dios en el querer bien* must rank among the most cunningly eventful thousand lines of verse in all Golden-Age *comedia*. Their essential motion is the violent inward thrust of the male into the female. Alvaro's sword, at the end of the act, turns against his dearly beloved sister. Only Juan's intervention parries it. That is essentially how the lover wrests her away from the brother.

A structural companion to *Fuego de Dios, ¿Cuál es mayor perfección?* elaborates itself about the theme of competition between body and mind. Angela has the body. Her cousin Beatriz has the mind. Having aided both cousins in a carriage accident, Felix is first drawn by Angela's loveliness but, upon learning to know both young women better, feels the force of Beatriz's intellect. He ends up courting Angela by day and Beatriz by night in a very clever variation on Lope's *La dama boba*. But the play begins with a social call paid by Beatriz and Angela on Leonor, Felix's sister, to the accompaniment of the trinkets and sweets that qualify an intensely feminine domestic scene. And the dramatic action once again gets moving with a male intrusion, that of Luis, Leonor's lover, who has been forbidden the house by her brother. The usual dreadful complications ensue; but Beatriz, with wonderful cleverness, puts all problems right so that she, though poor and plain, may marry the dashing Felix, Leonor may marry Luis, and Angela, Antonio. The triumph of Beatriz's *discreción* over Angela's *hermosura,* a basic conflict in the theatre of Calderón recurring allegorically, for example, in *El gran teatro del mundo,* produces this final and most un-Platonic summation, which issues from the lips of the assembled cast: "Que para dama la hermosa, / para mujer la prudente" (1: 1660). (Court the pretty girl but marry the smart one.)

Yet in these plays of Calderón, women are not only acted upon; they also act. Their resolve to assert themselves results directly and indirectly from male aggression and tyranny. Accordingly, Angela, in *Fuego de Dios en el querer bien,* is determined to leave her brother's house after he has nearly killed her. Leonor, in *¿Cuál es mayor perfección?* does leave Felix's protection and command. In the female emergent we have, therefore, the dynamic counterthrust to the male intruder.

And if a girl fears her brother, she fears her father more. To create the conditions of flight, Calderón regularly confronts two hostile male encroachers and brings the father down on them, the basic first-act situation of *Bien vengas,* but there without the father. In Madrid on legal business, Don Diego Centellas of *No siempre lo peor es cierto* assiduously courts Leonor, but with so little success that his love turns vengeful when he discovers that she has a more favored lover whom she admits to her house. Bribing his way to Leonor's bedroom, Diego hides there until Don Carlos, the other suitor, arrives. Carlos discovers Diego. They of course duel. The clash of arms brings Leonor's father running to the scene. Carlos gravely wounds Diego. In the confusion he and Leonor quit her father's house, an act of itself dishonorable for the woman. Carlos and Leonor chastely flee to Valencia, where the original situation repeats itself with variations and substitutions. Carlos acts as *voyeur* on the second occasion. And a full explanation by Diego clears the path to the altar. Yet in this play the woman, Leonor, is very much out, as much as the men are in. Carrizales' house has become a sexual companionway.

A brother as terrifying as a father is Beatriz's Diego of *Dar tiempo al tiempo.* But brother and sister are both the victims of circumstance. Diego thinks the worst when he returns home to find one man just outside his house and another within, Don Juan outside, Don Pedro inside. Don Juan is beating on Diego's door because, having returned late at night to Madrid after thirteen months in Seville without any news of Leonor, his beloved, he cannot wait an instant longer to see her. What Juan does not know is that Leonor has moved. Beatriz and Diego now occupy her house. And Beatriz has a lover, Pedro, whom she cannot for the moment marry because he has money troubles. Beatriz and Pedro spend each night in conversation, unknown to Diego. Juan arrives on the scene just as Pedro is slipping into the house which Juan believes to be that of his Leonor. Thus the enraged pounding on the door. Yet Diego's rage against his sister is still more powerful and murderous, and Beatriz runs away to take refuge with her friend Leonor. The usual wild confusions follow and culminate in two marriages, but here again woman is driven out into the open, and revealed.

Still another Leonor, in *También hay duelo en las damas,* has a similar experience. She has in Juan a welcome lover and in Pedro an unwelcome one. When Pedro jealously bursts in on the trysting Leonor and Juan, her father hears the racket and also rushes in with the sword of honor drawn. Leonor has to flee with Juan, who deposits her with his cousin Violante, whose lover is Felix, Leonor's brother. In this manner, Calderón joins the two halves of the plot into a perfect circle of dismay, insufficient, however, to prevent the marriages that resolve all immediate threat.

Calderón's liberated female is the *tapada* who ventures out on her own and is not driven to exposure. Such a one is Angela, of *La dama duende,* who does have legitimate business errands but who also makes it her business and pleasure to cross wits with men in public places, at great risk to herself and to others. Marcela of *Casa con dos puertas* is her twin for venturesomeness. But Doña Clara, in *Mañanas de abril y mayo,* exceeds them both. Her current cav-

alier, Don Hipólito, has jealously forbidden her to promenade in the park because he knows that she has no greater pleasure than to trifle with new men.
The prohibition merely whets Clara's appetite, and she and her servant, *em-
bozadas,* make a very early morning appearance. They encounter Hipólito and
his servant, who are mightily smitten with the strange ladies and closely pursue
them when they leave. To escape them, Clara bursts into a strange house and
there is received by Doña Ana, to whom she explains that her husband is following her in anger. No sooner has Clara hidden than Hipólito introduces himself and loses no time in paying his addresses to the lovely Ana, who coldly dismisses him as a philandering hypocrite. The novel element in the events that
follow is Clara's enterprise. She writes notes, makes assignations, and strikes
out in search of her goal—which is not marriage. For when final explanations
allow Ana to marry her true love Juan and even for the servants Arceo and
Lucía to unite, Hipólito and Clara desist for the pleasure of continuing their af-
fectionate rivalry.

But when Calderón constructs a play so that all its conflicts are in perfect
balance, and this is usually the case, marriage is the inescapable conclusion and
the concluding escape—from death or, worse, dishonor. *El escondido y la
tapada,* which can be reliably dated around 1636,[55] is his *summa* in the art of a
plot that extracts the highest yield from role reversal. The male protagonist is
Don César. He has courted two women, Celia and Lisarda. He cares more for
Lisarda, but he has killed her brother in a duel occasioned by Celia. César has
fled to Portugal to escape prosecution. Lisarda naturally looks with disfavor
on her brother's murderer. But Celia remains attached to her gallant, even to
the point of offering to shelter him in her house if he returns from Portugal.
César returns to Madrid with the intention of accepting this offer so that he can
continue his addresses to Lisarda. But Celia's brother Félix, with the Spanish
armies in Italy, has heard of his sister's discreditable connection with the duel
between César and Lisarda's brother and has rushed home to protect her reputation. Upon arriving in Madrid, Félix learns that his enemy César is also back.
Accompanied by Juan, Lisarda's betrothed, he searches Madrid and in so doing kills a man resembling César. Just as César reaches Celia's house and is de-
bating with her the wisdom of hiding in her quarters, Félix returns with the
news of the murder by mistake. At Félix's approach, Celia hides César in a
walled-off staircase joining her upstairs rooms to another set downstairs rented
by Octavio, an Italian businessman. César is of course accompanied by his servant. Félix, having been recognized at the killing, decides to pack up all of his
and Celia's belongings and take them to new lodgings for him, while Celia will
stay with her uncle. Immediately, all the servants set to work and with miraculous speed the household goods are dispatched to the new address. It is one of
the more extraordinary scenes in the *comedia.*

The bustle leaves Celia no time to release César and Mosquito. When all
has been silent for some time, they emerge into an empty and locked apartment. They are about to summon to their aid Octavio, the Italian living downstairs, when a violent banging at the outer door sends them back into the staircase. The new arrivals are *alguaciles,* peace officers, come to arrest Félix for
murder. Octavio unlocks the empty apartment for them to inspect and they retire in great disappointment. Mosquito and César are once again about to sum-

mon Octavio when Lisarda's father arrives to speak to Octavio on business. Noticing the spaciousness of Celia's empty rooms, he rents them on the spot from Octavio, so as to have quarters to accommodate his future son-in-law Juan. Lisarda and her entourage move in just as quickly as Celia and hers moved out, again trapping César and Mosquito. The rest of the play is given over to desperate efforts on the part of the men to break out, and on the part of Celia, the *tapada* of the title, to break in and release them. From these efforts terrible domestic strains arise, as when, for example, Lisarda sees Celia in Juan's room, while Juan sees César in Lisarda's room. In the end, Mosquito and César simply have to emerge and confess, and Celia must, correspondingly, show herself. And there is no other possible way *out* than for Celia and César to marry.

As a technical device, the closed-off staircase of *El escondido y la tapada* ranks with the tunnel of *El galán fantasma,* proving that Calderón is "inexhaustibly great as to theatrical technique." But Goethe's praise may also somewhat damn if it is taken to mean that Calderón was not more than a dramaturgical technocrat. That he was the greatest Golden-Age master of theatrical means is richly attested to internally by such things as his own marvelous stage directions for the *autos sacramentales* and externally by descriptions of spectacle plays such as the mythological *comedias.* [56] In addition, however, Calderón's technique has meaning. His most striking devices are stage properties that give access, that communicate. The *alacena,* or *vitrine,* of *La dama duende* enables Doña Angela to penetrate Don Manuel's rooms, as well as his luggage, clothes, letters, and private life. It is a novelizing stage property, allowing drama to look as deeply inward as prose fiction. It is the same with the tunnel in *El galán fantasma.* It brings together the lovers whom the prince had kept apart. The staircase in *El escondido* is a summation of significant technique because it completes the process of dramatic dislocation. Normally, in the light *comedias* of Calderón, the suitor breaks or slips in and as a result must hide in the lady's house and there undergo a brief sequestration, a brief feminization, until he can glide, jump, or fight his way out. Reciprocally, women who have been burst in upon make brief compensatory sallies out into the male world. But *El escondido* is a kind of Calderonian *Grande Bretèche,* with the lover faithfully immured, à la Balzac, and the mistress outside desperately striving to break in and set him free. César thus comes completely to occupy the play's inner feminine space, while Celia is forced by expulsion to occupy its major masculine dimension. This is absolute turnabout and a wonderful dramatic and psychological achievement.

With Calderón, then, plot is of a piece with his other combinations of mutually sympathetic and hostile elements. And Calderonian plot is fundamentally architectonic, a complex handling of solid and void, of outer and inner space. In the lighter *comedias,* anecdote takes the form of alternate interpenetrations of the feminine by the masculine, of the masculine by the feminine. There, narration conjugates female with male. And though in these structures man is drawn to woman and woman to man, the sexes also are just as regularly at odds with each other, loving enemies who in extreme cases cannot overcome their rivalry for the sake of matrimony. One principal pair of lovers fails to marry in *Mañanas de abril y mayo,* as we have seen. Furthermore, in the interests of an anecdotal architecture that fuses attraction with aversion, Calderón often builds upon a unique family situation, that of the parentless young brother and sister who are comely and marriageable both, but with the brother obliged to play the censor's role in the absence of the *paterfamilias*. These are the circumstances of *La dama duende,* of *No hay cosa como callar* and of many other *comedias* of every description. I have no doubt that there is a touch of autobiography here. Calderón's mother died when he was a boy, and his father when he was a youth. The Calderón brothers had to look after themselves and their sisters, and they had many financial and other difficulties. But in the peculiar relationship obtaining between brother and sister alone we have a myth older than personal history. Some Freudian-minded critics have seen incestuous longings in the pattern.[57] Their interpretation is mechanical and partial. The weddedness of brother to sister is such a persistent phenomenon that it calls for more comprehensive treatment.

One reason for questioning the idea of incest in Calderón is that, narratively speaking, the brother and the sister living together without parents are pre-sexual, which is to say that together they represent the least possible sexual differentiation between male and female. But no sooner does the play get into motion than sexual attractions draw other partners into their sphere and the siblings themselves out of it. As other males invade the domesticity of brother and sister, the brother becomes anxiously aware of his sister's awakening and growing sexuality. His protective concern for her feminizes him in the sense that the person who until recently has been his alter ego now breaks away spiritually from him and becomes another person of the opposite sex whom he seeks to control as if she were himself. He both possesses and does not possess her. Conflict is thus inevitable and so, from the twin nuclei of brother and sister develop those multiple and conflicting parts that so richly compose the lighter *comedias* of Calderón. To the sister, before the fact, the brother is all major male roles in her life. To the brother, equally before the fact, the sister is woman as beloved and wife. Brother and sister are thus a myth, like Aristophanes' in the *Symposium,* of undifferentiated or minimally differentiated sexual origin that, implanted in or before the play, develops from the harmonious mythic matrix into distinct and highly contrasted entities. These are the newly sexualized siblings and they seek other mates so as to reconstitute the old and peaceful union. Marriage is their goal; but, since it rests upon a highly developed sexuality and since the key to such growth is conflict, the pre-sexual sibling union remains a lost paradise that can never be truly regained. With the essential dramatic structure in the sibling-rooted plays dependent upon aversion and upon hostility's appearing and increasing between brother and sister, incest does not seem to me to be an adequate concept. Calderón's own fable is far more copious and complex than Freud's. Calderón derives sexuality from siblings of the opposite sex. The male takes the lead, is often in love before his sister, whose erotic development he, contradictorily, would like to repress. Yet, as he loves, he becomes the awakener in his sister of sexual awareness, introducing both maleness and, wittingly or unwittingly, males into her life, one of whom she is driven at the last to choose as the lifelong substitute for her brother, just as the brother replaces the sister with mistresses and a wife. Yet at the begining brother and sister are really one being with a dual consciousness divided between, on one side, the inner, pagan, and anarchical tendencies denominated as love, *amor,* and, on the other side, the outward-looking and social-autocratic forces labelled *honor.* Though contrasted and frequently in conflict, these awarenesses essentially are hemispheres of one single brain, the dramatic painfulness of whose separate functions stems from knowledge of the full-blooded existence of the opposing other. The sister risks her life in order to love, knowing that her brother is prepared to kill her for any serious breach of decorum even while he himself is involved with a mistress in such a way as possibly to impeach her honor. Such is the far from unusual dilemma of Félix in *También hay duelo en las damas,* but he expresses his agony with exceptional acuity:

Quien en sus locas quimeras
pudiera hacer que su amor
dentro del pecho viviera
sin que el honor lo supiera,
pudiera hacer que su honor,
sin que el amor lo alcanzara,
dentro del pecho también
viviera, porque no es bien,
si el estado se repara
en que me tienen los dos,
que los dos huéspedes sean
de una alma, donde se vean
tan ofendidos, ¡ay Dios!,
que, mal hallados e inquietos,
me está quitando la vida
la siempre mal avenida
familia de sus afectos:
lo que el honor quiere impide
amor; lo que amor desea
impide honor, porque sea mal
que a ninguno se mide, el mal
de mi frenesí, pues cuando
entre ambos me veo, conmigo
mismo peleo: ¡defiéndame
Dios de mí! [1: 1524-25]

One of my wildest dreams would be to be able to lodge love within my heart without honor's knowing about it and at the same time to shelter honor among my emotions without love's realizing it. Because, if you consider the state the two of them have gotten me into, it just won't do to have them both as boarders in a single consciousness where they are so at odds with each other that, ill-suited and turbulent, the constantly quarrelsome family of their feelings is driving me to my grave: love thwarts what honor strives for; honor thwarts what love desires, so as to make my sufferings unique, since, when I am torn between the two of them, I'm in conflict with myself. God preserve me from myself!

Félix's desire to have honor and love exist in ignorance of each other shows that those two sensitive areas are painfully conscious each of the other. The images he uses in describing them are, moreover, domestic, familial. They inhabit the same house and live amongst a swarm of conflicting emotions.

It takes only a step to incarnate such qualities in persons of the opposite sex living closely together, in brother and sister, loving as siblings often are, conflictive as they always are. Calderón knew family life and that knowledge hauntingly possesses a majority of his plays, not with the crude and Greco-Freudian gloom of O'Neill's dramas but rather with the incisive elegance of a myth of development. For in Calderón's plays, the fused male and female pain-fully and passionately sever from each other, maimed no doubt by that act of spiritual section yet at the same time thrust because of it into a world of inde-pendent action and judgment. There, however, the newly autonomous con-sciousness cannot operate without the tender and terrified recollection of the other, brother or sister.

Such a line of development provisionally solves, it seems to me, a tremen-dous dramatic and philosophical predicament, the relationship of the self to the other. In theatre, of course, as in society, there are myriad selves; but the play brings the mind to focus on only a small number of these. And of that number one or two come to be dominant. With Calderón the fundamental pair is man and woman, first as siblings, then as lady and gallant, *dama y galán,* and final-ly, in a dimension only just touching upon the standard play, husband and wife.

That is precisely the path of *¿Cuál es mayor perfección?* At its beginning Leonor is all women to her brother and he all men to her, except that he has al-ready begun to replace her with the lovely but stupid Angela. Angela is an un-worthy substitute, because Leonor is extremely clever. But Angela does ask a stupid question which elicits from Leonor an illuminating response. Peevishly, Angela inquires: "¿para qué tenéis hermano?" (Why do you even have a brother?) Leonor unhesitatingly replies: "Para tener el consuelo / de tener galán y esposo / en tanto que no le tengo." (So as to be consoled in him for not yet having a suitor or a husband.) Again, Angela asks: "¿Galán, hermano y es-poso?" (Suitor, brother and husband?) And Leonor confirms: "Sí, todo lo es Félix." (Yes Felix is all that.) Angela closes this far from brilliant exchange with the reflection: "¿Y eso / más? ¡Hermano, esposo y / galán y todo a un tiempo! / Mucho es para un hombre solo" (1: 1625). (All that? Simultaneously a brother, husband and suitor. Quite a lot for just one man.)

The point is that, as brother draws away from sister and reciprocally sister away from brother, the incorporation of an essential quality of each in the other—love for her, *amor,* persists in his involvement with the great world of society, while a concern for his public standing, *honor,* lives on in her every amorous complication—objectifies as each grows in individual stature but re-mains subjective because the one sibling can never utterly disregard a major preoccupation of the other. She and he have found in love and honor their major and minor modes, one subjective, objective the other. But each is a con-flictive function of the other. Brother therefore never loses, never annihilates sister (though he may with all seriousness threaten to do so), nor she him. *Amor* and *honor* perpetually struggle to maintain their eternally precarious balance. Each of the lighter *comedias* choreographs the shifting strengths of their battle lines. In the dramatic ranks, hostility clarifies the enemy, delineates her or him; but the fact that every major Calderonian character harbors a lov-ing inward vision of at least one other person binds him with affection to oppo-nents even in crises of hatred. In quarrels, duels, and warfare Calderón's men and women are hostile to the adversary but look as tenderly upon his existence as they do upon their own. Consequently, they can and do forgive and forget with what may strike readers oriented to another psychology as implausible speed. But the explanation is that every other, objectified as an opponent, is at root a sibling, a *moi*. The self and the other rarely live in harmony. That is one major reason why Calderón's art takes the shape of drama. His life at home taught him to understand and to express the "siempre mal avenida / familia de sus afectos." But neither does their hostility result in annihilation. Calderón discovered how to make the self immanent in the other and the other in the self, not serenely, with the majesty of a splendid Platonizing system, but with a wonderfully quarrelsome *Alltäglichkeit* essentially incorporating the frictions of domestic life shared day in and day out, Plato hard put to instruct his irrepressible family gathered around the hearth.

Or, to look impermissibly forward to the Henri Bergson of *Time and Free Will* (*Les Données immediates de la conscience,* Bergson's thesis), *honor* situates the Calderonian personage in the scientific, social, and quantifiable world of space, while *amor* places him in the inner and intuitive qualitative sphere of duration. Bergson teaches us that, at least when he wrote, space cannot be a measure of inner intensity, is rather its antithesis:

> Hence there are finally two different selves, one of which is, as it were, the external projection of the other, its spatial and, so to speak, social representation. We reach the former [i.e. the non-social] by deep introspection, which leads us to grasp our inner states as living things, constantly *becoming,* as states not amenable to measure, which permeate one another and of which the succession in duration has nothing in common with juxtaposition in homogeneous space. But the moments at which we thus grasp ourselves are rare, and that is just why we are rarely free. The greater part of the time we live outside ourselves, hardly perceiving anything of ourselves but our own ghost, a colourless shadow which pure duration projects into homogeneous space. Hence our life unfolds in space rather than in time; we live for the external world rather than for ourselves; we speak rather than think; we "are acted" rather than act ourselves. To act freely is to recover possession of oneself, and to get back into pure duration.[58]

Calderón is, however, rather less dualistic than Bergson in that Calderón dramatizes the two selves as reciprocals of each other. Neither is the ghost of its sibling. There are, nonetheless, ghosts in Calderón's plays. Yet these ghosts lack the ambiguity of Henry James's. They cede to flesh and blood in *La dama duende* and in *El galán fantasma.* And while Bergson finds the projection of the self into space to be the less real phenomenon, Calderón creates his ephemeral spirits in connection with inner consciousness. It does not occur to him to debate the solidity of the external world, which is the unquestioned point of departure for his voyages of discovery into inner space. There, in a novel and unfamiliar environment, certain phenomena may at first appear ghostly but are found to be human, all too human, on closer examination. Calderón's great achievement is thus dramatically to discover a great zone of awareness hitherto only dimly suspected (the inner rather than the outer ghost) and to expose its profound human density in connection with the most familiar modes of customary action. Calderón conflictively conjugates logos with deed, arms with letters, in the novelistic tradition of Cervantes.

What, then, is honor in the plays of Calderón? This phenomenon may artistically reflect a rather disagreeable state of affairs in Spanish society in accordance with the thesis of Américo Castro.[59] But corroborating evidence for Castro's view has not yet, so far as I know, come to light. Alexander Parker's suggestion that Calderón the Christian takes subtle but effective issue with his characters when they pervert the ideal of honor[60] acquits the dramatist of the charge of cruelty, but at the same time creates the enormous problem of the dramatist at odds with a central preoccupation of his own very numerous personages, in most of whom the devotion to honor is unquestioned. The most intelligent and still the freshest assessment of Calderonian honor is Peter Dunn's "Honour and the Christian Background in Calderón."[61] Dunn's notion that the honor code is a travesty of true Christianity has great appeal and is persuasively argued. Its weakness is, I think, that travesty calls for a near immediacy between the authentic and the inauthentic patterns. The travestied phenomenon lives in hostile but symbiotic intimacy with its host. Yet even Calderón's monsters of honor, in the plays that end murderously, act as exemplars of themselves and are contrasted to no other model. Nowhere in Calderón's secular plays do we find forgiveness for a wife thought to be unfaithful.[62] Nor am I convinced that Pedro Crespo in *El alcalde de Zalamea* has a truly Christian sense of honor in contrast to the captain's shallow societal feeling for it. *El alcalde,* as I hope we shall see, is far more subtle than that. Edwin Honig, in a series of studies collected as a book,[63] fundamentally extrudes honor from something like Freud's *Civilization and Its Discontents,* honor representing the repressive order from which the individual psyche seeks (with increasing success, as Honig sees it) liberation, especially in the direction of love. Honig basically is a translator, in fact as well as in criticism. Accordingly, he translates Calderón into Freud. This is refreshing and often revealing. But it is also a considerable falsification. Nonetheless, to see honor as the oppressive social adversary over which certain protagonists in the early plays triumph is an interesting formula that can make Calderón seem relatively contemporary, a kind of rebel. Here Honig is misleading but exhilarating. And he does discover rich psychological processes in the plays he scrutinizes. The disadvantage, as with much psycho-mythic criticism, is that the original text ceases to be its own best evidence and becomes ancillary to another system—Freudian, Jungian, Levi-Straussian—thought to be primordial. I myself take the literary text to be the fount of all meanings, structures, and systems associated with it, and would resist efforts to make it serve primarily as a witness to other constructs. Of course, to understand literature as drawing its meaning from other systems is the major tendency of the newer criticism.

Surely there are in Calderonian honor reflections of the tyranny of social codes. As a Christian artist Calderón must have questioned above all extreme applications to its rules. But if he did in fact represent the honor code as a travesty of true Christian conduct, that phenomenon would have to be limited to just a few plays, whereas honor is a fundamental motif in nearly all of the lighter dramas of the 1620s and 1630s. How it could operate untravestied in them yet travestied in a handful of others of the same period is a problem that Dunn does not undertake to solve. The fact is that we do not yet have a field theory for Calderonian honor, still less one for honor in Golden-Age literature.

But, moving in the direction of a general concept of honor in the theatre of Calderón, I would begin with Cervantes and especially with that wonderfully soothing speech which Leocadia's father pronounces in *La fuerza de la sangre*. Despite the mildness of its terms, exemplifying Cervantes' well-known mercifulness in such matters, the strictures of the code continue to operate with undiminished force. Leocadia "covers her head" for seven long years while Rodolfo feeds his many hungers in Italy, entirely oblivious of her. Cervantes, then, while correctly judging honor from the Christian point of view, artistically exploits it to the full not only in *La fuerza* but also in several other of the *Novelas ejemplares,* supremely in *El celoso extremeño,* where Carrizales' forgiveness and repentance come too late to affect the tale's tragic course. In this respect Lope's assertion in *El arte nuevo de hacer comedias* . . . that plays concerned with honor "mueven con fuerza a toda gente"[64] (tell upon every kind of person) suggests the potency of honor in art. Cervantes may have deplored the excesses of honor, but he found it irresistible in his work. Consequently, those who are morally uncomfortable with the murderous tendencies of honor really do not possess in Cervantes a true dissenter. His practice affirms what various pious statements appear to deny.

But Cervantes does provide the critic with an extraordinarily helpful clue in the struggle to elucidate the wider sense of honor. When in *La fuerza* father admonishes daughter, his terms are at one point so purely practical as to shock the moralist: "advierte, hija, que más lastima una onza de deshonra pública que una arroba de infamia secreta, y pues puedes vivir honrada con Dios en público, no te pene de estar deshonrada en secreto" (p. 126). (And remember, daughter, that an ounce of public dishonor does more harm than a hundredweight of secret shame and since you can live honorably in public with God, do not be disturbed by secret dishonor.) This is sensible advice, nonetheless. And it is perhaps equally sensible to turn away from its many moral contradictions to look at its elements.

In the first place, honor implies dishonor. It is a spiritual possession which takes a real force only when threatened with extinction. Metaphorically speaking, therefore, murder or the possibility of murder is its vital adjunct. Loss of honor is a mode of spiritual death which defines through its potentiality that dangerous plenitude which is the possession of honor, just as physical life can acquire heightened value when balanced against physical death. Dishonor is in consequence a metaphor rather than a morality. It is, moreover, a metaphor which in art constantly tends to take the concrete form of willed death, murder. Dishonor is a logical result of honor, and death a logical result of dishonor; logical, that is, in the deductive process that grows out of the artistic premise or hypothesis that is "honor." Bruce W. Wardropper has brilliantly demonstrated how the artistic syllogism operates in logical contravention of the moral law.[65] One reason honor so powerfully attracted the poet as well as the public was that it gave a firmly independent ground for the work of art, one not in the domain of the moral law, amoral if not immoral. In addition, those possessing honor— nobles—offered an extremely rewarding subject simply because they were, by definition, at risk. More could happen to them, internally and externally. Honor thus is to have and to be threatened, genuinely threatened, with not having. Dishonor validates honor, and Cervantes' practice in the *Novelas ejem-*

plares fully bears the statement out. Their great dynamic is the apparent loss of honor, its pursuit and recovery. Honor is not dramatically or artistically real until put to the test, and while in most cases it survives the trial, in others (*El curioso impertinente, El celoso extremeño, El médico de su honra*) it does not. But in all cases a testing of its strength is prescribed.

For Calderón, honor, like classical myth, is a ready-made literary hypothesis likely to enlist the belief of nearly anyone attending a play. The allurements of myth elicited acceptance from the cultivated few, but honor appealed to all, gentle and simple, lettered and unlettered. This appeal did not derive from the identification of honor with the official programs of the Spanish church and state. Duelling has always been thought detrimental to public order, and sovereigns in the honor plays move decisively to repress it, notably Pedro in *El médico de su honra* and Charles V in *El postrer duelo de España.* Moreover, it takes no profound grasp of even Spanish Catholicism to understand how odious to Christianity is the codified idea of murdering one's wife and shedding her lover's blood. Dunn's "Honour and the Christian Background" places the Calderonian formula in the clearest of non-Christian lights. Edwin Honig's sense of honor in Calderón, however, commits the fatal error of equating that artistic code with church and state:

> Thus in Calderón's plays where the exigencies of the honor code prevail, the hero's need to find release from a conscientious impasse makes for a temperamental type and a set of attitudes which are at once austere, melancholic, anarchic, conformist, hypocritical, schizophrenic and dehumanized. The determinism behind the type, which views life as cheap, evanescent and transitory, perpetuates both the rapacious imperialistic designs of the state and the deathbound consolations of religion. The tragic view of the Calderonian hero subsisting in an all-or-none credo is perfectly represented in those dramas where the motives of church and state coincide.[66]

Suppressed by the state, denounced by the church, Calderonian honor as a public phenomenon does participate to some degree in official modes. *Hidalgos* make brave soldiers who struggle to behave virtuously in questions outside their code. But the strength of honor in dramatic art comes from its capacities to found the individual noble consciousness on a canon not in the domain of the greatest public institutions. Honor is a sort of apostasy from these, a preserve set apart from their mandates. Everything that engages honor occurs separately from official commitments in, for example, *No hay cosa como callar.* Brothers in other plays leave the army when they hear unwelcome news about their sisters. Don Manuel in *La dama duende* is at a critical point in his professional career at the time when the action of the play occurs. He has left years of successful soldiering in Italy to take up a civil post but is no longer a soldier and not yet a governor during the action of *La dama.* In a great many of the cape-and-sword plays, moreover, the spirited *galanes* brush repeatedly with the police. Honor is a metaphysical enclave that necessarily occupies territories under the control of church and state for, except in art, it has no *patrimonium Petri.* Yet, though often co-terminous with church and state, it asserts its independence from them, often at the risk of death. The fact that, in *El alcalde de Zalamea,* King Philip confers life-long official status on Pedro Crespo should not confuse the reader into thinking that the state sanctions honor. Rather, the king recognizes in Crespo an extraordinary jurisdiction, quite outside his control, another kingdom, with its inalienable *fueros,* in his empire. And so it is that honor, while at times in harmony with the goals of church and state, really constitutes a third and artistic force quite apart from them, for it obeys its own laws. Its greatest edict, then, is that the man or woman of honor must gravely imperil that most prized possession in order to truly possess it.

Moreover, the very discreteness of Calderonian honor imbues it, even in its public manifestations, with an inwardness of retraction from other jurisdictions that notably eases transitions from the outer to the inner world. Calderón's man or woman of honor is, when visible to others, entirely self-possessed, not other-possessed. David Riesman would define his noble characters as "inner-directed," for they have absorbed a social code. It is therefore undiscerning critically to recast Calderón in the mold of Lope de Vega, who can so magnificently portray the conflict between instinctual cravings and the rigid rules of class-ridden society, nowhere more powerfully than in *El perro del hortelano,* where the Neapolitan Countess of Belflor can satisfy her imperious desire to marry her non-noble but very handsome and intelligent secretary only after he has provided himself with a false title. In that play, though it is superbly decorated with the higher literary and intellectual attainments, hunger triumphs over potent social forces after a protracted struggle, the terms of which are no less effective for being disarmingly simple. Diana, the countess, comes finally to curse honor while still perceiving its usefulness: "¡Maldígate Dios, honor! / Temeraria invención fuiste, / tan opuesta al propio gusto. / ¿Quién te inventó? Mas fue / justo, pues que tu freno resiste / tantas cosas mal hechas."[67] (God damn you, honor! You were a heedless sort of invention, completely at odds with what one wants. Who invented you? But it was right, because your curb represses many an ill-conceived project.) Clearly, Diana here experiences honor as a frustrating but valuable censor quite external to herself. The posture invites a Freudian or depth-psychological approach, instinct against society.

But with Calderón the psychological depths, while tending, as they define themselves, to actions and associations which the public spirit of honor must reprove, remain, under every separation and alienation, the possession of honor, its inner dominion. Love and honor in Calderón do clearly and unmistakably come into conflict with each other. And honor is the more outward mode while love is the more inward one. Yet Calderón's love and honor are Siamese twins, usually of the opposite sex, who are joined where prideful public consciousness and a longing psychological inwardness meet. Nor can they ever be severed, for Calderonian honor binds with consummate technique the world of outside space to the interior sense of duration, each being the often refractory and escapist possession of the other, ghosts and realities each of the other. This is a vastly different construct from Lope's and can far less easily be Freudianized because in it "individual" and "society," though often opponents, are really one.

And for Calderón Cervantes has once again shown the way. Leocadia's father's speech to her, in *La fuerza de la sangre,* organizes itself around the two poles of the public and the private: "deshonra pública," "infamia secreta"; "en público," "en secreto." Leocadia's disastrous experience has brought her inner and outer sense of her worth into radical disequilibrium. The private self has been profoundly wounded but the public person may express no sense of loss or shame. Her father tries to console her with the thought that her trauma is entirely unknown to the world at large and that it is public knowledge which does the damage. The observation is not very consoling, for it involves a terrible injustice. Leocadia's abduction has created for her an inner life, however, one shrouded in grief, to be sure, but nonetheless an intense inner existence which in its heights of pain seems oblivious to the passage of chronological time, seven years. Dishonor brings to life the psychological self which is an inverse function of the public dimension, varying as "onza" to "arroba." Morality and justice aside, Cervantes sees under honor the inner and outer worlds as functions of each other, the inverseness of which his art attempts to restore to a direct proportion. The loss of honor vivifies a potent inner personality that struggles to regain the esteem which the world has taken away. The psychological self is born among the ruins of the public person. It then undertakes to reconstruct the fallen social character. This is not an opposition between self and society but rather a complex collaboration between the two major modes of being. Calderón develops Cervantes' theory into a richly productive dramatic system.

There is in Calderón, moreover, a poetics of honor. The person afflicted under the code, man or woman, gains through suffering and adversity a heightened awareness that very closely resembles a poetic sensibility. And this new sensibility desires above all to find relief in expression, in confession. But untimely utterance will only increase the sufferer's burden and take from his or her hands the means of shaping events so that the decisive and binding utterance may at last be made. So it is that dishonor brings to life in the dishonored a poetry of grief that is disbarred from expression. Thus frustrated, poetry translates itself into action and becomes a rhetoric of silence, a ballet. Action is the silent poetic idiom of the honor plays, and this transposition from reflection to action helps explain the absence of a more visible poetry from the lighter honor plays. In them, action is voiceless utterance until love can dare to pronounce. Then poetry is restored to its accustomed medium. Accordingly, in Calderón the person suffering loss of honor gains in inner intensity but will express novel and painful perceptions only at a terrible risk. The dishonored are poets without publishers or public. But when their poetic action succeeds in controlling events to their liking, they speak with impressive power. It is the central preoccupation of poets to open to the public their private perceptions. But the poet's individual vision and the public's way of viewing the world usually differ considerably. The good poet bridges this gap with as little personal loss as possible. He brings others into his field of vision. Like poetic vision, honor fundamentally is a private perception suffering from its privateness and longing to emerge undiminished into the public eye and understanding. To do so successfully requires long preparation, a great silent rehearsal. But when it speaks, its voice is both terrible and sublime.

The Calderón play that speaks most eloquently and, in Isabel's case, most

terribly, about honor is *El alcalde de Zalamea*. Its relatively few critics have all
recognized that it is a work whose essential theme is honor, that in some way it
defines honor, as with C. A. Jones and Peter N. Dunn.[68] Among efforts to elucidate the concept,[69] Peter Dunn's remains the most nearly successful; but one
is left with an unsatisfied and uncomfortable feeling at the thought of a great
Christian dramatist's engaging so wholeheartedly and yet so ambiguously in a
parody of the faith.[70]

And just as we critics, while sensing the vital connection of *El alcalde* with
honor, have nonetheless not made the relationship clear, so have we also failed
to analyze satisfactorily this very strange play, neither light *comedia* nor yet so
complete a tragedy as to rank among the great tragedies of honor. *El alcalde de
Zalamea* is in fact a hybrid product, graver than the cape-and-sword plays, yet
sufficiently triumphant to escape the status of out-and-out tragedy. This generic ambivalence has occasioned one critic, at least, to declare the play anom-
alous. Margaret Wilson declares: "*El alcalde de Zalamea* is probably the only
one of Calderón's plays to which a criterion of realism is generally applicable.
It represents something of a freak in his production."[71] I believe that her conclusion is misguided but it does illustrate dramatically how great a stumbling
block the play has been.

If *El alcalde* is a freak, it is not because Calderón has exceptionally ven-
tured into a novel dramatic mode called "realism." The criticism of it based on
that assumption has been unsatisfactory, and quite invidious as a silent condemnation of Calderón's other plays. "¿Contra quién va dirigido este elogio?"
(Whom is this praise meant to denigrate?), as Unamuno's Joaquín Monegro
would inquire. Conceptually, the great difficulty is that the major participants
in *El alcalde,* the avatars of honor, the Crespo family, are not noble. And for
Calderón honor is a complex of awareness most fully and almost uniquely developed in the noble. To assert, therefore, that by some extraordinary demotic
deviation Calderón has in one play shown peasants to be as good as or better
than nobles is a *contresens.*

Nonetheless, *El alcalde* does offer us a definition of honor. And a good
definition requires at least two postures, both of them indispensable. In the
first place, the definer must wholeheartedly sympathize and identify with the
matter to be defined. He must project himself into the heartland of his subject.
Calderón qualifies for the first requirement by virtue of the comedies of honor
that he wrote for the *corrales* in the 1620s and 1630s. In these, all of which are
set in or near Madrid, the capital city of honor, the spirit essentially animating
them goes pretty much undefined. It is assumed. It is felt. It is common property.

The second major requirement for a successful definition is that, despite
the definer's affinities for his material, it must stand apart from the matter
needing to be made clear. Definition requires objectivity as well as subjectivity.
And since honor is immanent in the noble breast, the only way to break out of
those subjective confines is by resorting to the heart of the non-noble, of the
villano, that antithesis of Calderonian essence. This is precisely what happens
in *El alcalde de Zalamea*. It employs a kind of artistic geopolitics. It moves out
of the heartland of honor, away from Madrid, to the shifting borderlands
where the lack of clear definition makes passage from one region or one coun-

try to another rapid and easy. Fluid frontiers help to define nongeographical concepts, and I would venture to say that this is the reason why many of Calderón's greatest plays are actually situated on borders: *La vida es sueño* begins with a crossing of the frontier between Muscovy and Poland, and considerable of its structure is a dialogue—*limen* and *limes,* peaceful and hostile—between those two realms. *A secreto agravio* also begins with an anguished border crossing, part by land and part by sea. Castile and Portugal are, in that play, symbolic as well as actual realms and they too engage in a wonderfully complex conversation, criminal at bottom. Across the wide fluid expanse of the Atlantic and the Mediterranean, the kingdoms of Fez and Portugal talk, treat, and entreat in what is probably the most exalted conversation of all, that in *El príncipe constante.* The strategy of *El alcalde de Zalamea* is to irradiate from the center to the borders and beyond, and from that beyond, that exile, to look back upon the conceptual motherland and wonder at it and so define it. *El alcalde de Zalamea* is not a freak, but it is extreme. It shows honor *in extremis,* at and beyond the limits, very much as Cervantes' *El celoso extremeño* does.

The play as Calderón came upon it in rough-hewn form, in the version of the same title attributed to Lope, presented Calderón with one very difficult technical problem. How was he, *entiché de noblesse,* to treat non-noble characters in a serious fashion? Before him, in the theatre, only Lope had contrived occasionally to redeem the *villano* from his rather dull conventions. And even in Lope's drama, a Peribáñez, a Teodoro is exceptional. His standard cast of characters consists of *hidalgos* and above. Moreover, since classical antiquity the customary manner of representing the lower orders had been to deny them full seriousness by means of satire, irony, and humor. Petronius's *Satyricon* is a major example. Servants are not full size. They are funny little people.

Furthermore, to the figure of the *alcalde* in Spanish letters and folklore there attaches a tradition of hilarious incompetence that the critics of *El alcalde de Zalamea* have hitherto ignored. Pedro Crespo's immediate forbear is Martín Crespo,[72] also an *alcalde,* in Cervantes' *comedia Pedro de Urdemalas.* Martín has spent a considerable portion of his wealth to obtain the honor of office. But an *alcalde* is a magistrate as well as an administrator. He must therefore settle legal matters that are brought before him. To do so well calls for a readier wit and tongue than most literary rustics have at their command. The classic country *alcalde* accordingly is a fellow who absurdly and ridiculously apes legal and learned speech in his official pronouncements, this to the rather snobbish delight of his better-educated audience. Covarrubias makes precisely this point in his definition of *alcalde,* pointing out that there are two classes, a more exalted breed at court and a lesser group in the country: "los ínfimos los de las aldeas, los quales, por ser rústicos, suelen dezir algunas simplicidades en lo que proveen, de que tomaron nombre de alcaldadas" (those of lower standing being the village magistrates who, on account of their rusticity, usually come out with foolish pronouncements, from which the name *alcaldadas* derives).[73] Anticipating difficulties of this kind, Martín Crespo, upon being elected, chooses Pedro de Urdemalas as his "assessor" or spokesman. And Pedro uses his position of trust to bring Crespo's own daughter, disguised, before her father so that he may judge of the suitability of her projected marriage, which Crespo opposes. Pedro naturally finds for the lovers, and Crespo accepts his own decision when they reveal themselves. This episode is really an extremely clever variation on the proverb: "Tener el padre alcalde" (to have one's father as one's judge). Correas also lists: "Kien tiene el padre alkalde, no espere que le falte" and the most familiar version: "Kien tiene el padre alkalde, seguro va a xuizio."[74] (With one's father as the judge, one faces the sentence with confidence.) Pedro Crespo's statement to Isabel in the final act of Calderón's play, just after he has been named magistrate, echoes these several proverbs: "Hija, / ya tenéis el padre alcalde; / él os guardará justicia" (1: 563). (Daughter, now your father is your judge. He will render you justice.)

The most traditional *alcaldes* immediately previous to Calderón's are Cervantes' humorous bumblers in *La elección de los alcaldes de Daganzo,* who celebrate their uninspired choice of a magistrate with a gypsy festival and a tossing in the blanket of their parish priest. The *entremés* consists mainly in their malapropisms. But with Crespo in *Pedro de Urdemalas,* the usual expectation that the *alcalde de aldea* will mangle his lines as well as his duties reverses itself. Pedro's wiles help to effect the change, but Crespo confirms his own fit and proper judgment. Thus Cervantes begins the creation of a new type of village magistrate, one who, with or without help, overcomes his disabilities. That there was much to overcome in the reputation of the job itself is shown by two further *refranes* listed in the Autoridades dictionary: "Alcalde de aldea, el que lo desea, esse lo sea. Refr. que enseña no deben apetecerse oficios que ni son de honra, ni de provécho." (Anyone who wants to can be a village magistrate. A prov. that shows how one shouldn't desire office that is neither honorable nor profitable.) And, in the same vein, "Por falta de homres buenos à mi Padre hicieron Alcalde. Refr. que explica, que no pocas veces se dán los empleos a hombres poco inteligentes, por no hallar otros mas apróposito, que si los huviera no los eligieran." (For want of good men they named my father magistrate. A prov. which explains that, not infrequently, office is given to men of little intelligence because others more fit cannot be found; that if the fit were available, the unfit would not be named.) For my purpose the most telling observation is that the village magistracy is a charge of neither honor nor profit. That is indeed a heavy burden, with which Calderón will deal in his own way.

Cervantes' third round with the rural magistrate occurs in Part II of the *Quijote.* Martín Crespo assumes the form of Sancho Panza, and Pedro de Urdemales that of Don Quijote himself when Sancho, as a result of the contrivance of the duke and duchess, takes up his duties as governor of the island of Barataria. One reason for Sancho's downfall, no doubt, is Don Quijote's absence from his side. The master offers his fortunate servant sage advice but does not accompany him. The basic reason, though, is of course that the disturbances which expel Barataria's governor are as artificial as the post itself, created exclusively for the amusement of the ducal pair, a satire grafted upon a real political body. For Barataria is one of the duke's towns, and one of his bigger towns, with about a thousand inhabitants. It is fundamentally, then, a *lugarón,* a somewhat overgrown village. When Sancho, *lugareño* that he basically is, comes to run it, we have the essential ingredients for the traditional satire of the village magistrate.

With Sancho, however, the notable departure from tradition is the elevation of the tone of the proceedings, with satirical intent. Sancho is made to live and to discharge his duties in princely, almost royal, fashion. The resultant contrast between the style of Sancho's rule and Sancho's homely, humble self partly transforms events into a related form of irony, the *rusticus imperans,* the bumpkin briefly, usually for a day, dressed as and made to believe he is king, so as to provide human sport for bored courtiers. Almost as directly, the diction of Sancho's governorship takes aim at the *sermo grandiloquens* of Don Quijote himself, his highfalutin' rhetoric, princely and purple and therefore most unsuitable to a lowly country *hidalgo,* at least in the eyes of the duke. But, just as Don Quijote himself endures with melancholy dignity the elaborately rhetorical assaults which the ducal establishment makes upon his mind and body, so Sancho rather more than survives his so-called governorship, a graceless and hostile *merced.* In fact, Sancho acquits himself quite well, especially in those challenges to his acumen which present themselves in the form of tangled human problems, the Solomonic tradition, precisely the greatest peril for the standard tongue-tied rustic. Consequently, when Sancho discovers the ten gold *escudos* hidden in a hollow staff, "Quedaron todos admirados, y tuvieron a su governador por un nuevo Salomon" (p. 84). (Everybody was left astonished and thinking of the governor as a new Solomon.) Inevitably, of course, Cervantes does not find it possible to leave matters at this peak of clarity. The general decision is ambiguous: "Y el que escrivia las palabras, hechos y movimientos de Sancho, no acabava de determinarse si le tendria y pondria por tonto, o por discreto" (pp. 84-85). (And the person who was recording the words, deeds, and movements of Sancho could not make up his mind whether he would think of and portray him as a wise man or a fool.) Still, the fact that Sancho's scribe would even hesitate in the evaluation of a stock humorous figure shows how successfully Cervantes has given life and human stature to a parody, yet without destroying its satirical base.[75]

Lope (if it is Lope)[76] in his *Alcalde de Zalamea* also gives a new dimension to the flat tradition of the village magistrate. As in *Pedro de Urdemalas,* the father acts as judge in his own offspring's petition for justice but, in the play attributed to Lope, knowingly. In rendering justice, this Pedro Crespo adopts the solution of *El mejor alcalde, el rey.* He marries the offending captains to his daughters, and then executes the men by hanging them. And although he has technically exceeded his authority, Philip II confirms Crespo's decision. Philip visits Zalamea, drawn there by Don Lope's description of the magistrate: ". . . es hombre de humor / su alcalde: es hombre / extremado. . . . Tendrá vuestra majestad / gusto en verle, que el villano / tiene cierta autoridad / de más de juez cortesano.[77] (Its magistrate is a jovial, a humorous man. Your majesty will take pleasure in his acquaintance, for the rogue has a kind of authority that exceeds even a royal judge's.) Here again the portrait is a hybrid one. Don Lope presents Crespo to Philip as an amusing spectacle. The fellow is jovial but sharp, qualities quite consistent with received ideas about peasants and their crafty ways. Crespo, however, steps right out of the frame when he is credited with an air of authority greater than that of the royal breed of judges. This is quite a different man, a real man. He can deprive people of their lives quite as well as the king. Still, Lope or the pseudo-Lope does not quite let his *alcalde* grow up. The king will not release his creature from childish ways, and opines: "Valor es, / más que simpleza, el que tiene" (p. 228).

(He is, rather than a simpleton, a man of worth.) It is perceptive of the king to discern in a peasant real and large human stature. Yet he confines his important discovery to the tradition of peasant slow-wittedness by making Crespo mayor of Zalamea for life: "y a vos, por lo bien que hacéis / vuestro oficio, os hago alcalde / perpetuo." (And because you do your job so well I create you mayor in perpetuity.) Nonetheless, Crespo owes his office to his reversal of the usual expectations of an *alcalde,* that he can say and do nothing right. Sancho could make right judgments but failed when he had to act. Crespo can both think and act. He is far more secure in his job as *alcalde perpetuo* than Sancho was in his as *gobernador perpetuo.* There is a bitter irony here. Village mayors by literary definition do not, cannot, do their jobs well. If they do, they become other, new persons. Crespo has become a new man. In recognizing his transformation, the king rewards him by fixing him forever to that which he is not. The first *Alcalde de Zalamea* leaves this terrible issue quite unresolved, in the sense that it remains unexplained, unjustified.

Nonetheless, both Cervantes and the author of the first *Alcalde de Zalamea* have breathed new life into the tradition of the *alcalde de aldea.* As is so often the case both in wit and in literary renewal, reversal is the means by which surprise is obtained. Martín Crespo, Sancho Panza, and Pedro Crespo find it possible to make correct decisions, against all traditional expectations. Yet in affirming their individual capacities their creators find themselves in a very difficult situation. They are treating seriously members of a class and occupation whom there is no precedent to consider without humor, and they cannot entirely put the ironic focus aside. Thus their rustic Solomons remain ambiguous—half-comical, half-serious.

Accordingly, when Calderón took up *El alcalde de Zalamea* the village magistrate had already made half the journey towards three-dimensionality. In Calderón's hands he presses further still but does not complete the journey. He retains muted characteristics of the humorous bumpkin who can neither speak nor act properly. Calderón's audiences doubtless needed only broad hints in the play to recognize the type. Once he is established, the play, in the fashion of its predecessors, proceeds to work against the stereotype that is its heritage. To succeed, Calderón withholds from Crespo the staff of office until near the end of the play. I think, moreover, that the first title must have been *El garrote más bien dado*[78] rather than *El alcalde de Zalamea,* for in his work Calderón perfects the type of the rural magistrate redeemed. The essence of that perfection is to be found in the rustic's capacity to proceed with all justice of content and form against a nobleman who has broken the law. The tradition is that *villanos,* when they take matters into their own hands, perpetrate intolerable outrages against individuals and society. Not even Lope's obvious sympathy for the oppressed villagers of Fuenteovejuna can disguise his fear and distrust of popular disturbances when he recounts the story of the murder of the Comendador in *Fuenteovejuna.* Unlike them, Pedro Crespo handles his judicial murder properly, except for little matters like jurisdiction and the mode of execution. Still, the point is that Pedro Crespo has carried things out well, contrary to what might have been expected. The punishment was deserved and properly administered. Therefore the better title is *El garrote más bien dado* rather than the typological *El alcalde de Zalamea.* An artist who consciously delays conferring an undesirable and often ludicrous office would not impose it at the outset as a title.

But at the present time the title which has remained with the play no longer conveys its former attributes of ridiculousness. Later readers have found in Pedro Crespo's office a confirmation of the worth which Calderón created in despite of Crespo's *alcaldía* and its potentially attendant *alcaldalas*. Yet even outside the literary tradition of the village magistrate, Crespo belongs to another humorous type, the *villano rico* or rich, vainglorious peasant. Indeed, the first characterization of Crespo in the play precisely follows such a stereotype. Accordingly, when the sergeant describes for the captain that officer's billet in Zalamea, he tells him that he is lodged

En casa de un villano que el hombre más rico es del lugar, de quien después he oído que es el más vano hombre del mundo y que tiene más pompa y presunción que un infante de León. [1: 542]	in the house of a peasant who is the town's richest man and of whom I've also heard that he is the world's vainest man and that he's more conceited and arrogant than any princeling.

This is the first mention of Crespo in *El alcalde de Zalamea* and so quite important to the audience's sense of him. He comes into being, then, as an absurd type of person whom the captain instantly recognizes: "Bien a un villano conviene / rico aquesa vanidad." (That kind of vanity is just the thing for a rich peasant.)

And just as the original model of country magistrate served to amuse his better-educated and better spoken auditors, so the sergeant proposes to divert his captain with Crespo's daughter, if not by means of her beauty, which the captain scorns, then through the amusement-value of her clumsy speech: "¿Hay más bien gastado rato / (a quien amor no le obliga / sino ociosidad no más) / que el de una villana, y ver / que no acierta a responder / a propósito jamás?" (1: 542). (What better use is there of a bit of leisure time than to spend it with a peasant girl, not flirting, but being amused at how she can never answer anything right?) The key element here is the verb *acertar,* to do something right. Peasants, in the eyes of their noble beholders, can do nothing right. But Pedro Crespo is a notable exception. When King Philip questions his jurisdiction over the captain, he staunchly defends himself: "¿Y qué importa errar lo menos / quien acertó lo demás?" (1: 570). (What difference does a minor mistake make when somebody has got the main thing right?) For the king, this explanation is conclusive and, in reconciling his general Don Lope to the distasteful reality, Philip repeats Crespo's very words: "Don Lope, aquesto ya es hecho. / Bien dada la muerte está, / que no importa errar lo menos / quien acertó lo demás" (1: 570). (Don Lope, the deed is done. This death was properly administered, because a minor mistake doesn't matter when somebody has got the main thing right.) At the end of *El alcalde de Zalamea,* consequently, Crespo surmounts but does not eradicate his typological incapacity. Error remains a minor but significant aspect of his functioning. He is still a *villano* and an *alcalde* in perpetuity. Ridiculousness has not been entirely dispelled, even though it has been greatly diminished. On the whole, however, Crespo has amazed his public by managing matters well. This is the distance from humorous stereotype to almost complete humanity, from "no acierta . . . jamás" to "acertó lo demás" and is Calderón's solution, in part, to the problem of presenting a non-noble character in serious terms.

Yet there is another aspect to the problem. Real human depth is in the Calderonian canon exclusively a noble birthright. Pedro Crespo is a *villano* who grows to near-noble dimensions. His substance cannot come from nowhere, be created *ex nihilo*. It must have a source. That source is Don Mendo, an *hidalgo* who is treated with the flatness that is characteristic of literary satire. The two personages are thus complementary. Don Mendo is a noble without substance, without virtue of any kind, whereas Pedro Crespo is a man of substance without nobility. Both men are incomplete, but Don Mendo's wants are far graver. Nuño, Mendo's food-obsessed servant, exactly appreciates the needs of each party when he explains the advantages of a marriage between his master and Crespo's daughter Isabel: "Pues con esto tú y su padre / remediaréis de una vez / entrambas necesidades: / tú comerás y él hará / hidalgos sus nietos" (1: 543). (Because thereby at one stroke you will meet each other's needs: you'll eat and he will get noble grandchildren.) Nuño's speech shows Pedro Crespo to be possessed of that substance which Don Mendo lacks, while Mendo, though scarcely a human of any real proportions, does yet offer the title which appears to be Crespo's ultimate refuge and destiny. In addition, Mendo is just as much a departure from the norm as Crespo, for it is rare to encounter a satirical portrait of a gentleman. The critics, however, have had no way of avoiding Mendo's models. Calderón, to justify his unusual treatment, mentions Mendo's most prestigious predecessor:

Un hombre   A man who, around the corner, got
que de un flaco Rocinante   off his skinny Rocinante-like nag
a la vuelta desa esquina   and who in face and form resembles
se apeó y en rostro y talle   that Don Quijote whose adventures
parece aquel Don Quijote   Miguel de Cervantes wrote.
de quien Miguel de Cervantes
escribió las aventuras. [1: 542]

This is the most detailed reference to Cervantes of all that I have found in the plays of Calderón. The author, the character, the horse, and the book all emerge with what would seem undue clarity, for surely a phrase would have sufficed to establish Don Mendo's literary paternity. But those lines are for Calderón his personage's artistic *cédula* and justify the extreme caricature which we so easily accept but which might have unsettled a seventeenth-century Spanish audience. Cervantes acts as Calderón's apologist. Don Mendo and Don Quijote greatly differ, however. Like Crespo, Don Quijote grows from flat caricature—"un hidalgo de los de lanza en astillero, adarga antigua, rocín flaco y galgo corredor"—to human dimensions. Nor does either man ever throw off his satirical origins. But Mendo begins and ends in insubstantiality, shadow to Crespo's mass, unrelieved satire, pure literature, with a second great, but unnamed, predecessor in the *escudero* of the third *Tratado* of the *Lazarillo de Tormes*.

Far from being an aberrant reflection of actual experience, *El alcalde de Zalamea* points with pride to the literary sires of both Don Mendo and Pedro Crespo. Like many children, they pursue careers that differ from their parents', but there can be no question about their paternity. Moreover, in this play, both on the surface and in the deeps, Cervantes reveals his presence most pervasively. *El alcalde* is the final conversation in Calderón's long and fruitful dialogue with the author of the *Quijote* and the *Novelas ejemplares*. Along with the high-bred Mendo and with Crespo, one senses a very long dose of literature too in Don Lope, the irascible, bluff, foul-mouthed but fundamentally kind general. He is not a *miles gloriosus* but rather a *miles luctuosus,* groaning with the unremitting pain in his leg. That pain is significant, but it is also humorous and satirical. A less vivid Don Lope plays a small role in Calderón's *Amar después de la muerte,* which Valbuena Briones dates around 1633.[79] As a consequence, the general stands about halfway between caricature and deep humanity, so that a bond of competitive sympathy is forged between him and Crespo, who is travelling along the same road, from stereotype to autonomy. Calderón's own dramatic literature is thus Don Lope's sire. Ancestors are of vital importance in a play that defines honor, and parents and forbears are very much in evidence in *El alcalde de Zalamea*.

Logically, in striving for a dramatic definition of honor, Calderón attempts to make from the beginning the most comprehensive statement possible. But since the play is art, it declaims thematically rather than syllogistically, despite Calderón's well-known but deceptive penchant for pseudo-logical rhetoric, art masquerading as sorites. Honor as we find it in this play is an awareness that comes to life under the pressure of risk or danger. It is the consciousness that one has something to lose, therefore a paradoxical sense of possessing while being threatened with dispossession, simultaneously having and having not or dreading to have not. For example, in Act III of *Bien vengas, mal, si vienes solo,* Doña Ana appeals to her lover Don Diego and her father's house guest Don Juan to halt their duel for her honor's sake, in these terms:

mas cuando se ve culpada	But when a woman like me finds her-
una mujer como yo,	self compromised, she is compelled
siendo un átomo de ofensa	to risk everything, for even an atom
sobra de una presunción,	of suspicion is excessive grounds for
todo lo ha de aventurar,	conjecture. That is why she who is
que para aquesto nació	noble was born with honor and with
la que es principal mujer	obligations, so as to have, in a crisis,
con honra y obligación	something to loose.
para tener que perder	
cuando llegue la ocasión. [2: 624]	

Similarly, although the circumstances differ, Leonor, in *No hay cosa como callar,* expresses her fears for her reputation if she spends the night in Don Pedro's house after the fire in her rooms:

pero no
quisiera yo, porque tengo
mucho que perder, que alguno,
por objeción de suceso
tan extraño, me pusiera,
o bien malicioso o necio,
el que me quedé una noche
fuera de mi casa. [2: 1010]

But, since I have a great deal to lose,
I wouldn't at all care to have anyone
objecting, out of either malice or stu-
pidity, to the strangeness of my having spent a night away from my
house.

Don Pedro does not attempt to minimize the danger to Leonor's reputation. Rather, he emphasizes her need: "Un riesgo / tan preciso y tan forzoso / disculpa un atrevimiento / y más tan lícito y justo." (So urgent and necessary a risk excuses an unusual act, especially one that is so permissible and proper.) There follows the vital pledge of amends, if any are needed, by Don Pedro.

The noble individual, man or woman, is invested at birth with a pair of paradoxical properties. Honor is the *hidalgo*'s birthright, but this is a spiritual capital that must be put out at interest; otherwise the capital sum will itself waste away. *Obligaciones* are thus a necessity for the noble if he is to preserve and increase his inherited capital, *honra*. But every investment has a degree of risk, and *obligaciones,* being a commitment to people, involve a very high degree of risk. Ana's problems in *Bien vengas, mal* are characteristic. Her troubles begin when she accepts for safekeeping her friend María's love-letters and the portrait of her lover, Don Juan. Inevitably, Ana's own lover breaks in upon her just as she is hiding these compromising keepsakes; and when, to protect María, she will not reveal the names of the people involved, Don Diego suspects that Ana is deceiving him. The situation gets even more complicated when Ana's father takes Juan into his house so as to hide him from the police, who want him as the killer of his opponent in a duel. These are *obligaciones,* the commitments which honor compels the noble to make to other humans in need or distress. And they have an alarming tendency, once the noble generously responds, as he must, to bring the respondent into grave peril. Consequently, Calderón's nobles are terribly tried people. Their understandable sense of plenitude and pride as a result of their ancestry is almost exactly counterbalanced by a vulnerability to the accidents of adversity. Their very prominence exposes them to concatenations of misfortune, making high birth at once a blessing and a curse, the best and the worse of human lots. Pride in birth and a fair name is the great noble possession: *tener.* The disasters that result from the noble's exposed situation are the erosions that wear away his sense of proprietorship: *perder.* The essence of the noble experience, then, *tener que perder,* to have something, a great deal, to lose.

The date of composition of Calderón's *El alcalde de Zalamea* is hard to establish. Those who, like Margaret Wilson, find in the play an uncharacteristically experiential realism favor a date late enough in the 1640s for Calderón to have fought, as he did, in the Catalan campaign. The play itself, unlike the usual cape-and-sword drama, plunges into history headlong. The events that help to shape it are those of many years past, Philip II's acquisition of Portugal as the result of the extinction of its ruling house. So it is that Pedro Crespo explains to Isabel the need for her to go into seclusion:

Hija, el Rey nuestro señor,
que el cielo mil años guarde,
va a lisboa, porque en ella
solicita coronarse
como legítimo dueño,
a cuyo efeto marciales
tropas caminan con tantos
aparatos militares
hasta bajar a Castilla
el tercio viejo de Flandes
con un don Lope, que dicen
todos que es un español Marte.
Hoy han de venir a casa
soldados y es importante
que no te vean; asi, hija,
al punto has de retirarte
en esos desvanes donde
yo vivía. [1: 545-46]

Daughter, the king our master,
whom heaven spare for a millen-
nium, is on his way to Lisbon, undertaking to be crowned there as the
legal proprietor, to which purpose
troops of soldiers with many stores
are on the march until the veteran
Flanders regiment, under a certain
Don Lope, whom all declare to be
the Spanish Mars, can reach Castile.
Soldiers will be coming to the house
today and it is urgent that they not
see you. And so, daughter, you are
immediately to withdraw to those
upper rooms that I used to occupy.

The decision announced in this speech shows external historical events operating directly on the inner structure of the play. This immediate effect differs
markedly from the excursion to Fuenterrabía in *No hay cosa como callar* or the
many brief mentions, *en passant,* of events of the day in other Calderón cape-
and-sword dramas. They are exterior. Philip's impact on *El alcalde de Zalamea*
is deep and intimate.

In his introduction to the play, Peter Dunn makes the very reasonable and
very British remark, concerning *El alcalde's* date, that "we must assume that
the play was completed and performed before 1644, because that was the year
when the Spanish public became aware that Portugal was lost. We cannot
imagine that Calderón would have been tactless enough to present a play connected with the conquest of Portugal at the very moment when the new defeat
by Portugal was becoming public knowledge."[80]

In questions of honor, the king is out of bounds, for he is above honor.
Yet the sovereign is at the same time the fount of honor, its exemplar. Manifestly, King Philip breaks into the confines of *El alcalde* rather as King Pedro
so unfortunately does in *El médico de su honra.* His intrusions help to reinforce
the play's delimiting theme of possessing while yet not possessing. And the
theme becomes historical fact when we expand our period of awareness from
1580, with Portugal just moving into Philip's grasp, to precisely 1644, with
Portugal just out of Philip IV's control. The kingdom of Portugal is such an
excellent example of the noble's *tener que perder* that it would be astonishing
for Calderón not to capitalize on it, as he so richly and subtly does. My date
would therefore be 1644.

But a kingdom, like a golden chain, is a *bien de la fortuna,* fortune's gift,
and its loss does not necessarily entail dishonor. Even so, the disappearance of
a treasured possession that is in the receiving a spiritual conferral does give rise
to many questions of a moral nature. The winner is inevitably compared with
the loser, Philip II with Philip IV. Most of Calderón's experience, in Madrid,

at court, or in the field, was with the loser; and his whole dramatic philosophy is a loser's system. Yet material losses are not for him the major ones. His basic strategy is to draw a spiritual triumph from physical disaster. At all events, there is a clear and conscious parallel between Pedro Crespo and King Philip II. Both are sovereign personalities who, by a stroke of fortune, find a new and important jurisdiction placed within their grasp. Their right to exercise this new power is not unequivocal[81] but they have an overridingly legitimate claim. Each man accordingly advances resolutely to the assertion of his rights and is vindicated.

But in Calderón's art no victory is final. Defeat is the normal experience. Therefore, in honor's world of risk, where the noble is, by virtue of his contract with society and the moral universe, compelled to gamble, loss is a basic phenomenon and a key concept and word. In the first act of *El alcalde de Zalamea* the idea of gain and loss is developed symphonically, beginning with King Philip himself. And just as the play reaches us beyond its normal limits to the sovereign, so it falls below the customary social line in the persons of the soldiers, especially with Rebolledo and La Chispa. I believe *El alcalde* to be the only Calderón play in which a servant society comes to life. Usually Calderón ventures to create only a pair or two of servant lovers, narrowly and mockingly imitating their betters. But the soldiers and La Chispa in *El alcalde* form a real lower social stratum. They are granted this reality because, by soldiering, they have collectively taken a noble risk. They venture their lives in the service of a higher cause. Therefore they compel from the dramatist a far more serious contemplation of their destinies than he is elsewhere willing to concede. Characteristically, however, Calderón continues with surprising variations on this theme. For Rebolledo's pledge to the dangers of army life is much less wholehearted than that of his comrades, and in the significant opening scene he threatens to go "over the hill" if his company is not permitted to enter Zalamea. To abjure one's word in this way could cost as much as any military engagement. Moreover, death as a sentence for desertion brings the convicted person into dishonor. This is the warning of Rebolledo's companions when he boasts: "no . . . / será el primer tornillazo / que habré yo dado en mi vida" (1: 540). (It won't be the first time in my life that I'll have gone over the hill.) The grim response is: "Tampoco será el primero / que haya la vida costado / a un miserable soldado." (Neither will it be the first time that desertion has cost a wretched soldier his life.) Here is where we learn that Rebolledo is, as soldiers go, only half-noble. He makes the basic commitment and it confers *honra*. But along with the *galas del soldado* go the privations, as Cervantes is fond of reminding us. Rebolledo is unwilling to suffer, to tolerate. At first impression it appears that his companion La Chispa contemplates hardship with a far more virile countenance than Rebolledo. When he weakly protests that he would leave if he were not concerned for her, she cheerfully declares: "barbada el alma nací / y ese temor me deshonra, / pues no vengo yo a servir / menos que para sufrir / trabajos con mucha honra" (1: 541). (I was born with a bearded soul and his fear dishonors me, because I came for nothing less than to suffer hardships with much honor.) Rebolledo's inability to tolerate pain is first confirmed when he is accused of being the cause of the disturbance which Don Lope discovers when he enters Zalamea. Don Lope immediately orders that

Rebolledo be given "dos tratos de cuerda," a sort of hanging by the hands bound behind the back. Even though the captain begs "¡Ah, Rebolledo / por Dios, / que nada digas: yo haré / que te libren" (1: 549) (For God's sake, Rebolledo, don't say anything. I'll see to it that you're set free), he instantly confesses that he played a part so that the captain could see Isabel. La Chispa is a horrified bystander to all these events; but, as a participant in the abduction of Isabel and in the return of the wounded captain to Zalamea, she too is threatened with torture by Pedro Crespo; and then the apparent distinction between them disappears. After vainly and absurdly averring that she is pregnant (she is dressed as a man), La Chispa confesses just as readily as Rebolledo previously did and now again does. The other leading number of their society, the sergeant, escapes. Comparison of La Chispa and Rebolledo with the stalwart townspeople of *Fuenteovejuna* is instructive.[82] Calderón's pair were not born to *sufrir*. They are not noble even in the limited context of a soldier's dispensation from baseness.

But since they frequently resort to the lexicon of honor, their behavior is an ironic departure from their speech. La Chispa and Rebolledo parody honor by this means, and their major concern is with that key awareness which is risk, loss, danger. In short, they gamble, lose, and want to recoup their losses so as to repay their debts. Indeed, loss is the event which brings the captain and Rebolledo together and so prepares the peril that is the fundamental tension of *El alcalde de Zalamea*. Thus when the captain urges the soldier to make his wants known, Rebolledo declares:

Yo he perdido cuanto dinero
tengo y he tenido y he de
tener, porque de pobre juro en
presente, pretérito y futuro.

    Hágaseme merced de que,
por vía de ayudilla de costa,
aqueste día el alférez me dé
. . . .
el juego del boliche por mi
cuenta, que soy hombre cargado
de obligaciones y hombre al
fin honrado. [1: 546-47]

I've lost all the money I have, did have and ever will have, so that I'm taking the pauper's oath in the present, past and future.

    Please do me the kindness of having the ensign entrust to me, today, as a kind of slight per diem, the game of *boliche,* because I'm a man overburdened with debt and, in the last analysis, an honorable man.

Boliche, according to the Autoridades dictionary, is a kind of billiards in which the balls are thrown rather than propelled. Gambling is, at all events, a major concern in the lives of Rebolledo and La Chispa. They risk their lives and their property. Yet, in the last analysis, they are not honorable because they are unwilling to make good their pledges. They will not truly venture their only real capital, themselves. They have, in fact, nothing to lose even as they operate within the noble conceptual framework of loss and gain. This is in decided contrast to their comrades, who have pledged their lives. Thus they constitute a satirical extension of honor in depth, honor among thieves, and so fall beneath its lower pale, just as the king operates above its upper limits: *Del rey abajo, ninguno.*

Also below the customary social level of honor is a principal protagonist whom the critics have so far failed utterly to notice in Calderón's play. This is the town of Zalamea itself. Now, cities were in the habit of styling themselves in elevated terms: *la muy noble ciudad de Barcelona*. But for a hamlet to do so would have been as ludicrous as it was for Rebolledo to declare himself an "hombre, al fin, honrado." Yet Zalamea's claim to respectability is of the same nature and as valid as that of Rebolledo's companions who risk their lives in the king's service. Like them, Zalamea ventures its collective existence so as to perform what it conceives to be its duty. Many a town would have bought off the tired troops. Such is, indeed, Rebolledo's expectation as his company is marching towards the town where they hope to find rest and lodging:

Y aunque llegue vivo allá
sabe mi Dios si será
para alojar, pues es cierto
llegar luego al comisario
los alcaldes a decir
que, si es que se pueden ir,
que darán lo necesario.
Responderles, lo primero,
que es imposible, que viene
la gente muerta; y, si tiene
el Concejo algún dinero,
decir: "Señores soldados,
orden hay que no paremos:
luego al instante marchemos."

And even if I do get there alive, God only knows whether I'll get a billet, because the committeemen are sure to go right up to the commissariat and say that, if we possibly can take ourselves off, they'll give us what we need. The answer will be that, in the first place, it's impossible, since the men are exhausted; but then, if the town committee has any money, we'll hear: "Men, our orders are not to halt here. March on out immediately."

[1: 540]

Perhaps Zalamea has neither money nor provisions. But the more likely assumption is that the town, exceptionally, it would seem, chooses to do its duty by the tired troops. The captain takes the credit for himself when he announces: "Señores soldados, / albricias puedo pedir: / de aquí no hemos de salir / y hemos de estar alojados / hasta que don Lope venga" (1: 541). (Men, you have good news to thank me for. We stay, and are going to be billeted here until Don Lope arrives.) But the other soldiers must be as familiar as Rebolledo with the usual ways of getting rid of troops and must realize that it is the town committee that has taken them in, willingly.

Now Zalamea's peril begins. The first great danger to it occurs when the captain's ruse designed to discover Isabel provokes Crespo's wrath as well as his son's. Viewed in its own terms, the quarrel looks like simply the assault by one man on another's jurisdiction. Crespo's line of reasoning is that, within the sanctuary of his private moral values symbolized by his family and his house, his law is supreme. The captain, by invading its innermost recesses, has violated the law of hospitality and the law of sanctuary. In Pedro Crespo's house, with the captain as his invited guest, the question is: who is sovereign? Is the captain, as the representative of the king, *chez lui?* Or is Crespo absolute within his own precincts? As always with Calderón, the problem is hybrid, complex, ambiguous. But Crespo, perhaps owing to his natural air of authority, inherited certainly from the preceding play, seems to have the weight of evidence on his side. Yet when Rebolledo first confesses and Crespo triumphantly declares: "Ved agora / si hemos tenido razón" (1: 549) (Now you see how right we were), Don Lope counters with the sobering observation: "No tuvisteis para haber / así puesto en ocasión / de perderse este lugar." (You had no excuse for creating a situation that might have led to this town's destruction.) Unlike Crespo, Don Lope sees the larger issue and danger. The dispute is one between town and tunic. And Zalamea runs the very real risk of being sacked by the irate soldiery. Don Lope immediately takes measures to prevent such an occurrence by restricting the troops to their quarters. Temporarily, Zalamea survives the noble but deadly gamble. The key phenomenon again is loss, *perderse*.

Zalamea's second encounter with probable destruction occurs in Act III, when Don Lope, informed of the captain's arrest and imprisonment, returns in a rage to secure his officer's release by whatever means. During this crisis, as is often the case with ordinary speech in moments of extreme stress, the language of the play retreats to stereotype; but the stereotype of tragic anguish humorously and horribly enlarges and diminishes its subjects, in Cervantine fashion. Just as Crespo, in Act I, called Don Mendo an "hidalgote" because he lacked individual human substance, so now Don Lope identifies his rival in jurisdiction as "alcaldillo," and Crespo counters by describing himself as a "villanote." The increasingly heated exchange shows that both men have abandoned individuality for the simplistic categories of class. They both speak of Crespo in his functions as magistrate in the third person, until Crespo himself reverts to the first person pronoun. Then the battle of wills is truly engaged, with Don Lope's troops returned to Zalamea for the purpose of rescuing their comrades, Pedro Crespo's *villanos* barricaded in the jail and defending it with firearms. The town's annihilation seems inevitable as Lope orders: "Ésta es la cárcel, soldados, / adonde está el capitán; / si no os le dan, al momento / poned fuego y la abrasad, / y si se pone en defensa / el lugar, todo el lugar" (1: 568-69). (Soldiers, this is the captain's jail. If they won't release him to you, set fire to it immediately and burn it down; and if the town tries to defend it, burn down the whole town, too.) Only King Philip's arrival prevents the razing of Zalamea and the murder of its inhabitants. Thus does the ignoble *lugar,* as generically remote from high destiny as the *villano* was remote from the *hidalgo,* emerge from isolation and confront the dangers to which the patterns of history have exposed it. Though by definition lowly and humble, Zalamea has risen to the fearful occasion and miraculously survived it. In the perspective of its collective trial by fire, Zalamea performs as one of the play's principal protagonists and as a major comic element for having risked immolation and triumphed over it in another potent variation on the theme of *tener que perder.*

Awareness that the act of possessing simultaneously implies the risk of losing the thing possessed begins a chemical process of permutation by means of which the level of operations rises from the physical to the metaphysical, from the carnal to the psychological and spiritual, rather as intelligence, in the love theory of the time, spiritualizes the attractive image of a person of the opposite sex after it has impressed itself upon the consciousness, *alma:* seeing is supremely physical, but since vision is related to the higher faculties, images easily dematerialize, as Doña Gerónima explains in Tirso's *El amor médico:* "toda esta acción es corpórea. / Llega luego el alma y pide / al entendimiento agente / que las [especies] inmaterialice / y vuelva esperituales."[83] (This whole process [of seeing] is of the body. Then the soul takes over and asks the functioning intellect to immaterialize these corporeal images and to render them spiritual.) Honor, as Tirso's King of Naples tells us in *El burlador de Sevilla,* is the soul of the male human, residing in the female. Honor comes into being when loss threatens; and, since honor is a psychological operation of the higher awareness, it transposes physical preoccupations to the metaphysical. Honor, in short, metamorphoses. It is a species of love.

In *El alcalde de Zalamea* Pedro Crespo's first important speech naturally concerns itself with the harvest. It has been abundant and the wheat is being threshed. Crespo likens the piles of grain to heaps of gold. He also interprets winnowing symbolically, as a natural confirmation of the human social order: "que aun allí lo más humilde / da el lugar a lo más grave" (1: 544) (for even there the humbler sort make way for their betters). If Crespo himself reads agricultural activities in this way, then his auditors are authorized to view the final harvest effort in a similar fashion: "¡Oh, quiera Dios que en las trojes / yo llegue a encerrarlo, antes / que algún turbión me lo lleve / o algún viento me las tale!" (1: 544-45). (God grant that I may deposit it [the wheat] in the barns before some great downpour washes it away or some wind blows them [the barns] down!) In the material sense, Pedro Crespo is ripe for transmutation. He now sees his golden harvest with intellectual and spiritual eyes and fears its loss. But he has another harvest even more golden, "oro de más quilates." It is his children, a son and daughter carefully nurtured to near-maturity who are now of an age to make those choices that will shape the rest of their lives, a profession for Juan, marriage for Isabel. They are at the danger point—free, vulnerable, exposed like the wheat on the threshing floor.

And if gold has not transformed Pedro Crespo, it has transformed his children. Their manners and amusements are those of *hidalgos.* The first we learn of Juan is that he plays *pelota* and, like a genuine Calderón noble, has lost. In addition, the game itself is noble, as the Autoridades dictionary makes clear: "Juego de *pelóta.* Diversion y exercicio honesto, que ordinariamente usan los nobles y gente honrada" (The game of *pelota* is a respectable diversion and a form of exercise taken normally by nobles and people of standing.) In Lope de Vega's *El villano en su rincón* Juan Labrador is an immensely rich peasant not dissimilar in character to Pedro Crespo, for Juan Labrador refuses to be transmuted by his wealth into a nobleman. Nor does he wish his son and daughter, Feliciano and Lisarda, to change their country ways. But both young people are courtiers at heart, irresistibly drawn to Paris and the king. Indeed, the play opens with Lisarda's foray into the city in noble attire. In his way, Feliciano matches his sister; and when he and she meet to marvel over their father's obstinacy, Feliciano tells us that, whenever he can, he dresses like a courtier and goes off to Paris to mingle with gentlemen and to bet on their *pelota* matches, although he doesn't dare play for fear of his father.

Unlike Juan Labrador, Crespo has no apparent objection to his son's playing *pelota.* His quarrel with Juan takes up the matter of risk. According to the father, Juan ventures more than cash when he makes bets he cannot immediately cover; he needlessly endangers his reputation: "ni jugar / más de lo que está delante, / porque si por accidente / falta, tu opinión no falte" (1: 545). (Nor should you wager any more money than you have about you, so as to avoid blemishing your good name if by chance you couldn't pay.) The thematic unity of the apparently random progression from a rich but always endangered harvest to a son who has come to ask his father to pay his gaming debts is that gold is a noble metal which, when possessed in sufficient quantity, raises the consciousness of the possessor from physical to metaphysical preoccupations. *Opinión* is Pedro Crespo's entirely aristocratic obsession. But he wishes for his son to preserve his standing through peasant caution, never pledging more than he can immediately pay. Yet Juan has moved far more deeply into aristocratic values and knows that the noble, in wagering all, risks the loss of all.

Further elaboration of this theme propels the reader to the fundamental contradiction of Pedro Crespo's condition. Even though his wealth promotes social modification and upward mobility, he absolutely insists upon remaining a peasant. Juan surely reasons better than his father when he urges Crespo to buy a patent of nobility at the bargain price of five or six thousand *reales*. Once ennobled, Crespo will no longer have the inconvenience of being required to billet soldiers in his house. Crespo's reply, that a title bought with money is like a wig, covering but not concealing the wearer's baldness, is a brilliant simile; but the son's counter-assertion, that a wig, as well as a title, has protective properties, really carries the day, although it fails to convince his father.

Paradoxically, Crespo's obstinacy in retaining lowly status imbues him with a quality essential to the high-born. Peasants have no sense of obligation and must be compelled to render service. But nobles should spontaneously offer to their king their lives, their fortunes, although not quite, as Crespo will soon maintain, their sacred honor. *Noblesse oblige:* "Quien nació / con obligaciones, debe / acudir a ellas" (1: 548). (A person born to responsibility must discharge it.) Such is Don Alvaro's highly ironic account of his *hidalgo* self. Crespo was not born to this lofty sense of duty but, partly through wealth, has acquired it. A title would excuse him from the peasant's obligations. In buying one he would be sparing himself, much as village *alcaldes* spare their town by bribing the king's troops to move elsewhere. Like Zalamea, Crespo scorns to avoid responsibility, in fact willingly and eagerly accepts it and all its perils. His attitude is ideally noble, and it is virtualized by his insistence upon remaining a peasant, a *pechero*. Thus a conscious and deliberate persistence in the lowly role (Crespo likes to speak of *humildad,* although he is marvellously proud) creates the conditions of willing, generous service which ideally characterizes the noble. No wonder that Don Alvaro de Ataide has such difficulty in interpreting the Crespo family. Their social signals are sublimely crossed.

El alcalde de Zalamea is a play constructed on parallels. Its most obvious one is that between Crespo and Don Lope de Figueroa. With each man, the fundamental consciousness is that of a willing submission to discomfort and danger. One verb in the play most fully conveys the sense of the noble mind's often painful conformity with fate. It is *sufrir*. We first encounter it as a somewhat debased expression in the mouth of La Chispa: "no vengo yo a servir / menos que para sufrir / trabajos con mucha honra" (1: 541). (I came for nothing less than to suffer hardships with much honor.) But it acquires fuller value with Don Lope, Crespo, Juan, and Don Alvaro. They all make their submissions, the old and the young soldier to war, Crespo to the peasant's obligation, Juan to his father. Don Lope's throbbing leg represents in a physical way the price in pain a proud spirit must pay when it takes up its harsher responsibilities. For the committed nobleman like Don Lope, the pain is unremitting; and Crespo's sympathy for the general is all the more genuine because his own sufferings are spiritual rather than physical.

But there are things which the proud spirit cannot tolerate, cannot *sufrir*. Any blemish of one's reputation is unbearable. Thus do rebellious rages rise up in the general context of the nobleman's willing subjection. Crespo and Juan flare up when they discover the captain's stratagem to catch a glimpse of Isabel. They particularly resent the officer's readiness to discipline Juan in place of Crespo himself:

Crespo: ¡Detened, señor capitán! que yo puedo tratar a mi hijo como quisiera y vos no. *Juan:* Y yo sufrirlo a mi padre mas a otra persona no. [1: 548]	Hold it, captain, I can treat my son as I please, but not you. And I'm willing to take it from my father but not from anybody else.

And when the captain, amazed at the men's resistance ("tan hidalga resistencia," as he later calls it in Isabel's case), asks what they were planning to do, Juan makes the perfect reply: "Perder / la vida por la opinión." (Stake our lives in defence of our reputation.) Inevitably, Don Alvaro asks how a peasant can have a sense of honor. He is told by Juan that honor in a peasant is the same as that in a captain. The statement is inordinate, revolutionary, and brings Don Alvaro into action with the oath: "¡Vive Dios, que ya es bajeza / sufrirlo!" (By God, it's abject to put up with this any longer!)

Don Lope's arrival prevents a first recourse to arms and also completes the parallelistic structure, for now Don Alvaro has in his presence a surrogate father to whose orders he can properly submit, as Juan does to Crespo. In addition, while castigating his officer, Lope strenuously objects to any outside interference, just as Crespo had in the case of his son. But in thanking the general for his timeliness, Crespo once again adverts to the terrible sense of risk animating *El alcalde de Zalamea:* "Mil gracias, señor, os doy / por la merced que me hicisteis / de excusarme una ocasión / de perderme" (1: 549). (Sir, a thousand thanks for the favor you did me by making it unnecessary for me to go the limit.) The general is understandably amazed and asks: "¿Cómo habíais, decid, de perderos vos?" (And just how was it going to be necessary for *you* to go the limit?) The resultant dialogue produces Pedro Crespo's famous riposte describing honor as an inviolable spiritual preserve, one which, by the way, has already been seriously impinged upon. But the critics have tended to overlook the question which provokes that response. It is a marvel of ambiguity, for Don Lope asks Crespo: "Sabéis que estáis obligado / a sufrir, por ser quien sois, / estas cargas?" (1: 549). (Don't you know that because you are who you are, you have to put up with these exactions?) The English rendering conveys none of the resonances of the key phrase in Don Lope's question, "por ser quien sois." That phrase almost invariably in Golden-Age literature refers to the moral obligation of the noble arising from his conscious and cultivated sense of his own nobility. Accordingly, when Isabel innocently pleads with the captain for Rebolledo's life, she bases her appeal on the obligation of the noble to protect women. Rebolledo has asked for Isabel's protection. She consequently asks Don Alvaro to extend the obligation from herself to Rebolledo, and clinches her argument with: "que esto / basta, siendo vos quien sois" (1: 547). (So much is quite enough, because you are who you are.) In other words, a simple appeal to the nobleman from a woman is quite sufficient. But now Don Lope applies the same consecrated phrase to Pedro Crespo, whose condition is that of a peasant but whose essence is noble and who therefore merits the unconscious tribute of being reminded of the duties of the base-born in terms reserved exclusively to the aristocracy.

Such is, indeed, the ambiguity of the whole Crespo family, especially Juan and Isabel, whose appearance is confusing. So it is that the captain, when he bursts in upon the women in concealment, must call Isabel a lady, *dama,* even though he knows she is a *labradora.* Crespo irritatedly reminds the captain: "Isabel is my daughter and a peasant, sir, not a lady."

This same ambiguity characterizes Don Lope's parting gift to Isabel. It is a *venera* thickly set with diamonds. Don Lope asks his host's daughter to take and wear it as a *patena.* We have already seen the very large significance accorded by Calderón in art and in life to the *venera,* a scallop-shell ornament worn by pilgrims to Santiago and, in far more elegant form, by knights of the Military Orders, that is to say, by men whose nobility has been investigated and found to be soundly based. It is therefore for Calderón the very symbol of true nobility, but one which can, as it is used for example in *No hay cosa como callar,* attest both to high rank and to base behavior. In *El alcalde* Don Lope transmutes this noble ornament into the country girl's characteristic paten, which the Autoridades dictionary describes as a "lámina ò medalla grande, en que está esculpida alguna imagen, que se pone al pecho, y la usan por adorno las labradoras." (A metal surface or medallion carved into an image, worn at the breast, and which peasant girls use as an ornament.) In Don Lope's gift, Isabel's refinement seems to solicit a response which, while witnessing her highborn manner, confirms her in her lowly condition, much as Philip's naming Crespo perpetual *alcalde* fixes him forever outside the ranks of the noble.

With Juan it is different. He is the dynamic member of the family, in transition. When Rebolledo announces to Don Alvaro the good news that, with the son's departure, there is one less enemy to fear, he describes Juan in a most striking way: "En la calle le he topado / muy galán, muy alentado, / mezclando a un tiempo, señor, / rezagos de labrador / con primicias de soldado" (1: 557). (In the street I met him, very handsomely dressed, very virile, simultaneously combining, sir, the last gleanings of the peasant with the first blooming of the soldier.) Father, son, daughter are thus hybrid creatures with a noble inwardness but a humble outwardness. Juan, however, is in the process of a metamorphosis that very likely will result in noble grandchildren for Pedro Crespo.

And, with the exception of the ridiculous Don Mendo, the largest common conceptual denominator in the play is a general willingness to "perder la vida por la opinión." Normally in Calderón plays the protagonists are not called upon to cover their bets, to make the ultimate sacrifice, although they often come quite close to doing so. *El alcalde de Zalamea,* exceptionally, as the instrument of definition, does make this demand of the two people who in a less serious environment would have been the work's young lovers happily united at the last. Don Alvaro literally perishes. He is very much Pedro Crespo's noble counterpart. Like Crespo, he stubbornly and haughtily persists in refusing to marry the lowly girl, Isabel, whom he has raped and dishonored. And, just as Crespo's rigid adherence to peasant rank creates for him an atmosphere of willing submission to duty that ideally characterizes the nobleman, so the captain's adamant refusal to marry Isabel dishonors him. The same attitude produces opposite results: *De una causa, dos efectos.* Nonetheless, in Don Alvaro's distorted understanding of honor, he would degrade himself by marrying Isabel. That view leads to his execution. Thus, quite literally, he sacrifices his life to his honor. The act, though cruelly misconceived, puts Don Alvaro on quite another plane than that of the craven Don Mendo, who will take no risk whatsoever and is therefore simply ignominious.

Isabel's rearing as a gentlewoman of the spirit has raised her to a height (she occupies the attic at the time of her fateful first encounter with the captain) where her existence is exposed to the workings of fortune. History is frequently disaster, and history horribly breaks in upon the interlude of her existence in the form of kingdoms, wars, and soldiers. A part of her tragedy is her father's excusable imprudence. As many critics have noted, Crespo is not wise to hide Isabel away. Moreover, he is too moved by and absorbed in Juan's departure to be as alert as he might have been at dusk, when a retreat into the house would have been a safer action. But Isabel is fundamentally a victim to fate. And she is compelled to sacrifice the expectations of a career as wife and mother to an understanding of honor which makes the helpless victim of rape unfit for the usual feminine role. Thus her life, in the customary sense, is lost to honor. Calderón would probably defend her lot by describing it as providential, the nunnery offering a spiritual wealth far exceeding the potential of an ordinary existence. Despite that, one mourns Isabel's sacrifice. Like Don Alvaro, she has lost, really lost. Honor in Calderón is not just a game. The pity is that Isabel had to be the sacrificial guarantor of *El alcalde's* mortal seriousness, though she survives, as her companion in dishonor, Don Alvaro de Ataide, does not.

Pedro Crespo is both the conscience and the consciousness of Zalamea. He takes pride in his humility and looks forward to a perpetuity of risk no greater than the material, crops and barns. This existence is an idyll in comparison with the agitations of those who live in the mainstream. But Crespo and Zalamea are surprised by history and time. The grand design violates their autonomy. This violation takes the form of various kinds of rape. Zalamea itself is entered. Crespo opens his house but reserves his daughter. She too, however, is exposed; and Crespo feels included in the invasion of her domain: "El se me entró en mi opinión, / sin ser jurisdición suya" (1: 568). (He invaded my honor without having any jurisdiction.) In the decisive culmination, then, Isabel is torn from her father's grasp and publicly violated. She unwillingly joins the company of La Chispa, a *mujer pública.* Historic time thus enters into private life, even into the private parts, and makes these intimacies public knowledge. Rape, cruel and shameful, is the instrument of this highly Cervantine penetration. It is the terrible price paid for a raising of the psychological consciousness which is called honor when it stirs in the minds of the high and therefore dangerously born.

Like Lope's Juan Labrador, Pedro Crespo would avoid every unnecessary engagement with historic time. But both peasants have children and consequently are inalterably committed. Pedro Crespo's paternity frames in Juan and Isabel the two major dimensions of human awareness, inwardness with the daughter, outwardness with the son. Because he profoundly identifies with each child, Pedro Crespo represents honor, which is the psychological corridor that links, most often conflictively, the female psyche with the male. Crespo is the vicar who richly participates in the full awareness of each of his offspring. Psychologically speaking, then, he is the psychiatrist exploring with equal versatility the problems of the female and the male. Or in a Platonic vein his consciousness is the original mold in which maleness and femaleness most closely and contentedly coexist. It is the monad of bisexuality that Aristophanes slyly describes in the *Symposium*. Nonetheless, as any father must, Crespo stands off from his daughter and son. His awareness of them is a constant, a continuum, a perpetuity. But they live in historic human time and are compelled to go their tragically different ways. These ways deprive Pedro Crespo of his children forever. Juan gladly goes off to the wars with a new and authentically noble surrogate father, Don Lope de Figueroa. He is lost to his father because he disappears in the masculine outer world of war. Isabel, dishonored, retreats absolutely into inwardness, into a marriage which, whatever its spiritual recompense, separates her altogether from her father without offering the consolation of grandchildren. Their respective fates are separate intensifications of the masculine and the feminine to the absolute, war on the one hand, prayer on the other.

In Calderón's cape-and-sword plays of the 1620s and 1630s, the father is a nonexistent or minimal frame to the conflicting masculine and feminine models which, at the last, are always joined and reconciled. Fathers intervene by accident or as an aid to the concluding resolution, as in *No hay cosa como callar*. The extraordinary feature of *El alcalde de Zalamea,* which owes so much to its less serious predecessors, is that the father dominates the action and is not noble, while in truth his own children have to be called noble. This painful situation does, however, create ideal circumstances for definition. Crespo resolutely keeps his distance from honor and so is objective with respect to its workings. At the same time he is passionately commited to his children, the consciousness of whose fate creates in Crespo's mind a complex of preoccupations that is equivalent to honor in the noble sensibility. Accordingly, through his children, Pedro Crespo has the subjectivity necessary for a great dramatic definition: the objective and subjective modes are Crespo's major functions. He is both a parent and a judge: "Hija, / ya tenéis el padre alcalde." Crespo thus not only frames but also participates in the action of *El alcalde de Zalamea.*

The play's ultimate paradox still is, of course, that the definer of honor is not noble. The explanation must be mythic. The creator, especially in a pagan sense, can create more than he himself is. Jove can think of himself as the maker of mankind, who as future Christians have a higher destiny than his own. Moreover, honor, as we have seen, is the second of Calderón's major fables. It is spun off by the Prometheus myth itself, is ancient myth made contemporary, an *aggiornamento* which actually occurs in *La estatua de Prometeo*. Honor in the technical sense is a principal Calderonian *mythos,* like classical myth a ready-made artistic hypothesis which the less cultivated are as ready to accept as the more cultivated are trained to accept the classical. Honor is an extended myth which easily translates into plot. But that plot almost always deals with events contemporary, more or less, with the time of the writing of the play. Honor is modern myth.

And Pedro Crespo is in Calderón the great mythic figure of honor, its definer. He is the Tantalus of honor, which he does and yet does not possess. Psychologically, considerations of honor govern him. But biologically he has no honor. And as he, like Tantalus, reaches out for honor, it eludes his grasp, taking the form of dishonor. Through Isabel, Crespo is perpetually afflicted and shamed, while through Juan honor lies just beyond his grasp. Crespo's sufferings are infernal, mighty, and tragic. He is as much the Prometheus as he is the Tantalus of honor.

Time is what has condemned Crespo to his purgatory of pain. It bursts in upon his world with a tragic impetus. Time in *El alcalde de Zalamea* is particularly historical and involves the person exposed to it in a whole dimension of adversity. History is, in fact, the third of Calderón's major fables. *El alcalde de Zalamea* is a dramatic border region between those plays in which the private myth of honor predominates and those in which a countervailing plot—history—is uppermost.

PART III

POETIC PRINCIPALITIES

The Private and the
Public Person in Calderón

"He [Lorenzo de Medici] was the
prince of his own poetic soul."

Ernest Hatch Wilkins

Two sovereign modes condition the rise and development of drama in Spain. In the first place there must be a personal mastery of circumstance, dominion over the outer world such as one finds in the Duke and Duchess of Alba when Juan del Enzina begins to write to and for them. Spanish theatre really begins at court. But service such as Enzina's was grudging, not because the servitor was surly but rather because the conscious artist, in fashioning a private universe which he alone commands, inwardly establishes himself as the rival and peer of the lord of the outer world, duke or king. Poets, cultivating power in privacy, can more easily avoid conflict with temporal might than can dramatists, who must depend on expensive public means to convey their message. Dramatists are therefore bound to the prince for and against whom they strive. Their vision is at heart poetic and private but it cannot be realized without the public purse. Accordingly, the dramatic poet engages power in a most complex way, needful of its support, resentful of its control, eager to create in art an independent and autonomous kingdom. The plays of Spain's first complete playwright, Juan del Enzina, reveal his long artistic struggle with his several sponsors, spiritual and temporal, church and state. They demonstrate his progressive liberation from the artistic dictates of both and culminate in the declaration of independence that is *Plácida y Victoriano,* a work in which the artist rules as absolutely as king or God, depriving man of life, like the king, and, like God, restoring him to it. *Plácida* is the first great *comedia.*

After Enzina, Spanish drama, contending with many masters, does not until Calderón regularly confront the supreme power of the state. On memorable occasions, however, Tirso and Lope do address themselves to the problems of political as against individual supremacy, Tirso most compellingly perhaps in *El vergonzoso en palacio* and *El burlador de Sevilla.* Both plays begin at a notable remove from their proper king and court but are inevitably drawn to the center of power. In three of his greatest dramas, Lope de Vega similarly studies the relationship between mastery of the self and mastery of others. In *Peribáñez,* a naturally noble peasant proves his superiority to a nobleman who cannot control his sexual passions. Here the prince is drawn to and conquered by the poet. The artist remains sovereign. But in *El mejor alcalde, el rey,* the sexual depredations of a provincial lord against his vassal draw the king of Castile into a disordered private feudal sphere which the monarch, representing himself, is compelled to annex. Thus a poetic individual anarchy is repressed and absorbed by greater might. The prince triumphs over the licentious poet.

El villano en su rincón, however, provides the richest spectacle of sympathy and struggle between the artist and the ruler. Juan Labrador has created from his own peasant family and holdings what appears to be the perfect private enclave, one that acknowledges the overlordship of the King of France without ever admitting the person of the king into its consciousness. The sovereign is kept out, so that he may not truly preside. Yet the barriers between public domain and private preserve have already broken down because Juan's children, like Peribáñez, are natural aristocrats who are powerfully drawn to the city and the court. In almost equal measure the king is drawn to his peasant rival, whom he visits incognito, but to destroy as much as to honor him. King Louis, then, simply exerts an irresistible counter-attraction, taking to himself the peasant's wealth, his offspring, and finally the man in person.

With Juan Labrador's installation as a great officer in the household of the king, Spanish theatre, symbolically and in fact, returns to the court which it left in the form of *Plácida y Victoriano*. Despite the profound spiritual distance of their art from the palace, Lope and Tirso nonetheless felt the enormous attractiveness of power, even though Philip II and Philip III did not care for plays and kept dramatists off. With the advent of Calderón, however, the prince has his poet at hand. The effect on Calderón's theatre, as distinct from Lope's and Tirso's, is notable. All three measure their distance from dangerous but indispensable political supremacy. Yet Calderón does so in close proximity to, in easy intimacy with, the power that he admires and fears.

One major spiritual situation of Calderón's drama is precisely at court, and this well before his extensive involvement with royal entertainment that began in the mid-1630s and lasted all his life. Literally and figuratively, then, Calderón is the poet who went to court, as Lope and Tirso (though for differing reasons they may have powerfully wished to do so) did not. A courtier's study is the king and may extend, if he is thoughtful, to kingship. In his drama Calderón studied, first with a spiritual kinship and then from first-hand observation, the sovereign and the institutions of sovereignty. His profound grasp of the many aspects of supreme power and of its effect on the king himself and on his courtiers and subjects surely is an essential feature and quality of his dramatic art. No other great Spanish dramatist of his time knew the king and kingship so well. For today's reader that may be a disadvantage. But this dimension of power and history in the royal individual is one of the great Calderonian deeps. His most penetrating analysis of kingship is *La vida es sueño*. But that play belongs to a little known and still less studied series of works which in plot and theme engage the complex of problems posed by the royal task of governance. In these, as in *Peribáñez, El mejor alcalde, el rey,* and *El villano en su rincón,* a ruling individual competes with his subject for the love of a beautiful young woman, also the ruler's subject. In perhaps the most complex elaboration of this basic conflict, in *Basta callar,* Calderón shows his own awareness of having developed a kind of dramatic subgenre by having Carlos remark in Act II: "Esto de amar el señor / y el criado una belleza / siempre para en que desista / generosa la grandeza. / Pues, empiécese esta farsa / por donde ha de acabar" (2: 1728). (When the lord and vassal love the same beautiful woman, it always comes to the eminence's nobly forbearing. So, let this farce begin where it ought to end.)

In each play of the series now being considered, the sovereign does always desist, but at the last, at the very last. His reluctance to surrender the woman creates the conflicts which in large measure constitute the play, so that, like marriage in most nontragic *comedias,* the ruler's act of self-sacrifice must be delayed until the end. In addition, Carlos's confidence that the duke in *Basta callar* will yield his claim may be appropriate to his own dramatic environment. His is what one might call a comedic confidence. But the king does not always obey the laws of comedy in Calderón. A powerful example is the rivalry which develops in the first part of *La hija del aire* between King Nino and his general Menón over Semíramis. Nino, when he discovers the woman's marvellous beauty and her engagement to Menón, behaves very much as Tello does towards Elvira and Sancho in *El mejor alcalde*. On the pretext of honoring his general's marriage with suitable festivities, the king delays the union of Semíramis with Menón and, using the time thus gained, arrogates her to himself. But Semíramis is as cunning as she is willing, and, Ann Boleyn to his Henry VIII, succeeds in getting the king to marry her. Menón is destroyed in the process. His fatal blunder was to entertain, in the face of a tragic royal reality, comedic illusion. Menón thinks that he is an actor in that series of plays in which the king finally does give way:

No, señor, cansado está
el mundo de ver en farsas
la competencia de un rey,
de un valido y de una dama.
Saquemos hoy del antiguo
estilo aquesta ignorancia
y en el empeño primero
a luz los efectos salgan.
El fin de esto ha sido—
después de enredos, marañas,
sospechas, amores, celos,
gustos, glorias, quejas, ansias—
generosamente noble
vencerse el que hace el monarca.
Pues, si esto ha de ser después,
mejor es ahora: no haga
pasos tantas veces vistos. [1: 736]

No sire, people are tired of situation comedies in which the king and his minister compete for a lady. This time, let's change that old routine of everybody's being in the dark and bring the whole thing out at the first encounter. The dénouement has always been for the one playing the king—after complications, involvements, suspicions, declarations of love and jealousy, satisfactions, delights, complaints, desires—to get himself under control with a noble liberality. So, if this is how things are going to turn out later, why not now? Let's not repeat something that is very old hat.

Nino, however, cannot and will not overpower his passion for Semíramis, and the tragedy of *La hija del aire,* a study in misgovernment, develops from Menón's misplaced confidence in a comedic outcome. *La hija del aire* is thus a comedy that has miscarried, consequently a new kind and concept of tragedy.[1] As such, it guarantees the seriousness of the conflict in the genuine comedies. It shows that the king is so powerfully tempted that he may not be able to overcome desire, may instead destroy his rival and appropriate the woman. The tragic potential in a comic situation provides Calderonian comedy with a considerable portion of that seriousness which critics have seen as one of its peculiar features.[2] Nor is Calderón the originator of the kind of play that fails to take shape in *La hija del aire.* Inevitably, Lope preceded him in Spain with *La mayor victoria,* probably written between 1620 and 1622, in the opinion of Morley and Bruerton. Lope's play perfectly expresses the basic formula—at the end of Act III, of course—where Otón renounces Casandra to Octavio: "Desto la Italia se asombre, / no de las armas y gloria / que me dan eterna historia, / pues sólo quien se venció / a si mismo, ése alcanzó / sólo *La mayor victoria.* "[3] (Let Italy be astonished not at those glorious feats of arms which give me historical eternity but rather at this [sacrifice], since the only person to attain the greatest victory is the one who has conquered himself.) Not only is the full formula present here but also its inherent association with history, which is a basic motif in the theme of the self-conquering king.

Theme and motif are not purely Spanish, either. Indeed, for obvious reasons, the flawed monarch tends to be a non-Spaniard, an Italian in Lope's play. All of Calderón's aberrant rulers in this series are likewise foreigners to Spain. By title, the plays constituting it, in rough chronological order, are: *Amor, honor y poder; Nadie fíe su secreto; Amigo, amante y leal; La banda y la flor; El galán fantasma; El secreto a voces; Darlo todo y no dar nada; Basta callar;* and *El segundo Escipión.* The first and last of these nine plays can reliably be dated 1623 and 1677.[4] Thus they span fifty-four years, practically the entire creative lifetime of Calderón. Their lustful rulers are King Edward III of England, Prince Alexander of Parma (in both the second and third works), the Duke of Florence, the Duke of Saxony, the Duchess of Parma, Alexander the Great, three *grandezas* in *Basta callar* (the Count of Montpelier and the Duke of Béarn and his sister Margarita), and finally Scipio Africanus in *El segundo Escipión.* Furthermore, both *La hija del aire* and *La vida es sueño* belong in the list for peculiar reasons, *La hija* as the antithesis of its comic thesis, *La vida* as the surpassing culmination of its problematics. They too portray foreign monarchs. Many other Calderón plays which examine rulers and princes in love (for example, *La cisma de Ingalaterra* or *Las manos blancas no ofenden*) might be included so as to extend the list. But the category would then lose its clarity. For this kind of court play develops the courtiers' awareness of the monarch, their constant study of her or him, into the monarch's awareness of himself.

These nine plays probe the conscience of the king in terms of self-consciousness. The dimension is, I would submit, a new one for the ruler in a Golden-Age play, where before Lope the sovereign existed but was not real in a problematical sense. Thus in a number of Lope's plays—*Peribáñez, El villano en su rincón*—country people, when they set eyes upon the king, are astonished to discover that there is human flesh beneath the robes of state, or a beard growing upon the august visage. Indeed, one central study of Golden-Age drama, as it also is with Shakespeare, is the nature of the ruler, of the king's two bodies, natural and politic. And one great discovery is that rulers are *menschlich, all zu menschlich.* But the artist probably finds himself even more fascinated by the monarch's engagement with time, with history, similar to his own struggle to extract from the wasting asset of a single brief life span an achievement that will endure, the *monumentum perenne.*

No figure seems better to illustrate the struggle with time that the artist and ruler have in common than Alexander the Great, who is a kind of archetype standing as colossal model for royal ambition. Lope in *El villano,* subtly alludes to Ludovico's predecessor when the French king calls Juan Labrador Diogenes. The peasant's unwillingness to look upon his king neatly parallels Diogenes' refusal to wait upon the victorious Alexander, who, like Ludovico, then feels obliged to go to the subject who will not go to him, although Alexander assumed no disguise. Still, Lope's monarch is more imperious than legendary Alexander. Alexander respected Diogenes' independence. Ludovico annexes Juan Labrador and his world.

Perhaps I violate a chronological notion of literary history by beginning to study the series of self-conquering kings with the Alexander of *Darlo todo y no*

dar nada. Hilborn dates the play 1651,[5] thus late in its class. But Alexander has
a primacy which may excuse my ordering. Calderón's play has, moreover, an
English predecessor in John Lyly's *Campaspe,* which was performed at court
on January 1, 1583/4.[6] Good in itself, Lyly's play has extrinsic interest. Lyly's
English editor, R. Warwick Bond, wrote at the beginning of this century that
"In *Campaspe* . . . Lyly may claim to have produced the first English histor-
ical play. . . . It is further remarkable as the earliest original prose-play in
England."[7]

I very much doubt that Calderón knew *Campaspe.* He surely had no English, if *Honor amor y poder* and *La cisma de Ingalaterra* are any indication, for
no echo of the actual English language is heard in either work, or, as far as I
know, anywhere in Calderón. My guess is that eighty years apart in time Lyly
and Calderón composed original plays by drawing, each in his own way, on the
same sources. Lyly's "chief source is undoubtedly the passage in Pliny's *Natural History,* bk XXXV. C. 10, narrating the surrender of Campaspe by Alexander to the painter."[8] Bond cites Pliny's Latin, in which the key phrases seem
to me to be those characterizing Alexander's self-control in giving his concu-
bine *(pallaca)* to Apelles: "magnus animo, major imperio sui: nec minor hoc
facto, quam victoria aliqua. Quippe se vicit." The last three words are the key
expression: "Indeed, he overcame himself." But the corollary that his sacrifice
was the equivalent of some victory on the field of battle also provides a basic
ingredient. Bond identifies the remaining sources of *Campaspe* as follows:
"For the historical matter, the relations of Alexander with Timoclea, Hephaes-
tion, Clitus, Parmenio, etc. Lyly drew on Plutarch's *Life of Alexander* in
North's translation. . . . We must look for the materials for Lyly's Diogenes
chiefly in the life of him included in Diogenes Laertius' *Vitae philosophorum,*
lib. VI. Ch. 2."[9] Those are the same sources suggested by A. Julián Valbuena
Briones in his introduction to Calderón's *Darlo todo y no dar nada.* But in contradistinction to Valbuena's ascription of the proverbial summation to a long
aphoristic tradition, all the materials for the phrase with which the self-
conquering king habitually closes the play lie to hand in Pliny's Latin, from
where they move easily into Lyly's English in the final dialogue between
Hephestion and Alexander:

> *Alex.* How now *Hephestion,* is Alexander able to resist love as he
> list?
> *Hep.* The conquering of Thebes was not so honourable as the sub-
> duing of these thoughts.
> *Alex.* It were a shame *Alexander* should desire to command the
> world, if he could not command himself.[10]

These concluding remarks, so strategically placed in *Campaspe,* suggest a
critical line which students of the play have not failed to grasp. Peter Saccio
quotes T. W. Baldwin's structural question: "Shall Alexander choose love or
arms?" and G. K. Hunter's broader theme for debate: "Wherein lies true king-
liness? Is it in the power to command others or in the power to command ourselves?"[11] Command, *imperium,* is certainly a vital element of *Campaspe,* as is

the conflict between love and war. But both questions somewhat narrow and distort Lyly's play. A choice between love and warfare, a gift for leadership coupled with an unsure hold on one's self, these formulations suggest a kinesis of conflict, inward and outward struggle. But *Compaspe* does not express itself in terms of energy. Instead, it is curiously static, visual. It arranges itself in scenes which, unlike Lope or Calderón, Lyly very clearly and Latinately demarcates: *Schaena Prima,* etc. This nonlinear and pictographic mode of narration, very suitable to a play featuring a painter and his beloved model, calls to mind church windows that relate the life of a saint. After all, Alexander is in this kind of play a secular saint, and the events proving his heroic virtue culminate in a renunciation that approximates martyrdom. Alexander immolates the commands of the body so as to liberate again his all-conquering spirit. In all of this there is a question of scale. Both in war and in love, Alexander is outsize, and he reproaches the frigid Hephestion for his failure to perceive the imperial intensity of his passion for Campaspe:

> Little do you know, and therefore sleightly do you regard, the dead embers in a private person, or live coles in a great prince, whose passions and thoughts do as far excede others in extremitie, as their callings doe in maiestie . . . none can conceive the torments of a king, unlesse hee be a king, whose desires are not inferior to their dignities.[12]

Here Lyly shows essentially a nonrelationship between Alexander and Hephestion. In war, Alexander has friends. In peace he has none, in Hephestion least of all, from whom his grandeur and depth of feeling separate him. In a window Alexander would be much larger than anyone in attendance upon him and would glow much more richly than his army or his court, as a result of the "live coles." This speech also places him in the dominant position which he rightly occupies. All events in *Campaspe* are scenes that compose themselves in clusters around his commanding figure, from which a tracery rib of incomprehension divides the lesser world. Martyrdom so far surpasses ordinary human experience as to be inconceivable to the witness. But it can and does evoke admiration, in the sense of both respect and wonder. Lyly portrays Alexander as wholly admirable, in love or out of it. But his sexual foible does not lead him into a commoner human scale. It too is part of his Jovian mandorla. Indeed, the passion for Campaspe expresses itself as admiration for her perfect proportions, echoing Pliny: "Namque cum dilectam sibi ex pallacis suis praecipue, nomine Campaspem, nudam pingi ob admirationem formae ab Apelle jusisset. . . ." (For when he commanded one of his concubines named Campaspe, to whom he was especially attached, to be painted nude, because of his admiration for her form, by Apelles. . . .) Thus both Campaspe and Alexander have subjectivity. But it is impenetrable. She is something on the order of a hardboiled virgin and resists all sexual advances. He will accept only kings as peers. We cannot understand sovereigns. Campaspe surely would have been wise to yield. But virtue is peerless and, especially when coupled with art, compels us to admire rulers, Alexander most of all. By forbidding comprehension, Lyly creates for us the spectacle of pure entertainment. Alexander has charismatic skills so far surpassing the normal that one cannot project oneself into his role. But one is not thereby deprived, because the elevation of his feats makes them all visible, although there is little or no human or logical connection between them. And this lofty and unapproachable visibility fills the spectator with wonder and awe, as if Alexander were an aerialist at the circus. His virtue is an incredible virtuosity. And Lyly's play, while of an exemplary classicism as to content, retains with powerful effect a medieval narrative technique based on visual display. All of this, though excellent in its own way, is very far from the Shakespeare of the Chronicles. It seems almost as if Lyly had failed somehow to make for himself the Renaissance discovery of time.[13] His play has, rather, the quality of the most classicizing Byzantine mosaics, those in the church at Daphne, for example, with Alexander as pantocrator.

Like Shakespeare, Calderón works very differently from Lyly, and even from Lope. Now, all the plays that portray the self-conquering king must in some very explicit way intone the phrase that epitomizes them. It is the theme that gives them their essential character. Calderón's formula varies significantly from Lope's in *La mayor victoria*. The adjective changes from *mayor* to *alto:* "Ea, valor, la más alta / victoria es vencerse a sí" (1: 1064). Lope stresses the moral dimension, Calderón its loftiness. But in *Darlo todo* this elevation does not serve to separate the supreme sovereign from all others, as in the case in *Campaspe*. On the contrary, the magic, defining phrase is a construction built on lower foundations, a pinnacle reached by dramatic process, so that the prince's ultimate sublimity expresses profound relations with his subordinates. The fundamental motion of these plays is, then, ascent.[14]

Because it powerfully assists the dramatic process of ascent, painting also plays an important part in *Darlo todo*. In Spain, even as late as Calderón's time, painters held low social rank and were taxed as artisans. Calderón himself wrote an eloquent defense of the nobility of the painter's calling, of its supreme position among the arts. Yet, despite Curtius, *Darlo todo* is not a *Traktat,* or treatise, on painting.[15] Portraiture has a clear dramatic function in the play, one closely connected with its structural tendency to rise. Good painting also involves an ascent from the physical person or thing depicted to the meaning or spiritual quality of what is portrayed, Leonardo's "motions of the mind." The kind of painting that characterizes *Darlo todo* is portraiture, art at its most humanistic and spiritual. Calderón's portraits accordingly begin with the physical but from there mount to a higher and deeper penetration of his sitters, so that in the end their very souls are persuasively painted.[16] Since fine painting strives, in Calderón's view, for this high goal, it is, though physical in origin, a noble art. On this point the critics often cite Don Juan Roca of *El pintor de su deshonra;* but his is, because of his tragic history, a dubious and complex example. *La fiera, el rayo y la piedra* presents the clearest defense of painting, although even it is not entirely unambiguous. Pygmalion joins Don Juan Roca and Apelles in the tiny but notable company of artists who have important parts in the *comedias* of Calderón. Toward the beginning of Act II he presents himself to Céfiro, who, once he has pronounced the name Pygmalion, interrupts him with the question:

Sois vos aquel a quien dieron	Are you the man whose painting and
la pintura y la escultura	sculpture brought him so much re-
tanta opinión que es proverbio	nown that it is proverbially said of
decir de vos que partís	you that you share with Jupiter the
con Júpiter el imperio	power of creating life and conscious-
de dar vida y de dar alma	ness, in metal as well as on canvas?
así al metal como al lienzo?	

Pygmalion replies that he blushes to acknowledge his excellence as an artist because some consider painting and sculpture to be a trade or craft unworthy of a
gentleman. Pygmalion defends his devotion to art by contrasting his leisured
and voluntary cultivation of it with the craftman's need to get a living from his
work. The gentleman artist is, literally, a dilettante, an amateur, whose
achievements the eighteenth and nineteenth centuries would call an accomplishment, a *gala,* or ornament, as Pygmalion describes it. Céfiro exalts Pygmalion's ability still more by ascribing to him a life-giving competence that approaches the divine ability to create life (1: 1609-10). The artist can, like God,
animate the inanimate. Góngora's sonnet on El Greco comes forcefully to
mind.[17] At the same time the mechanical skills involved in painting and sculpture have caused them to be classified as mechanical arts, *oficio.* In Golden-
Age Spain, the census lists generally divided citizens into the two categories,
taxpayers and nontaxpayers. Nobles did not pay taxes. Calderón's support of
the painters' petition to be exempt from taxes is not simply a generous mark of
esteem or an effort to help artists financially. It attempts as well to put painters
on a legally recognized noble level. Artistically, *Darlo todo y no dar nada*
amounts to a parallel enterprise. It establishes painting as a noble rather than a
mean or mechanical art. Calderón's Campaspe and Apelles are therefore quite
different from Lyly's. Both are of gentle birth and scrupulously observe an
aristocratic code of conduct. Apelles has recourse to elegant and courtly self-
effacement when his love for Campaspe collides with Alexander's. It is a manifestation of a whole phenomenology of moral refinement characteristic of the
later plays. Such acts of civilized self-sacrifice in connection with the competi-
tions of love at court or in a courtly atmosphere Calderón terms *fineza.* A quite
late play, *Fineza contra fineza,* is constructed on an increasing scale of clear
though muted sexual sacrifice. *Fineza,* a concept which I despair of rendering
into English with even several words, springs from sexual rivalry and transmutes the crassness particularly of the struggle between two men for a woman's
body into an elevating, ennobling process powered by the apparent renunciation by one competitor. Such renunciation is tantamount to a gift. And gifts
from one aristocrat to another, in the Calderonian code, subordinate the receiver to the giver. To give up the woman to one's rival is consequently to place
him in a morally inferior position, from which he can recover only by a greater
gift than the one he has received. The conflict of *Fineza contra fineza* is a basic
structural principle of *Darlo todo y no dar nada.* Artistically and morally it ed-
ifies the play, which rises on the joint framework of portraiture passing from
body to mind and of renunciation ascending to imperial heights. Noble in Calderón's lexicon means elevated; and for him the loftier a concept is, the greater
its reality, for he is, like most post-Renaissance writers, a philosophical idealist

who finds the greatest truth, vitality, and vividness in operations of the mind and soul rather than in the manifestations of matter.

In *Campaspe,* Apelles paints only Campaspe and gives her portrait a blemish so as to extend the sittings. In his play Calderón notably broadens the role of art to a point where one may say that *Darlo todo* is itself a portrait of Alexander. Now, according to Calderón, blemishes, defects, help the portrait painter. Apelles explains to Campaspe:

Como pintarse no pueden las perfectas hermosuras sin que el crédito se arriesgue cuando en un rostro hay lunar o desproporción que acuerde, cuando se mira el retrato, de su dueño las especies, es fácil el retratarle. Mas cuando es tan excelente que no hay término en sus partes que, desordenado, deje especies a la memoria, no se imita fácilmente. [1: 1046]	Because one cannot paint perfect beauty without risking one's reputation. It is easy to paint the portrait of a sitter in whose face is a blemish or asymmetry which reminds you of her features when you look at the picture. But when the face is so goodly that no single feature, by discordance with the others, prompts a recollection of the whole image, it is not easy to reproduce it.

Guido da Montefeltro's nose makes him easy to paint. But Campaspe's flawless beauty challenges Apelles' talent. He rises to its demands and depicts her with breathtaking accuracy and liveliness. Don Juan Roca, in *El pintor de su honra,* a talented amateur painter, throws down his brush in despair, for he cannot record the unblemished beauty of his wife Serafina. In marrying, the husband ventures his honor against the risk of his wife's infidelity. A beautiful wife, as Pedro in *Peribáñez* discovers, greatly increases her husband's danger. A painter wagers his reputation when he undertakes to portray perfect beauty. Maritally and artistically, the odds against Don Juan Roca are extremely high. He loses first at the easel. That failure prepares and announces his marital disaster. But even though Don Juan's acceptance of unreasonable odds involves him and Serafina in tragedy, the principle from which he acted remains sound. In life and art, nothing noble can be attained without risking one's dearest and most vital interests. Don Juan Roca is a noble and an artist who fails in both his enterprises. Apelles is an artist and noble who succeeds in both. They have in common the terrible danger to which they necessarily expose themselves.

In painting Alexander's portrait, Calderón begins with the blemishes. The play opens with a return to Athens after the first and partial Macedonian conquest of the Persian empire. The *gracioso* Chichón is a soldier of Alexander's and in his search for water encounters Diogenes. Calderón prefaces Alexander's appearance with that of the philosopher who is his opposite and who, like Juan Labrador, scorns to gawk at the all-conquering king. Between Alexander and Diogenes there is a poetics of desire and non-desire, of esteem and scorn, which, as in a Góngora sonnet, compares and contrasts value systems. Both Diogenes and Alexander have set *imperium* as their goal. Both are therefore seekers after supreme power. Their methods of achieving it radically distinguish them. Alexander employs force and government, Diogenes moral science, *ciencia,* knowledge which in its ultimate implications is Christian theology. A pre-Christian anchorite living in solitary contentment in his cave, the philosopher represents pure and independent ratiocination, pure consciousness. But mind like his has immense power, so that Alexander, positive, and he, negative, are royal reciprocals. Diogenes portrays his mastery of inner circumstance in Alexandrian terms: "este pobre albergue, donde / yo reino, y rey de mí mesmo, / habito solo conmigo, / conmigo solo contento" (1: 1022) (this poor retreat over which I rule and where, king over myself, I live by myself and am content with my solitary self). Ego very forthrightly emerges from this declaration. But it is a self which Diogenes has perfectly mastered through renunciation, noble renunciation. Thus he has risen to power through scorn while Alexander wears the diadem of desire. And his command is greater than the king's, so that he enjoins Chichón to inform Alexander that: "si él es dueño / del mundo, yo lo soy más, / pues en contrarios extremos, / él lo es porque lo estima / y yo porque le desprecio" (1:1024). (If he is the ruler of the world, I am more so, because, each at his opposite extreme, he rules because he values the world, I because I despise it.)

Here we have a pre-Christian reformulation of the struggle between the King of Fez and Don Fernando in *El príncipe constante,* inner sovereignty clashing with outer. Both plays work with a field of hostile and sympathetic elements, Calderón's basic construct. In *Darlo todo,* however, the sympathetic elements have greater weight. Alexander esteems Diogenes. Diogenes coolly inspects Alexander with the practiced gaze of a great diagnostician and finds his faults. The king lacks the power to correct these. The first is a physical blemish and is the prime feature in Alexander's dramatic portrait by Calderón: "con cuanto puede, no / puede enmendar un defecto / con que, para desengaño / de lo poco que es su imperio, / le dio la naturaleza en los / ojos" (1: 1023). (With all his power, he is powerless to correct a defect of the eyes which nature caused in him to show him how trifling his rule is.) In Chichón's rejoinder we pass immediately from the physical to the spiritual, perceiving that Alexander's crossed eyes symbolize his imperfect command of himself and that in this region also he is not yet able to overcome his faults. Chichón's description, almost disgustingly vivid, is the verbal equivalent of Guido da Montefeltro's nose: *ut pictura poesis:*

Yo confieso que, atravesados, es grande la fealdad que tiene en ellos, mayormente, encarnizado y lagrimoso el izquierdo, sobre cuyo hombro derriba la cabeza quizá el peso del laurel. Pero ¿qué importa ser horroroso su aspecto, si no le pasan al alma imperfecciones del cuerpo?	I admit that the crossed eyes are quite ugly, particularly so with the left one red and watery, perhaps because the head allows the weight of the laurel wreath to rest on its brow ridge [hombro]. But what does it matter if his appearance is horrible, as long as his physical imperfections do not become psychological?

[1: 1023-24]

But Diogenes' point is precisely that Alexander's physical blemishes represent psychological disorders: "con cuanto puede, no / puede enmendarse a sí mesmo" (1: 1024). (For all his power, he is unable to put himself right.)

And when Alexander does himself appear on stage, his first business is to cut the Gordian knot. Once that is done, however, portraiture again becomes a major concern. Efestión announces the successful conclusion of marriage negotiations with Rojana, the queen of Cyprus. Alexander has been in love with her ever since seeing her portrait. Efestión has promised Rojana a painting of Alexander and has commissioned one from each of Greece's three greatest painters, Timantes, Zeuxis, and Apelles. They now present themselves and their likenesses so that Alexander may choose the one representation that he prefers. Here again physical defect is the major issue, a blemish on the king's face. Timantes, in his portrait, suppresses it, to Alexander's wrath: "Infame ejemplo / da ese retrato a que nadie / diga a su rey sus defectos. / Pues ¿cómo podrá enmendarlos, / si nunca llega a saberlos?" (1: 1026). (This portrait sets a bad example. Following it, nobody would tell the king his faults. Well, how can he correct them if he doesn't know what they are?) Moral imperfections manifestly are the issue here, even though the physical is the point of departure for a discussion of them. On the other hand, Alexander takes offense at Zeuxis's too blatant depiction of the same blemish. Only Apelles finds a proper courtly *mezzo termino* by posing his subject in three-quarter view, with the blemished area in shadow, so that it does not appear, although the artful avoidance of it declares to the sitter that the painter is well aware of the problem. In satisfaction Alexander states to Apelles: "Buen camino habéis hallado / de hablar y callar discreto." (You have discreetly found a good way to speak and to remain silent.)

Applied broadly, this praise defines visual art which, though mute, can be eloquent. It also anticipates Apelles' response to the impossible conflict which arises when he and Alexander are both in love with Campaspe. Then the painter's fits of madness offer behavior that resembles painting. Even in madness, Apelles does not dare reveal to Alexander the cause of his illness. But he does find the means of unburdening himself to Diogenes, who informs Alexander. Apelles himself thus maintains silence and yet reveals the nature of his malady. In the traditional Alexander and Campaspe material, the central event is the portrait which Alexander has Apelles paint of her. Calderón retains this indispensable commission. But in his play he wonderfully expands the modes and functions of portraiture. First Diogenes and Chichón draw a verbal image of the king. Then the play involves itself deeply with actual portrayal, the pictures of Rojana and Alexander. Beyond that, Calderón compels behavior that communicates in the way painting does.

A similar richness of invention is to be found in Campaspe. For one thing, Calderón, drawing from the traditional material, compounds her and Timoclea. Timoclea is found in Plutarch's *Life of Alexander*. She was a noble and virtuous lady from Thebes. Soldiers looted her house and their captain raped her. When he asked her where she had hidden her jewels and other valuables, she showed him the well. And when he peered down into it, she pushed him in and stoned him to death. Alexander noticed her when the maruading soldiers brought her in as a prisoner. Impressed by her proud bearing and moved by her story, he granted her and her children freedom and immunity. Timoclea appears pretty much intact in Lyly's *Campaspe,* but Calderón takes large liberties with her, using her name as that of Campaspe's mother and altering the story. A sword replaces the well. About to be raped by the captain, Campaspe seizes his weapon and kills him with it. When his soldiers discover the body, they set out after Campaspe, and she makes her first appearance battling with them, wounded. Of course, Apelles intervenes to save her and falls seriously hurt just before the captive daughters of Darius, Estatira and Seroes, emerge from their quarters and stop the engagement. They order the soldiers to carry Apelles away, to hospital or to burial, and take Campaspe in. She knows neither the fate nor the identity of the man to whom she owes her life, but assumes that he is dead.

Complicating social and moral relationships by having one person save another's life is a favorite device with Calderón. For him life is the supreme gift, and so a second bestowal of it imposes supreme obligation. Typically in Calderón plays, the obligation which the receiver owes the giver conflicts with other commitments, so that the life-saving device helps to create a symmetrically rising structure of struggle which Max Oppenheimer has called the baroque impasse.[18] Alexander too is caught up in this web of contradictions. Like Heraclio in *La exaltación de la Cruz,* he has fallen in love with Rojana because of her portrait. But he holds Darius's daughters captive, even though their ransom has been paid. And now Campaspe, after her rescue by Apelles, adds a further complication by saving Alexander's life when his horse runs away while he is hunting. Campaspe owes Apelles her life because he protected her from Teágenes' soldiers. She owes Alexander at least great gratitude for condoning justifiable murder. For his part, Alexander knows that Campaspe has saved him and he commissions Apelles to paint her portrait so that he may hang it in a temple as a thanksgiving and votive offering. So it is that the series of lives saved leads to the play's central act of portraiture. This is proper, because Calderón thinks of artistic creation as a second making, divine like the first, a supreme gift. On the physical plane, saving a life is tantamount to the act of second creation that occurs in superb portraiture. Céfiro, in *La fiera, el rayo y la piedra,* hails Pygmalion for his artistic gifts as Jupiter's coadjutor: "partís / con Júpiter el imperio / de dar vida y de dar alma." Great art is, then, an imperial gift on a nearly equal plane with the divine.[19] Pygmalion shares Jupiter's *imperium.* In that perspective, Apelles equals and even surpasses Alexander. And when he shows Campaspe the marvelous portrait he has painted of her, the noble, the divine likeness, she upbraids her artist-lover for pandering to his Maecenas's desire by creating her image for him:

¿Qué es lo que miro? ¿Es por dicha	What is this I see? Is it canvas, or is
lienzo, o cristal transparente	what you place before me window
el que me pones delante,	glass which conveys my image so
que mi semblante me ofrece	vividly that it resembles me as well
tan vivo, que aun en estar	by being mute, because the voice ex-
mudo también me parece,	pires on the lips at the sight of it, so
pues, al mirarle, la voz	much so that not even my heart

en el labio se suspende
tanto que aun el corazón
no sabe cómo la aliente?
¿Soy yo aquélla o soy yo yo?
Torpe la lengue enmudece,
quizá porque el alma en medio
de las dos dudando teme
dónde vive o dónde anima,
no sabiendo, a un tiempo
entre una y otra imagen
mía, de cuál de las dos es huésped.
¿Esta habilidad tenías?
¿Segundo ser darle puedes
a un cuerpo? ¿Pues ¿cómo,
cómo, si tan divino arte ejerces,
tan bajamente le empleas,
que para otro dueño engendres
la copia de lo que dices que amas?
[1: 1050-51]

knows how it inspires voice? Am I she or myself? The fuddled tongue falls silent, perhaps because my soul, hesitating between the two, misdoubts as to where it abides or draws life in, unable to know as between one image and the other, which one shelters it. You had this power? You can give the body a second existence? Then how, oh how, if you practice so divine an art, can you so basely employ it that you would sire for another man the likeness of her whom you say you love?

Campaspe here reveals the essential contradiction of Apelles' situation. His art places him higher than Alexander. The subservience of this position as painter to the king, "pintor de mi cámera," sets him among the lowest, as a kind of domestic. Only Alexander's magnanimity can release Apelles from the insanely perfect balance between his exalted talent and the baseness of its applications. But, as Curtius has impressively seen, *Darlo todo y no dar nada* does evaluate the art of portrait painting and, by extension, its companions in creation, at the highest possible price. Alexander tells the great rival painters that: "los tres, sutiles y diestros / ejercéis el mejor arte, / más noble y de más ingenio" (1: 1027). (You three, subtle and skilled, practice the best of arts, the noblest, and the one requiring the most talent.) Calderón's moving appreciation would alone make the play in which it occurs memorable. But he has gone much further. He has, very early among artists, made another artist a protagonist in one of his own creations. *Darlo todo* is itself a fine achievement in verbal portraiture, dominated by Alexander's blemished but awesome image. To us, however, accustomed to the artist as hero, Apelles may offer still greater interest, for in him Calderón studies the functions of art, unforgettably and in a way uniquely descriptive of Calderón's own creative modes.

Art in the first place offers a very great contradiction between its goals, spiritual, and its means, physical. The handiness with materials that a competent artist must have makes of him a skilled craftsman, goldsmith, jeweller, whose social position was in Calderón's time quite low and an insurmountable impediment to nobility. When Philip IV nominated Calderón to Santiago, Calderón's father's profession as an *escribano* had presented an obstacle which the Pope had had to overcome, so that there was something of the artistic contradiction in Calderón's personal experience. Owing perhaps to the lesser role of matter in painting, Calderón, like Alexander, considered it to be the most spir-

itual of the visual arts. Yet it constitutes a paradoxical alliance between the inanimate means, canvas, paint, brushes, and the effect of animation which
painting attempts to achieve. Art, then, deals in the shifting patterns and pol-
icies of tendencies that Calderón categorizes as life or death. He also likes to
classify experience under the same headings, so that a summary of Campaspe's
history would begin with Teágenes' threat to her life, her murder of him, his
soldiers' attempt to capture or kill her, Apelles' lifesaving intervention, Estatira's appearance to the same effect, Alexander's merciful remission of the
death penalty, and finally Campaspe's saving of Alexander's life. There the
physical alternation between life and death ends and a metaphysical interca-
dence replaces it, especially in the recognition scene of the portrait. Apelles'
and Campaspe's misfortune is that they find each other only to lose each other,
are born to each other only to die to each other. Similar to her vital experience,
their emotional history involves a shifting array of the forces of life against
those of death. The scene of the portrait, in that perspective, posits supreme
agony and irony, for no sooner has Apelles brought the woman he loves to life
in enduring art than he must consign her image into the keeping of his competitor, a surrender that is spiritual death.

But the vital process, the historical process, teaches in its inflictions much
about the essential place and function of art. Art mediates, even though in and
through a maze of contradiction and paradox, between opposites, is a *coincidentia oppositorum.* Therefore, art lives along the moving line of battle, and
sympathy, between adversaries. This frontier, *limen* of attraction, *limes* of repulsion, is the very site, fluctuate though it must, more like tide than rank, of
Calderonian dramaturgy, of Calderón's poetics. The structure of the relationship between Apelles and Campaspe draws precisely such a tidal line, a waver-
ing rhythm of plenitude and emptiness, of rise and recession. He first possesses
her unknown beauty when he intervenes to save her, only to lose her, and himself to wounded unconsciousness. And Campaspe, having seen her deliverer
fall, likewise believes him dead. So each has experienced possession and be-
reavement in the first stage of their parallel history. Their second encounter
draws and crosses a familiar but essential Calderonian border, the metaphysical counterpart to the physical frontier between life and death that is traced in
the first encounter. This is the line between sleeping and waking, between unconsciousness and consciousness. It has already been explored in the discussion
of *No hay cosa como callar.*

Here in *Darlo todo y no dar nada,* Apelles has regained consciousness and
has been released without having to reveal his identity. But he has no notion as
to what Campaspe's fate may have been and, ruminating over her, wanders
aimlessly off into the woods. He does not yet know that Campaspe lies asleep
nearby. She has just saved Alexander's life and is obsessed with worry over
Apelles. So she escapes into sleep, with apologies to Apelles:

Permite, infelice joven,   Ill-starred youth, you who constant-
que horroroso representas   ly present in horror your dark image
siempre tu sombra a mi vista,   to my fancy, grant to so many appre-
siquiera un instante treguas   hensions an instant of respite, since

a tantos temores,
que no te hago ofensa,
pues son muerte y sueño
una cosa mesma
. . . . oh, tú,
intricado seno, alberga
vivo un cadáver. . . . [1: 1042]

I do not desert you, because death
and sleep are one. . . . Shelter, o
matted wilds, a living corpse.

Apelles, talking out loud to himself, hears Campaspe even before he sees her. Her exclamations from the depths of sleep coincide with his musings. So they embrace verbally. But only when he discovers her asleep is the narrowness of their intimacy revealed: "¿Cómo es posible que, siendo / ella la que está durmiendo, / sea yo el que estoy soñando?" (How is it possible for me to be the one who is dreaming, when she is the one who is asleep?) The question is strikingly reminiscent of Don Juan's observation in *No hay cosa como callar,* when he finds the beautiful Leonor asleep in his bedroom: "tú durmiendo y yo soñando" (you asleep and I dreaming). Thereupon Apelles apostrophizes this *belle au bois dormant* in language which might strike the casual reader as irritatingly conceptist but which in fact mentally perambulates the shifting ground between life and death which is both the zone and the chronology of their relationship:

¿Cómo puede ser, o bella
deidad, si eres homicida,
que yo te busque con vida
y que tú te halles sin ella?
Si a mi me toca el perdella
y a tí el haberla guardado,
¿cómo sin ella te he hallado?
                    [1: 1043]

If you are a murderer of men, how is it possible, oh lovely divinity, for me, alive, to seek you out and for you to be found lifeless? If it is my part to lose my life, and yours to have preserved it, how can it be that I have found you lifeless?

Apelles awakens Campaspe, who takes him to be the ghost of his dead self. But with considerable effort he convinces her that he is indeed alive. To her question: "¿no te vi a mis pies / muerto?" (Did I not see you lying dead at my feet?) he replies: "Ahora también me ves / aún más que la vez primera?" (So you see me again now, even more so than the first time?) The explanation of this second metaphorical death is perhaps the ultimate distillation of the poetic language of the *cancioneros:*

Como allá la herida
del cuerpo me dejó en calma
y aquí la herida del alma,
o bellísima homicida,
ha vuelto a darme la vida,
para que de una manera
aquí viva y allá muera,
sin morir y sin vivir. [1: 1044]

There, a bodily wound left me comatose and here, oh most beautiful murderess, a wound in the soul has restored me to life, so that, through a single mode, here I live and there I die, without dying or living.

Though complicated as an epitome of experience, Apelles' summation makes a
fairly simple point. Death interpenetrates life. The heightened consciousness of
the lover, like that of the artist, participates deeply in the two major modes of
being and non-being. With each breath drawn, the person who is fully alive expands to new plenitude and with each breath released expires into emptiness.
The artist takes the pulse of experience, finds the median of the sines of inhalation and exhalation, mediates between the extremes of vitality at its fullest and
mortality at its emptiest, purest.

And just as in his love Apelles' profound awareness probes the whole dimension of desire as well as that of desire's nullification, so in objective human
circumstance his artist's perceptions mediate between two kinds of attack upon
history, the positive assault of Alexander, the negative tactics of Diogenes.
Time is the enemy. It defeats all men. But certain men, before making that
final surrender, wish to fashion from history itself a fame that will outlast their
brief span, thus shaping victory from the very matter of defeat. Towards this
goal one may follow two principal routes, that of time itself, a course of ambitious self-realization along annuated paths of glory, or through withdrawal
from time, away from people and roads into the concavities of theological
meditation. To refuse to yield to the temptations of glory, to accept no gifts
from fortune, not to develop, suffer or mature, to remain unborn, childish, to
have no history—this second and negative possibility has the highest of high
values in the dramatic system of Calderón. The life of nullification of life
through the meditative intellect he calls *ciencia.* Only extraordinary individuals
develop it fully but it remains a potential in all superior humans, who, except
for servants, are the only people Calderón considers artistically (but not morally or socially) worthwhile. *Ciencia* in Calderón looks very much like the familiar face of Christian asceticism, except for its choice of foe, who is not the
medieval adversary, the world, the flesh, and the devil, but rather time itself in
the form of continuing consciousness, in the form of history. Majesty conquers
history by beating it at its own game, by outrunning it. *Ciencia* wins by not
competing at all. Majesty represents the broadest compass of the outer world,
ciencia the deepest penetration of inner truth. Even though Calderón values
ciencia more highly than he does majesty, he venerates both, so that a basic
conjuncture in his plays is that of the outwardly supreme person with the inwardly supreme, of the king with the anchorite, as when, in *La exaltación de la
Cruz,* the two princes of Persia seek out their former tutor Anastasio in his
cave, time coming to timelessness. And their initiative is significant, too, for
they go to him, not he to them. They need him, not he them.

So it is in the case of Alexander as against Diogenes. Two value systems
clash when they encounter each other. Alexander is an economic man. He desires to possess, and as soon as one desire is satisfied, another replaces it. In
short, he values and appreciates infinitely what this world has to offer. It is not
desire, however, which distinguishes him but rather the heroic scale of his aspiration and achievement. Like those who before him had tried and failed to un-
tie the Gordian knot, his enterprise is "noble codicia" (a noble covetousness).
Its grandeur makes it so. Diogenes represents Alexander's undertaking in a
profoundly negative aspect. Between them, the verbal play is that of *apreciar* in
contrast to *despreciar,* to function economically, setting a price on all things, as

against completely noneconomic functioning, refusing to put a price on any material or vital thing, refusing to live in the common way at all.

In his first conversation with Chichón, Diogenes, unwilling to seek Alexander out, explains that a man much more to his liking would be: "un hombre / tan sabio, prudente y cuerdo / que llorara que no había / otros muchos mundos nuevos / sólo para despreciarlos / más que para poseerlos" (1: 1023) (so sage, prudent and wise that he would weep only because there were not many other new worlds to despise rather than to possess). Turning Alexander's legendary regret about in this fashion is a wonderful touch which reveals the heroic goal that Diogenes, in his way, shares with Alexander. Yet those who strive to attain the same aim are competitors, and it is as competitors that they meet. Alexander neatly defines what both contend for: "la posteridad / de una heroica fama eterna / ¿será vuestra o será mía?" (1: 1038). (Will a heroic fame lasting for all posterity be yours or mine?) Diogenes' reply shows that his mind sees farther than contention, into the symbiosis of their conflict:

Diog. – Será mía y será vuestra.	It will be yours *and* mine.
Alej. – ¿Cómo?	How?
Diog. – Como quien dijere	Because anyone who will speak of
que vino Alejandro a Grecia	Alexander's coming to Greece will
dirá cómo visitó	also tell how he visited Diogenes on
a Diógenes en ella,	the occasion, so that, historically
con que en la historia vendremos	speaking, we will be running neck
a correr los dos parejas,	and neck, you because you made the
vos por hacer la visita,	visit, I because it left me indifferent.
y yo por no agradecerla. [1: 1038]	

Alexander's visit to Diogenes answers another purpose. It helps to rank the three kinds of sovereign male personality in the play—emperor, philosopher, and artist. Between Alexander and Diogenes, the question is as to who is more self-sufficient; and the philosopher wagers that the monarch will need his wisdom but that he himself will have no need of Alexander's wealth. And such is the case when, in Act II, Alexander summons Diogenes to diagnose the cause of Apelles' insanity. Desire is needful, but the vacuum of non-desire is absolutely self-sustaining, therefore more nearly perfect. Diogenes clearly outranks Alexander. Yet when Alexander asks Diogenes what he can do for him, Diogenes asks him to make another flower like one that he points to. Alexander of course cannot, and comments: "Eso fuera ser criador. / No cabe en la humana esfera / tan soberano atributo" (1: 1038). (That would involve being a creator. So sovereign an attribute is not within human competence.) But it is, because the artist, like God, can bestow what appears to be life, the "noble mentira" that is artistic creation. And so he, like Pygmalion in *La fiera,* shares supreme power with Jupiter and even with the succeeding Christian God. In consequence of that "soberano atributo," the artist outranks by far the ruler and the philosopher.

At the same time he serves them. Art produces delightful objects which kings commission and purchase because they covet all things that have value, all *riquezas.* A visit to any large museum will prove that painting has historically been a royal appanage celebrating the splendors of the sovereign. The more accomplished the artist, however, the greater his psychological penetration, particularly in the genre that most concerns *Darlo todo,* the portrait. The psychological acuity of the great portraitist can reveal the tragic emptiness of power and grandeur, as in Goya's portrait of the Countess of Chinchón. In probing such depths of disabusement, the painter serves the philosopher with eloquently mute testimony as to the hollowness of majesty. Thus the artist mediates between imperial pomp and philosophical disillusionment, creating illusions and disillusions, much as Apelles the sensitive man treads his painful way in love between the sea of death and the shores of life, partaking of each, struggling with each. In art and in life Calderón is illustrating through Apelles the principle of the balanced conflict between creation and destruction, being and nothingness. Though Christian in every conscious context, this structure and these notions much more nearly resemble formulations like yin and yang or a Manichean field of force. Artistically, Calderón is a Manichean, but gross opposition cannot do justice to his exquisite sense of the balance of opposites, of the commingling in opposition, and to his supreme portrayal of consciousness on the borderline between exaltation and extinction, a rhythmic line of oscillation that he draws with oriental force and delicacy. These abstractions take vivid, concrete form in the love that joins and divides Apelles and Campaspe, in the rivalry that merges and distinguishes Diogenes and Alexander. Yet the greatest aesthetic pleasure comes rather from a return to a delighted contemplation of the abstract pattern. Still, Calderón is simultaneously vital and stylized. Experience counts for as much as design.

And the hierarchy of monarch, philosopher, and painter has an experiential purpose. In the material ranking common to most societies, king comes first, followed by the philosopher and then the artist. By exploring the nature and attributes of painting, *Darlo todo y no dar nada* succeeds in painting a verbal portrait of Alexander the Great. It reveals his blemishes. It changes the conventional hierarchy by showing that Diogenes and Apelles possess qualities signally lacking in Alexander—the philosopher's self-control, the painter's constancy and self-sacrifice. Alexander's solution is simple and familiar. He absorbs Diogenes' and Apelles' virtues much as Ludovico absorbed Juan Labrador. But Alexander rejects their persons, sending Diogenes back to his cave and Apelles and Campaspe off to consummate their union out of his sight. Nonetheless, as a result of this merger, a new monarch appears, compounded of sovereign, philosopher, and artist, an extraordinary amalgam. Moreover, the play ends daringly, with a denial of sovereignty when Campaspe refuses to be disposed of in marriage by Alexander, even though she loves Apelles. She stoutly maintains that her love is not within Alexander's gift. True, she later explains to Apelles that she pretended not to love him as a stratagem, *fineza,* designed to ward off Alexander's royal rage. Nonetheless, her insistence that love is a privileged region of the free will exempt from royal rule creates a dimension of spiritual liberty that sharply distinguishes Calderón's Campaspe from Pliny's or Lyly's. With them, Pliny especially, she is a beloved object—an *objet d'art*—of which Alexander at great cost to his acquisitive instinct dispossesses himself: "dono eam dedit" (he made a gift of her). Lyly better approximates the ground broken by Calderón. Lyly's Alexander puts himself at some pains to determine the true feelings of the lovers, explaining to Campaspe: "I will not enforce marriage, where I cannot compel love" (5: 4). But both she and Apelles, once they are sure of Alexander's benevolence, freely admit their attachment to each other. The lesson is clear. Alexander, speaking of himself in the objective third person, remarks, not without bitterness, to Hephestion: "I perceive *Alexander* cannot subdue the affections of men, though he conquer their countries."

Lyly's Campaspe has less need of self-assertion than Calderón's. But Calderón's comes much more to life by adapting the main metaphor of the play to her independence. She begins as lovely pawn or chattel, a slave of the powerful, like the Persian princesses held in captivity for ransom, and to whom Calderón compares here by association. In the eyes of both Apelles and Alexander, Campaspe is an *objet d'art,* Pygmalion's statue. One miracle of art and love in the play is that she comes to life. But to come to life simply to love the artist who has called her into existence would mean for the living flesh to assume a bondage not unlike that of the statue's. Campaspe's freedom and independence derive from her unwillingness to be bestowed or at once to bestow herself upon Apelles. She conceives herself to be separate, distinct. She can make a true gift of her love and of herself only if she possesses herself, however briefly. Her refusal to be awarded, that modicum of disobedience, creates the independent person who can unhesitatingly choose her lover. Freedom is a major theme of *Darlo todo y no dar nada.*

Yet the only absolutely free person in the play is Diogenes. The others are all considerably bound, Alexander to his ambition, Apelles to his art, Campaspe to her love. Still, they all win greater freedom than they previously had. Campaspe and Apelles are able to love each other openly. Alexander, however, in accordance with his heroic scale, wins the most freedom of all by learning from Diogenes how to control his passions and his vices. In subjecting these he frees himself from servitude to them. Thus Diogenes enables Alexander to carry out that inner conquest of himself which is the most notable of his victories, "la más alta victoria." One paradox of *Darlo todo* is that the slaves are free and the master bound. Alexander learns from his underlings how to be free, or partly so. For the king is like the artist. He must serve history just as the artist must serve him. Freedom and disabusement come from whatever depth of psychological penetration they may achieve. Alexander's sacrifice of his love for Campaspe is meant to serve his image in time and history, to give his portrait substance: "no diga de ti mañana / la historia que toda es plumas, / el tiempo que todo es alas, / que tuvo en su amor Apeles / más generosa constancia que yo" (1: 1064). (I am not willing for history, which is pure insubstantiality, and time, which is pure passage, to record that Apelles in his love displayed a nobler perseverance than I.)

In performing the governance of himself, Alexander adopts the modes of the philosopher and the artist, who deal with the timeless inner world. But the ruler and the artist also have, even though it may be two-dimensional, large commitments to historical time. In this play, Alexander and Apelles collaborate to produce a portrait from which evanescent pomp—"plumas," "alas"—

is not absent. Alexander did after all have fantastic *grandezas,* and accuracy requires that they be shown. Yet certain actions of his suggest that his spirit surpassed the royal conventions. One, his generosity in connection with Campaspe, helps to bring the stylized hierophant to life, to free him from the bonds of a received image. The result is *Darlo todo y no dar nada,* a verbal portrait of Alexander the Great, in depth.

I have dealt with *Darlo todo y no dar nada* first and at some length because, although it is a late play, it is the only play in the series to deal directly with the historical Alexander the Great, who is the prototype of the flawed monarch. And for Calderón, to a considerable and surprising degree, blemish defines the monarch. One reason for his insistence on the failings of kings is technical. It is, as we have seen, easier to portray the great man whom passion at first overpowers than it is to describe the perfect prince, and far more amusing. But it is difficult not to feel that imperfection precisely characterizes the features of the prince. These Calderón calls "las especies." Such traits seem to brand the breed, to constitute the species of which Calderón is so pitiless and attentive an observer in his function as poet at court. And of course these plays do show important people compelled to face and correct rather gross faults. They therefore investigate psychological humiliation and self-discovery. In the course of such experiences, blemish is itself a *cognitio,* a datum from which the discoverer can refer to his old and new selves. The flaw is, as a result, essential. But the subject, the technique, the boldness of the treatment, Calderón's freedom and independence, all of these reveal a master exploring new and dangerous ground with the brilliance and autonomy of Velázquez and Goya. Indeed, the plays on the theme of the self-conquering king may be considered as something on the order of a Titianesque royal portrait gallery, a grouping easy to imagine in the case of a man who himself collected, in a fairly modest way, religious art.

Chronologically, the first subject to "sit" for Calderón was King Edward III of England in Calderón's first play, *Amor, honor y poder,* already discussed in connection with Edward's attempts to rape and seduce Estela, sister of his youthful subject Count Enrico of Salveric and daughter of the king's first minister. Edward conceives a violent sexual passion for Estela after her brother saves her life when her horse bolts and he stops it, much as Campaspe saves Alexander but with the sexual roles reversed in the later play. Edward's lust for Estela is matched by Enrico's love for the Infanta Flérida, who reciprocates, although the count and the princess are inept at expressing their feelings and furthering their cause. Edward's determination to bed Estela nonetheless dominates the play. Her brother naturally intervenes in defense of the family honor, except that the rank of his adversary greatly inhibits his freedom of action. In perhaps the best scene of a highly accomplished play, the two couples find themselves in the royal gardens. Estela accompanies Flérida. The two men have hidden themselves in the hope of an interview with their mistresses. Flérida and Enrico meet and quarrel. While they are thus engaged, Estela notices the king hidden in the shrubbery near the fountain of Venus, whose statue is the principal ornament of this part of the grounds. Estela hits upon the clever idea of warning Edward off by speaking to him as though she were addressing Venus:

Hermosa madre de amor,	Beauteous mother of love, who do
que aun entre mármoles fríos	still, even in cold marble, enjoy with
gozas de Adonis los brazos	many a lascivious embrace the arms
con tantos nudos lascivos,	of Adonis, tell that child god, if as
dile a aquese niño dios,	your son he obeys you, that I alone,
si te obedece por hijo,	to his despite, do free myself of his
que yo sola, a su pesar,	deceits, for if it were possible that the
de sus engaños me libro,	king himself should love me, and if
porque si fuera posible	the king were to undertake the slight-
que me quisiera el rey mismo,	est thing to the detriment of my
si el rey quisiera intentar	honor (yet he could never wish to in-
cosa contra el honor mío	jure honor that is most illustrious
(que no es posible que ofenda	and immaculate), I would say to the
al honor más claro y limpio),	king himself that I value my honor
al misme rey le dijera	more highly than his kingdom, more
que en más que su reino estimo,	highly than even the world.
y más que el mundo, mi honor. [2: 78]	

Unfortunately, Estela's tactic only increases Edward's ardor so that when, inevitably, Enrico blunders by, the king is struggling to raise Estela's hand to his lips. Now Enrico, enraged at his sovereign's temerity, pretends to take the living man for a statue and verbally excoriates it for the sins of the model:

Este es del rey tan natural retrato	This likeness of the king is so true
que, siempre que su imagen con-	that, whenever I look upon his
sidero,	image, I approach him with hat re-
llego a verle quitándome el som-	moved and on bended knee; thus do I
brero,	show my respect. And if the king
con la rodilla en tierra, así le acato.	were to offend in a way involving my
Y si el rey me ofendiera	honor, I would speak my grievance
de suerte que en la honra me tocara,	to this likeness and then I would tell
viniera a este retrato y me quejara,	it that very Christian monarchs
y entonces le dijera que tan cristianos	ought not to transgress the law, that
reyes no han de romper el límite a las	he should bear in mind that my an-
leyes,	cestors were perhaps the preservers
que mirase que tiene sus estados	of his kingdom, acquired with their
quizá por mis mayores conservados,	blood equally in conquest and in de-
con su sangre adquiridos,	fense.
tan bien ganados como defendidos.	
[2: 79]	

Edward cannot tolerate either the ruse or the reprimand, and slaps Enrico in the face. Unable to strike out at his king, Enrico wounds in his stead a courtier, Teobaldo. Edward has Enrico arrested and tried by the count his father for *lèse-majesté.* The count finds his son guilty and sentences him to death. Now only Estela can save him and, knowing how Estela will have to save him, Enrico forbids her to make any appeal. She disobeys and recites a long and highly operatic speech to Edward, brandishing a dagger, threatening to take her own life. But Estela does succeed in moving the king to forgiveness. He pardons Enrico, offers himself in marriage to Estela, and pairs Enrico with Flérida. Thus all organizes itself emblematically in anticipation of the inditement of the essential line, Edward's, of course: "Ya solamente he sido / quien vencedor se coronó vencido" (2: 88). (Only now have I become the victor crowned by defeat.) The verse sounds enigmatic but it expresses a fundamental dramatic posture and inquiry. Calderonian drama is an adversary system. Its heroes oppose time, and history in particular, and bend every effort to carry out their will. But more often than not they are defeated. Yet even in defeat the vanquished will seeks and finds advantages greater than those of victory, here in Edward's case, as in Alexander's, a moral triumph.

Victory in defeat and defeat in victory constitute a paradoxical pattern that fascinates Calderón, provides one of his basic dramatic structures.[20] As such it readily addresses itself to the problem of man in time. Yet the man most immersed in time, history's greatest captive, is the monarch. Calderón's kings all struggle mightily to break the embrace of temporal succession, and in defeat they succeed. Edward is not the third but the first of his dramatic line. Through him we also learn that art almost necessarily accompanies the royal progress. In that garden scene, the play's most novel and effective, Enrico approaches his sister with the disingenuous question: "Hermana, ¿qué mirabas en las fuentes / con tantos artificios diferentes, / mármoles y figuras?" (2: 79). (Sister, what were you looking at in the fountains, with so many different inventions, marbles, and forms?) She replies: "Estaba contemplando sus pinturas." (I was studying the paintings.) He then comments: "Es propio de los reyes / tener grandezas tales. / Bultos hay que parecen naturales." (It beseems sovereigns to possess such splendors. There are statues that seem alive.) Calderón, his art also a royal accompaniment, brings stage figures into intense dramatic existence, like the flesh and marble statues[21] that Estela and Enrico not in vain apostrophize.

Alexander the Great dons modern dress in two early plays that examine youthful amorous involvements of Alexander Farnese, Duke of Parma, Philip II's nephew. Alexander, Alejandro Farnesio to the Spaniard, was the son of Margaret of Parma and her second and much younger husband, Ottavio Farnese. Margaret was the natural daughter of Charles V and Margaret van der Gheenst,[22] a Flemish noblewoman. Philip named Margaret of Parma his first regent of the Netherlands, but took her son off to Madrid as a kind of hostage, and Alexander was raised in Spain in the company of Philip's son Carlos and Alexander's other uncle, Don Juan of Austria. At twenty, Alexander married Princess Maria of Portugal and established himself with her in Parma. But his father was still quite young and vigorous, and from youth Alexander inclined to warfare, chafed at inaction. He fought as a private gentleman at Lepanto in 1571 and greatly distinguished himself. Finally, in 1577, Philip sent him to the Netherlands with reinforcements; and when Don Juan of Austria died shortly after his arrival, Alexander replaced him as commanding general in Flanders, where he remained in that capacity until his own death in 1592. Farnese succeeded in recapturing for Philip all of the southern Netherlands, and it is generally felt that only his diversion by Philip from the northern provinces to the Armada and its allied land operations against England prevented the reconquest of the whole of the country. Alexander certainly was the ablest general sent against Flanders, and his reputation in Spain was exceedingly glorious, particularly for the sieges of Maastricht and Antwerp.

Lope chose Maastricht as the subject of his *El asalto de Mastrique,* judged by Morley and Bruerton to belong probably to the years 1600–1606.[23] The work suffers from the disadvantages common to siege plays, tendencies to pageantry and immobility. But it does very vividly portray the cursing general Don Lope de Figueroa, who also appears in Calderón's *El alcalde de Zalamea.* And Calderón may owe to Lope's piece the idea of beginning *El alcalde* with a loudly complaining soldier. Alonso opens *El asalto* by exclaiming against the hardships of war, hunger most of all. His lines: "¿no hay más de andar sin comer / tras una rota bandera?" (Isn't there anything but following unfed a tattered flag?)[24] strongly resemble Rebolledo's outcries at the beginning of Calderón's play: "¿Somos gitanos aquí / para andar de esta manera? / ¿Una arollada bandera / nos ha de llevar tras sí / con una caja?" (1: 540). (Are we gypsies, to have to go wandering around like this? Can a furled flag drag us along behind it, and a drum?)

As far as Alexander himself goes, Lope, when he introduces him, makes the obvious historical comparison between the two generals, to the Greek's disadvantage: "generoso príncipe de Parma, / Alejandro Farnesio, cuyos hechos / oscurecen las glorias de Alejandro"[25] (noble prince of Parma, Alexander Farnese, whose deeds darken those of Alexander). Calderón makes the same comparison, uninvidiously, towards the end of *Nadie fíe su secreto,* the first of his two Alexander of Parma plays, when the prince, about to yield Doña Ana to César, his favorite, remarks: "que hoy a Alejandro en grandeza, / como en el nombre, le imito" (2: 124) (for today I shall imitate Alexander in magnanimity as well as in name). This marking is much more discreet. But of course Calderón's play deals with the period in Alexander's life just previous to his departure for Flanders and glory. It ends with the events forming Lope's play in clear view: "Yo he de partir luego a Flandes / a servir el gran Filipo / Segundo, donde Mastrique / venga a ser el blasón mío" (2: 124). (I must soon leave for Flanders to serve the great Philip the Second, whereby Maastricht may turn out to be my shield of arms.) Certainly, Calderón's knowledge of Lope's play is more than a possibility.

But *Nadie fíe su secreto* is based in part on a myth of Alexander in private life at Parma. John Lothrop Motley, drawing heavily upon Strada's *De bello belgico* (Rome, 1653), tells the tale in Volume III of *The Rise of the Dutch Republic:*[26]

> His father, still in the vigor of his years, governing the family duchies of Parma and Piacenza, Alexander had no occupation in the brief period of peace which then existed. The martial spirit, pining for a wide and lofty sphere of action, in which alone its energies could be

fitly exercised, now sought delight in the pursuits of the duellist and gladiator. Nightly did the hereditary prince of the land perambulate the streets of his capital, disguised, well armed, alone, or with a single confidential attendant. Every chance passenger of martial aspect whom he encountered in the midnight streets was forced to stand and measure swords with an unknown, almost unseen, but most redoubtable foe, and many were the single combats which he thus enjoyed, so long as his incognito was preserved.

Motley goes on to tell how a Count Torelli recognized his prince even while duelling with him and so threw down his sword and begged Alexander's forgiveness. After that, the duke's nocturnal habits became notorious and he had to abandon them.

Calderón employs only a pale reflection of this anecdote.[27] In *Nadie fíe* the plot turns about sexual rivalry between prince and subject, as in *Darlo todo.* For two years Alexander's closest friend and first minister, César, has secretly been courting Doña Ana de Casteloí with, until recently, indifferent success. But now the lady has granted honorable assignation at her *reja.* Unfortunately, Alexander has just seen and fallen in love with the same Doña Ana. Unaware of this, César confesses his secret to Don Arias, another intimate of Parma's. Don Arias aggravates the initial blunder by telling Alexander of César's feelings. The prince determines to thwart his friend's love at all costs. Knowing that César's tryst is fixed for that night, Alexander, pretending to alleviate César's melancholy, keeps him with him all night as he makes the rounds of Parma in disguise. Here is the dim reflection of Strada's Farnese, without real swordplay, although the *gracioso* duels with a weapon of straw. Matters continue in this vein, with events favoring now the lovers and now the prince. But at the last, not unsurprisingly, Alexander masters his jealousy and his passion. From his point of view, the experience encompassed by the play is a successful trial in private life which prepares him for the much greater trials on the stage of history. For César the title surely is the message. Inopportune disclosure invites calamity. Thus the play works itself out against a background of broken silence.

Amigo, amante y leal is a reprise of *Nadie fíe su secreto,* featuring once again Alexander and Don Arias. The unlucky lovers are Félix and Aurora. And the problem is the familiar one of rivalry between the prince and his *privado* over the same lady. But *Amigo* has the complex structure and inverse hierarchy of *Darlo todo,* as *Nadie fíe su secreto* does not. Félix has three orders of obligation: love, friendship, and duty. He loves Aurora, is Don Arias's best friend, and owes the prince absolute loyalty. Since both Arias and Alexander have designs on Félix's lady, the going gets rather thick, especially when Félix is commanded to arrange Aurora's abduction and rape. However, he regularly disentangles himself and her by stratagems showing the greatest ingenuity. The solution comes when Félix arranges his commitments in a new sequence. When he returned to Spain, the order of his preference was love, friendship, duty. By the end of the play he is able to place himself last in the new ranking: duty, friendship, love. The capacity for self-sacrifice in an inferior has here the same didactic value as in *Darlo todo.* After Félix has—brokenheartedly, one must allow—renounced Aurora, Alexander finds the example edifying and applies it: "Como él se vence, podré / vencerme yo" (2: 382). (I will be able to conquer myself as he has himself.) But Félix is not done once Alexander has given up Aurora. He offers to renounce her again in favor of Don Arias, his friend. Disposing of one's beloved in this noble way may be rather grand in Félix but seems to make a chattel of Aurora. Fortunately she does not witness the two acts of self-sacrifice. If she had, she might have made a speech like Campaspe's. In the final scene she does come out after Félix with an unsheathed sword, understandably, for she has throughout been much put upon. But of course he and she make up. Still, she does come last, Alexander first. His name alone provides in this play the historic aura. *Amigo, amante y leal* shows how dangerous, exciting, and crushing an experience it can be to compete with one's prince. Somehow, Alexander always wins.

History recedes further still in *La banda y la flor* as, compensatorily, love and rivalry play an even greater part. In fact, the play modulates from the theme of competition between prince and private gentleman by creating a false struggle for Clori between Enrique and the Duke of Florence. Enrique really loves Lísida, Clori's sister. But as a purported adept at the game of love he has determined that the best way of securing Lísida's affection is to court Clori. The result has been an impossible situation, because now Clori is in love with Enrique, who does not dare abandon Clori. The duke's passion for Clori, to which he makes Enrique privy, adds new complications, as Clori does everything discreet in her power to encourage Enrique and discourage the duke. Enrique gets himself into increasingly greater difficulties until finally all parties descend upon the duke's country house—the girls' father and one of their suitors, as well as the duke himself—all resolved to have it out with Enrique. The duke gets to him first and wrings from him the confession that Lísida, not Clori, is his choice. The duke immediately awards her to him and also joins a second couple in marriage. But, though the way is clear, he abstains from taking Clori as his wife. Her disdain has killed his love. Nonetheless, Clori's interpretation does not seem quite right: "Pues sirva este desengaño / para todos de saber / que hacer del amor agravio / poco tiempo puede ser, / porque como dios, en fin, / triunfa de todo después" (2: 456). (Let all learn from my disillusionment that taking love as an insult can only last a short while, because, since love is a god after all, in the end he triumphs over all.) The meaning probably is that love triumphs vengefully, by depriving the person who has injured him (the offender being Clori) of any partner. But the fact is that revenge arises out of extinguished love and that once again victory resides with the prince, who disproves the emblem *omnia vincit amor: dux amorem vincit.*

This conclusion practically amounts to a rematch between Eros and the prince after the manner of Enzina's *Egloga décima,* in which Amor truculently challenges all comers: "Ninguno tenga osadia / de tomar fuerças comigo."[28] (Let no one dare a trial of strength with me.) Both Clori and the duke accept the challenge, with the result that Clori stands reproved and deprived (but not, one assumes, for long) while the duke enjoys both revenge and supremacy. Of course, implicit in all these tales of sacrifice and renunciation is the notion that love ought to be considered as an expendable though extremely powerful inclination. In a play somewhat reminiscent of Tirso's *Palabras y plumas,* entitled

Para vencer amor, querer vencerle, two noble cousins advance nearly equal claims to Ferrara upon the death of their uncle, the duke. To avoid litigation and warfare, the obvious solution would be for the couple, Margarita and César, to marry. César loves Margarita; but Margarita cares not at all for him and is disinclined to men in general, preferring power to love. César's response is to try to win his cousin's love by an incredible series of gallant sacrifices. When, despite all these and a long separation, Margarita still treats César with icy disdain, he resolves to destroy his love and cultivate in its place an affection for Matilde, a Hungarian noblewoman whose life he has saved and who loves him. Just as it is too late, Margarita begins to feel warmly disposed towards César and is punished by having to suffer his refusal to marry her so that he can marry Matilde. Here love is not absolutely, though it is no doubt temporarily, overcome as it is with the Duke of Florence. Rather, *Para vencer* shows the greater strength of reciprocated love as against love unrequited. However, all these plays do test the relative strength of love with respect to other deep feelings, and as we have seen it does not always prove the most powerful of them. Calderón, indeed, can hardly conceive of a phenomenon without its equal and opposite manifestation. In contradictory response to César's love, Margarita therefore harbors an anti-love which in the end destroys his dedication, as part of a conflict between Eros and Anteros.

In contrast to the extinction of unrequited love in *Para vencer amor,* in *El galán fantasma* the prince is only just able to stifle his jealous desire for a beautiful subject. The scene now changes from Florence to Saxony. Its duke is Federico, and he may reflect the Frederick the Wise who ruled at the beginning of the Reformation, or John Frederick the Magnanimous, whom Charles V captured at Mühlberg and forced to sign the capitulation of Wittenberg, probably John Frederick, although the direct impress of history on this play is slight. Protestantism plays no discernible part in it. Calderón mentions Guelphs and Ghibellines as the factions which have caused serious divisions in the country and among its great houses. This may be an indirect way of alluding to the wars of religion which devastated Saxony even more than other parts of the Holy Roman Empire. Protestantism may, moreover, help to explain the character of Duke Federico, Calderón's least estimable prince of the estimable ones. But his violent viciousness furnishes an essential element in one of Calderón's cleverest, most stageworthy, and most breathlessly exciting plays. If *Darlo todo y no dar nada* is the interpretive masterpiece of the series, *El galán* is technically the greatest, suspenseful from the first to the last, and a worthy theatrical successor to its more meditative companion piece, *La dama duende.* But *El galán* lacks the ambiguities of *La dama.*

Duke Federico and Astolfo are rivals for the love of the noble and beautiful Julia. Julia loves Astolfo deeply and openly. When she learns that the duke plans to remove Astolfo by murdering him, she begs her lover not to keep their usual tryst and begs his father Enrique to restrain him. But Astolfo's own jealousy drives him to go to Julia. At her house, the duke has gained admittance through suborned servants and comes into Julia's presence as Astolfo. No sooner does he reveal his true identity than the real Astolfo bursts in upon them. He and Federico duel; and Astolfo falls, apparently dead. The first act ends in a chorus of lamentation. Federico feels not the slightest remorse at having murdered a subject: "si mil veces viviera / le diera muerte otras tantas" (2: 646). (If he had a thousand lives, I would give him a thousand deaths.)

Julia deeply mourns her dead lover, and the duke continues his suit, now even more importunate. She seeks solace in the garden where so often she met Astolfo, while Federico prowls its walls and the street. Just as a servant is about to play some music to ease her sorrow, thumping sounds are heard to come from underground. Then from the earth emerges a terrifying figure— Astolfo. Julia's servants run away screaming. Julia faints. Astolfo returns to the tunnel. Hearing the disturbance, Federico and his little guard of servants break down the doors to Julia's house and rush into the garden. The duke ascribes the vision of Astolfo to the melancholy and disordered imagination of a sorrowing woman's mind. He dismisses all the servants, and, about to rape Julia, suggests that she call Astolfo to her defense. Unseen, he comes out from under the ground again, extinguishes the garden light, and moans and speaks most unnervingly. The duke commands lights to be brought. Their illumination reveals Carlos, Astolfo's best friend, who explains that, upon hearing cries of alarm, he rushed over and jumped the garden wall. Vexed and frustrated, the duke has no choice but to go home.

Once he has left, Carlos explains that Astolfo is not dead. And soon Astolfo himself appears to tell the whole story. His father, when he withdrew the body, discovered that his son still breathed. He placed Astolfo in a secret room, where a skilled and silent doctor tended him. And, to avoid any suspicion, funeral services were promptly held. Then Astolfo's father took him to a wild and remote place in the country to complete his convalescence. When Astolfo was well, his father came again with a horse and much of his fortune in the form of jewels. He told Astolfo to leave the country, but Astolfo could not leave without Julia. In secret he returned to town, staying with Carlos, his closest friend. Carlos's family and Julia's had been hereditary enemies and his ancestors had at one time dug a tunnel from their house to Julia's. The plan had been to make a surprise assault, but the opportunity for it passed, and the tunnel had remained a secret from Julia's family because the last few feet had not been dug away. It was the sound of Carlos's and Astolfo's final excavations that Julia had heard beneath her garden. Julia happily agrees to run off with her lover. Of course, they will marry when they are safe. But they will need to wait a while for Julia to prepare, and to convert her holdings into cash or jewels. In the meantime, they will again meet every night in the garden, thanks to the tunnel.

The complications of the third act defy summarization. But they would stage extremely well. Federico gives up open attack on Julia and instead plans an abduction. It miscarries when his henchmen carry off Laura, Astolfo's sister, rather than Julia. Moreover, the duke, in the confusion, discovers the tunnel. It leads to that final confrontation which characterizes most of the less serious plays of the 1620s and 1630s, and to Federico's very reluctant decision to sanction the marriage of Julia and Astolfo. But, like Alexander in *Darlo todo y no dar nada,* who wants Campaspe and Apelles to enjoy their blessedness out of his sight, he banishes the happy pair from Saxony. *El galán fantasma,* in addition to its technical virtuosity, places the errant ruler in the harshest light. His irruption into the lyric love of private existence is, like that of the *hombres salvajes* in the *Diana,* a murderous incursion, unrestrained and unrepentant. In this atmosphere, personal consciousness and public power have almost no correspondence, are nearly irreconcilable. Carlos and Laura do remain at court, but the principal actors must leave and are glad to leave. Calderón could only portray a foreign Protestant prince with such features. Yet Federico's traits—*especies*— are generic. Any prince is tempted horribly to oppress those around him. And they, with the heightened awareness that comes from honor and from art, are the least able to tolerate oppression that opens their lives to the leering public gaze. Often, then, as the agony of the encounter between a bestial ruler and a sensitive courtier draws to its close, either the ruler or the subjects must depart, to obscure exile or historic fame. Consequently, in these plays Calderón shows tyrant princes who shatter social structure and who, though by abnegation they may somewhat mend the damage, are destructive of order because their power is intolerably great.

Such monarchs are so often impelled to rape female subjects that it is not amiss to see their rule as a politics of rape in which the protective lover sacrificially intervenes—almost always successfully, it is true, but genuinely risking life in the process. With Calderón, in fact, death delimits even the cape-and-sword plays like *La dama duende.* The technical difference between it and *El galán fantasma,* is, first, the mortal presence of the prince. When he is around—Jove and his thunderbolts—we know that death presides, for execution is the prince's ultimate temptation, is in many respects *his* history. So death is the active presence, while life and love are the passive reciprocals. One ought really to call Federico and his breed the Black Prince, for he imparts, communicates destruction. In the first act of *El galán,* Astolfo receives death like an involuntary chalice. But, drinking of it unwillingly in the unthinkable duel, he himself becomes a black prince because, not having died altogether, and craft and circumstance aiding, he can wear death like an actor's protective clothing, Hamlet's mourning. Since death is the prince's principal weapon, one can thwart him only through death *and* resurrection. And this is the principal theme, the principal rhythm of *El galán fantasma,* whose nocturnal garden with its feeble light, extinguished and rekindled, recalls Mencía's fateful garden in *El médico de su honra.* She tragically flickers to a final extinction. But Astolfo is a Lazarus of love who flares his flame with the last exhalation of death. In the excitement of his perambulations as a soul who cannot yet go to rest—like Hamlet's father's ghost—we ought not to forget his real agony. Medieval legend had it that Lazarus's second life was a torment of grim expectation of the second encounter with death. Astolfo dies metaphorically several times in *El galán fantasma.* His agony was all for love. But where, even in exile, can he escape the death that defines his life and happiness? Calderón is the Black Prince of Poets.

In *El secreto a voces,* the lethal quality of supreme power is veiled but no less certain. Since, however, it depicts an unsuitable passion in a princess rather than in a prince, the battle is fought more with words than with swords. This play, then, offers a variation on the theme of the self-conquering king. The ruler here is a woman, Flérida, Duchess of Parma, a name with only novelistic echo, nothing historical except the duchy itself. Flérida loves Federico, her secretary, who loves Laura, one of Flérida's ladies. The same situation obtains in Lope's *El perro del hortelano* and in Tirso's *El vergonzoso en palacio,* except that neither Teodoro of *El perro* nor Mireno of *El vergonzoso* cares for another woman than his employer. Moreover, Teodoro is of lowly birth, while Mireno may be. But Federico is noble, although not of ducal rank. Flérida, therefore, would not create a shocking misalliance by marrying him. Their union is possible though probably not politic. Still, both of Federico's predecessors marry their high-born ladies, Teodoro by a grossly comical and *commedia-del-arte* kind of deception, Mireno seduced by his Madalena but opportunely revealed just afterwards as the son of a duke. Comic illusion in both cases makes up for a real and an apparent social inequality.

In *El secreto a voces,* a play quintessentially of the court, the lyric relationship between Laura and Federico runs many of the same dangers as that between Astolfo and Julia in *El galán fantasma.* The lovers must communicate. But in the closed world of the court, any communication is exposed to public scrutiny, especially on the part of its most public figure, the jealous and frustrated duchess. Language in *El secreto* thus plays a dual role, like that of the tunnel in *El galán.* It allows communication but conceals it. Speech and behavior throughout the play, though by and large speech is behavior, are encoded, use a cypher. In fact, Federico does contrive a cypher for him and Laura to use in public. In the end, during the last act, Flérida absolutely breaks that code and learns that Federico loves Laura and does not care for herself, whom he reviles to her face as "esa fiera, esa tirana / de Flérida" (2: 1242) (that bitch, that tyrant of a Flérida). Bitch is not an inappropriate name for the duchess, who, like the Duke of Saxony, goes to all lengths to keep Federico from his mistress, whose identity is not known to her with certainty until almost the end. But her power so terrifies the lovers that they attempt to flee her realm, though they fail. In addition, Flérida has Federico arrested by Laura's father. An essential further complication is that Enrique Gonzaga, Duke of Mantua, betrothed to Flérida but unknown in appearance to her, comes to Parma as a close relative of the Duke of Mantua, to inspect his bride and press his suit. Federico knows the duke, keeps his secret, and advances his cause, which is also Federico's. But the duke's presence as someone other than himself greatly augments the role of language in *El secreto a voces.* Letters fly back and forth between the duchess and the duke with a wonderful celerity, concealing more than they reveal. At the last Flérida must of course make the ritual sacrifice, with rather a better will than Federico of Saxony, for she does not banish the culprits and closes the incident by icily bestowing her hand on the proper and panting Enrique of Mantua.

In *Basta callar* Calderón combines the masculine world of *El galán fantasma* with the feminine dimension of *El secreto a voces.* The masculine side occupies a county, Mompeller (Montpelier) and the feminine a duchy, Bearne (Béarn). Background events begin in Mompeller. Count Federico of Mompeller and his subject Ludovico both love and court Serafina, daughter of Roberto, the ambassador of Bearne to Mompeller. Serafina prefers Ludovico to the count. Inevitably the two men fight over her, but Ludovico does not know the identity of his rival. In a duel, Ludovico wounds one of the count's servants and must flee Federico's jurisdiction. The count sends hired assassins after him. They attack him in a lonely place and leave him for dead.

But Margarita, sister of the Duke of Bearne, happens upon the grievously wounded Ludovico while she is out hunting and has him properly looked after. He recovers and takes service with the duke, whose *privado* he rapidly becomes. Margarita loves the man whose life she has saved. But her brother plans to marry her to the Count of Mompeller. Such indeed was Roberto's mission to the count. When the play opens, all the major parties are assembled in Bearne, even Federico, who has come incognito, ostensibly to learn more of Margarita but in reality to move ahead in his seduction of Serafina, who has returned home with her father. In addition, the duke himself is in love with Serafina. So he, Ludovico, and Federico are all rivals for her favors, while Margarita nurtures an unavowed but violent penchant for Ludovico, who at her court calls himself César. Frustration is once again, in this situation, the main action, the main weapon. Fearful to confess her love, Margarita does her best to keep Ludovico-César and Serafina apart. In parallel fashion, Duke Enrique succeeds in blocking every interview of Serafina with Ludovico. His rivalry with the count results in a second duel. Though it is stopped before either adversary can be hurt, the duke has Ludovico put in prison and Ludovico fears that his penalty may be execution. The Black Prince once more. At last, in a nocturnal garden scene with music, Serafina gathers the courage to declare her and Ludovico's love to the discomfited Margarita. The darkness also conceals, within hearing distance, all of Serafina's suitors—Ludovico, Federico, Enrique. Her act of utterance liberates her and her true lover. Out of a suffocating silence, Serafina has spoken. All the others, from noble or ignoble motives, have held their tongues but now speech defeats silence. Duke Enrique in response sanctions the union of Serafina with Ludovico and commands the joining of his sister Margarita to Count Federico of Mompeller. He himself is left out, and Federico and Margarita clearly are considerably less than overjoyed but consign their reluctance to a definitive silence.

Once again in *Basta callar,* Calderón has constructed a play on the musical basis of sound and silence. Nor is time, that third essential element of musical composition, lacking. It is present as a humorous notation in the person of Capricho, one of Calderón's most memorable *graciosos.* With him time is a magnificent obsession as soon as Margarita, very early in the play, has made him the gift of a sumptous watch, all enamel and diamonds. From then onwards, every act in which he takes part is viewed by him as a function of the watch and of chronometric time. But, more seriously, all other major participants in the play feel pressed for time, by time. So in Act III Serafina cries to Ludovico:

no en quejas desaproveches con celosos desvaríos este breve, este pequeño instante que el cielo quiso, a ruego de mis tristezas, mis lágrimas y suspiros, conceder a mis lealtades, que es muy precioso, muy rico el veloz metal del tiempo para hacer dél desperdicios. [2: 1738]	Do not abuse with accusations and jealous rantings this brief little instant of time that heaven, in response to my sad, tearful, and sighing entreaties, has been inclined to grant my steadfastness, for the fleeting metal of time is too terribly precious and rare to waste.

"El veloz metal del tiempo" is a novel image and suggests the costliness of time as it takes the concrete form of Capricho's watch, which, just following this scene, breaks because he has wound it too tight. Thus, in the next interview between Serafina and Ludovico, in the garden of her father's house, the lovers are again interrupted and Ludovico complains of the father's untimely arrival: "¡Que hubiese / de llegar ahora a romper / el hilo de tu discurso!" (2: 1742). (Why did he have to arrive now and break the thread of your argument?) To which Capricho, idiotically obsessed, adds: "Mi reloj debe de ser, / que también ha roto el hilo / de los suyos." (It must be my watch, because it has also broken the thread of its [arguments, i.e., mechanism].) Here Calderón contrapuntally juxtaposes the serious and the jocose apprehensions of the passage of time.

Stronger than time in *Basta callar,* however, is silence, paradoxical because, as in *El secreto a voces,* it speaks in its own cipher of suffering. Language for the mighty—*los poderosos*—becomes in *Basta callar* a prison house[29] from which they, unlike Ludovico and Serafina, cannot escape by means of liberating utterance. Their muteness is of course eloquent as dramatic technique. Yet even more startling is Calderón's ability to probe what one hesitates to call zones of repression, the dimensions of stifled utterance, that which people would speak but dare not, the unspoken. I believe that with this play Calderón has shown us that power rests upon the unspoken, the unspeakable. Those in power long for the gratification of free expression but know that to speak out will rob them of their strength. Therefore, they shut up. And the play leaves one in frightened contemplation of three silent sufferers who have a talent for inflicting pain and death, rather than in the presence of the joy of the happy lovers. Like sleep, silence is a mode of death and as it closes over duke, duchess, and count, the princes are laid in the blackness of their living tombs, *vivos cadáveres.*

It is fitting that the most finely orchestrated study of conflictive temporality in the sovereign personality should come last chronologically in the list of the eleven plays that centrally concern themselves with the problem of the inner as against the outer person. Like *Amor, honor y poder, El segundo Escipión* was first and probably last performed at the Royal Palace on November 6, 1677. Since poor Charles II's birthday was November 11, one assumes that this was the occasion;[30] and perhaps it gave rise to melancholy remembrance on Calderón's part. The physical contrast between Calderón's recollection of the eighteen-year-old Philip IV in 1623 and the nearly sixteen-year-old Charles II in 1677 must have been dismaying. But of course no hint of unhappy comparison is to be found in the play. Quite the contrary. As a kind of subtle flattery to the young king, who, I fear, could not understand it, *El segundo Escipión* chooses as its characteristically Calderonian subject a conflict between father and son in which the son, though chronologically later and therefore lesser, emerges superior to the father. There is a decided echo between *El segundo Escipión* and Carlos Segundo. The first address to Scipio, Flavia's in Act I, augments and intensifies this echo, unmistakably, anaphorically: "Segundo Escipión, segunda / vez digo, sin ofenderte, / pues ser segundo a tu padre / es ser primero a tus gentes" (1: 1414). (I say Scipio the Second a second time, intending no offense, because being your father's second means being first to those people in your keeping.) The remainder of Flavia's speech is built on the rhetoric of first and second as applied in particular to the first city of Carthage and *Cartago nueva* (Cartagena), the second Carthage, in Spain, the city which Scipio is now besieging and from which Flavia and the women for whom she speaks have been expelled.

The question of rank as a function of time, as a matter of seniority, grows perplexed when one considers that there were three Scipios of historical importance: father, son, and adoptive son, and that both the son and the adoptive son bore the epithet *africanus*. Publius Cornelius Scipio fought against Hasdrubal in Spain for seven years and died there in battle in 211 B.C. His son, Publius Cornelius Scipio Africanus (236–184/3 B.C.) is our hero and one of the very greatest generals. Polybius describes him as "almost the most famous man of all time."[31] The elder son of this Scipio, Publius, who because of poor health did not enter public life, adopted his cousin. The cousin, being adopted, took the name Publius Cornelius Scipio Aemilianus. In 146 B.C. he destroyed African Carthage and created a Roman province in its stead. For his victory, he also received the epithet *africanus;* but history distinguishes between him and the first *africanus* by designating the older and greater man *maior* and the younger and lesser *minor*. All of this, I believe, bears lightly but significantly upon the implied comparison in Calderón's play between Carlos Segundo and Scipio, second of that name but, according to Polybius, the preserver of his father's life during the engagement on the Ticinum, as well as the resplendent victor in precisely the same region where his father had met disaster and death. Thus, reversing biology and time, in a very Calderónian twist, the first Africanus surpassed his parent and, by saving his life, became his spiritual progenitor, a stature reflected in the term *maior*. By means of such comparisons, Calderón's history plays, though as historical works they submit to time, nonetheless attempt to reverse history, to rise above it: "yo valgo más que yo," and "la más alta victoria" are anti-historical phrases, defeatist, sublime.

As Valbuena points out in the "Observaciones preliminares" to *El segundo Escipión,* Calderón drew exclusively perhaps on Livy (26: 41-51) for his historical materials. These he characteristically fashions into instruments to serve his own idiom and purposes: Livy, using accounts other than Polybius or perhaps inventing (he himself exclaims, "There is really no limit to historians' lies"),[32] describes a violent rivalry between Trebellius, a soldier, and a marine, Digitius, for the mural crown, a gold ornament awarded the first man to get over the wall. In Livy, Scipio solves the problem by awarding each man a crown. Polybius speaks of Scipio's promise to his troops of mural crowns, plural. Calderón has Scipio, Solomonlike, break the prize in two, awarding one half to Egidio, the admiral, and the other half to Lelio, the general. These two friends, in *Escipión,* engage in an amicable but ferocious competition which derives from Calderón's basic understanding of the structure of the universe. The general and admiral represent each a natural element, land and water. These are both sympathetic and hostile: "unidamente contrarios y contrariamente unidos." Similarly, the men are firm friends but determined rivals.

In one case Calderón marvellously alters his source. Historically, Scipio conquered Cartago Nova in a day. One reason for the rapidity of his success was that the defenders did not man that portion of the city walls which faced what they thought was a deep lagoon, fed by the sea. In Polybius, the Roman soldiers notice the tide quickly ebbing from the lagoon. Scipio understands at once what is happening and sends his forces across the now shallow waters to scale the undefended walls. They spill into the city and help to bring about its prompt fall. Livy—and now he seems consciously to expand on Polybius so as to give Scipio a handsomer part—gives this account:

> He [Scipio] had already been told by fishermen from Tarraco who had been all over the lagoon in boats, or wading when there was not enough water to float them, that he could easily get across the wall of the town on foot. So now, when a message came to him that the tide was ebbing, he started for the lagoon with a party of 500 men. It was about midday, and a brisk northerly wind which had got up was helping to drive the water in the lagoon in the same direction as the natural fall of the tide, uncovering the shoal patches and leaving depths in some places up to a man's navel, in others scarcely up to his knees. What Scipio had found out by careful inquiry he now proceeded to attribute to the miraculous intervention of the gods, who, he declared, to let the Romans cross, were turning the sea, draining the lagoon, and opening ways never before trodden by the foot of man. He ordered his men accordingly to follow Neptune as their guide and make their way across the lagoon to the walls of the town. [p. 415]

Calderón combines this bit of inspired tactics with another incident, reported in nearly identical terms by both Polybius and Livy, who describe how an old woman, the wife of Mandonius, threw herself in tears at Scipio's feet and begged him to have the guards look after the women, her nieces, in their charge. At first Scipio did not understand that the woman feared that the lovely young prisoners were in danger of being raped. When he did, he gave orders for them to be protected. Of this incident Calderón creates Flavia and the women she leads after their expulsion from Cartago. In *Escipión* Flavia's gratitude to Scipio moves her to reveal Cartago's principal defensive weakness: "Esta es la puerta del mar, / porque como sobre arena / corre su cortina, a tiempos / derrubiada, suele en quiebras / ruina amenazar" (1: 1434). (It is the sea gate, because since its palisade is built on sand, which on occasion erodes away, it regularly threatens to collapse into the eroded faults.) Polybius shows a Scipio who masterfully seizes upon an unexpected opportunity and turns it to his advantage; Livy, a careful gatherer of intelligence who ascribes the fruits of reconnaissance to divine aid. Calderón takes away from him the whole plan of battle and puts it into the mind of a grateful woman, who describes it complete to Scipio and assures him of its accuracy by pledging herself and her followers to battle along with the Romans: "ya fieramente apacibles, / ya apaciblemente fieras" (now ferociously peaceful, now peacefully ferocious). The figure of speech, this chiasmus, forms a fundamental Calderonian paradigm of attraction and revulsion, sympathy and hostility. These women, though women still, *apacibles,* have been transformed by wrath into fighting men, *fieras.* Thus they peacefully make war and are warlike in peace. Their structure is built to the same specifications as the relationship between Lelio and Egidio, and Scipio uses Flavia's speech as an instrument for minimizing the rivalry between general and admiral, who interrupt Flavia's interview with their quarrel.

In *El segundo Escipión* as in *Darlo todo y no dar nada,* moreover, an incident which for an ancient author, Livy or Pliny, threw light on the temperance and magnanimity of the great man under discussion becomes for Calderón the essential challenge of the play. And *Escipión* develops this challenge even further than does *Darlo todo,* because in the latter Alexander does not learn who his rival is until nearly the end. Scipio finds himself faced with Egidio and Lelio as rivals early, although he does not discover that he has a powerful third competitor in Luceyo until the third act. But the point is that *Escipión,* unlike *Darlo todo,* which fills an interlude between Alexander's campaigns, deals with the battle in a very great variety of its manifestations, and that battle in this expanded, orchestrated sense begins with the play itself. The first line of *El segundo Escipión* is: "¡Arma, arma! Guerra, Guerra!" (To arms, to arms! To battle, to battle!)

Escipión's most public manifestation of strife is of course the Second Punic War between Rome and Carthage, as a function of which Mago and Scipio stand historically opposed at Cartago Nova. But Calderón, the great poet of adversity, generally presents conflict not only in conventional public terms but also in intimate, domestic, and private forms. Consequently, Flavia and her women fight the first skirmish of the siege. Sent out from the city, they immediately encounter a band of Roman soldiers who capture and despoil them and who clearly intend to use them sexually and enslave them. Flavia's troop, though weaponless, have a military bearing that moves Turpín to address them as "hermoso escuadrón" (lovely platoon). With these words the first set of reciprocals falls into place. The unexpected appearance of a group of females in the masculine world of siege warfare strikes a domestic note of privacy in circumstances of the most public nature. At the same time, these helpless females have a fierce devotion to their personal integrity which gives them a bellicose and masculinized air. In addition, once captured, the women in their despair voice an appeal for mercy that is fundamental to Calderonian dramatic structure, its second and superior motion. In most Calderón plays, the first movement proceeds, explicitly or implicitly, from the operations of time as history and fate, both of which tend, like the human span itself, to a mortal and disastrous conclusion. Individual and collective destinies are a timepiece, a mechanism that drives mortals to an inexorably appointed hour from which there is no escape, to which all must submit. Even in submission, however, the struggle with fate takes the form of mute or voiced appeal. With this appeal begins the second operation, the real and the vital one, of Calderonian dramaturgy. For if it is heard, the appellant is remitted from his irreversible sentence.

The two motions, in *Escipión,* figure most forcefully in Scipio himself. As the great general, as the man whose appointed place in history we ironically know before he himself does, he embodies the fateful effects of time as disaster for his enemies. Because of him, they are defeated, are destroyed, and die. He causes them to know the horrors of history, which for men and nations means, sooner or later, death, defeat, and disappearance. This, then, is the *first* Scipio. The deterministic pattern that he represents and executes Calderón calls *rigor*. But, like every other prime Calderonian phenomenon, it has its equal and opposite, in fact engenders its equal and opposite: *de una causa dos efectos*. The reciprocal of *rigor* is *piedad,* mercy to its justice, a personal antidote to awful public necessity, a "feminine" motion contrasting with a "masculine" one. Calderón's plays take place in a field of operations ambiguously and inseparably delimited, defined, by these two fundamental forces, which in normal sequence take form first as *rigor* and then as *piedad* and which, like the elements, are essences in Calderón's dramatic universe. When Sheba asks Solomon to forgive Joab and Semey in *La sibila de oriente,* Solomon replies with a definitive explanation of the ambiguous interrelationship of these two qualities:

Sabá, justicia y piedad
en igual línea se ven,
que son virtudes las dos
que no pueden exceder
una de otra, como efectos
participados de quien
ni puede ser más ni menos
y siempre vive en un ser.
Sabio es el rey que castiga
y poderoso es el rey
que venga agravios de Dios
ministro de su poder,
sin que deje la justicia
ofendida por hacer
lisonjas de la piedad
si virtud también lo es. [1: 1174]

Sheba, justice and mercy have to be seen in the same perspective, for both are virtues such that the one may not exceed the other, like the participatory phenomena that they are, the one unable to be greater or less than the other and both always aspects of a single essence. Wise is the sovereign who punishes and powerful the king who avenges wrongs offered to God, as a minister of his might, without leaving justice offended as a result of his paying his respects to mercy, if it also is a virtue.

Critics attempting to determine whether King Peter of *El médico de su honra* is cruel or just should ponder this passage.[33] Like Solomon, he is both and neither.

Here obviously, is another significant and important Calderonian border region, that between *rigor* and *piedad*. But what most concerns us now is their sequence. Flavia's troop first experience a *rigor* from which there appears to be no appeal. Their despair expresses itself in an authentically tragic course:

Todas. – ¡Socorro, dioses
  clementes¡
Todos. – No hay socorro.
Todas. – ¡Piedad, cielos!
Todos. – No hay piedad.
Todas. – ¡Hados crüeles, favor!
Todos. – No hay favor. [1: 1414]

Women in chorus. – Help us, oh
  benignant gods!
Soldiers in chorus. – There is no help.
Women. – O heavens, mercy!
Soldiers. – There is no mercy.
Women. – Defer, cruel fate!
Soldiers. – There is no deferral.

These choruses summon, conjure Scipio, who hears the appeal and spares the women. His penchant for mercy, springing from his first harsh self, engenders a creative second consciousness, a second person, son of the first but opposed to the necessarily cruel and dictatorial sire. This is the *second* Scipio, in creative conflict with his prime historical and deterministic self; and Flavia, rightly divining in her savior a new incarnation, properly proceeds to address him, in the speech previously analyzed for its objective historical resonances, as "Segundo Escipión."

Thus, temporally speaking, there are two Scipios: Escipión Segundo, a historical person who falls into his appointed ordinal place after his father, whose main theater of operations is the public arena of war and government, who has hereditary enemies like Hannibal and the Carthaginians whom he considers it just to wreak vengeance upon; and Segundo Escipión, the alter ego of the first, whom he transcends from history into immortality, whose base of operations is the inward consciousness, who from there, in a victory over the historic self, transmutes hatred and jealousy into forgiveness. The major drama of *El segundo Escipión* is the conflict between Scipio Africanus's first and second selves. It addresses the usual palace audience but most particularly and eloquently apostrophizes the unfortunate Charles II, for whom Calderón vainly hopes a second being as glorious as Scipio's:

mudando	Since fame and fate have already
el cántico su sentido,	drawn the curtain on the Second
puesto que Fortuna y Fama	Scipio, the unconquerable Caesar of
tienen ya el velo corrido	Spain, let them all, shifting the sense
el Segundo Escipión,	of the canticle, exclaim: Long live
español César invicto,	the Second Charles!
digan que el Segundo Carlos . . .	
Todos y Mús.—¡Viva! [1: 1457]	

There are, then, in *El segundo Escipión,* two theaters of operations, the outer campaign against Cartago Nova and the inner one that pits Scipio's second against his first self. The outer battle ends fairly soon, with the defeat and surrender of the city. But the inner struggle, beginning in Act I with the appearance of the beautiful Arminda, whom Scipio desires for himself, endures longer. Scipio delays his triumphal entry into Cartago as he wrestles with conflicting inclinations which he himself calls "esta interior guerra" (1: 1451) (this inner war). Though on a heroic scale (and our time has little liking for that dimension), Scipio is a fully realized psychological personality, richly developed in the public domain as a great general to whom all may have access through his fame, but even more richly developed in the private sphere. The public and the private selves obviously are symbiotic modes of each other. The structure of the play reveals their relatedness by timing the two triumphs so that they will occur simultaneously in a joint manifestation of victory and defeat. But their paces differ. The inner struggle is slower, more arduous, so that the outer must wait for it. And their techniques diverge. The intrepidity that wins the skirmish outside can lose the whole engagement within, so that the outer and the inner are hostile as well as sympathetic.

With conflict concentrated thus on Scipio in his first and second incarnations, the rest of the play repeats, develops, and modifies his definition into two conflictive selves. The first Scipio is natural. Talent, appetite, and inclination draw him along the highway to fame. The second Scipio is anti-natural, a product of civilized doctrines which curb, correct, and improve the natural impulses. The second self is thus an artifact, a work of art, related to the original of course but in certain ways, though not in all ways, superior to it. Accordingly, in all Calderón plays where it is a question of a second and regenerative self, one also finds a dialogue between original and copy, between the natural and the artificial being. Art is terribly important to Calderón, but not simply because he was a connoisseur of painting and sculpture. Rather, these re-presentations combine in a single new projection both the aesthetic and the moral. Redemptive inner consciousness, to be successfully cultivated, requires all the talent and application of which a highly skilled artist is capable. The civilized moral being is a work of art, faithful to the uncouth original and yet quite unlike it, each related to the other as the father is to the son, relatives who can be both like and unlike, physically and spiritually.

As it does in *Darlo todo y no dar nada,* art has major functions in *El segundo Escipión.* In the person of Luceyo, the Celtiberian prince who was captured on land by the Romans at the same time that their naval forces captured Arminda, his bride-to-be, it takes the precise form of a *noble mentira,* a noble lie. For Luceyo, as an ally of the Carthaginians, is fearful of revealing his true identity to Scipio, both for his own sake and for Arminda's. Consequently, he calls himself Uliceo, explaining that his involvement in the death of a man forced him to leave Spain for Africa, where he has been working as a sculptor:

me hube de valer de arte,	I had recourse to art. Learning it was
que siendo aprenderle gala	an accomplishment of the easy cir-
de ociosa juventud, más	cumstances of my youth, cultivated
por agilidad y gala	as a skill and adornment rather than
que por profesión (si bien	as a profession, although so noble a
tan noble que aunque le usara	one that even if I were to practice art
por profesión, me sería	professionally, I would consider it an
más que objeción alabanza	honor rather than a disadvantage,
por ser el de la escultura). [1: 1424]	since it is sculpture.

Again in this passage Calderón defends the visual arts as a noble calling, suitable for the gentleman both as avocation and vocation, but perhaps preferable as an avocation. And Luceyo uses sculpture as a forgivable deceit to protect himself and Arminda from Scipio. When Arminda's uncle reveals the true identity of the captive Uliceo, Scipio does experience great difficulty in checking his impulse to take revenge on his prisoner for an inherited grievance, Roman-Carthaginian enmity, the death of his father. But the point is that Luceyo's lie serves both an inherently dramatic and an apologetical purpose.

Luceyo and Scipio are not the only men in love with Arminda. Egidio and Lelio, admiral and general, have also been captivated by her beauty, and both hope that Scipio will prevent her marriage to an ally of Carthage and award her to them. The question between them is: which one? Lelio insists that he has the prior claim because while in Rome he had visited a famous painter's studio, when he came upon the portrait of an unknown beauty with whose image he

fell in love. When he saw Arminda, he realized that she was the woman portrayed. Egidio, for his part, maintains that he saw the actual person first, when
he took Arminda prisoner, so that his claim is the stronger. Lelio had shown
Egidio Arminda's miniature portrait, and when Egidio refuses to return it, the
friends unsheathe their swords. Scipio passes by at just this moment and con-
fiscates the portrait, which, like the original, remains in his possession until the
end of the play, when he delivers it to Luceyo as part of Arminda's dowry, in
the culminating action of his struggle with himself.

   The portrait adds another element of difficulty to Scipio's creation of his
second self. After the victory over Cartago Nova and Luceyo's exposure as an
ally of the enemy, Lelio and Egidio again appear before Scipio to press three
petitions—their competing claims to the mural crown, to the portrait of Arminda, and to Arminda herself. They argue forcibly along the lines of Scipio's
own first desire, to avenge his father, to protect the state, to satisfy his craving
for Arminda. In these several dialogues, the portrait plays a fundamental role
and almost succeeds in convincing Scipio that the rivals' reasons are as valid
for him as they are for Lelio and Egideo:

Lelio un retrato que vio	A portrait that Lelio saw subjugated
le rindió a su celestial	him to its celestial beauty. Egidio
belleza: el original	saw the original and lost his mind to
vio Egidio y también rindió	her beauty. Do I, who have seen both
a su belleza el sentido.	the portrait and the original, then,
Pues yo que el retrato vi	not have the excuse of both? Yes.
y el original. ¿no fui	Why then do I try to counter my own
quien de uno y otro ha tenido	inclination when the original and the
entrambas disculpas? Sí.	copy together plot against me?
Pues ¿cómo vencerme trato,	
si original y retrato	
se conjuran contra mí? [1: 1451]	

Scipio's soliloquy shows how the idea of portraiture connects with the difficult
emergence of his second self from the first. The whole dialogue—and consciousness is inner dialogue—is sustained between the original and the copy.
There is also a fleeting recollection of a Garcilaso sonnet here, particularly in
the verb "se conjuran." Its most famous line has already been recited, humorously. For Calderón has made a comical reprise of the rivalry between Lelio
and Egidio in the ignoble competition between the two *graciosos* Brunel and
Turpín. Turpín has stolen a jewelry box from Libia which she by chance recovers from him, but on opening it she finds only worn and worthless trifles, so
that she exclaims, slightly altering Garcilaso's first line: "¡Ay dulces prendas,
por mi mal halladas!" (1: 1438). (Dear treasures, discovered to my grief, alas!)
In the context of the original sonnet, the "dulces prendas" are things associated
with a mistress either dead or departed, but most likely dead: "¡Oh dulces
prendas por mi mal halladas, / dulces y alegres cuando Dios quería, / juntas
estáis en la memoria mia / y con ella en mi muerte conjuradas!"[34] (Oh sweet
features which to my grief I have found, gay and sweet as long as God did will,
in my memory you are one and along with it do plot against my life!)

   In these lines the poet comes across powerful reminders of a vanished love whose loss he feels with almost mortal bitterness. "Prendas" is a maddeningly vague term but must refer primarily to those gifts which lovers exchange; it translates quite nicely into English as "keepsakes," except for the English word's romantic and Victorian associations. It seems to me rather certain that the lady is dead[35] because of the phrase "cuando Dios quería." One lives or dies in obedience to the will of God. The "prendas" had a happy sense in life but bitter connotations in death. Verses 453-55 of Manrique's *Coplas* appear quite firmly to support the hypothesis of death: "que querer ombre vivir / quando Dios quiere que muera / es locura."[36] (For a man to want to live when God wills his death is insanity.)

Usually the "prendas" are assumed to refer to a lock of hair because in Garcilaso's *First Eclogue,* stanza 26, Nemoroso describes the lock of hair which he keeps about his person at all times in grieving memory of the dead Alisa. But this is hardly a necessary correlation. Indeed, I would suggest that in the sonnet the "prendas" are the features of the poet's lady as they appear in a miniature portrait, surely the basic gift exchanged by proper lovers. At the same time, as with the portrait, the lady's features are indelibly preserved in the poet's memory, so that there are two likenesses present in the poem, a mental and a physical one, the physical one comes across by chance and so painfully quickening the mind's recollection. Both, therefore, give rise to bitter reflections, like conspirators in an assassination plot, "con ella en mi muerte conjuradas." The "ella" refers to "memoria" which is the repository of the mental image.[37]

Likewise, in Scipio's soliloquy, two images are present, his impressions of Arminda in person and as depicted in the miniature. The effect of each image on Scipio is precisely the effect Arminda's portrait had on Lelio, that her person had on Egidio. This double appeal to the senses is another assassination plot in which the two representations of Arminda conspire to stifle Scipio's creation of a greater, timeless self out of and in opposition to his historical persona. He and Calderón ultimately are iconoclasts, since image subjugates and the person who breaks the spell of image breaks the image. Heraclio does precisely that in *La exaltación de la Cruz.* Scipio, on the other hand, destroys his image of Arminda by sanctifying it. He makes of it a votive offering in the temple of her union with Luceyo, a union metaphorically alluded to by Luceyo as the carving of a statue of Venus. And so he donates both the ransom money for Arminda and her portrait to Luceyo as an offering to Venus, Coelestis rather than Naturalis.[38] "Luceyo, haz de él sacrificio / a aquella hermosa deidad / que tu metáfora dijo, / al colocarla en su templo / y en vez del trasunto vivo, / pon en su ara ese retrato" (1: 1456). (Luceyo, sacrifice it [the ransom] to that lovely goddess alluded to in your metaphor, when you set her up in her temple and, in place of her living likeness, put this portrait on her altar.) Like the traveller who has safely reached home after a hazardous sea voyage and so hangs a miniature of his vessel in the temple of Castor and Pollux,[39] or the afflicted person healed of his malady, Scipio nobly casts away the passion that has tormented him, its image threatening to destroy the creation of his second and higher image of himself, sensual art in conflict with temporal art, time against immortality.

Since *El segundo Escipión* is the only historical play of Calderón's to allude to the reigning sovereign, and I believe his only play of any description directly to address either Philip IV or Charles II, the analysis of time should perhaps end with it. It does not. One last play remains to be considered. But, before turning to it, one ought to measure the range of *Escipión,* which, rather than a single study, is a whole portrait gallery. Charles's ultimate sire, as Calderón would have it, is Alexander the Great, in part because of the close traditional association of him with Scipio. Antiquity saw in Scipio the spiritual descendant of Alexander. Calderón brings Alexander/Scipio home to Spain and so repatriates the entire subgenre on the theme of the self-conquerer. In so doing, anachronistically, he calls his young Roman general "invicto César español" and thus adds to the list Julius Caesar and that other "invicto César español,"the Emperor Charles V, Carlos Primero of Spain, therefore Charles II's ordinal predecessor and great peninsular model. Together with his own father Philip IV, Alexander, Scipio, Caesar, and Charles V are the goodly company among whom Calderón places the youthful Charles II, last of his line. Such is the long temporal span of *El segundo Escipión,* a play that engages and submits to time in the form of history so as to escape from and triumph over it.

  Escipión has at least one other span, operating in space rather than in time as a kind of moral and aesthetic perspective. This is the distance that separates nature from art, "lo vivo" from "lo pintado." In contrasting the intensity of his passion, for Arminda with Lelio's, which originated in the miniature portrait, Egidio declares:

Cuando el bajel entró,	When the vessel came into port, he
también en suspensa calma	[Egidio, speaking of himself in the
la libertad, vida y alma	third person], like it, in a state of ar-
a su original rindió,	rest, yielded his freedom, life, and
de suerte que aquel cuidado	soul to its [the portrait's = Armin-
tan distante de éste está	da] original, so that Lelio's feelings
cuanto la ventaja va	are as far from mine as the advan-
de lo vivo a lo pintado.[40] [1: 1450]	tage of the living person is great over
	the painted one.

Egidio here expresses the normal, unreflecting assumption that the "real" thing is far superior to its counterfeit in art and that "lo vivo" and "lo pintado" differ widely. The whole tendency of *Escipión* inclines to the contrary, however, to a showing of the superiority of the anti-natural and civilized image over original nature, even though original and copy, like first and second nature, are nonseparable concepts. And since one's second nature comes into existence in a painterly fashion, art also expresses moral evolution, indeed absorbs it, for, although Scipio on several occasions makes the ritual declaration that he has won the greatest victory of all by mastering himself, his final act is the iconoclastic *envoi* of Arminda's portrait, in which the aesthetic overmasters even the moral, "lo pintado" outranks "lo vivo." Here, Calderón conquers morality by submitting to it, by so fully incorporating it into his dramatic aesthetic that it ceases to operate autonomously and becomes a function of art. Thus also does Cervantes solve, in the *Persiles,* the problem of the conflicting *imperia* of religion and art. In both works art triumphs by means of annexation.

El segundo Escipión dramatizes the deepest struggle of the sovereign personality with its primary and secondary natures. As a result, the identifying marks of inner conflict appear sooner and are more varied. The minimal expression of a ruler's throttling of his own desires in favor of more important interest is the formula: "Vencerse a sí mismo es la más alta victoria," voiced with small preparation almost at the end of the play, whose characters, when they learn of it, are amazed at the prince's change of heart. *Escipión* tellingly replaces this near-spontaneous conversion with a protracted inner siege. Scipio, observing Egidio and Lelio narcissistically in love with Arminda, is about to base his conduct on their flawed example when he experiences a revulsion from his rush of desire, and the final apothegm is pronounced, but well before the play's conclusion. This early enunciation extends the span of battle, greatly increasing *Escipión*'s dramatic intensity: "Mas ¡qué digo! / El que venció a su enemigo / ¿no sabrá vencerse a sí? / No, que en esta interior guerra / el vencedor el vencido / viene a ser / . . ."(1: 1451). (But what am I saying? If a man has defeated his enemy, can't he defeat himself? No, because in this psychological kind of warfare, the winner turns out to be the loser.)

Here Calderón transforms a hierarchical statement into vivid and as yet unresolved dialogue. Scipio hesitates to enter Cartago for his triumph because he has not got used to the presence in himself of two contrasting entities, the one externally victorious and at the summit of honor, the other defeated from within and thus in public terms, though not in private ones, without honor. Scipio must learn hypocrisy: "(Aunque más discurriré / qué medio habrá, qué partido, / en que, hipócrita, mi honor / no entre como vencedor / pues ya sé que va vencido)" (1: 1452). (Although I will give more thought to the way or means by which I can keep my hypocritical honor from making its entry as a victor, because I now know that it marches to defeat.) In this variation of the formula, the key word is "hipócrita," that awareness which perceives and measures the distance between seeming and being, between "lo pintado" and "lo vivo." Its Greek etymon, of course, means actor; and just as soon as Calderón's ruling personalities become aware of their two natures, they become actors, in their own frame of reference as well as from the point of view of the audience. The painful imbalance between Scipio's outwardly triumphant sense of himself and the vanquished inner man produces this magnificent portrait of a great personality at variance with himself, this splendid psycho-literary image:

¡Qué de cosas revuelvo en mi imaginación,
si es que a unir vuelvo!
¿Cómo mi honor, hipócrita, fingido,
triunfará vencedor yendo vencido?
Y más, habiendo, ¡ay cielos!,
en muda muestra sido
del reloj de un silencio adormecido
en callados desvelos,
despertado el ruido de los celos.

[1: 1453]

How many things beset my imagination when I bring them all together! How can my false and hypocritical honor go victorious to its triumph in defeat? All the more difficult, alas, because a jealous clangor has stirred, by the mute expostulation of its clockface, a silence nodding over its voiceless vigil.

When Scipio at last must act, the formula multiples, taking the new form of a hypothesis, a step forward from the previous agonized questions: "Mucho haré si lo consigo / y consigo que vea el mundo / que, de mí mismo vencido, / de mí mismo vencedor, / valgo yo más que yo mismo" (1: 1454). (I will accomplish much if I can do it, and make the world understand that, defeated by myself, victorious over myself, I exceed my own worth.) Scipio carries out his projected act of sacrificial self-transcendence, so that he can return to the syntax of simple declaration, expressing finally the basic formula in its essential culminating place:

y pues habéis visto	And since you all have seen that I
que he vencido no	have defeated the enemy not only in
sólo al campal enemigo	the field but also within, because I
sino al doméstico, pues	have conquered myself, the most
a mí mismo me he vencido,	notable victory consisting in the mas-
siendo la mayor victoria	tery of the self, let the triumph now
el vencerse uno a sí	proceed.
mismo, prosiga ahora el triunfo.	

[1: 1456]

Technically, one of the wonders of *El segundo Escipión* is Calderón's regenerative handling in it of a banality. Unfamiliar variations of it lead us, surprise by surprise, to the accustomed tonic intonation, now seen afresh owing to the novel variants. This development begins with self-interrogation through a question answered inconclusively in the negative. Since the negative is inconclusive, the questions revive even more compellingly in the indirect discourse of the second citation. They continue in the third but now contain an affirmation which shifts the balance of the debate from victory to defeat, from outer to inner. The phrase is "yendo vencido." The next step recasts the problem in the shape of a hypothesis, in the fourth citation. And finally, in the fifth citation Scipio's struggle, resolved, declaratively voices itself in the usual manner. This, his last utterance, reveals that the awakening, developing, and proper positioning of Scipio's inner being have constituted a parenthesis in the flow of outward historical time, that in fact the fashioning of the inner consciousness has held history at bay, given it pause, moved into timelessness. Therefore, when the play ends, we return to historical time: "prosiga ahora el triunfo."

Yet *El segundo Escipión* demonstrates more clearly and variously and brilliantly than its companion pieces how a single sentence, which is also a *sentencia*,[41] can define a species of play. This dramatic subgenre of Calderón's is novel and illuminating because it analyzes the psychological self of a historically notable person on a heroic scale, a feat which the epic is not prepared to accomplish. These plays are, then, psychological epics.

The best known of them is *La vida es sueño,* and its essential dialogue is, like *Escipión*'s, a constant exchange between the inner and outer phases of man on the heroic scale, a psychological Odyssey fitted into an Iliad on the conquest of kingship, a feminine rhythm flowing insensibly into a masculine one. I do not believe that it has ever before been made really clear to what dramatic

species *La vida es sueño* belongs.[42] Jackson I. Cope attempts an explanation in
the chapter on the play in *The Theater and the Dream,*[43] but from him we learn
what we needed no help to know, that Segismundo forms himself into a
philosopher-king or, better, king-philosopher, possibly, as Cope would have it,
on a Platonic model but much more probably in the Aristotelian[44] vein.

   La vida offers a fascinating variant on the theme of the conquered self, because the action and growth are here shared, as nowhere else in Calderón, between two persons, Basilio and Segismundo, father and son. Basilio decisively
influences the evolution of his son, and the key to Segismundo's behavior is his
father. Accordingly, the phrase that, in one major sense at least, defines the
play begins with reference to the father who, in *La vida*'s last few moments,
abandons all thought of further resistance and surrenders to the victorious
Segismundo. Then action stops while the son uses the prostrate father as an object lesson, a negative one at first but one which then gives way to a positive
recommendation: "La fortuna no se vence / con justicia y venganza, / porque
antes se incita más. / Y así, quien vencer aguarda / a su fortuna, ha de ser / con
prudencia y con templanza" (1: 532). (Fortune cannot be overturned by injustice and vengeance, for they only further arouse it. And so if one expects to
counter fate, he must do so with prudence and moderation.)

   The next prefatory occurrence of *vencer* is interrogative: "Y podré yo / que
soy menor en las canas, / en el valor y en la ciencia, / vencerla?" (1: 533). (And
will I, who am less experienced, less worthy and less learned, be able to overcome it?) After another mention of Basilio's erroneous methods, Segismundo
makes his submission to his father, answering his own question as to whether
the lesser person can perform the greater deed, whether the *minor* can excel the
maior. Segismundo's success elicits from him this paternal benediction: "A ti el
laurel y la palma / se te deben. Tú venciste; / corónente tus hazañas." (You de-
serve the laurel and the palm. You have conquered. Let your deeds crown you.)
The way is now clear to the final and familiar sacrifice, in which Segismundo
surrenders Rosaura to Astolfo, making us realize that one basic plot has been
rivalry between the prince and his subject[45] for the favors of a lady, Segismundo vying with Astolfo for Rosaura: "Pues que ya vencer aguarda / mi valor
grandes victorias, / hoy ha de ser la más alta: / vencerme a mí" (1: 533). (Since
in my valor I still expect to win great victories, the moment has come for the
greatest triumph of all, that gained over the self.)

   Like Scipio, Segismundo engages himself in a lengthy debate before he repeats the tonic formula, although his inward struggle is less richly developed
here than the Roman general's is. But, anticipating the juxtaposition of the two
kinds of strife in *Escipión,* "campal" and "doméstico," Segismundo does
plunge himself into what is probably the play's most crucial soliloquy-dialogue
when Rosaura appears before him on the field of battle and he must decide
whether to rape her or to help her. A theatregoer accustomed only to the drama
of Ibsen and after would find the situation wildly implausible, absurd. But Calderón, as the great symphonic poet of strife, uses the meeting with Rosaura to
place inner anguish and indecision against its proper background of outward
battle, "interior guerra" against *guerra exterior, campal*. In reaching his decision, Segismundo argues both scholastically and poetically, the logical
method consisting in a *sic-et-non* comparison of the two courses of action, the

poetical a more complex manipulation of the theme of *carpe diem,* in which the urge to take one's pleasure now inevitably though often reluctantly must express the reciprocal notion that it is well to defer immediate gratification in the interest of a higher pleasure.[46] With the poetic theme of *carpe diem,* both approaches are present, although one of them may be only implicit. Segismundo amply develops both ideas and chooses the second: "¡Vive Dios! que de su honra / he de ser conquistador / antes que de mi corona." (By heaven, my mission is to reconquer her good name even before reconquering my crown.) The military metaphor, a psychological conquest concomitant with victory on the field of battle, is most appropriate; and the insight Calderón affords into the inner processes of Segismundo's personality is extraordinary, contemplation even at the height of action. Scipio suspends the triumphal procession into Cartago Nova until he can so order his interior self that his satisfaction with it is equal to the satisfaction he takes in victory over the Carthaginians. Segismundo brings time to a stop in the midst of all the uncertainties of battle itself, creates an enclave of timelessness in time itself. But both heroes belong to history in Calderón's special sense of what is truly historic, time transcended. And *La vida es sueño* is the greatest in his series of plays which deal with man at his most temporal, as sovereign. Time presses down heavily on the monarch. He is its captive. He attempts heroic escape. But *La vida* is not the only great play of its group. *Darlo todo y no dar nada* and *El segundo Escipión* rank among Calderón's finest works. The point is that *La vida es sueño* is not unique, not *sui generis,* but clearly belongs to a dramatic species. The identifying phrase which Segismundo pronounces at his supreme moment proves the play's affiliation, as do many other of its features, above all the fundamental triangle of sovereign, subject, and berivalled lady. This information ought to change the critic's point of view and thus his interpretation.

For one thing, *La vida es sueño* belongs to history. It is not abstracted from time or place. Consequently, assessments like Joaquín Casalduero's, which positions the play in a symbolic twilight, are inaccurate: "The action occurs in imaginary time. Being bound by an oath is mentioned. Basilio is an astrologer-king. Poland and Muscovy are places that correspond to this time, that is, beyond the geographical experience of the audience. The spatiotemporal medium removes us from all concrete data. Within this nonspecificness, we have two sites, wilderness and the palace, the lair of the beast and the dwelling of man. The two poles of action—sleeping and waking—relate to each other in terms of light and time: nightfall, dawn, shadow, and light. This is the twilight world of the Baroque, the "confused" world of the Second Part of the *Quijote.*"[47]

It was in the sixteenth and seventeenth centuries that Western Europe began to form more precise notions of Russia and Poland, to acquire *datos particularizadores* concerning countries which had previously been on the periphery of the European consciousness. Drawn into northern European politics by Charles's accession to the imperial throne, Spain also participated in this new awareness of the East. Maximilian sent an ambassador to Ivan III of Muscovy in 1517. He was Sigismund von Herberstein. In 1519 Herberstein made himself known to the new emperor, Charles V, by travelling to Spain as the bearer of a petition from the Styrians. Charles sent Herberstein on a second mission to Muscovy in 1526. The fruit of the two ambassadorships was a book, Herberstein's *Commentarii rerum Moscoviticarum,* published in Vienna in 1549. Richard Pipes calls it "the most important of . . . early accounts" and adds: "It was based on good knowledge of the written sources as well as intelligent personal observations, and it provided westerners with the first serious description of Russian history, geography, government, and customs. Herberstein's book was the main source of continental knowledge of Russia in the sixteenth century, but by no means the only one." Pipes further notes that Italian, German, and Czech translations of the *Commentarii* appeared shortly after its publication in Latin.[48]

Another important early description of Russia was Giles Fletcher's *Of the Russe Commonwealth,* published in English in 1591.[49] Fletcher was an English merchant who had been to Russia. His book could scarcely have had much effect on Spain. But he does most interestingly and confusingly describe the house of the Grand Dukes of Muscovy, the house of Beala, as he calls it: "The chiefe of that house that advanced the stocke, and enlarged their dominions, were the three last that raigned before this Emperour [Fedor Ivanovich], to wit, *Ivan Basileus,* and *Ivan* father to the other that raigneth at this time. Whereof the first that tooke unto him the name and title of Emperour, was *Basileus* father to *Ivan* and grandfather to this man" (p. 15). Fletcher seems to be referring to four rulers: "this Emperour" and "the three last that raigned before" him but actually names only "Ivan Basileus," "Ivan," and "this man." What interests me most in Fletcher's discussion is the word *"Basileus,"* Basil in contemporary English, Vasily in Russian, Basilio in Spanish.

Three Basils ruled in Russia during the period that concerns us: Basil I (1389–1425), Basil II, "the Blind" (1425–1462), and Basil III (1505–1533). Until the accession of Fedor ("this man") Ivan was the only other name which Muscovite sovereigns bore. Thus, in a little over two hundred years, we have three Basils and two Ivans. My point is simple. If in the sixteenth or early seventeenth century one needed to choose an appropriate name for a Russian ruler, the informed choice would, in Spanish, be either Basilio or Juan, more probably Basilio, considering the Russians' use of the patronymic, which would make both Ivan III and Ivan IV Ivan Vasilyovich. Spanish did not render this peculiarity, so that Ivan IV (the Terrible) is denominated Juan Basilio in Lope's *El Gran-Duque de Moscovia.* Indeed, it was in the form of Ivan the Terrible that Russia perhaps most horribly impressed itself upon European awareness. The years 1560–1584 comprehended the second and "evil" phase of his reign. Their culminating event was the tsar's murder of his elder surviving son, also Ivan, in November of 1580. Ivan deeply loved his heir but struck him dead in a fit of rage. Fletcher's description is arresting: "As for the other brother that was eldest of the three, and of the best towardnesse, he died of a blowe given him by his father upon the head in his furie with his walking staffe, or (as some say) of a thrust with the prong of it driven deepe into his head. That he meant no such mortall harme when hee gave him the blow, may appeare by his mourning and passion after his sonnes death, which never left him till it brought him to the grave."[50]

But, since the ducal and imperial line apparently ended with Fedor, who died childless, Ivan's murder was only the prelude to a sensational chain of events which, in the early seventeenth century, startled all Europe. The Ivan the Terrible had a third son, Dimitry, born in 1582 to his seventh wife, Maria Nagaya. With his oldest brother dead and Fedor without issue, he was the heir to the throne. But Fedor's weakness as a ruler permitted his brother-in-law, Boris Gudunov, to exercise the real power and to aspire to the crown. Dimitry, however, stood in the way. He died in 1591, under suspicious circumstances. He was said to have slashed his own throat during an epileptic fit. After Fedor's death in 1598, Boris accepted nomination as tsar. To Boris's consternation, in 1603 in Poland a young man came forward claiming to be the tsarevich Dimitry, miraculously escaped. He found a significant following among the Polish magnates, although the king, Sigismund III, was cautious of him. Dimitry invaded Muscovy with a small force in 1604. Within eighteen months he succeeded in defeating the troops sent against him, occupied Moscow, and was crowned tsar. Boris Gudunov had died and his son had been murdered. In Poland, the Jesuits and the papal nuncio had secretly converted Dimitry to Catholicism. Rumors of this conversion and Dimitry's otherwise unorthodox behavior helped his enemies incite a mob against him. Less than a year after his coronation, they invaded his apartments in the Kremlin and hurled him to his death. The fortunate first part of this incredible tale, including Ivan's murder of his son, provides the plot for Lope's *El Gran-Duque de Moscovia,* one of his better plays.[51] But Lope either composed *El Gran-Duque* before learning of Dimitry's fall or chose not to reckon with it. Ignorance of his hero's fate is the more likely possibility. At all events, his play, published in the *Parte VII* in 1617 and presumably performed at some time close to its date of composition, probably 1605,[52] represents the broadest, most popular depiction of recent Russian history in Spanish. And in this work Ivan the Terrible figures as Juan Basilio, as we have seen.

For *El Gran-Duque* Lope was able to draw upon abundant documentation. His precise sources remain a matter of dispute.[53] However that may be, several very widely diffused and exciting accounts existed. The earliest and most perfervid was Juan de Mosquera's *Relación de la señalada, y como milagrósa conquista del sereníssimo principe Ivan Demetrio . . .* (Lisbon, 1606). There is evidence of a Valladolid edition as well. Mosquera's work was not original but rather a translation of Barezzo Barezzi's *Relazione della segnalata e come miracolosa conquista del paterno imperio conseguita dal serenissmo Giovine Demetrio* (Venice, 1605). Mosquera and Barezzi had not yet learned of Dimitry's death. But the author of the *Légende de la vie et mort de Demetrius, grand-duc de Moscovie* (Amsterdam, 1606) clearly had. So had the person responsible for the *Tragoedia Muscovitica: sive de vita et morte Demetrii, qui nuper apud Ruthenos imperium tenuit . . .* (Cologne, 1608). If Spaniards had no access to these accounts, they had to wait until 1613 when Dr. Luis de Bavia published the *Quarta Parte* of his *Historia Pontifical, y Católica.* Already in the *Tercera Parte* (Madrid, 1608) Bavia had recounted Ivan's killing of his heir and the death of Ivan himself. In the *Quarta Parte,* musingly and bemusedly, Bavia tells Dimitry's whole disturbing and inconclusive story, repeating much of the tale of Ivan the Terrible. After his discussion, the publication of *El Gran-Duque de Moscovia* in 1617 must have seemed reasonably timely and topical. The *Historia* was quite popular.[54]

Late sixteenth-century history, however, linked Muscovy with Poland. In the second half of his reign Ivan fought a long and ultimately unsuccessful war with Poland in an effort to win access to the Baltic. Indeed, from the time of Ivan III, Muscovy had been a major adversary of Poland, and the Russian danger subsided only with the collapse of the Russians, after the death of Boris Godunov and the so-called Pseudo-Dimitry, into their Time of Troubles. Poland was, of course, Dimitry's base of operations. He married a Polish woman and his main supporters were Polish. In addition, Polish Jesuits had converted him from his Orthodoxy to Catholicism. Their powerful presence in that remote land climaxed a long clash between Protestantism and Catholicism. Polish Protestants tended to be a noble and intellectual elite, while the ordinary people remained Catholic. By skillful maneuvering and adroit management, however, the pope and his representatives were able to return the country to the Catholic fold after a period of Reformation which, at the outset, resembled the English Henrician model. The Polish kings, unlike Henry VIII, also remained firm Catholics but were forced to accommodate themselves to their largely Calvinist nobles. The papal nuncios and the Jesuits greatly assisted the sovereign in adhering to the old faith, and it is no accident that Barezzi's translator Mosquera was a Jesuit, *"religioso de la Compañía de Jesus,"* as his title plainly declares. Through Dimitry, the Jesuits and the pope obviously hoped to complete their Polish triumph by a conversion of the schismatic Russians. Poland accordingly was the West's prime vantage point for a Catholic look at Russia, Poland both hostile and sympathetic to Russia. In fact, the prime source for Barezzi and Mosquera, Luis de Bavia and Lope de Vega probably is the dispatch which Claudio Rangoni, the nuncio to Poland, addressed to Paul V. Dated July 2, 1605, it gives a very complete account of Dimitry, one which conforms in almost every particular to Barezzi-Mosquera and to Lope's *Gran-Duque*. It concludes with news of Dimitry's successes against Boris and in expectation of his ultimate triumph. At the beginning, the major events of Ivan IV's reign are rapidly reviewed, including the famous murder, with some extenuation: "mentre era travagliato dalla guerra che gli faceva il re Stefano, datosi in prede alla tirannide, amazzò Giovanni, su figluolo maggiore." (At a time when he was preoccupied with the war that King Stephen was waging against him, he gave way to wrath and struck down Ivan, his eldest son.)[55] But the point is that the nuncio to Poland is conveying to the pope his interpretation of past, present, and future events in Muscovy, thus linking the two countries as they were already linked through Polish support of Dimitry. His story forces one to consider the two countries together, especially since Dimitry's attack on Boris could not have been launched without the tacit condonation of it, and even connivance at it, of King Sigismund III. And just as a probable choice of name for a Muscovite ruler would have been Basilio, so a Polish sovereign in literature in the sixteenth and early seventeenth centuries was likely to have been called Segismundo. From 1506 until 1632, three Sigismunds reigned in Poland: Sigismund I (1506–1648), Sigismund II Augustus (1548–1572), and

Sigismund III (1587–1632). Dimitry's behind-the-scenes proponent therefore was Sigismund III.[56]

This historical linking of Poland to Muscovy, in friendship and in strife, carries over into Calderón's *La vida es sueño,* where the two kingdoms have many bonds and much hostility: Polish Clotaldo's tenebrious affair with Violante, the beauteous Muscovite, that "mal dado nudo / que ni mata ni aprisiona, / o matrimonio o delito" (1: 528) (ill-tied knot that neither binds as marriage nor convicts as concubinage); Astolfo's claims to the crown of Poland in competition and conjunction with those of his Polish cousin Estrella; Rosaura's descent into Poland from Muscovy as she seeks either revenge on or marriage to Astolfo. However, that great separation which the royal names Basilio and Segismundo symbolize no longer exists as a political boundary in *La vida,* where the father is Basilio and the son is Segismundo and both are Poles. Nonetheless, those same two names, when examined in terms of the considerable knowledge of the sixteenth and seventeenth century history of Muscovy and Poland which reached and spread through Spain in vivid and popular recitals, purportedly factual as well as imaginative, point to a wealth of concrete events, places, and persons connected with the actual Poland and Russia of Calderón's time, especially during the period from 1580 to 1632. Calderón feels perfectly free, of course, to fashion his historical material to the specifications of artistic need. In that respect he exactly resembles nearly all Golden-Age dramatists, who do not feel bound by "history." Even so, *La vida es sueño,* in its major and essential outlines, emerges from a history and a geography which, although remote, were *known* and familiar to very many Spaniards. Poland was not to them the coast of Illyria or Arcadia but a real and tormented and tragic place.

It also seems to me that if the popular mind retained any single event from Russian history, it was that hideous blow that Ivan struck his son. Basilio delivers no physical blow against Segismundo in *La vida.* But the father is cruelly pitted against the son, and later the son against the father. To be sure, father-son conflict is a constant in Calderón. Yet this particular manifestation of it has a telling factual reinforcement. It is too careless, too simple, then, to say that in *La vida es sueño* Calderón leads us into a historically, geographically, and humanly generalized landscape. That Poland is a symbolic land where symbolic battles are fought would be difficult and useless to deny. Still, it is also quite dangerous to deny a masterpiece its primordial self, one that exists first—savagely, relentlessly, cruelly—in the horrors of historic time and place and fact and face. Calderón's Poland of the first casting is a wild and bloody place, inhospitable and frightening.[57] It is the Poland of history. From it another country emerges, a second Poland created by all the conscious counter-tendencies of art. The second is abstracted—stolen—from the first but never loses the memory of its historical horrors. Thus *La vida es sueño* is both in and against time, historical and anti-historical, specific and abstract. These seeming antitheses it fuses, but it does not wholly confuse them. Each retains a separate identity in interaction. The sense of confusion comes from the sum of *La vida*'s conflictive entities, its entire landscape of struggle.

La vida es sueño's commitment to time and place is thus fundamental to a critical appreciation of the play, is one of the qualities that make it, despite many attachments to the medieval past, a markedly post-medieval work. "Acudamos a lo eterno" (1: 530) (Let us cleave to eternity) is an aspiration which both the medieval and the Renaissance spirit can share. But Segismundo rises to that perception through profound personal experience of the transience even of royal splendor. He had himself to observe the withering effect of the passage of even a few hours or days to arrive at a truism, meaningless in the abstract, highly significant as an individual awareness. He and his companions in the play are therefore in time against time. And temporality in *La vida es sueño* is far from abstract, far from imaginary. The hours and the days and the years have tremendous weight. One can see it; one can feel it. Time triumphs. Man must yield. Astolfo tellingly describes his aged uncle, in Act I, before the king's first appearance, as "Basilio, que ya, señora, / se rinde al común desdén / del tiempo" (1: 505) (Basilio, who now, my lady, bends before time's contempt for any man). The king himself, in his long first speech, avows his age at the outset: "me confieso / rendido al prolijo peso [de los años]," (1: 507). (I allow that I am bent under the overbearing weight [of the years].) Consequently, Basilio first emits a semiotic signal with his body. Time has warped it into an unwilling literal *humilitas* or closeness to the ground. But the royal spirit rears with evergreen impetuosity of youth and pride: "pues, contra el tiempo y olvido, / los pinceles de Timantes, / los mármoles de Lisipo, / en el ámbito del orbe / me aclaman el gran Basilio" (1: 507) (for, in opposition to time and oblivion, Timanthes in paint and Lysippus in stone acclaim me, throughout the breadth of the world, as Basilio the Great).

Aided by the art that celebrates his deep learning, Basilio resists and tries to overcome time through a reputation for great wisdom. This compulsion to win out over the inevitable weakening and disappearance of the body through lasting fame is at root an artistic impulse. Calderón has already shown us Alexander in the revealing society of the great painter Apelles. He has also presented Luceyo in the congenial guise of a professional sculptor. Art accompanies prideful power as intimately and as easily as Titian associated with the Emperor Charles V. The sovereign and the painter are both struggling against time and oblivion. Theirs is therefore a natural collaboration.

Basilio's engagement with time, however, is considerably more pertinacious than the already compulsive yearning for immortality that produces greatness. The King of Poland, heavily involved under any circumstances with destiny, has, through the study of astrology, fashioned himself into a kind of Prometheus who steals the secrets of the future, with benign intent. His is a dangerous business because even a noble theft cannot, in an exemplary universe, go unpunished, and because a terrible power, far greater than Basilio's, guides in Calderón the course of time. By attempting to anticipate the gradualities of revelation, the slow and secret unfolding of fate, Basilio usurps, or would usurp, a prerogative that is God's. God controls history, not Basilio; but the king's competition with God, even though indirect, adds a sublimely misdirected grandeur to his stature, imbuing it with a further Promethean quality. Indeed, like Prometheus's fire, Basilio's knowledge is ambiguous—hurtful and helpful both: "¡que a quien le daña el saber, / homicida es de sí mismo!"

(1: 507). (For when a person's own learning does him harm, he is a suicide.) The thirst for fame can and does induce its seekers to perform suicidal acts. So Basilio proudly declaims that:

son las ciencias que más curso y más estimo, matemáticas sutiles, por quien al tiempo le quito, por quien a la fama rompo la jurisdicción y oficio de enseñar más cada día; pues cuando en mis tablas miro presentes las novedades de los venideros siglos, le gano al tiempo las gracias de contar lo que he dicho. [1: 507]	it is science which I study and appreciate the most, higher mathematics, by means of which I take away from both time and fame the right and duty to make new things manifest each day. Because when in my tables I see as present the events of ages to come, I wring from time permission to tell what I have told.

In Basilio, then, the struggle with time has assumed unprecedented proportions. Not only does he resist it, as sovereign and artist may and will, but also he believes he has arrogated to himself its principal functions. Basilio thinks that he has eclipsed time as the agent of revelation and yielder of secrets. He looks upon the future as a present certainty. Consequently, with a mind that in its own estimation easily overleaps the distance between present and future, the king can find no meaning in history. He has, as he supposes, stopped history by the exercise of an intellect so skilled and artful that its calculated images ("tablas") usher the beholder into the presence of a vision caught for all time, after the manner of a portrait painting or statue. His astrological reckonings are a magnificent self-portrait that steals the royal soul away from time. Basilio is a mathematical artist (*matemático* was the correct technical term for astrologer in seventeenth-century Spain and Europe) who, like Pygmalion in *La fiera, el rayo y la piedra,* and more so than he, would share divine power, ultimate power. The artist competes with God in his desire to create timelessness, life everlasting. Basilio's science, as he delineates it in his first speech, creates the illusion of just such a timelessness for himself. Astrology is his lyric voice, his lyric consciousness. The poet truly is at court; but now a king harbors in himself an artistry which, while perhaps pardonably narcissistic with respect to himself, becomes anti-art when he applies it to his major subject, his son. By scientifically perpetuating his own image, the king plays a positive role. He preserves. But when he turns his art to the depiction of Segismundo's future and a hideous form seemingly promises to come into being, Basilio attempts to suppress the ugliness which he foresees, becomes an iconoclast, an anti-historian. He then would destroy.

The father as creator and destroyer is essential to an understanding of the son. As Segismundo's father, Basilio is his creator. But as an astrologer-artist the king, by preventing the flow of time for Segismundo, prevents his unpredictable story from telling itself. The tale may be tragic or comic. But if art and history are to have any meaning it must be told. Consequently, just as Basilio feels that he has, with science, triumphed over time, so he strives to arrest his son's development in time, out of fear that the outcome will be a tragic humiliation for himself. The lyric halt in time that, with the father, expresses itself as pride in a wonderful reputation for wisdom, takes, in the case of the son, the form of a furious and agonized meditation on the reasons for his own suppression and eclipse. Segismundo's terribly moving first soliloquy is a lyric utterance, an expression of inner consciousness in near total isolation. But it lacks the civilized ease that one may expect in even the most aggrieved of personal poetic statements, in Garcilaso's *First Eclogue,* for example, There, Salicio and Nemoroso really are cruelly afflicted lovers, but their suffering has come as a natural consequence of time's passage, so that they bear the hurt as best they can, in highly controlled exclamations of grief, grief told with practiced grace. In contrast, Segismundo's outburst has the volcanic force of power long and wrongfully suppressed, of a narration not granted any voice. Segismundo is enwombed and entombed in his father's tragic mind, a prisoner of Basilio's vision of terror. But he does not know even that much of his own story. Nor can he be civilized without some sense of his personal and mankind's collective past, or without some notion of the future. The king's tyranny with time, his abolition of the prince's past and future, has built around Segismundo a poetic prison house by immuring his consciousness within walls of timelessness. Prisoners can often make their captivity tolerable by reliving the pleasures of the past and by looking forward to the new life that the future may bring. Segismundo has, as far as he knows, neither past nor future. His imprisonment is therefore unendurable.

The force of the first soliloquy comes from this agony. As the interrogative refrain clearly shows, the prince's first utterance does deal with freedom. Yet if we take the freedom that Segismundo has in mind to mean simply physical or spatial liberty, the speech seems confused and confusing. Birds, animals, fish, and streams are not usually thought of as free but rather as determined by instinct, chance, or physical law. Though they are more or less unfettered, they are not free to choose. Theirs is then a severely circumscribed liberty. Segismundo envies even that, however. He of course longs for the absence of physical restraints. Yet here he seems instinctively to grope not so much for freedom as for the deterministic preconditions to freedom. In brute creation, at least, things are allowed to follow their course. The animals live out their lives. The stream flows until it empties into the sea. But Segismundo has been mysteriously denied his destiny. He is not even free to be determined by whatever passions and astral influences may wish to govern him. Before freedom, necessity exists. Segismundo first longs for the freedom to be determined. Thereafter he can, if he will, construct freedom against necessity. The human qualities to which the prince refers in his soliloquy mostly have to do with the faculties that make choice possible: *alma, distinto, albedrío.* Choice operates against fatality. In order for it to engage its adversary successfully, however, fate also must be free to operate. Segismundo's first soliloquy is, then, a kind of enraged lyric counterspell hurled against the invisible sorcery and sorcerer that hold him a fast prisoner from time at the foot of his magic mountain.

Indeed, as the play begins, Basilio's spell, which like those in fairy tales is designed to ward off some future evil, the princess's fatal pricking of her finger, for example, is beginning to break up as a result of pressures from both without and within. Thrown from her horse, a bruised and shaken Rosaura crosses the border from Muscovy into Poland: "sin más camino / que el que me dan las leyes del destino" (1: 501) (with no course except that set for me by fate). Her arrival is portentous because she releases time, simultaneously with, it must be allowed, that relaxation of severity which experimentally occurs in the conscience of the aged Basilio. His is the inward unfreezing. By entering Poland, Rosaura unknowingly violates the taboo that guards against knowledge of Segismundo's existence. She is the first outsider to learn his grim secret. Her acquisition of this information, the simple fact that Segismundo does exist, naturally gives rise to a desire to know more about the wretched prisoner she has discovered, thus setting in train the revelatory thrust of the play, its will to disclose, a tendency incarnate with gallows humor in Clarín, the *gracioso* who cannot and will not keep a secret. And Rosaura is revelation both objectively and subjectively, for she has come to Poland not only on the track of love and vengeance but also in search of her complete story, essentially in search of her father. Just as Segismundo has been maimed by the denial to him of his past, so Rosaura comes to Poland wounded and uncertain because she has no acknowledged father. He is the key element in her story, as Basilio is in Segismundo's. Yet even though Basilio reveals himself to his son early in the second act of the play, Clotaldo keeps his secret from Rosaura throughout most of *La vida*. In Act I her sword discloses their relationship, and of course the audience knows that they are father and daughter from that moment on. Still, Clotaldo does not publicly and officially acknowledge Rosaura until the final critical moment when Astolfo protests her dubious background: "ella no sabe quién es" (1: 533). (She doesn't know who she is.) Clotaldo then rather enigmatically explains that: "yo hasta verla / casada, noble y honrada, / no la quise descubrir. / La historia desto es muy larga; / pero, en fin, es hija mía" (1: 533). (I did not want to reveal her identity until I found her honorably married to a nobleman. The history of all this is pretty long; but, in sum, she is my daughter.)

"La historia desto es muy larga" indeed, and readers or viewers of the play never come to know it all. But narration in *La vida es sueño* is progressive, if inexhaustible, revelation, time's burden of unfolding more each day. This is precisely the undertaking that Basilio would resist because he reads the future as a tragedy and would therefore like to suppress it, for personal and for public reasons. Yet forces far more powerful than a king have broken into the hermetic circle of royal consciousness that is Poland. Intrusions like Rosaura's presage the end of a long and powerful incantation in tales of magic, as when, in C.S. Lewis's *The Lion, the Witch and the Wardrobe,* Lucy "accidentally" ("sin más camino / que el que me dan las leyes del destino") wanders into Narnia through the wardrobe in which she had hidden, and meets Mr. Tumnus the fawn. For a very long time Narnia, under the White Witch's spell, has lain in a perpetual winter which, unprogressing as winter is, does not even progress as far as Christmas. The arrival of Lucy and her brothers and sister sets in train a process that thaws the witch's spell, after which season and time return to the liberated landscape. Before Rosaura, Poland seems locked in Basilio's timeless intellectual grasp. After Rosaura, time begins to flow, holding out possibilities of regeneration such as those envisaged by Faust in the spring scene of "Vor dem Thor": "Vom Eise befreit sind Strom und Bäche / Durch des Frühlings holden belebenden Blick; / Im Thale grünet Hoffnungs-Glück; / Der alte Winter, in seiner Schwäche, / zog sich in rauhe Berge zurück."[58] (Because of spring's graciously invigorating gaze, brook and stream flow free of ice. In the valley happiness greens expectant. Aged winter in his weakness has retreated to his mountain redoubt.)

Unlike these lines, or Lewis's tale, *La vida es sueño* has no explicit myth of season. It in no way suggests the time of year. But through the confrontation of Basilio and Segismundo, the white-maned father as the oppressor of his vigorous son, it does implicitly create a seasonal opposition. Basilio's rule is the winter season that holds even his son frozen in its astrological and intellectual grasp. When Rosaura arrives Segismundo stirs, awakens, and explodes. But Basilio's laws are designed to prevent such meteorologies. Just as Rosaura is about to tell her story after the fashion of an ill-omened heroine in Cervantes, Clotaldo and his marked guards seize her and Clarín, and her portentous "Yo soy . . ." dies without a predicate. Those stilled words, that silence, in a sense, opens a parenthesis that occupies the rest of the play. In it, Rosaura strives to recover herself, her past, her full story and history. The sword she shows to Clotaldo is itself historic, for, when Segismundo's jailer sees it, he and the whole narration revert to the past: "Esta espada es la que yo / dejé a la hermosa Violante" (1: 505). (This sword is the one I left with lovely Violante.) This reversion from the present to the past, with the utmost slowness and difficulty in Rosaura's case, finally compels the confession of her secret, the most stubbornly concealed one in the play. And, since there is from the first in *La vida es sueño* a profound modal link between Rosaura and Segismundo, her conjuration of the past also provokes his and through it he also strives to recover himself.

But the heir-apparent to the crown of Poland is absent from *La vida*'s first consciously historical recitation, that made by Astolfo of the background of his and Estrella's claims to succeed Basilio. Basilio himself repairs the omission by revealing to the whole Polish court the obliterated story of Segismundo. When he comes to discuss his son in that long, elegant, and terrible speech, the king shifts from the bemused present to the grievous past: "En Clorilene, mi esposa, / tuve un infelice hijo" (1: 507). (By my wife Clorilene I had an ill-starred son.)

For Rosaura, as for Segismundo, the paradox is that, even though she helps to set in motion the mechanism of temporality, she is herself still subject to its laws, so that in Act II when Clotaldo inquires after Rosaura of Clarín, he declares: "ella está esperando / que ocasión y itempo venga / en que vuelvas por su honor" (1: 512). (She is waiting for the time and opportunity for you to vindicate her honor.) Clotaldo approvingly replies: "Prevención segura es esa, / que al fin el tiempo ha de ser / quien haga esas diligencias." (Hers is a proper anticipation, since, after all, time will have to be the agent of such undertakings.) Rosaura and Segismundo are both the agents of time—actors—and acted upon by it, thus active and passive, masculine and feminine in mode, dual, double.

From their doubleness and that of others like Basilio springs *La vida*'s theatricality. Jackson Cope scores intuitively when he brings Artuad's concept of *Le théâtre et son double* to bear on Calderón's play and its cruelties.[59] A primary duality in Calderón is the sense of acting and being acted upon, of being actor and spectator. Characteristically, it is Clarín who first introduces the idea of theatre when, just after Rosaura has pleaded with Clotaldo for her life by playing upon the contrast between humility and haughtiness, Segismundo's haughtiness and *her* humility, he ignominiously tries to split the difference between humility and pride:

Y si Humildad y Soberbia no te obligan, personajes que han movido y removido mil autos sacramentales, yo, ni humilde ni soberbio, sino entre las dos mitades entreverado, te pido que nos remedies y ampares. [1: 504]	And if humility and pride, players who have moved and stirred a thou- sand religious allegories, have no ef- fect on you, I, neither humble nor proud, but rather split between the two of them, do beg that you will help and protect us.

The human situation of the drama also involves doubleness as one goes into the theater and finds the self in actors reproduced and sits in silent judgment on them and on oneself. This is a simultaneous doubleness, spectator with actor. It is, however, based on the distinct successions of experience, seeing first one role and then another contrasting with it, now Humility, now Pride, in a thousand allegories. Time, in short, is essential to duality. Logically, then, just as she introduces temporality into *La vida es sueño,* so Rosaura brings in duality.

Its first manifestation is situational. Rosaura crosses the wild frontier between Muscovy and Poland. She is thus on the border between two kingdoms. But when she enters one, she can scarcely be said to leave the other behind. Her whole unhappy past lies in Russia, but Poland promises an answer to its riddle. With respect to the two countries that concern her she is, then, like Clarín, "entre las dos mitades / entreverado"—split, partaking of each, yet not altogether in the one or the other. Another situation at the beginning of *La vida es sueño* has to do with Rosaura and time, her "lumínico-temporal" function in the play. She and Clarín advance into Poland at the day's end, in its fading light, "a la medrosa luz que aún tiene el día" (1: 501) (in the uncertain light that the day still retains). The first scenes thus occur on another frontier, that between day and night. Throughout, *La vida es sueño* employs an enormously complex chiaroscuro technique. The metaphor of its title is in the idiom of dark and light. Man is a diurnal animal and conducts most of his conscious activity in the light of day. At night he sleeps and dreams. To say that life is a dream-sleep is to place consciousness in the context of unconsciousness, waking in the realm of sleep, light in a region of dark. Metaphorically again, Segismundo is the sun, the Polish sun, "sol de Polonia." Basilio's suppression of him has, however, hidden him in a timeless eclipse. But the whole tendency of the play is to reveal the prince in all the horror and brilliance of his emergent majesty. Astolfo explains: "salís como el sol / de debajo de los montes!" (1: 514). (Like the sun you emerge from beneath the mountains.) Segismundo, in this metaphorical process, is, as the play unfolds, a splendor hidden in the dark that inevitably comes to shine unobstructed. But the guiding notion that *la vida es sueño,* that life itself and its activities which seem fully conscious in the light of day are really the figments of a fleeting somnolence, projects a darkness into light even in the noonday blaze of Segismundo.

Rosaura limns Segismundo. In one phase, he is the blackness of total eclipse, in another the sun at zenith. To him, she is the light intervening between total darkness and total illumination. Accordingly, in their second encounter, at court, Segismundo remonstrates with Rosaura for her attempt to evade him in twilight terms, light that is "entreverado":

Oye, mujer, deténte.	Woman, listen; wait. Don't join
No juntas el ocaso y el oriente,	dusk to dawn by running off just as
huyendo al primer paso;	we meet, because, with dusk joined
que juntos el oriente y el ocaso,	to dawn and light to chill shade, you
la lumbre y sombra fría,	will surely be the cause of curtailing
serás sin duda síncopa del día.	the day.

[1: 516-17]

Rosaura's dawning functions are suggested by her name, which brings to mind the roseate light of sunrise and sunset both, sunrise with its vital and conscious associations, sunset with its ebbing and unconscious attributes. Indeed, Rosaura appears before Segismundo each time in an uncertain light, with the darkness coming on in Act I, in the early morning of Act II, and in the dubious illumination of Act III, in the tumults of which Estrella remarks: "El sol se turba" (1: 525). (The sun is clouded over.) Some of the sense of the superimposition of sunset on sunrise have already been discussed in Part I of this study. These Calderón further amplifies in *La vida es sueño,* probably his greatest borderland work. For in this play the borderlands ceaselessly witness an intellectual, an imagistic, and a moral traffic between a whole array of dualisms— light and dark, life and death, consciousness and unconsciousness. So swift are the transfers from one to another that entire realms of apparent distinctness come to be superimposed each upon the other, to be seen, therefore, in terms of each other.

On the literal level, physical existence manages to have itself interpreted as a deadly function. The major life in the play, Segismundo's, so accelerates its course in his father's mind that he presents it publicly as a tragically absolute shortening of man's allotted span: "Publicóse que el Infante / nació muerto" (1: 508). (It was given out that the Prince was born dead.) In addition, Basilio, accelerating, anticipating, saw the son as the cause of the mother's death: "dio muerte a su madre" (1: 507). (He killed his mother.) And finally he sees Segismundo as the agent of at least his moral if not his physical extinction. For Basilio the most fearful part of his offspring's horoscope is the dreadful scene in which he will lie prostrate, trampled, at the young man's victorious feet, a king dishonored if not physically dead. Thus the king's mind, in a tragic poesis of his son's fate, so outstrips time that Basilio has come to the end of Segismundo's story before it has fairly begun, joining, in his astrological fashion, sunrise to sunset.

Basilio's interpretation of Segismundo's potential story is an uneven work of criticism. The king correctly apprehends the facts, on the whole, although exaggeratedly. The prince's few hours at the palace hardly give him time to become the monster that his father anticipates; but one murder carried out plus two attempts and an attempted rape are a rather unsettling record. Once Segismundo is known to exist, moreover, the kingdom does divide into factions, one loyal to the father, the other to the son. And that most searing assault on the king's pride, Segismundo's harrowing of him, is carried out figuratively. The prince does not literally trample on his father. Still, the horoscope that Basilio has cast is pretty accurate factually. Where Basilio fails is in the interpretation of his son's personal motive. The prince overcomes his tendency to cruelty, so that two Segismundos, at the last, confront the king. One he knows. The other is his son. And while the king has misapplied his doctrine of unreality to the rearing of his heir, that doctrine remains sound in the abstract, false as a method, or anti-method, true as a description of actuality. Basilio has thus abused his learning, but it remains solid and genuine: life must be seen in terms of death, consciousness in terms of unconsciousness, reality in terms of dream.

But what organizes these elements, apparently opposed, is experience, time, history. Existence as primordial experience is a process that leads to extinction. All things that live necessarily incline to death. Basilio is right: "el nacer / y el morir son parecidos" (1: 507) (birth and death are similar), for the one inevitably entails the other. If history is the story of living persons and institutions, it is a narration of horror, always, always concluding, sooner or later, in death. And no force can change that melancholy physical fact, so that a correct literal perspective of the new-born child places his dawning life in the sunset of death: "Babies in their baskets / soon will be in their caskets." Thus there is in all the works of Calderón a fundamental perception of this inevitable fact, to which, as fact, one must submit. If one is born heir-presumptive to the crown of Poland, one must sooner or later take his place in the succession of dead rulers.

But Calderón knows that death-bound humans are born possessed of an inner consciousness that aspires to eternity. His most profound personages are lyric beings who seek artistic perpetuity. They are like and ultimately derive from Garcilaso's wonderfully afflicted shepherds Salicio and Nemoroso, creatures of the light who should emerge in joy to perform sunlit deeds in the eclogue's traditional span of a single working day, but who sink to the ground in their grief and sing night-shaded songs of desertion and death. They could go on forever. But darkness closes in to stop their lamentations, which in substance are a miraculously successful protest against death. They tell their melancholy story, at the emotional summit of which is Elisa's death in childbirth. Nothing can change her disappearance, or Galatea's; but art brings them spiritually back. Their art submits to and rebels against fate. It is compounded of two modes of perceiving time. The one might be called linguistic and the other historical. What sustains the shepherds is a continuum of utterance that would offer itself as the model for an eternity of grief, grief splashed with light from an inexhaustible source, emanating from the endlessly present day. Salicio and Nemoroso, for the length of their song, believe that they have absorbed death and time by incorporating death and its surrogates, abandonment, absence, into the texture of their narration, which, although its verbs use past and even future modalities, focuses relentlessly on the present, which dominates to the point of annihilation the past and the future by making them empty into it. Their grief is now. But while in the *First Eclogue* this lyric consciousness, this eternal linguistic present, utterance oblivious of the history of utterance, strives to absorb all actuality, it is being overtaken by temporal progress in the form of light, as the day expands and then slowly falters. At the end, the poem is horribly sundered when its principal inner effect, the night of grief exposed to the full light of day, is erased by an objective phenomenon—the sinking sun. Functioning as historic time, it dissolves the lyric illusion by moving the reader from within the *Eclogue*'s timeless verbal bounds back out into a phenomenological world where death will overtake, not somebody else, but him. The consciousness that encompasses gives way to the consciousness that is encompassed:

Nunca pusieran fin al triste lloro
los pastores, ni fueran acabadas
las canciones que sólo el monte oía,
si mirando las nubes coloradas,
al tramontar del sol bordadas de oro,
no vieran que era ya pasado el día;
la sombra se veía
venir corriendo apriesa
ya por la falda espesa
del altísimo monte, y recordando
ambos como de sueño, y acabando
el fugitivo sol, de luz escaso,
su ganado llevando,
se fueron recogiendo paso a paso.[60]

The shepherds would never have put a stop to their terrible lament nor would the songs to which nature was the only listener ever have ended if, noticing the clouds aflame as the setting sun edged them with gold, they had not realized that the day was done. Night already had come on, running in haste down the thickly-wooded slope of the towering mountain; and both, as if waking from a dream, with the retreating sun a miser of light, driving their herd before them, slowly made return.

This is the moment at which *La vida es sueño* begins: "The plowman homeward plods his weary way, / And leaves the world to darkness and to me."[61] Calderón calls this numinous borderland period of time "el aurora de la tarde," dusk's dawning.

If Garcilaso had written only one eclogue, the critic would be less certain about his desire to engage the multiple modes of time and, above all, historic time. But his three long essays in the sense of duration attest to an ambition to come to grips with poetry both flowing and fixed. The strategy of the *Egloga primera* is to lull, to neutralize, epic and historical duration into a kind of soporific interregnum, during which its intense energy can be turned inward to the profit of a new poetry of aggrieved contemplation whose creative postulate is an *als ob,* a condition contrary to fact that permits the Eclogue's fundamental metaphor to function. That metaphor is singular only in one respect. It bridges the immense gap between antithetical polarities. It links exact opposites. The key phrase in the final stanza of the *Egloga primera* is: "recordando / ambos como de sueño." The function of the whole stanza is to return Salicio, Nemoroso, and the reader to historic time. But this is done at an extraordinary moment, not at the dawn of consciousness, at the beginning of the day, but rather at the onset of darkness and the night, when it is unusual, even metaphorically, to wake up. In the retrospect which these last verses compel us, then, to take, we perceive that the *Egloga primera* has been in poetic figure, in its own inner reality, a long dark night of pain. Appropriately, Nemoroso voices best this blackness of affliction, describing himself as: "solo, desamparado, / ciego, sin lumbre en cárcel tenebrosa" (294-95) (alone, bereft, blind in a lightless dungeon), and in stanza 23 extending darkness to include the rest of his life in the "tenebrosa / noche de tu partir . . ." (317-18) (the shadowed night of your departure). Further citation is not needed to show how the poem, in a fundamental operation, turns day into night and sleep and dream, the exquisite nightmare that is the *Egloga primera*. It thus involves a complex and diplomatically hostile relationship between *Wahrheit* and *Dichtung*. In Garcilaso's campaign, *Wahrheit* is poetry's powerful opponent whom it is not possible to take on in direct confrontation. Thus the victorious subtleties already discussed, which turn weakness into strength. True, the poem does at the last surrender itself under highly controlled conditions to an implacable foe, who has won by lasting out. But the work's essential insistence is that epic modes can be made to yield a lyric voice, that phenomenological historical actuality can be made to shelter a timeless illusion, that *Wahrheit,* after the performance of proper maneuvers, can become *Dichtung.* Here, then, we have the poetic premise of *La vida es sueño.*

Yet its situation with respect to actuality is vastly different from that of the *Egloga primera.* The poem, because the *moi lyrique* has not yet been firmly established, must by apostrophe halt phenomenological flow so as to place in the resultant interstice a linguistic realm apart from time yet in it, aware of its passage as one is aware of an object in the periphery of vision. In the Eclogue, day is phenomenological, night linguistic or poetic. Its whole tendency is towards a translation of the energies of the one into the other, even though they seem opposed. Therefore day is "in" the poem, since it must be present to be transmuted into night. Night—the *Dichtung*—is all the more for this the poem's major emphasis, its sense of its own central reality. Even so, the poesis of night is a hostage to phenomenology and must bow to history when outer night comes on.

When *La vida es sueño* begins, the *moi lyrique* already is quite firmly but strangely and artificially established. Segismundo exists in a timeless present of deprivation, a historical vacuum into which phenomenology in the person of Rosaura is fatefully drawn. She brings to him movement, change, and passion. As these things come to him and he to them, the lyric consciousness becomes a historical one; and in the historical order of events Segismundo assumes that hideous secondary rank, one that is lesser and worse than his father's, which temporal sequence, when unmodified, ordains. His horoscope was Basilio's dream. In Act II the father's dream becomes a nightmarish actuality in the son. But Act III teaches Segismundo that his bipartite nature, poetic and historical, once he is in firm possession of both, can be used to reverse the historical hierarchy. The lesser ruler can become the greater man, the second Scipio the first. Even though the product of this revulsion against time is intended to be proof against its effects, time is of course essential to the shaping of the awareness that brings the second and suprahistorical Segismundo into being. History, Calderón tells us, is essential to poetry; and drama is the portrayal of their fruitful conflict.

Much might be made of the prince's faulty preparation for his two major roles. In fact, Segismundo makes much of it himself when he denounces Basilio's method of rearing him, a suppression that produced the effect feared rather than the one desired. But once Rosaura comes into Segismundo's presence, once he begins to live in a public and social context, he exhibits ultimate political and artistic power. With Rosaura helpless before him, he can destroy or spare her. He can kill or create. Because he still lives, when the play begins, mostly in his artificially imposed linguistic environment, Segismundo there gives life by not murdering Rosaura. But when, in Act II, he regains possession of his historical self, he murders easily and attempts other murders as well as rape in the case of Rosaura. Then history is a murderous nightmare and the prince its unfettered agent. But the point is that, from the start, despite his deprivations, Segismundo disposes of supreme power, the power to destroy and the power to create. He uses both weapons and comes to be, in consequence, simultaneously a historical and a suprahistorical person, not a philosopher-king but a poet-king.

Art, not philosophy, is what shapes the second and triumphant self. No artist figures in *La vida es sueño*. With respect to Segismundo, none is necessary, for he is Alexander and Apelles both, the original and the copyist, sitter, artist, and portrait. But, precisely as in *Darlo todo y no dar nada* and *El segundo Escipión,* art centers upon the beautiful and berivalled woman, Rosaura. Astolfo wears her portrait, and his cousin Estrella jealously desires him to yield it up to her. In the scenes that follow Segismundo's disastrous day at court, during which nonetheless he gains possession of himself, thus acquiring the possibility of fashioning a superior person to himself, Rosaura unwillingly intervenes between Astolfo and Estrella and ingeniously gets her miniature back from him, to Estrella's great disgust with her unfortunate suitor. Despite the unpleasantness, this is a victory for Rosaura. Like Segismundo, she has recovered herself, retrieved her historical individuality, in part, at least. Yet the historical Rosaura, the child of a highly ambiguous union and the dupe of a Muscovite prince who for political reasons must prefer his cousin and the crown of Poland to an adventuress, is only the first and not necessarily the authentic version of the woman. At the play's end we perceive her in quite a different light: "casada, noble y honrada." The first may be called the original and the second the copy. Physically the two women are quite perfectly like, but morally they are as far from each other as *lo vivo* is from *lo pintado,* the first unmarriageable, the second suitable for a reigning duke. Together, Rosaura, Segismundo, and Clotaldo have created the second Rosaura out of the materials that constituted the first, realizing an artistic rehabilitation of the historical personage. Their art is decidedly superior to her nature, and decidedly like it.

All the principal actors in *La vida es sueño* are thus summoned to form a more enduring character—*monumentum perennius*—fashioned out of their primary, natural, and rather feral natures. Those who do not, perish utterly. Clarín's purely opportunistic temperament encourages him always to act in conformity with the power that currently prevails, in contradistinction to that noble stance which places higher human consciousness "contra el tiempo y el olvido," the basic artistic posture that attempts to deliver man from the horrors of history. Clarín has not the slightest notion of the suprahistorical self and the arduousness of achieving it. He is a hostage to fortune, and fortune in the form of a stray bullet finds him out in his place of concealment and kills him. Similarly the rebel soldier[62] functions in a purely historical sense by fomenting rebellion and its consequence, Segismundo's restoration to his role as heir-apparent. In the soldier's perspective, Segismundo has triumphed as the result of a historical process. But the very moment at which the soldier makes his petition finds Segismundo at the height of his second and suprahistorical self-creation. This the soldier threatens in his limited awareness, so that Segismundo literally imprisons him in historicity. His only meaning is temporal. He served to strengthen temporal processes that aided in the contrary construction of the anti-historical Segismundo. His time of usefulness has passed. And no significant second self endures beyond that instant of opportunity, so that the prince simply removes the soldier from a flow of time in which his meaning has already perished. The soldier is an artist who deservedly has survived his reputation.

Of course—and here is the inevitable ambiguity—Segismundo's prison tower is an incubator of both historic and anti-historic enterprise. It thrives on sequestration but invites invasion. Therefore, the structure of events at the conclusion of *La vida es sueño* is anything but definitive. The whole sequence might repeat itself but with another ending, Segismundo in chains again and the soldier or his substitute a victorious usurper. Yet the same forces that would have impelled another and far less fortunate history for Segismundo would also have fostered its antidotal anti-history in the form again of a second self that was just as much proof against time as the victorious suprahistorical personality that we do in fact witness. Segismundo naturally prefers the form of events in which he finds himself. Yet he has an excellent chance of surviving a less favorable concatenation. The necessary submission to time makes possible a deliverance from it.

Finally, if there is a philosophy in *La vida es sueño*,[63] it is a strangely empirical one. Segismundo's greatest deprivation is experience. When, each unaware of the other, Rosaura and Basilio free him to live in time, he is able to approach and ponder the mystery of sequence, the passage from a first apprehension of phenomena to a second sense of them and so to a comparison of original and copy. The whole ambiguity of *La vida es sueño* lies in this puzzling distance between primary and secondary. But, like Hume when he is discussing the relationship between cause and effect in *An Inquiry Concerning Human Understanding*,[64] Calderón posits no necessary inherent connection between primary and secondary. Clarín and the rebel soldier are proof of that. Though they partake fully of the same events as the play's major figures, they fail to evolve as the others do. Thus nothing determines the development of the secondary from the primary. But experience is essential to the cultivation of the will to endure beyond the repetitions of history. Segismundo must feel and see the closeness of the first manifestation to the second, of the original to the copy, to want to construct a more lasting nature, just as in Hume's philosophy causality can be grasped by experience alone, which is to say through historical awareness: *post hoc, propter hoc,* a logical fallacy, a phenomenological truth.

Accordingly, the philosophy of *La vida es sueño* is an anti-philosophy, a pragmatism that defies systematic expostulation. That is why Segismundo must live in the original in order to live on in the copy. Consequently, though premised on the metaphor that governs Garcilaso's *Egloga primera,* the play changes the poem's emphasis, which is a passage from history to poetry, by making the historical and poetic selves hostile yet sympathetic coadjutors in the work's entire enterprise. This is, of course, after long and rich elaboration, an ultimate and in some senses terrible consummation of the struggle in Spanish drama between the lyric and the politic, between poet and sovereign. Each has annexed the other into a continuum of strife that makes them inseparable for as long as either may survive.

NOTES

PART I

1. With the dates proposed by Harry W. Hilborn in *A Chronology of the Plays of D. Pedro Calderón de la Barca* (Toronto, 1938), they are: *El mayor encanto, amor* (1635); *Los tres mayores prodigios* (1636); *Amado y aborrecido* (1650-1652); *El monstruo de los jardines* (1650-1653); *La fiera, el rayo, y la piedra* (1652); *Fortunas de Andrómeda y Perseo* (1653); *El golfo de las sirenas* (1657); *El laurel de Apolo* (1658); *La púrpura de la rosa* (1660); *Eco y Narciso* (1661); *Apolo y Climene* (1661); *El hijo del sol, Faetón* (1661); *Celos, aun del aire, matan* (1662); *Ni amor se libra de amor* (1662); *Fieras afemina amor* (1669); *La estatua de Prometeo* (1669); and *Fineza contra fineza* (1671). Hilborn's date for *La estatua* is questionable, along with others. In the preface to his edition of the play (Paris, 1965), p. vii, Charles Aubrun writes: "*La estatua de Prometeo,* 'comedia famosa,' was presented for the first time before the Queen-Mother Mariana of Austria on the occasion of her birthday, the 21st or 22nd of December of a year that may have been 1670, 1671, 1672, or 1674 at the royal Coliseum of the Palace of the Buen Retiro." (My translation.)

2. Two general articles are W.G. Chapman's "Las comedias mitológicas de Calderón," *Revista de Literatura* 5 (1954): 35-67, and Charles V. Aubron's "Estructura y significación de las comedias mitológicas de Calderón," *Hacia Calderón, Tercer Coloquio Anglogermano* (Berlin, 1976), pp. 148-55. N. Erwin Haverbeck Ojeda discusses *El mayor encanto, amor, El golfo de las sirenas, Fieras afemina amor,* and *La fiera, el rayo, y la piedra* in "La comedia mitológica calderoniana: soberbia y castigo," *Revista de Filología Española* 56 (1973): 67-93. *Los tres mayores prodigios* is briefly but discerningly examined by A.I. Watson in "Hercules and the Tunic of Shame: Calderón's *Los tres mayores prodigios,*" *Homenaje a William L. Fichter* (Madrid, 1971), pp. 773-83. A tantalizing account of this same play's staging is that in N.D. Shergold's *A History of the Spanish Stage* (Oxford, 1967), pp. 285-86. Describing *Las fortunas de Andrómeda y Perseo* as "an Ovidian romance of the noble soul" (p. 237), C.A. Merrick studies it most fruitfully, with the help of León Hebreo and mythographers such as Pérez de Moya in "Neoplatonic Allegory in Calderón's *Las fortunas de Andrómeda y Perseo,*" *Modern Language Review* 67 (1972): 319-27. Her only predecessor apparently is H.M. Martin, with "Corneille's *Andromède* and Calderón's *Las fortunas de Perseo,*" *Modern Philology* 23 (1925-1926): 407-15. Everett W. Hesse offers a psychological interpretation of *Eco y Narciso* in his *Análisis e interpretación de la comedia* (Madrid, 1968), pp. 69-83. Charles V. Aubrun finds in *Eco* an unconscious political allegory in "Eco y Narciso," *Homenaje a William T. Fichter,* pp. 47-58. It is also studied by William R. Blue in "Dualities in Calderón's *Eco y Narciso,*" *Revista Hispánica Moderna* 39 (1976-1977): 109-18. Jorge Aguilar Mora briefly takes up first the *loa* of *Fieras afemina amor* and then the play itself in "Nota sobre la loa a *Fieras afemina amor,* Jornada primera," *Nueva Revista de Filología Española* 23 (1974): 111-15, 268-326. An exhaustive treatment of Prometheus in literature, with a su-

perb study of Calderón's *La estatua de Prometeo,* is Raymond Trousson's *Le Thème de Prométhée dans la littérature européenne* (Geneva, 1964). Anne M. Pasero also examines the play in "Male vs. Female: Binary Opposition and Structural Synthesis in Calderón's *Estatua de Prometeo," Bulletin of the Comediantes* 32 (1980): 109-15.

3. The dates are Morley and Bruerton's from their *Cronología de las comedias de Lope de Vega* (Madrid, 1968).

4. *The Idea of a Theatre* (Princeton, 1972), p. 15.

5. Prometheus's creative rhythm of withdrawal and return is similar to the relationship, described by Arnold Toynbee, between the innovating individual personality and the society he seeks to modify. Toynbee further defines the "movement of withdrawal-and-return" as "a disengagement and temporary withdrawal of the creative personality from his social milieu, and his subsequent return to the same milieu transfigured: in a new capacity and with new powers. The disengagement and withdrawal make it possible for the personality to realize individual potentialities which might have remained in abeyance if the individual in whom they were immanent had not been released for a moment from his social toils and trammels. The withdrawal is an opportunity, and perhaps a necessary condition, for the anchorite's transfiguration; but, by the same token, this transfiguration can have no purpose, and perhaps no meaning, except as a prelude to the return of the transfigured personality into the social milieu out of which he has originally come: a native environment from which the human social animal cannot estrange himself without repudiating his humanity and becoming 'either a beast or a god.' The return is the essence of the whole movement, as well as its final cause." Arnold J. Toynbee, *A Study of History* (Oxford, 1951), 8: 248. In connection with original solutions to the problems of growing societies, Toynbee also speaks of the genetic function of "Promethean *élan,*" p. 246.

Toynbee's pattern clearly is a basic one in Calderón. It would be too tedious to enumerate the examples of individuals, held in isolation, often in a cave, who emerge from inwardness with a disastrous or beneficent effect. A major negative case is that of Semíramis in *La hija del aire.* Her appearance from a cave signals tragedy for her kingdom and herself. Segismundo's situation in *La vida es sueño* is more complex. His first and involuntary plunge into society is a horrendous mistake. But when, returned to prison, the prince analyzes his experience, a transfiguration takes place and he goes forth a second time to triumph.

The rapid passage from deepest seclusion to glaring publicity is, of course, also a major feature of the mythological plays. Thetis, Achilles' mother, keeps him a virtual prisoner in a cave so that death will not overtake him. But music draws him out. It is the same with Eco in *Eco y Narciso.* Climene, in *Apolo y Climene,* has been brought up not in a cave but in a rural retreat so isolated as to be tantamount to one. And she and Apollo withdraw to Fitón's magic cave, where Phaeton is born. Like their enchanted retreat is the cave of marvels in which Psyche enjoys Cupid's faceless love in *Ni amor se libra de amor.* The list is highly extensible.

6. Yupanquí is a convert to Christianity who, in celebration of his new faith, fashions a lamentably crude image of the Virgin.

7. For simplicity's sake, all citations of Calderón in this book list volume and page numbers of the Aguilar edition of the *Obras completas,* volumes 1 and 2 edited by Angel Julián Valbuena Briones (Madrid, 1969, 1973), volume 3 edited by Angel Valbuena Prat (Madrid, 1967). I have regularly changed the punctuation somewhat. All translations are my own.

8. *Politics,* 1. 1. 9-12, as quoted and translated by Toynbee, *History,* 1: 173.

9. For a study of the relation of thought to image in Calderón, see my "Calderonian Cartesianism: The Iconography of the Mind in *La exaltación de la Cruz," L'Esprit Créateur* 15 (1975): 286-304.

10. Insofar as faith and Catholic Christianity are a fundamental ingredient of the

art of Calderón's theatre, *all* his plays are what might be termed "religious." But, apart from the one-act allegorical works—*autos sacramentales*—there is a small but distinct corpus among the plays in which the central event is conversion from paganism or Islam to Christianity. These can appropriately be termed "religious plays," *comedias religiosas,* although a better description would be "dramas of conversion." Perhaps the first work on the list is a negative example, a play in which a Christian can*not* be converted, not so much to Islam as to non-Christian uses. I mean Don Fernando in *El príncipe constante.* Others in the conversion category are *El mágico prodigioso, Las cadenas del demonio, La exaltación de la Cruz, Los dos amantes del cielo, El José de las mujeres, La aurora en Copacabana,* and *El gran príncipe de Fez.*

11. The ninth verse of Quevedo's sonnet "Cerrar podrá mis ojos. . . ." Quevedo speaks here of his "soul which has been a place of detention for a god altogether." The god is Eros and the sense is that the poet has entirely abandoned himself to earthly love during his lifetime.

12. In citing this passage I have omitted the musical reprise in the text in order to bring out the rhetorical figures more clearly. In a performance, of course, the music would reinforce the rhetoric.

13. These passages are from the second version of Calderón's *auto sacramental alegórico* (one-act play based on religious allegory) entitled, like the famous secular drama which it somewhat resembles, *La vida es sueño.* The first scholar to discuss in print the importance of the four elements to Calderonian physics was E.M. Wilson in "The Four Elements in the Imagery of Calderón," *Modern Language Review* 31 (1936): 34-47. It is odd that no one has followed on in this fruitful direction.

14. And are of course to be found, vigorously deceiving, in the dramas of conversion: Astarot in *Las cadenas del demonio,* Idolatría in *La aurora en Copacabana.*

15. Similar to my proposition with respect to Fernando's trust in the night is Elias L. River's "Fénix's Sonnet in Calderón's *Príncipe constante,*" *Hispanic Review* 37 (1969): 452-58. Rivers convincingly shows that Fénix's comparison of fixed stars to fading flowers is a misapprehension on her part.

16. From Gerald Brenan, *St. John of the Cross* (Cambridge, England, 1973), p. 144.

17. My "The Economic Parable of Time in Calderón's *El príncipe constante,*" *Romanistisches Jarhbuch* 23 (1972): 294-306, discusses in detail a number of matters related to the present investigation, but from a somewhat different perspective.

18. *Poesías líricas en las obras dramáticas de Calderón* (London, 1964), pp. 88-89.

19. *Eckermanns Gespräche mit Goethe* (Basal, 1945), 1: 148, 168. (My translation.) Goethe is one of the few critics of Calderón who could knowledgeably discuss technique and stagecraft in producing his plays, for in his later years as director of the Weimar court theatre Goethe mounted three productions of Calderón in German translation. (Goethe did not read Spanish, which is surprising, since his Italian was fluent.) On January 30, 1811, he presented *El príncipe constante (Der Standhafte Prinz)* with great success. Less successful but far from a failure was the March 30, 1812, production of *La vida es sueño (Das Leben ein Traum).* But the performance of *La gran Cenobia (Die grosse Zenobia)* in January of 1815 on the occasion of the Grand Duchess's birthday must be accounted a total failure, although Goethe felt that the first three of five acts had been well received. Soon afterwards, in April of 1817, Goethe resigned as director of the theatre, and Calderón's brief blooming in Weimar was over. I am indebted to Swana L. Hardy's *Goethe, Calderón und die Romantische Theorie des Dramas* (Heidelberg, 1965), especially pp. 34-41, for this valuable information.

20. Cristóbal Pérez Pastor, *Documentos para la biografía de D. Pedro Calderón de la Barca* (Madrid, 1905), pp. 425-28.

21. Curtius's "Calderón und die Malerei," *Romanische Forschungen* 53 (1939): 145-84, abridged and revised as "Excursuses" XXII and XXIII in *European Literature*

and the Latin Middle Ages (New York, 1953), is the estimable initial study. Other such studies include Helga Bauer's *Der Index Pictorius Calderóns* (Hamburg, 1969).

22. Cf. Bauer, *Index,* p. 88.

23. My text is from Biruté Ciplijauskaité's edition of Góngora's *Sonetos completos* (Madrid, 1969), p. 212. For useful background information, see J.F.G. Gornall, "Art and Nature: Góngora's Funerary Sonnet for El Greco," *Bulletin of Hispanic Studies* 55 (1978): 115-18.

24. In "From Comedy to Tragedy: Calderón and the New Tragedy," *Modern Language Notes* 92 (1977): 181-201, I attempt to show the general relationship between Golden-Age comedy and tragedy, with Calderón as prime example.

25. In Ovid's telling (*Metamorphoses,* Book 14) Iphis, spurned and mocked by Anaxarete, hangs himself from the lintel of her door. As Iphis's funeral procession is drawing near, pity moves Anaxarete to go up to a high room and look out upon his bier. She changes to stone as she gazes down at her dead lover. Ovid's account of Pygmalion (Book 10) is that the bachelor Pygmalion, repelled by prostitutes, shuns women and carves a lovely white female statue with which he falls in love. Venus grants his prayer that it come to life and marry him. Anaxarete's is a cautionary tale, and Garcilaso cunningly employs it as his most convincing argument in favor of the lady of the "Cancion V^a" responding to the love of Mario Galeota: "Hágate temerosa / el caso de Anajárete. . . ." (Take the case of Anaxarete as a frightening example.)

26. The definition is: "Dios es una bondad suma, / una esencia, una sustancia, / toda vista, todo manos" (1: 610). (God is supreme goodness, of one essence and substance, omniscient, omnipotent.)

27. "In the scene in which the ghost of the Prince lights the way for the advancing army, he became so carried away by the beauty of the poetry that he flung the book on the table so forcefully that it fell to the floor." Hardy, *Goethe, Calderón,* p. 36. (My translation.)

28. Bruce W. Wardropper's eloquent "The Dramatization of Figurative Language in the Spanish Theatre," *Yale French Studies* 47 (1972): 189-98, analyzes this fundamental process in the major works of Spanish Golden-Age drama.

29. Like religion, literature is a total system that asserts its primacy over all other structurations and constructs. In its purview, the function of faith, if it has one, is to bear witness to the originality of art, whereas in religion faith is the original, art the copy or *speculum.* Calderón's theatre consistently exploits this tension between original and copy, primary and secondary, nature and art, faith and art.

30. Rainer Maria Rilke, *Das Stunden-Buch von Mönchischem Leben,* in *Ausgewählte Gedichte* (The Hague, 1948), p. 59.

31. *Goethes Faust,* II, ed. Calvin Thomas (Boston, n.d.), p. 337.

32. *Faust,* I: "Vor dem Thor," 1112.

33. C. Hubbard Rose questions Calderón's authorship of the second play, in "Who wrote the *Segunda Parte* of *La hija del aire?*" *Revue belge de philosophie et d'histoire* 54 (1976): 797-822. Although she advances plausible arguments, no solid evidence supports the conjecture. Moreover, Calderón's later mention of the very incident with which the second play begins, the lines from *Mujer, llora y vencerás* quoted below, strongly supports his authorship.

34. The play's major critic to date is Gwynne Edwards, whose thesis first resulted in two articles: "Calderón's *La hija del aire* in the Light of His Sources," *Bulletin of Hispanic Studies* 43 (1966): 177-96; and "Calderón's *La hija del aire* and the Classical Type of Tragedy," *Bulletin of Hispanic Studies* 44 (1967): 161-94. Then the Tamesis critical edition of the play, with a considerable introduction, appeared in London in 1970. While largely descriptive, these three efforts are extremely useful.

35. A rather unsatisfactory account, because of its bizarre order of treatment, is Sven Stolpe's *Christina of Sweden* (New York, 1966). The "historical" Christina is, none-

theless, every bit as remarkable as Calderón's, at least as she is portrayed in Stolpe's book.

36. Not always, however. One striking example, soon to be discussed, is *Para vencer amor, querer vencerle.*

37. William M. Whitby's "Rosaura's Role in the Structure of *La vida es sueño,*" most conveniently consulted in Bruce W. Wardropper's *Essays on the Theatre of Calderón* (New York, 1965), pp. 101-13, establishes Rosaura as the key factor in Segismundo's conversion.

38. Calderón's use of the energetics of hatred and love is not unlike that attributed to Racine by Ronald W. Tobin in "The Too-Faithful Reflection: Self-Hatred in the Tragedies of Racine," *L'Esprit Créateur* 8 (1968): 102-15. With Calderón, however, we have a conservation of energy that converts the destructive passion of hatred into the constructive one of love. Indeed, self-hatred is not a factor in the plays of Calderón, except in the tragedies of honor, where the offended husband, because of his suspicions, comes to hate his *alter ego,* his cherished spouse, and destroys what is best in himself in destroying her. In short, Racine does not employ the *odi-amo* interlock as a fundamental structural design. With him, hatred prevails over love; with Calderón, love over hatred.

39. By "secular religion" I do not mean to suggest, after the fashion of Peter N. Dunn in his "Honour and the Christian Background in Calderón," in Wardropper's *Critical Essays,* pp. 24-60, that the comedies of honor parody Christian precept. My point is, rather, that they incorporate the divine into the secular world.

40. *The Allegorical Drama of Calderón: An Introduction to the Autos Sacramentales* (Oxford, England, 1943).

41. Such is, roughly, the thesis of Bruce W. Wardropper's "Calderón's Comedy and his Serious Sense of Life," in *Hispanic Studies in Honor of Nicholson B. Adams* (Chapel Hill, North Carolina, 1966), pp. 179-93.

42. See my "Economic Parable of Time."

43. Horace, *Carmina,* 3. 30. 1.

44. Jacob Burckhardt, *The Civilization of the Renaissance in Italy* (Oxford, England, 1945), p. 2: "Between the two [Papacy and Empire] lay a multitude of political units—republics and despots—in part of long standing, in part of recent origin, whose existence was founded on their power simply to maintain it. In them for the first time we detect the modern political spirit of Europe, surrendered freely to its own instincts, often displaying the worst features of an unbridled egotism, outraging every right and killing every germ of a healthier culture. But, wherever this vicious tendency is overcome or in any way compensated, a new fact appears in history—the State as the outcome of reflection and calculation, the State as a work of art."

45. This interpretation differs markedly from A.A. Parker's "The Father-Son Conflict in the Drama of Calderón," *Forum for Modern Language Studies* 2 (1966): 99-113. Parker's emphasis in that fine analysis is fundamentally biographical, experience transfused into art. Mine is theoretical. Nonetheless, conflict is a common point. The relationship of father to son is indeed central to *La vida es sueño.*

46. The historical background is discussed at some length in Part III of this book.

47. *Rigor* and *piedad* constitute a fundamental Calderonian rhythm of governance, with *rigor* a kind of deterministic quantum, in *La vida es sueño* the horoscope, while *piedad* represents the subjective quality of fated events, often taking the form of a successful appeal from them. The horoscope comes literally true, but when it actually occurs it does not mean what Basilio thought it would mean. In such fashion *rigor* engenders *piedad* and both constructs function as diastole and systole, contraction and relaxation.

48. Parker rightly stresses the essentialness of this dialectic and its felicitous resolution. *La vida* is not a tragedy *manquée.*

49. Stanislavsky describes the finest uncontrolled performance as a triumph of intuition: ". . . the very best that can happen is to have the actor completely carried away by

the play. Then regardless of his own will he lives the part, not noticing *how* he feels, not thinking about *what* he does, and it all moves of its own accord, subconsciously and intuitively." *An Actor Prepares* (New York, 1946), p. 13. Stanislavsky's blessed interpreter is of course the Segismundo of Act II. He *is* the prince of Poland. But Diderot's actor is a second version of this unconscious artist: "The man of feeling obeys nature's impulses and the only thing that he expresses is pure emotion. The moment he modifies or compels emotion, he is no longer himself but rather an actor performing." "Paradoxe sur le comédien" in *Oeuvres* (Paris, 1957), p. 1056. (My translation.) This controlled and self-conscious personage is the Segismundo who emerges from prison at the beginning of Act III and who by its end has come both to accept and to doubt his role.

50. Lionel Abel, *Metatheatre* (New York, 1963).

51. Thomas A. O'Connor, "Is the Spanish *Comedia* a Metatheater?" followed by Arnold G. Reichenberger's enthusiastic endorsement, *Hispanic Review* 43 (1975): 275-91. The most thoughtful of the detractors probably is Stephen Lipmann, in "Metatheater and the Criticism of the *Comedia,*" *Modern Language Notes* 91 (1976): 231-46.

52. *Le Cru et le cuit* (Paris, 1964); *Du Miel aux cendres* (Paris, 1966); and *L'Origine des manières de table* (Paris, 1968).

53. G.S. Kirk, in *Myth: Its Meaning and Function in Ancient and Other Cultures* (Berkeley, 1975), writes (p. 228) of Prometheus's theft of fire: "Presumably the tale goes back long before Hesiod, and we can recognize some possible Near-Eastern prototypes, especially in the myth of Adapa."

54. Raymond Trousson comments, in *Le Thème de Prométhée,* 1: 11: "In comparing the two texts, one realizes that, to a certain degree, the *Theogony* and *Works and Days* complement each other with respect to the Prometheus myth. Nonetheless, gaps and unclear passages remain for a modern reader. No doubt the explanation is that Hesiod was addressing a well informed audience, which is proved by the highly abbreviated abstract of the adventures of Prometheus that he makes at the beginning of the Pandora myth." (My translation.)

55. Philip Whaley Harsh, *A Handbook of Classical Drama* (Stanford, 1944), p. 52.

56. See Trousson, *Le Thème de Prométhée,* pp. 40-55.

57. Seznec, *La Survivance des dieux antiques* (London, 1940); in English translation, *The Survival of the Pagan Gods* (New York, 1961); Allen, *Mysteriously Meant: The Rediscovery of Pagan Symbolism and Allegorical Interpretation in the Renaissance* (Baltimore, 1970).

58. See especially Allen, *Mysteriously Meant,* pp. 53-59.

59. *Adversus Marconium* 1.1.247.

60. See particularly Trousson, *Le Thème de Prométhée,* pp. 73-77.

61. He prefers a "philosophical" approach but perceptively refers to the play's synaesthesia: "It has been well observed that *La estatua de Prometeo* offers a veritable Wagnerian concept of theatre, a synthesis in which literature, music, and the plastic arts all have their place. Such abundance produces complexity but also riches" (p. 172). (My translation.)

62. Graves (Baltimore, 1955), in his introduction, remarks that he has tried to "explain" all myth in anthropological and historical terms. Kirk, after declaring that his book attempts to deal with the relationship of myth to folktale, to ritual, to structuralism, the function of myth, culture and myth, Near-Eastern and Greek myth, the unconscious and myth, etc., observes: "Almost none of these problems has been convincingly handled, even in a provisional way, up to the present" (p. v). Nor is his own intelligent and conscientious effort entirely satisfactory.

63. Quoted from *The Original Poems of Fray Luis de León,* ed. Edward Sarmiento (Manchester, England, 1953), pp. 18-20.

64. Trousson, *Le Thème de Prométhée,* p. 102.

65. Kirk, *Myth,* p. 78.

PART II

1. I became aware of the presence of Cervantes independently but owe to the kindness of Dr. Patricia Kenworthy knowledge of Alberto Sánchez's article "Reminiscencias cervantinas en el teatro de Calderón," *Anales Cervantinos* 6 (1957): 262-70. Sánchez has been quite helpful in making my own haphazard list somewhat precise.

Cervantes is evoked in Calderón mostly by direct mention or allusion, but on at least three occasions Calderón plots occurrences similar to events in Cervantes' works. Such references to Cervantes occur in at least 22 plays of Calderón. Here is my list, probably not entirely accurate or complete (volume and page numbers refer to A. Julián Valbuena Briones' edition): *Los empeños de un acaso,* Act I (2: 1045); *Las manos blancas no ofenden,* Act III (2: 1115); *El astrólogo fingido,* Act I (2: 136-37) (here, although Cervantes is not named, the reference clearly is to *El curioso impertinente* and to the world of *Don Quijote*); *El alcaide de sí mismo, Act II (2: 823); Mañana será otro día,* Act I (2: 765) and Act II (2: 774); *Antes que todo es mi dama,* Act I (2: 879); *El escondido y la tapada,* Act II (2: 686); *Casa con dos puertas mala es de guardar,* Act I (2: 282) and Act III (2: 306); *La banda y la flor,* Act I (2: 426); *El maestro de danzar,* Act I (2: 1541, 1542); *También hay duelo en las damas,* Act III (2: 1523); *Dicha y desdicha del nombre,* Act I (2: 1810); *Los hijos de la fortuna,* Act I (2: 1234); *El sitio de Bredá,* Act I (1: 114) and Act III (1: 130); *Basta callar,* Act I (1: 1713); *La dama duende,* Act I (2: 241) and Act II (2: 250); *El alcalde de Zalamea,* Act I (1: 542); and *La niña de Gómez Arias,* Act II (1: 805).

Finally, there are the situations reminiscent of Cervantes. In *El astrólogo fingido,* it is the *Clavileño*-like episode featuring Otáñez in Act III (p. 162). In *No siempre lo peor es cierto* it is the silent and suffering trip of the lovers, while *No hay cosa como callar* patterns itself broadly on *La fuerza de la sangre.*

2. See Edward M. Wilson and Duncan Moir, *A Literary History of Spain, The Golden Age: Drama 1492-1700* (London, 1971), p. 103; and N.D. Shergold, *A History of the Spanish Stage* (Oxford, 1967), 288-89.

3. Here is the letter, which I am not equal to translating:

> "Fermosa dueña, cualquier que vos seáis la condolida de este afanado caballero, y asaz piadosa minoráis sus cuitas, ruégovos me queráis facer sabidor del follón mezquino, o pagano malandrín, que en este encanto vos amancilla, para que segunda vegada en vueso nombre, sano ya de las pasadas feridas, entre en descomunal batalla, magüer que finque muerto en ella; que non es la vida de más pro que la muerte, tenudo a su deber un caballero. El dador de la luz vos mampare, e a mí non olvide.
>
> El caballero de la Dama Duende"

4. Louise George Clubb, *Giambattista Della Porta, Dramatist* (Princeton, 1965), p. xi: "The two greatest tourist attractions of Naples about the year 1600 were, according to contemporary report, the baths at Pozzuoli and Giambattista Della Porta."

5. Ibid., p. xi: "In his spare time, Della Porta wrote plays. Seventeen of them have survived: a tragicomedy, a sacred tragedy, a secular tragedy, and fourteen comedies." One of the comedies is entitled *L'astrologo,* but resembles Calderón's play only in the element of elaborate deception. Yet it does not seem unlikely that Calderón knew Della Porta's work.

6. Wilson and Moir, *Literary History,* p. 112.

7. Valbuena Briones, 2: 25.

8. Cristóbal Pérez Pastor, *Documentos para la biografía de D. Pedro Calderón de la Barca* (Madrid, 1905).

9. See A. Julián Valbuena Briones, "Revisión biográfica de Calderón de la Barca," *Arbor* 94, no. 365 (1976): 25. Calderón was first called up to accompany the king on a voyage of pacification to Catalonia and later to serve in combat. However, I can find

no mention of a royal trip proposed for 1640 in John H. Elliott's *The Revolt of the Catalans* (Cambridge, England, 1963).

10. Calderón left five *veneras,* a very costly one valued at 1800 reales, and four others much less expensive. See Pérez Pastor, *Documentos,* 424-25.

11. *Novelas ejemplares* in Rodolfo Schevill and Adolfo Bonilla, eds., *Obras completas de Miguel de Cervantes Saavedra,* 2 (Madrid, 1923): 114. All quotations from Cervantes are from this edition. All translations are my own.

12. The second verse of Góngora's sonnet "Mientras por competir con tu cabello," no. 149, in *Sonetos completos,* ed. Biruté Ciplijauskaité (Madrid, 1969), p. 222.

13. Although my emphasis and purpose are distinct from hers, this reading of *La fuerza* is to a degree complementary to that of Ruth El Saffar in *Novel to Romance* (Baltimore, 1974), pp. 128-38. I find especially striking the following observations: "In no other story is the period of 'courtship' so foreshortened, nor the period of anguish so extended. Only in the period of dismay and anxiety is a character creatively engaged with his own life in Cervantes's works" (p. 131). "Rodolfo's bedroom also appears twice in Leocadia's life, the second time inverting while duplicating the meaning of the first time. It is on the bed where she was raped that Leocadia, seven years later, finds Luisico, who has been trampled by a horse and rescued by Rodolfo's father. The repetition of the room and its site as the place where Luisico is twice given life establishes a parallelism and at the same time suggests a reversal of themes" (p. 137).

14. In his celebrated "Algunas observaciones acerca del concepto del honor en los siglos XVI y XVII," *Revista de Filología Española* 3 (1916): 1-50, 357-86, Américo Castro ponders honor in Cervantes at length and cites the speech of Leocadia's father. His conclusion seems to be that Cervantes, while accepting the idea of honor that cries out for vengeance as a social reality, modifies such a mistaken precept with forgiveness. The discussion of the speech I cite is summary and superficial. And what evidence is there to support the notion that Calderonian honor was a social reality? It seems to me that Cervantes' view of honor was entirely conventional but the fictional environment he fashioned for questions of honor was so novel and extreme that it simply could not function "normally" there. How could Leocadia's elderly father take revenge on her unknown assailant? Since he cannot, he musters what consolation he can. And what he does offer is pretty poor, in view of Leocadia's torment.

15. In "Calderón y Fuenterrabía: el 'Panegírico al Almirante de Castilla,' " *Boletín de la Real Academia Española* 49 (1969): 253-78, E.M. Wilson has succinctly summarized the military operations connected with the siege. Calderón's brother Joseph distinguished himself at Fuenterrabía and, possibly to further Joseph's military career, Calderón wrote the "Panegírico" in praise of the admiral of Castilla. At all events, *No hay cosa como callar* incorporates an occurrence very close to Calderón personally. Moreover, as Wilson points out, Don Juan, frivolous in his private life, engages our sympathy by conducting himself well in battle.

16. Elliott, *Revolt of the Catalans,* p. 335: "Fuenterrabía had become for Olivares the symbol of national unity, of the achievement of the Union of Arms on which he had set his heart. From all over Spain, troops were flocking to the town's defence."

17. Edward Friedman's work in elucidating Cervantes' dramatic technique presents us with a very different method from Lope's highly narrative one. See, for example, p. 43, note 6, of Friedman's "Cervantes' Dramatic Development: From *Los tratos de Argel* to *Los baños de Argel,*" *Revista de Estudios Hispánicos* 10 (1976): 31-55. Cervantes' technique, in Friedman's exposition, avoids direct narration and works in associative clusters. Calderón achieves a not dissimilar result by complicating lineality, by adding plot to plot. Encounter occurs when the multiple strands emerge.

18. See Valbuena, "Revisión biográfica de Calderón," pp. 19, 21-22.

19. The question of Don Juan Roca's age is a vexed one and, as I shortly point out, the difficulty is more one of temperament than of time. At all events, Juan is no longer in

his *première jeunesse* but can scarcely be called old. His terms for the situation are "divertido / en varias curiosidades / dejé pasar la primera / edad de mi primavera" (1: 868). (Absorbed in various pursuits I allowed my first youth to slip away.)

20. *La desdicha de la voz,* Act II (2: 938):

Que debe de ser comedia, sin duda, ésta de don Pedro Calderón, que hermano o padre siempre vienen a mal tiempo y ahora vienen ambos juntos.

This has just got to be one of Don Pedro Calderón's plays, where a brother or father always comes back home at the wrong time, and now here they both come.

21. The name provides a touch of local color and may be a reminiscence of Enrique de Aragón, sixth duke of Cardona and three times viceroy of Catalonia (1630-1632, 1633-1638, and 1640).

22. Edward M. Wilson, in a lengthy analysis of water and fire in the play, musters in evidence most of the references to fire. "Hacia una interpretación de *El pintor de su deshonra,*" Ábaco 3 (1970): 49-85. See especially pp. 72-77.

23. "The Unconscious Mind in Calderón's *El pintor de su deshonra,*" *Hispanic Review* 18 (1950): 285-301.

24. The Greek who burned down the temple of Diana at Ephesus, apparently in 356 B.C., so as to give his own name immortality. See *Paulys Real-Encyclopädie der classischen Altertumswissenschaft* (Stuttgart, 1912). He figures as Eróstrato in Calderón's mythological play-opera *Celos, aun del aire, matan* (1660).

25. See, for example, in the Pléiade edition of the *Mémoires* 3 (Dijon, 1950): 52, his description of the Prince de Conti: "His mentality was unaffected, brilliant, vivid; his sallies well timed, amusing, never offensive; unconstrained graciousness characterized his every act; all this together with the inanities of society, of the court, of women, of speaking their language to them, with a solid and inexhaustibly sensible mind." (My translation.)

26. Words of art denoting, especially, illicit sexual intercourse.

27. From Muley's speech in praise of Don Fernando, a gloss, in part, of these lines, which occur near the end of Act I of *El príncipe constante* (1: 257).

28. Aristotle has, in fact, a somewhat distinct hierarchy. See, for example, H. Wijsenbeek-Wyler's *Aristotle's Concept of Soul, Sleep and Dreams* (Amsterdam, 1978), p. 69.

29. Such would seem to be the definition of Jorge Manrique in "Coplas por la muerte de su padre," Stanza XXXV, from the Anaya edition of the *Poesías completas,* ed. J.M. Alda-Tesán (Madrid, 1965), p. 107.

"Non se vos haga tan amarga la batalla temerosa
    qu' esperáis,
pues otra vida más larga
de la fama glorïosa
    acá dexáis,
(aunqu' esta vida d'honor
tampoco no es eternal
    ni verdadera);
mas, con todo, es muy mejor
que la otra temporal
    peresçedera."

Do not greatly fear the outcome of the awful battle that awaits you, since you leave behind fame that will endure for some time, even though it is neither everlasting nor absolute. It is nonetheless far superior to mere existence.

30. See, for example, Julio's conmment to Don Fernando in Lope's *La Dorotea,* ed. Edwin S. Morby (Berkeley, 1958), pp. 105, 118.

31. In Act III of *El médico de su honra* (1: 344): "Dos horas tienes de vida, cristiana eres; / salva el alma, que la vida es imposible." (You have two hours to live. Save your soul [by confession], since there is no hope for the body.)

32. Rosaura is dressed as a man and Segismundo is as closely confined as Carrizales' wife.

33. Most of these plays are analyzed in Part III of this book.

34. These lines are from *Casa con dos puertas* (2: 282) and *Los empeños de un acaso* (2: 1045).

35. Tomás Rodaja, in *El licenciado,* embarks upon a lengthy grand tour of Italy and Flanders. As with most tourists, food, drink, lodging, and the "sights" are his major concerns.

36. Lope de Vega, in *La dama boba,* brilliantly and cynically explores the Spanish marriage market of his time. His fundamental postulate is that what the male lacks in himself creates the demand for female qualities. The poor nobleman will need an heiress as his wife. The rich suitor can afford beauty. But no man looking out for a wife is willing to pay for a woman's cleverness and wit. See my "The True Mind of Marriage: Ironies of the Intellect in Lope's *La dama boba,*" *Romanistisches Jahrbuch* 27 (1976): 347-63.

37. Ruth El Saffar, in a brief but searching analysis of *La fuerza de la sangre* in *Novel to Romance,* pp. 128-38, does not comment on the portrait interview. My understanding of it seems to strengthen her notion that "the union of Leocadia and Rodolfo is a hymn to the ultimate reconcilability of all things" (p. 139). Rodolfo, unlike Recaredo, can approach the spiritual only through physical beauty; but his Italian sojourn has at least taught him that much.

38. El Saffar, *Novel to Romance,* p. 139: "Rodolfo's acceptance of Leocadia as his wife is viewed with benevolence and is taken as sacramental, despite the fact that it was motivated by desires originating out of his lust and love for beauty."

39. Don César, in Act II of *Peor está que estaba* likens first love to a painter's preliminary sketch:

no espero
que se pueda borrar amor primero.
Enseña la moral filosofía
que una forma donde otra forma había
no se puede estampar tan fácilmente.
Explíquelo un ejemplo claramente:
cuando un pintor procura
linear una pintura,
si está lisa la tabla,
fáciles rasgos en bosquejo entabla;
mas si la tabla tiene
primero otra pintura, le conviene
    borrarla,
no confunda
con la primera forma la segunda.
Ya me habrás entendido:
tabla lisa al primer amor ha sido
mi pecho; mas si hoy quiere
introducir segundo amor, espere
a ver borrado aquella
imagen que adoró divina y bella.

I don't expect that a first love can be effaced. It is a doctrine in ethics that a later form cannot easily impress itself upon an earlier one. An example should make this clear. If the surface on which a painter intends to rough out his painting is clean, it is easy for him to sketch in a draft. But if his surface shows first another picture, he needs to rub it out, so that the first won't get mixed up with the second. You must already have taken my meaning. My heart was a clean surface for the first love; but if it now wants to portray a second love, it should wait until that first image, whose divine beauty it adored, is effaced.

[2: 331-32]

This speech has large implications for understanding *El pintor de su deshonra* better. We see another reason why Serafina's husband cannot paint her. Another image intervenes. There is, moreover, in Serafina herself a tragically painterly process of attempting and failing to replace a first image with a second.

40. This process has already been described with reference to *La fiera, el rayo y la piedra*. The zone between life and art is one of the great borderlands in Calderón's theatre.

41. Henri Bergson, *L'Evolution créatrice* (Paris, 1929), p. 1.

42. Although my language seems to suggest it, I am not aware of any debt to René Girard's *Violence and the Sacred* (Baltimore, 1977) or to his follower, Cesáreo Bandera, who applies some of Girard's notions to Cervantes and Calderón in *Mímesis conflictiva, ficción literaria y violencia en Cervantes y Calderón* (Madrid, 1975).

43. Pérez Galdós's *Doña Perfecta* perhaps provides a parallel. The protagonist of that novel is a civil engineer who leaves a gridded urban world of rectilinearity and railroad tracks for the curvilinear maze of a backward, Gothic country place called Orbajosa. There his aunt, a mystic tyrant, thwarts and finally murders him. She is an evil Psyche.

44. Mary Magdalen was a popular subject for Golden-Age artists. In one of his less inspiring efforts Velázquez painted her, and she is also presented in Fray Luis de León's original poem sometimes entitled "De la Magdalena," as in the Biblioteca de Autores Cristianos edition, and sometimes simply "Otra," as in the Sarmiento edition.

45. For a much more "existential" discussion of the burning of Don Quijote's books, see Stephen Gilman's "Los inquisidores literarios de Cervantes," *Actas del tercer congreso internacional de hispanistas* (Mexico City, 1970), pp. 3-25, especially p. 9.

46. Scott Fitzgerald felt that his wife had no right of access to their joint biography as elements of fiction, and banished her as an artist from their lives. See Andrew Turnbull, *Scott Fitzgerald* (New York, 1962), pp. 207, 235.

47. The major discussion is Herman Iventosch's "Cervantes and Courtly Love: The Grisóstomo-Marcela Episode of *Don Quijote*," *PMLA* 89 (1974): 64-76. Before Iventosch, Américo Castro had analyzed the episode in *Hacia Cervantes* (Madrid, 1967), pp. 262-301; and J.B. Avalle-Arce in *Deslindes cervantinos* (Madrid, 1961), pp. 97-119. A significant step forward in the understanding of Cervantes' pastoral is taken by Javier Herrero in "Arcadia's Inferno: Cervantes' Attack on Pastoral," *Bulletin of Hispanic Studies* 55 (1978): 289-99, especially p. 289. My sense of pastoral in Cervantes does not take up the moral issue treated by Herrero, but it is akin to his reading, especially in the view of Grisóstomo as a *poète maudit*.

48. Thomas G. Rosenmeyer, *The Green Cabinet: Theocritus and the European Pastoral Lyric* (Berkeley, 1969). In his introduction Rosenmeyer calls his title something of a misnomer, but for my purposes it is splendidly exact, a green cabinet and a greenroom both.

49. From the Garnier edition of *Les Fleurs du mal* prepared by Antoine Adam (Paris, 1961), p. 24.

50. I am, of course, thinking of Plutarch's *Parallel Lives*.

51. Patrick Gallagher, in "Garcilaso's *First Eclogue* and the Lamentations of Love," *Forum for Modern Language Studies* 9 (1973): 192-99, studies the lachrymosity of Garcilaso and ascribes it to biblical reminiscence as well as to his fellow poet Garci Sánchez de Badajoz, from whom Garcilaso no doubt adapted the refrain. And I am convinced by Gallagher's evidence that Garcilaso's sources are not all that purely classical. But the issue of the *function* of the tears remains unsolved. My article, "Time and the Tactics of Suspense in Garcilaso's *Egloga primera*," *Modern Language Notes* 83 (1968): 145-63, attempts an explanation of the presence of unrestrained subjectivity in a poem thought by some to be marked by classical restraint.

52. The refrain of the *First Eclogue*. Its sense has been best examined by Brian Dutton, "Garcilaso's 'sin duelo,' " *Modern Language Notes* 80 (1965): 251-58. The fundamental meaning would seem to be: "Flow forth, tears, without hindrance." Gallagher's rendering as "effortlessly" is precise. But I still believe there is some basis for understanding "sin duelo" in the sense of "painlessly."

53. Robert Graves summarizes all the extant classical sources in two brief paragraphs. *The Greek Myths* (Baltimore, 1955), 2: 280-81.

54. Hilborn, *Chronology,* pp. 11-12.

55. See Valbuena Briones' "Nota preliminar," 1: 674.

56. See, for example, N.D. Shergold, *Spanish Stage,* pp. 285-86.

57. Most notably in the case of Edwin Honig, whose "Flickers of Incest on the Face of Honor: Calderón's *Phantom Lady,"* *Tulane Drama Review* 6 (1962): 69-105, discovers, as the title suggests, incestuous drives in *La dama duende.*

58. *Time and Free Will* (London, 1959), pp. 231-32.

59. "Algunas observaciones acerca del concepto del honor en los siglos XVI y XVII," *Revista de Filología Española* 3 (1916): 1-56, 357-86.

60. Parker defines Calderón's anti-honor (in the debased sense) stance most clearly in his article "Santos y bandoleros en el teatro español del Siglo de Oro," *Arbor* 13 (1949): 395-416. His concluding remarks about *La devoción de la Cruz* (p. 409) are categorical: "The whole play is, in the first place, a condemnation of an overly rigid notion of paternal authority and in the second place a condemnation of an extravagant notion of honor that perverts the ideal of individual moral uprightness into a totally self-seeking exaltation of one's rank in society." (My translation.)

61. It first appeared in *Bulletin of Hispanic Studies* 38 (1960): 75-105, and was reprinted in Bruce W. Wardropper's *Critical Essays in the Theatre of Calderón* (New York, 1965), pp. 24-60.

62. Although God forgives in the allegorical version of *El pintor de su deshonra.*

63. *Calderón and the Seizures of Honor* (Cambridge, Mass., 1972).

64. From Federico Sánchez Escribano and Alberto Porqueras Mayo, *Preceptiva dramática española* (Madrid, 1965), p. 134, verse 328.

65. "Poetry and Drama in Calderón's *El médico de su honra,"* *Romanic Review* 72 (1958): 3-11.

66. *Calderón de la Barca, Four Plays* (New York, 1961), xxiv.

67. *El perro del hortelano,* A. David Kossof, ed. (Madrid, 1970), pp. 190-91.

68. C.A. Jones, "Honor in El alcalde de Zalamea," *Modern Language Review* 50 (1955): 444-49; Peter N. Dunn, "Honour and the Christian Background in Calderón," *Bulletin of Hispanic Studies* 36 (1960): 90-105; idem, "Patrimonio del alma," *Bulletin of Hispanic Studies* 40 (1964): 78-85.

69. See Jenaro Artiles, "Bibliografía sobre el problema del honor y la honra en el drama español," in *Filología y crítica hispánica: Homenaje al Prof. Federico Sánchez Escribano,* ed. Alberto Porqueras-Mayo and Carlos Rojas (Madrid, 1969), pp. 235-41.

70. Frank P. Casa's "Honor and the Wife-Killers of Calderón," *Bulletin of the Comediantes* 29 (1977): 6-23, originates in precisely such unease with Dunn's perceptive and really unequalled judgments.

71. *Spanish Drama of the Golden Age* (Oxford, 1969), p. 153.

72. Another of the disadvantages under which magistrates surnamed Crespo may have had to labor was the imputation of cowardice or timidity. See Lope's *Dorotea,* note 128, 11.1.15: "Es muy usual la asociación entre el pelo crespo y la cobardiá o timidez." A copious list of authorities follows; the Spaniard Gerónimo Cortés interests one particularly with the observation that "los cabellos crespos denotan rudeza de ingenio y simpleza en el varón" (in the male curly hair means slow-wittedness).

73. Sebastián de Covarrubias, *Tesoro de la lengua castellana,* ed. Martín de Riquer (Barcelona, 1943).

74. The phonetic spelling, Correas's original orthography, is that of the 1967 edition of the *Vocabulario de refranes,* ed. Louis Combet (Bordeaux).

75. John J. Allen, in "The Governorship of Sancho and Don Quijote's Chivalric Career," *Revista Hispánica Moderna* 38 (1974-75): 141-52, describes (p. 147) Sancho's actions while governor as a "surprisingly laudable performance" but does not lose sight

of his absurdity, either. Allen sees the governorship as a moment of individual truth for Sancho which parallels Don Quijote's experience of self-knowledge in the cave of Montesinos. He finds in Sancho the same compound of seriousness and satire that I do, obviously with different critical intent.

76. Morley and Bruerton, in their *Cronología de las comedias de Lope de Vega* (Madrid, 1968), pp. 411-12, question Lope's authorship on purely metric grounds. These alone do not seem to me sufficient to reject the attribution. Some other evidence is needed.

77. From the *Biblioteca de Autores Españoles,* 28: 228. I have modernized the capitalization.

78. In his Pergamon edition of the play (Oxford, 1966), Peter Dunn observes that when the work appeared as one of *Doze comedias de las más grandes que hasta ahora han salido* (Lisbon, 1653), it was called *El garrote más bien dado,* "a title which continued in use into the nineteenth century" (p. 26).

79. "Nota preliminar," 1: 350. Hilborn definitely dates the play in 1633 (p. 20).

80. Dunn, *El alcalde,* p. 7.

81. Anthony Watson, in *Juan de la Cueva and the Portuguese Succession* (London, 1971), pp. 26-35, records a modicum of opposition to the annexation of Portugal.

82. This is precisely what J.M. Sobré does in "Calderón's Rebellion? Notes on El alcalde de Zalamea," *Bulletin of Hispanic Studies* 54 (1977): 215-22. His emphasis, however, is on the conflict between Philip and Crespo and the need for authority to have a solid moral foundation.

83. Tirso de Molina, *Obras completas,* ed. Blanca de los Ríos (Madrid, 1962), 2: 1005.

PART III

1. For further discussion of this point, see my "From Comedy to Tragedy: Calderón and the New Tragedy," *Modern Language Notes* 92 (1977): 181-201.

2. Especially Bruce W. Wardropper, in "Calderón's Comedy and his Serious Sense of Life," *Hispanic Studies in Honor of Nicholson B. Adams* (Chapel Hill, North Carolina, 1966), pp. 179-93. Far less convincing is J.E. Varey's *"Casa con dos puertas:* Towards a Definition of Calderón's Comedy," *Modern Language Review* 67 (1972): 83-94.

3. *Nueva Biblioteca de Autores Espanoles* (Madrid, 1950), 3: 323c.

4. "Fue estrenada el 29 de junio de 1623" (Briones, 2: 53), and *"El segundo Escipión* fue representado el seis de noviembre de 1677 en el Palacio Real" (1: 1412).

5. *Chronology,* p. 51.

6. Peter Saccio, *The Court Comedies of John Lyly* (Princeton, 1969), p. 225.

7. *The Complete Works of John Lyly* (Oxford, 1902, 1967), 2: 251, 252.

8. Ibid., p. 306.

9. Ibid., pp. 307, 309.

10. Ibid., p. 358.

11. Saccio, *Court Comedies,* p. 27.

12. Bond, *Complete Works of John Lyly,* 2: 331.

13. Ricardo Quinones, *The Renaissance Discovery of Time* (Cambridge, Mass., 1972).

14. John Portera's "Amor y lealtad en Lyly y Calderón," *Bulletin of the Comediantes* 28 (1976): 96-99, although beautifully written, does not persuade me that Lyly's play reflects the greater freedom of Elizabeth's court, Calderón's the near-total reduction of freedom to the single phenomenon of love.

15. For Calderón's actual treatise, see Ernst Robert Curtius, "Calderón und die Malerei," *Romanische Forschungen* 50 (1936): 89-136. Calderón in 1677 wrote a defense

of the nobility of painters specifically to help them become exempt from required military service. The sincerity of his conviction is strengthened in the subsequent discussion here. A better text is provided by Edward M. Wilson in "El texto de la *Deposición a favor de los professores de la pintura* de don Pedro Calderón de la Barca," *Revista de Archivos, Bibliotecas y Museos* 77 (1974): 709-25.

16. "Hizo segundo reparo en que, transcendiendo sus relieves de lo visible a lo no visible, no contenta con sacar parecida la exterior superficie de todo el universo, elevó sus diseños a la interior pasión del ánimo; pues en la posición de las facciones del hombre (racional mundo pequeño) llegó su destreza aun a copiarle el alma, significando en la variedad de sus semblantes, ya lo severo, ya lo apacible, ya lo risueño, ya lo lastimado, ya lo iracundo, y ya lo compasivo; de suerte que retratado en el rostro el corazón, nos demuestra en sus afectos, aun más parecido el corazón que el rostro." Wilson, pp. 717-18.

17. "el pincel niega al mundo más suave, / que dio espiritu a leño, vida a lino." Luis de Gongora, *Sonetos completos,* ed. Biruté Ciplijauskaité (Madrid, 1969), p. 212.

18. "The Baroque Impasse in the Calderonian Drama," *PMLA* 65 (1950): 1146-65. This essay needs cautious handling.

19. "halló, que la mas significativa era, ser la pintura un casi remedo de las obras de Dios." Wilson, "El texto de la Deposición," p. 717.

20. My "Calderonian Cartesianism: The Iconography of the Mind in *La exaltación de la Cruz,*" *L'Esprit Créateur* 15 (1975): 286-304, especially explores the interplay of the modes of victory and defeat.

21. Here again, in his earliest play, Calderón already is reconnoitering and crossing the boundaries that seem to separate art from life.

22. Variants of the spelling of her name are many.

23. *Cronología,* p. 287.

24. *Nueva Biblioteca de Autores Españoles,* 27: 36.

25. Ibid., 27: 8.

26. (Philadelphia, n.d.), p. 391.

27. Unaware of the at least legendary historicity of Alexander's life in Parma before his Netherlandish glory, Edward Nagy, in "Los soportes de ficción y la sátira social en *Nadie fíe su secreto* de Pedro Calderón de la Barca," *Duquesne Hispanic Review* 9 (1970): 87, sees *Nadie fíe su secreto* as a process in which the prince emerges from the insubstantialities of a frivolous social life to the sense of reality that is history: "esta vez no servirá sin blasón al público—como hizo hasta ahora—que esperaba divertirse, sino al Rey en unas circunstancias históricas, reales, y no artificiales como lo era su mundo y el de la comedia en el tablado." This conclusion strikes me as unbalanced. Calderón, like Cervantes, knew history far too well to consider it merely real and art unreal. What the history plays of Calderón essentially do is try to bring into harmony the private and public myths of the self.

28. *Eglogas completas,* ed. Humberto López-Morales (Madrid, 1968), p. 201.

29. To use the phrase of Fredric Jameson, *The Prison-House of Language* (Princeton, 1972).

30. The text of the play makes the assumption nearly certain.

31. *Histories* (New York: Putnam's, 1925), 6: 103.

32. Livy, *The War with Hannibal* (London: Penguin, 1965), p. 419.

33. The bibliography is extensive: A. Irvine Watson, "Peter the Cruel or Peter the Just? A Reappraisal of the Role Played by King Pedro in Calderón's *El médico de su honra,*" *Romanistisches Jahrbuch* 14 (1963): 322-46. D.W. Cruickshank, "Calderón's King Pedro: Just or Unjust?" *Gesammelte Aufsätze zur Kulturgeschichte Spaniens* 25 (1970): 113-32. Idem, "Pongo mi mano en sangre bañada a la puerta: Adultery in *El médico de su honra,*" in *Studies in Spanish Literature of the Golden Age Presented to Edward M. Wilson* (London, 1973), pp. 46-62. Lloyd King, "The Role of King Pedro in Cal-

derón's *El médico de su honra,"* *Bulletin of the Comediantes* 23 (1971): 44-49. Everett W. Hesse, "Los tribunales de honor en *El médico de su honra* de Calderón," *Homenaje a Guillermo Guastavino* (Madrid, 1974), pp. 201-12.

34. Garcilaso de la Vega, *Poesías castellanas completas,* ed. Elias L. Rivers (Madrid, 1969), p. 46.

35. For a different reading, that the lady is temporarily ill-disposed towards the poet, rather than dead, see Judith Georgette Kim, "Garcilaso's Sonnet 'O dulces prendas,' " *Kentucky Romance Quarterly* 21 (1974): 229-38.

36. From *Poesía elegíaca española,* ed. Bruce W. Wardropper (Salamanca, 1968), p. 62.

37. For a revolutionary (political) interpretation of this sonnet and of much of Garcilaso's poetry, consult Frank Goodwyn, "New Light on Garcilaso's Poetry," *Hispanic Review* 46 (1978): 1-22. Goodwyn's evidence makes the love affair between Garcilaso and Isabel Freyre, already questioned by Kim and others, seem very suppositious indeed. But death and early sorrow are a constant poetic theme, so that the uncertainty as to whether Garcilaso loved a lady who later died in childbirth does not preclude his poetry from referring to a young lady's death. Whether Garcilaso loved Isabel or not, Elisa of the *Egloga primera* has died while giving birth, causing Nemoroso dreadful grief.

38. See Kenneth Clark, *The Nude: A Study in Ideal Form* (New York, 1956), p. 71: "Plato, in his *Symposium,* makes one of the guests assert that there are two Aphrodites, whom he calls Celestial and Vulgar, or, to give them their later titles, Venus Coelestis and Venus Naturalis."

39. Gaius Valerius Catullus, *Poems,* trans. Celia and Louis Zukovsky (London, 1969), p. iv: "Phasellus ille quem videtis, hospites." The "phasellus" is the nimble little pinnace in which the poet has sailed safely home from Bithynia.

40. At root the expression is of course proverbial.

41. A brief statement thick with meaning of a common-sensical or moral kind, very close to, often the same as, a proverb.

42. The most valiant effort to date, and a not unsuccessful one, has been Arturo Farinelli's in *La vita è un sogno,* 2 vols. (Turin, 1916). His idea was that the metaphor itself is a genre. The notion is very close to the operative one of *The Theatre and the Dream.*

43. (Baltimore, 1973).

44. This judgment is probably unjust. Cope's Platonic, rather than ancient or modern neo-Platonic, technique for viewing the play does allow great coherence and freshness. The Platonic approach has a specificity which the neo-Platonic has not. But I am still not comfortable with it or convinced of its basic applicability. The most persuasive brief discussion of the Platonic view of *La vida es sueño* is Harlan Sturm's "From Plato's Cave to Segismundo's Prison: The Four Levels of Reality and Experience," *Modern Language Notes* 89 (1974): 280-89. But I believe this present book has shown a richer and broader function for the cave in Calderón than the Platonic, itself rich. Moreover, in a purely philosophical vein, the dialogue in Calderón between Aristotelian and Platonic modes has yet to be mentioned, although it profoundly exists.

45. Astolfo is of course a reigning sovereign in his own right; but as Basilio's nephew and Estrella's potential husband he assumes a slightly subordinate role. His sovereignty seems pale next to Basilio's or Segismundo's. He takes orders rather than giving them.

46. Segismundo's line of thought at this point is far from being purely rational, although Everett Hesse gives that impression in "La dialéctica y el casuismo en Calderón," reprinted in Manuel Durán's and Roberto González's *Calderón y la crítica: Historia y antología* (Madrid, 1976), pp. 563-81. Hesse's reduction mixes methods, hypothetical reasoning with straight syllogistic thinking. These methods have different rules. But, much more significantly, beneath the surface of reason flows a stream of passion that ex-

presses itself poetically. It far more deeply influences the surge to decision. The true nature and form of reason in Calderón remain to be studied.

47. Joaquín Casalduero, *Estudios sobre el teatro español* (Madrid, 1962), p. 161.

48. P. [5] of his introduction to *Of the Russe Commonwealth,* facsimile ed. with variants (Cambridge, Mass., 1966).

49. Ibid.

50. Ibid., p. 16.

51. Duncan Moir, *The Golden Age: Drama, 1492-1700* (London, 1971), p. 58: "And there is another good play by Lope on events in eastern Europe in his own times, *El Gran-Duque de Moscovia y Emperador perseguido* (M and B: 1606?)."

52. The basic positions with respect to the date are taken in Gertrud von Poehl's "La fuente de *El Gran Duque de Moscovia,*" *Revista de Filología Española* 19 (1932): 47-63, and in J.A. van Praag's "Más noticias sobre la fuente de *El Gran Duque de Moscovia* de Lope de Vega," *Bulletin Hispanique* 39 (1937): 356-66.

53. Of the available theories, von Poehl's seems the sounder.

54. According to van Praag, "Más noticias" p. 357, the *Tercera Parte* had the following editions: Madrid, 1608; Barcelona, 1609; Madrid, 1613; Barcelona, 1621; Madrid, 1652. The *Quarta Parte* appeared in Madrid, 1613; Barcelona, 1621; Madrid, 1652.

55. Published as an appendix in the four-volume *La Russie et le Saint-Siège* (Paris, 1901) by Paul Pierling, 3: 431-48. The quotation is from p. 432.

56. Two important articles support a number of my assertions as to Poland's presence in *La vida es sueño.* They are Ervin C. Brody's "Poland in Calderón's *Life Is a Dream:* Poetic Illusion or Historical Reality," *Polish Review* 14 (1969): 21-62; and Henry K. Ziomek's "Historic Implications and Dramatic Influences in Calderón's *Life Is a Dream,*" *Polish Review* 20 (1975): 111-28.

57. Such is, precisely, Rosaura's first impression of the place: "Mal, Polonia, recibes / a un extranjero, pues con sangre escribes / su entrada en tus arenas" (1: 501).

58. *Faust,* ed. Calvin Thomas (Boston, 1892), l.903-07 (p. 43).

59. Cope, *The Theatre and the Dream,* pp. 8-11.

60. *Spanish Poetry of the Golden Age,* ed. Bruce W. Wardropper (New York, 1971), pp. 147-48.

61. The third and fourth lines of Thomas Gray's "Elegy Written in a Country Churchyard."

62. A dispute, now apparently settled, flared up over the rebel soldier. It began with H.B. Hall's questioning the defensibility of Segismundo's treatment of him in "Segismundo and the Rebel Soldier," *Bulletin of Hispanic Studies* 45 (1968): 189-200. A.A. Parker replied in defense of the prince in "Calderón's Rebel Soldier and Poetic Justice," *Bulletin of Hispanic Studies* 46 (1969): 120-27. Hall rejoined with "Poetic Justice in *La vida es sueño:* A Further Comment," *Bulletin of Hispanic Studies* 46 (1969): 128-31. As far as I can judge, the tradition favoring Parker's defense has been conclusively demonstrated by Daniel L. Heiple in "The Tradition behind the Punishment of the Rebel Soldier in *La vida es sueño,*" *Bulletin of Hispanic Studies* 50 (1973): 1-17. Despite this tradition, so effectively traced by Heiple, the disposition of the soldier remains an unsettling element in the play.

63. Attempts to treat of *La vida es sueño* "philosophically" usually bring rather thin commonplaces to light, as is the case with Jack S. Bailey's "Algunas ideas filosóficas en *La vida es sueño* de Calderón," *Abside* 40 (1976): 381-92.

64. (Indianapolis, 1977), especially "Of the Idea of Necessary Connection," pp. 72-89.

INDEX